George Chetwynd Griffith

The angel of the Revolution; a tale of the coming Terror.

By George Griffith. With illus. by Fred. T. Jane

George Chetwynd Griffith

The angel of the Revolution; a tale of the coming Terror.
By George Griffith. With illus. by Fred. T. Jane

ISBN/EAN: 9783337024123

Printed in Europe, USA, Canada, Australia, Japan

Cover: Foto ©ninafisch / pixelio.de

More available books at **www.hansebooks.com**

Drawn by Edwin S. Hope.

... NATASHA ...

THE ANGEL OF THE REVOLUTION

A Tale of the Coming Terror

BY

GEORGE GRIFFITH

WITH ILLUSTRATIONS BY FRED. T. JANE

EIGHTH EDITION

LONDON
TOWER PUBLISHING COMPANY LIMITED
91 MINORIES, E.C.
1894

TO

CYRIL ARTHUR PEARSON

TO WHOSE SUGGESTION

THE WRITING OF THIS STORY

WAS PRIMARILY DUE

THE FOLLOWING PAGES ARE INSCRIBED

BY

THE AUTHOR

CONTENTS.

CHAP.		PAGE
I.	AT THE ELEVENTH HOUR,	1
II.	AT WAR WITH SOCIETY,	8
III.	A FRIENDLY CHAT,	16
IV.	THE HOUSE ON CLAPHAM COMMON,	23
V.	THE INNER CIRCLE,	30
VI.	NEW FRIENDS,	37
VII.	THE DAUGHTER OF NATAS,	46
VIII.	LEARNING THE PART,	54
IX.	THE BEGINNING OF SORROWS,	63
X.	THE "ARIEL,"	70
XI.	FIRST BLOOD,	78
XII.	IN THE MASTER'S NAME,	85
XIII.	FOR LIFE OR DEATH,	91
XIV.	THE PSYCHOLOGICAL MOMENT,	98
XV.	A VOYAGE OF DISCOVERY,	103
XVI.	A WOOING IN MID-AIR,	110
XVII.	AERIA FELIX,	119
XVIII.	A NAVY OF THE FUTURE,	127
XIX.	THE EVE OF BATTLE,	135
XX.	BETWEEN TWO LIVES,	141
XXI.	JUST IN TIME,	153
XXII.	ARMED NEUTRALITY,	162
XXIII.	A BATTLE IN THE NIGHT,	169
XXIV.	THE NEW WARFARE,	179
XXV.	THE HERALDS OF DISASTER,	188

CHAP.		PAGE
XXVI.	AN INTERLUDE,	193
XXVII.	ON THE TRACK OF TREASON,	201
XXVIII.	A SKIRMISH IN THE CLOUDS,	208
XXIX.	AN EMBASSY FROM THE SKY,	216
XXX.	AT CLOSE QUARTERS,	225
XXXI.	A RUSSIAN RAID,	233
XXXII.	THE END OF THE CHASE,	241
XXXIII.	THE BREAKING OF THE CHARM,	247
XXXIV.	THE PATH OF CONQUEST,	251
XXXV.	FROM CHAOS TO ARCADIE,	258
XXXVI.	LOVE AND DUTY,	267
XXXVII.	THE CAPTURE OF A CONTINENT,	276
XXXVIII.	THE BEGINNING OF THE END,	289
XXXIX.	THE BATTLE OF DOVER,	295
XL.	BELEAGUERED LONDON,	301
XLI.	AN ENVOY OF DELIVERANCE,	308
XLII.	THE EVE OF ARMAGEDDON,	315
XLIII.	THE OLD LION AT BAY,	323
XLIV.	THE TURN OF THE BATTLE-TIDE,	331
XLV.	ARMAGEDDON,	339
XLVI.	VICTORY,	347
XLVII.	THE JUDGMENT OF NATAS,	355
XLVIII.	THE ORDERING OF EUROPE,	366
XLIX.	THE STORY OF THE MASTER,	375
	EPILOGUE.—"AND ON EARTH PEACE!"	386

THE ANGEL OF THE REVOLUTION.

CHAPTER I.

AT THE ELEVENTH HOUR.

"ICTORY! It flies! I am master of the Powers of the Air at last!"

They were strange words to be uttered, as they were, by a pale, haggard, half-starved looking young fellow in a dingy, comfortless room on the top floor of a South London tenement-house; and yet there was a triumphant ring in his voice, and a clear, bright flush on his thin cheeks that spoke at least for his own absolute belief in their truth.

Let us see how far he was justified in that belief.

To begin at the beginning, Richard Arnold was one of those men whom the world is wont to call dreamers and enthusiasts before they succeed, and heaven-born geniuses and benefactors of humanity afterwards.

He was twenty-six, and for nearly six years past he had devoted himself, soul and body, to a single idea—to the so far unsolved problem of aërial navigation.

This idea had haunted him ever since he had been able to think logically at all—first dimly at school, and then more clearly at college, where he had carried everything before him in mathematics and natural science, until it had at last become a ruling passion that crowded everything else out of his life, and made him, commercially speaking, that most useless of social units—a one-idea'd man, whose idea could not be put into working form.

He was an orphan, with hardly a blood relation in the world. He had started with plenty of friends, mostly made at college, who thought he had a brilliant future before him, and therefore looked upon him as a man whom it might be useful to know.

But as time went on, and no results came, these dropped off, and he got to be looked upon as an amiable lunatic, who was wasting his great talents and what money he had on impracticable fancies, when he might have been earning a handsome income if he had stuck to the beaten track, and gone in for practical work.

The distinctions that he had won at college, and the reputation he had gained as a wonderfully clever chemist and mechanician, had led to several offers of excellent positions in great engineering firms; but to the surprise and disgust of his friends he had declined them all. No one knew why, for he had kept his secret with the almost passionate jealousy of the true enthusiast, and so his refusals were put down to sheer foolishness, and he became numbered with the geniuses who are failures because they are not practical.

When he came of age he had inherited a couple of thousand pounds, which had been left in trust to him by his father. Had it not been for that two thousand pounds he would have been forced to employ his knowledge and his talents conventionally, and would probably have made a fortune. But it was just enough to relieve him from the necessity of earning his living for the time being, and to make it possible for him to devote himself entirely to the realisation of his life-dream—at any rate until the money was gone.

Of course he yielded to the temptation—nay, he never gave the other course a moment's thought. Two thousand pounds would last him for years; and no one could have persuaded him that with complete leisure, freedom from all other concerns, and money for the necessary experiments, he would not have succeeded long before his capital was exhausted.

So he put the money into a bank whence he could draw it out as he chose, and withdrew himself from the world to work

Year after year passed, and still success did not come. He found practice very different from theory, and in a hundred details he met with difficulties he had never seen on paper. Meanwhile his money melted away in costly experiments which only raised hopes that ended in bitter disappointment. His wonderful machine was a miracle of ingenuity, and was mechanically perfect in every detail save one—it would do no practical work.

Like every other inventor who had grappled with the problem, he had found himself constantly faced with that fatal ratio of weight to power. No engine that he could devise could do more than lift itself and the machine. Again and again he had made a toy that would fly, as others had done before him, but a machine that would navigate the air as a steamer or an electric vessel navigated the waters, carrying cargo and passengers, was still an impossibility while that terrible problem of weight and power remained unsolved.

In order to eke out his money to the uttermost, he had clothed and lodged himself meanly, and had denied himself everything but the barest necessaries of life.

Thus he had prolonged the struggle for over five years of toil and privation and hope deferred, and now, when his last sovereign had been changed and nearly spent, success—real, tangible, practical success—had come to him, and the discovery that was to be to the twentieth century what the steam-engine had been to the nineteenth was accomplished.

He had discovered the true motive power at last.

Two liquefied gases—which, when united, exploded spontaneously—were admitted by a clockwork escapement in minute quantities into the cylinders of his engine, and worked the pistons by the expansive force of the gases generated by the explosion. There was no weight but the engine itself and the cylinders containing the liquefied gases. Furnaces, boilers, condensers, accumulators, dynamos—all the ponderous apparatus of steam and electricity—were done away with, and he had a power at command greater than either of them.

There was no doubt about it. The moment that his trembling fingers set the escapement mechanism in motion, the model that embodied the thought and labour of years rose into and round in obedience to its rudder, straining hard at the string which prevented it from striking the ceiling. It was weighted in strict proportion to the load that the full-sized air-ship would have to carry. To increase this was merely a matter of increasing the power of the engine and the size of the floats and fans.

The room was a large one, for the house had been built for a better fate than letting in tenements, and it ran from back to front with a window at each end. Out of doors there was a strong breeze blowing, and as soon as Arnold was sure that his ship was able to hold its own in still air, he threw both the windows open and let the wind blow straight through the room. Then he drew the air-ship down, straightened the rudder, and set it against the breeze.

In almost agonised suspense he watched it rise from the floor, float motionless for a moment, and then slowly forge ahead in the teeth of the wind, gathering speed as it went. It was then that he had uttered that triumphant cry of "Victory!" All the long years of privation and hope deferred vanished in that one supreme moment of innocent and bloodless conquest, and he saw himself master of a kingdom as wide as the world itself.

He let the model fly the length of the room before he stopped the clockwork and cut off the motive power, allowing it to sink gently to the floor. Then came the reaction. He looked steadfastly at his handiwork for several moments in silence, and then he turned and threw himself on to a shabby little bed that stood in one corner of the room and burst into a flood of tears.

Triumph had come, but had it not come too late? He knew the boundless possibilities of his invention—but they had still to be realised. To do this would cost thousands of pounds, and he had just one half-crown and a few coppers. Even these were not really his own, for he was already a week behind with his rent, and another payment fell due the next day. That would be twelve shillings in all, and if it was not paid he would be turned into the street.

As he raised himself from the bed he looked despairingly round the bare, shabby room. No; there was nothing there that he could pawn or sell. Everything saleable had gone already to keep up the struggle of hope against despair. The bed and wash-stand, the plain deal table, and the one chair that comprised the furniture of the room were not his. A little carpenter's bench, a few worn tools and odds and ends of scientific apparatus, and a dozen well-used books—these were all that he possessed in the world now, save the clothes on his back, and a plain painted sea-chest in which he was wont to lock up his precious model when he had to go out.

His model! No, he could not sell that. At best it would fetch but the price of an ingenious toy, and without the secret of the two gases it was useless. But was not that worth something? Yes, if he did not starve to death before he could persuade any one that there was money in it. Besides, the chest and its priceless contents would be seized for the rent next day, and then—

"God help me! What *am* I to do?"

The words broke from him like a cry of physical pain, and ended in a sob, and for all answer there was the silence of the room and the inarticulate murmur of the streets below coming up through the open windows.

He was weak with hunger and sick with excitement, for he had lived for days on bread and cheese, and that day he had eaten nothing since the crust that had served him for breakfast. His nerves, too, were shattered by the intense strain of his final trial and triumph, and his head was getting light.

With a desperate effort he recovered himself, and the heroic resolution that had sustained him through his long struggle came to his aid again. He got up and poured some water from the ewer into a cracked cup and drank it. It refreshed him for the moment, and he poured the rest of the water over his head. That steadied his nerves and cleared his brain. He took up the model from the floor, laid it tenderly and lovingly in its usual resting-place in the chest. Then he locked the chest and sat down upon it to think the situation over.

Ten minutes later he rose to his feet and said aloud—

"It's no use. I can't think on an empty stomach. I'll go out and have one more good meal if it's the last I ever have in the world, and then perhaps some ideas will come."

So saying, he took down his hat, buttoned his shabby velveteen coat to conceal his lack of a waistcoat, and went out, locking the door behind him as he went.

Five minutes' walk brought him to the Blackfriars Road, and then he turned towards the river and crossed the bridge just as the motley stream of city workers was crossing it in the opposite direction on their homeward journey.

At Ludgate Circus he went into an eating-house and fared sumptuously on a plate of beef, some bread and butter, and a pint mug of coffee. As he was eating a paper-boy came in and laid an *Echo* on the table at which he was sitting. He took it up mechanically, and ran his eye carelessly over the columns. He was in no humour to be interested by the tattle of an evening paper, but in a paragraph under the heading of Foreign News a once familiar name caught his eye, and he read the paragraph through. It ran as follows:—

RAILWAY OUTRAGE IN RUSSIA.

When the Berlin-Petersburg express stopped last night at Kovno, the first stop after passing the Russian frontier, a shocking discovery was made in the smoking compartment of the palace car which has been on the train for the last few months. Colonel Dornovitch, of the Imperial Police, who is understood to have been on his return journey from a secret mission to Paris, was found stabbed to the heart and quite dead. In the centre of the forehead were two short straight cuts in the form of a T reaching to the bone. Not long ago Colonel Dornovitch was instrumental in unearthing a formidable Nihilist conspiracy, in connection with which over fifty men and women of various social ranks were exiled for life to Siberia. The whole affair is wrapped in the deepest mystery, the only clue in the hands of the police being the fact that the cross cut on the forehead of the victim indicates that the crime is the work, not of the Nihilists proper, but of that unknown and mysterious society usually alluded to as the Terrorists, not one of whom has ever been seen save in his crimes. How the assassin managed to enter and leave the car unperceived while the train was going at full speed is an apparently insoluble riddle. Saving the victim and the attendants, the only passengers in the car who had not retired to rest were another officer in the Russian service and Lord Alanmere, who was travelling to St. Petersburg to resume, after leave of absence, the duties of the Secretaryship to the British Embassy, to which he was appointed some two years ago.

"Why, that must be the Lord Alanmere who was at Trinity in my time, or rather Viscount Tremayne, as he was then," mused Arnold, as he laid the paper down. "We were very good friends in those days. I wonder if he'd know me now, and lend me a ten-pound note to get me out of the infernal fix

I'm in? I believe he would, for he was one of the few really good-hearted men I have so far met with.

"If he were in London I really think I should take courage from my desperation, and put my case before him and ask his help. However, he's not in London, and so it's no use wishing. Well, I feel more of a man for that shillingsworth of food and drink, and I'll go and wind up my dissipation with a pipe and a quiet think on the Embankment."

CHAPTER II.

AT WAR WITH SOCIETY.

HEN Richard Arnold reached the Embankment dusk had deepened into night, so far, at least, as nature was concerned. But in London in the beginning of the twentieth century there was but little night to speak of, save in the sense of a division of time. The date of the paper which contained the account of the tragedy on the Russian railway was September 3rd, 1903, and within the last ten years enormous progress had been made in electric lighting.

The ebb and flow in the Thames had at last been turned to account, and worked huge turbines which perpetually stored up electric power that was used not only for lighting, but for cooking in hotels and private houses, and for driving machinery. At all the great centres of traffic huge electric suns cast their rays far and wide along the streets, supplementing the light of the lesser lamps with which they were lined on each side.

The Embankment from Westminster to Blackfriars was bathed in a flood of soft white light from hundreds of great lamps running along both sides, and from the centre of each bridge a million candle-power sun cast rays upon the water that were continued in one unbroken stream of light from Chelsea to the Tower.

On the north side of the river the scene was one of brilliant and splendid opulence, that contrasted strongly with the half-lighted gloom of the murky wilderness of South London, dark and forbidding in its irredeemable ugliness.

From Blackfriars Arnold walked briskly towards Westminster, bitterly contrasting as he went the lavish display of wealth around him with the sordid and seemingly hopeless poverty of his own desperate condition.

He was the maker and possessor of a far greater marvel than anything that helped to make up this splendid scene, and yet the ragged tramps who were remorselessly moved on from one seat to another by the policemen as soon as they had settled themselves down for a rest and a doze, were hardly poorer than he was.

For nearly four hours he paced backwards and forwards, every now and then stopping to lean on the parapet, and once or twice to sit down, until the chill autumn wind pierced his scanty clothing, and compelled him to resume his walk in order to get warm again.

All the time he turned his miserable situation over and over again in his mind without avail. There seemed no way out of it; no way of obtaining the few pounds that would save him from homeless beggary and his splendid invention from being lost to him and the world, certainly for years, and perhaps for ever.

And then, as hour after hour went by, and still no cheering thought came, the misery of the present pressed closer and closer upon him. He dare not go home, for that would be to bring the inevitable disaster of the morrow nearer, and, besides, it was home no longer till the rent was paid. He had two shillings, and he owed at least twelve. He was also the maker of a machine for which the Tsar of Russia had made a standing offer of a million sterling. That million might have been his if he had possessed the money necessary to bring his invention under the notice of the great Autocrat.

That was the position he had turned over and over in his mind until its horrible contradictions maddened him. With a little money, riches and fame were his; without it he was a beggar in sight of starvation.

And yet he doubted whether, even in his present dire extremity, he could, had he had the chance, sell what might be made the most terrific engine of destruction ever thought of to the head and front of a despotism that he looked upon as the worst earthly enemy of mankind.

For the twentieth time he had paused in his weary walk to and fro to lean on the parapet close by Cleopatra's Needle.

The Embankment was almost deserted now, save by the tramps and a few isolated wanderers like himself. For several minutes he looked out over the brightly glittering waters below him, wondering listlessly how long it would take him to drown if he dropped over, and whether he would be rescued before he was dead, and brought back to life, and prosecuted the next day for daring to try and leave the world save in the conventional and orthodox fashion.

Then his mind wandered back to the Tsar and his million, and he pictured to himself the awful part that a fleet of airships such as his would play in the general European war that people said could not now be put off for many months longer. As he thought of this the vision grew in distinctness, and he saw them hovering over armies and cities and fortresses, and raining irresistible death and destruction down upon them. The prospect appalled him, and he shuddered as he thought that it was now really within the possibility of realisation; and then his ideas began to translate themselves involuntarily into words which he spoke aloud, completely oblivious for the time being of his surroundings.

"No, I think I would rather destroy it, and then take my secret with me out of the world, than put such an awful power of destruction and slaughter into the hands of the Tsar, or, for the matter of that, any other of the rulers of the earth. Their subjects can butcher each other quite efficiently enough as it is. The next war will be the most frightful carnival of destruction that the world has ever seen; but what would it be like if I were to give one of the nations of Europe the power of raining death and desolation on its enemies from the skies! No, no! Such a power, if used at all, should only be used against and not for the despotisms that afflict the earth with the curse of war!"

"Then why not use it so, my friend, if you possess it, and would see mankind freed from its tyrants?" said a quiet voice at his elbow.

The sound instantly scattered his vision to the winds, and he turned round with a startled exclamation to see who had spoken. As he did so, a whiff of smoke from a very good cigar drifted past his nostrils, and the voice said again in the same quiet, even tones—

"You must forgive me for my bad manners in listening to what you were saying, and also for breaking in upon your reverie. My excuse must be the great interest that your words had for me. Your opinions would appear to be exactly my own, too, and perhaps you will accept that as another excuse for my rudeness."

It was the first really kindly, friendly voice that Richard Arnold had heard for many a long day, and the words were so well chosen and so politely uttered that it was impossible to feel any resentment, so he simply said in answer—

"There was no rudeness, sir; and, besides, why should a gentleman like you apologise for speaking to a "—

"Another gentleman," quickly interrupted his new acquaintance. "Because I transgressed the laws of politeness in doing so, and an apology was due. Your speech tells me that we are socially equals. Intellectually you look my superior. The rest is a difference only of money, and that any smart swindler can bury himself in nowadays if he chooses. But come, if you have no objection to make my better acquaintance, I have a great desire to make yours. If you will pardon my saying so, you are evidently not an ordinary man, or else, something tells me, you would be rich. Have a smoke and let us talk, since we apparently have a subject in common. Which way are you going?"

"Nowhere—and therefore anywhere," replied Arnold, with a laugh that had but little merriment in it. "I have reached a point from which all roads are one to me."

"That being the case I propose that you shall take the one that leads to my chambers in Savoy Mansions yonder. We shall find a bit of supper ready, I expect, and then I shall ask you to talk. Come along!"

There was no more mistaking the genuine kindness and sincerity of the invitation than the delicacy with which it was given. To have refused would not only have been churlish, but it would have been for a drowning man to knock aside a kindly hand held out to help him; so Arnold accepted, and the two new strangely met and strangely assorted friends walked away together in the direction of the Savoy.

The suite of rooms occupied by Arnold's new acquaintance was the beau ideal of a wealthy bachelor's abode. Small, compact, cosy, and richly furnished, yet in the best of taste withal, the rooms looked like an indoor paradise to him after the bare squalor of the one room that had been his own home for over two years.

His host took him first into a dainty little bath-room to wash his hands, and by the time he had performed his scanty toilet supper was already on the table in the sitting-room. Nothing melts reserve like a good well-cooked meal washed down by appropriate liquids, and before supper was half over Arnold and his host were chatting together as easily as though they stood on perfectly equal terms and had known each other for years. His new friend seemed purposely to keep the conversation to general subjects until the meal was over and his pattern man-servant had removed the cloth and left them together with the wine and cigars on the table.

As soon as he had closed the door behind him his host motioned Arnold to an easy-chair on one side of the fireplace, threw himself into another on the other side, and said—

"Now, my friend, plant yourself, as they say across the water, help yourself to what there is as the spirit moves you, and talk—the more about yourself the better. But stop. I forgot that we do not even know each other's name yet. Let me introduce myself first.

"My name is Maurice Colston; I am a bachelor, as you see. For the rest, in practice I am an idler, a dilettante, and a good deal else that is pleasant and utterly useless. In theory, let me tell you, I am a Socialist, or something of the sort, with a lively conviction as to the injustice and absurdity of the social and economic conditions which enable me to have such a good time on earth without having done anything to deserve it beyond having managed to be born the son of my father."

He stopped and looked at his guest through the wreaths of his cigar smoke as much as to say: "And now who are you?"

Arnold took the silent hint, and opened his mouth and his heart at the same time. Quite apart from the good turn he had done him, there was a genial frankness about his unconventional host that chimed in so well with his own nature that he cast all reserve aside, and told plainly and simply the story of his life and its master passion, his dreams and hopes and failures, and his final triumph in the hour when triumph itself was defeat.

His host heard him through without a word, but towards the end of his story his face betrayed an interest, or rather an expectant anxiety, to hear what was coming next that no mere friendly concern of the moment for one less fortunate than himself could adequately account for. At length, when Arnold had completed his story with a brief but graphic description of the last successful trial of his model, he leant forward in his chair, and, fixing his dark, steady eyes on his guest's face, said in a voice from which every trace of his former good-humoured levity had vanished—

"A strange story, and truer, I think, than the one I told you. Now tell me on your honour as a gentleman: Were you really in earnest when I heard you say on the embankment that you would rather smash up your model and take the secret with you into the next world, than sell your discovery to the Tsar for the million that he has offered for such an air-ship as yours?"

"Absolutely in earnest," was the reply. "I have seen enough of the seamy side of this much-boasted civilisation of ours to know that it is the most awful mockery that man ever insulted his Maker with. It is based on fraud, and sustained by force—force that ruthlessly crushes all who do not bow the knee to Mammon. I am the enemy of a society that does not permit a man to be honest and live, unless he has money and can defy it. I have just two shillings in the world, and I would rather throw them into the Thames and myself after them than take that million from the Tsar in exchange for an engine of destruction that would make him master of the world."

"Those are brave words," said Colston, with a smile. "Forgive me for saying so, but I wonder whether you would repeat them if I told you that I am a servant of his Majesty the Tsar, and that you shall have that million for your model and your secret the moment that you convince me that what you have told me is true."

Before he had finished speaking Arnold had risen to his feet. He heard him out, and then he said, slowly and steadily—

"I should not take the trouble to repeat them; I should only tell you that I am sorry that I have eaten salt with a man who could take advantage of my poverty to insult me. Good night."

He was moving towards the door when Colston jumped up from his chair, strode round the table, and got in front of him. Then he put his two hands on his shoulders, and, looking straight into his eyes, said in a tone that vibrated with emotion—

"Thank God, I have found an honest man at last! Go and sit down again, my friend, my comrade, as I hope you soon will be. Forgive me for the foolishness that I spoke! I am no servant of the Tsar. He and all like him have no more devoted enemy on earth than I am. Look! I will soon prove it to you."

As he said the last words, Colston let go Arnold's shoulders, flung off his coat and waistcoat, slipped his braces off his shoulders, and pulled his shirt up to his neck. Then he turned his bare back to his guest, and said—

"That is the sign-manual of Russian tyranny—the mark of the knout!"

Arnold shrank back with a cry of horror at the sight. From waist to neck Colston's back was a mass of hideous scars and wheals, crossing each other and rising up into purple lumps, with livid blue and grey spaces between them. As he stood, there was not an inch of naturally-coloured skin to be seen. It was like the back of a man who had been flayed alive, and then flogged with a cat-o'-nine-tails.

Before Arnold had overcome his horror his host had re-adjusted his clothing. Then he turned to him and said—

"That was my reward for telling the governor of a petty Russian town that he was a brute-beast for flogging a poor decrepid old Jewess to death. Do you believe me now when I say that I am no servant or friend of the Tsar?"

"Yes, I do," replied Arnold, holding out his hand, "you were right to try me, and I was wrong to be so hasty. It is a failing of mine that has done me plenty of harm before now. I think I know now what you are without your telling me. Give me a piece of paper and you shall have my address, so that you can come to-morrow and see the model—only I warn you that you will have to pay my rent to keep my landlord's hands off it. And then I must be off, for I see it's past twelve."

"You are not going out again to-night, my friend, while I have a sofa and plenty of rugs at your disposal," said his host. "You will sleep here, and in the morning we will go together and see this marvel of yours. Meanwhile sit down and make yourself at home with another cigar. We have only just begun to know each other—we two enemies of Society!"

CHAPTER III.

A FRIENDLY CHAT.

OON after eight the next morning Colston came into the sitting-room where Arnold had slept on the sofa, and dreamt dreams of war and world-revolts and battles fought in mid-air between aërial navies built on the plan of his own model. When Colston came in he was just awake enough to be wondering whether the events of the previous night were a reality or part of his dreams—a doubt that was speedily set at rest by his host drawing back the curtains and pulling up the blinds.

The moment his eyes were properly open he saw that he was anywhere but in his own shabby room in Southwark, and the rest was made clear by Colston saying—

"Well, comrade Arnold, Lord High Admiral of the Air, how have you slept? I hope you found the sofa big and soft enough, and that the last cigar has left no evil effects behind it."

"Eh? Oh, good morning! I don't know whether it was the whisky or the cigars, or what it was; but do you know I have been dreaming all sorts of absurd things about battles in the air and dropping explosives on fortresses and turning them into small volcanoes. When you came in just now I hadn't the remotest idea where I was. It's time to get up, I suppose?"

"Yes, it's after eight a good bit. I've had my tub, so the bath-room is at your service. Meanwhile, Burrows will be laying the table for breakfast. When you have finished your tub, come into my dressing-room, and let me rig you out. We are about of a size, and I think I shall be able to meet your most fastidious taste. In fact, I could rig you out as anything—from a tramp to an officer of the Guards."

"It wouldn't take much change to accomplish the former, I'm afraid. But, really, I couldn't think of trespassing so far on your hospitality as to take your very clothes from you. I'm deep enough in your debt already."

"Don't talk nonsense, Richard Arnold. The tone in which those last words were said shows me that you have not duly laid to heart what I said last night. There is no such thing as private property in the Brotherhood, of which I hope, by this time to-morrow, you will be an initiate.

"What I have here is mine only for the purposes of the Cause, wherefore it is as much yours as mine, for to-day we are going on the Brotherhood's business. Why, then, should you have any scruples about wearing the Brotherhood's clothes? Now clear out and get tubbed, and wash some of those absurd ideas out of your head."

"Well, as you put it that way, I don't mind, only remember that I don't necessarily put on the principles of the Brotherhood with its clothes."

So saying, Arnold got up from the sofa, stretched himself, and went off to make his toilet.

When he sat down to breakfast with his host half an hour later, very few who had seen him on the Embankment the night before would have recognised him as the same man. The tailor, after all, does a good deal to make the man, externally at least, and the change of clothes in Arnold's case had transformed him from a superior looking tramp into an aristocratic and decidedly good-looking man, in the prime of his youth, saving only for the thinness and pallor of his face, and a perceptible stoop in the shoulders.

During breakfast they chatted about their plans for the day, and then drifted into generalities, chiefly of a political nature.

The better Arnold came to know Maurice Colston the more remarkable his character appeared to him; and it was his growing wonder at the contradictions that it exhibited that made him say towards the end of the meal—

"I must say you're a queer sort of conspirator, Colston. My idea of Nihilists and members of revolutionary societies has always taken the form of silent, stealthy, cautious beings, with a lively distrust and hatred of the whole human race outside their own circles. And yet here are you, an active member of the most terrible secret society in existence, pledged to the destruction of nearly every institution on earth, and carrying your life in your hand, opening your heart like a schoolboy to a man you have literally not known for twenty-four hours.

"Suppose you had made a mistake in me. What would there be to prevent me telling the police who you are, and having you locked up with a view to extradition to Russia?"

"In the first place," replied Colston quietly, "you would not do so, because I am not mistaken in you, and because, in your heart, whether you fully know it or not, you believe as I do about the destruction that is about to fall upon Society.

"In the second place," if you did betray my confidence, I should be able to bring such an overwhelming array of the most respectable evidence to show that I was nothing like what I really am, that you would be laughed at for a madman; and, in the third place, there would be an inquest on you within twenty-four hours after you had told your story. Do you remember the death of Inspector Ainsworth, of the Criminal Investigation Department, about six months ago?"

"Yes, of course I do. Hermit and all as I was, I could hardly help hearing about that, considering what a noise it made. But I thought that was cleared up. Didn't one of that gang of garotters that was broken up in South London a couple of months later confess to strangling him in the statement that he made before he was executed?"

"Yes, and his widow is now getting ten shillings a week for life on account of that confession. Birkett no more killed Ainsworth than you did; but he had killed two or three others, and so the confession didn't do him very much harm.

"No; Ainsworth met his death in quite another way. He accepted from the Russian secret police bureau in London a bribe of £250 down and the promise of another £250 if he succeeded in manufacturing enough evidence against a member of our Outer Circle to get him extradited to Russia on a trumped-up charge of murder.

"The Inner Circle learnt of this from one of our spies in the Russian London police, and ——, well, Ainsworth was found dead with the mark of the Terror upon his forehead before he had time to put his treachery into action. He was executed by two of the Brotherhood, who are members of the Metropolitan police force, and who were afterwards complimented by the magistrate for the intelligent efforts they had made in bringing the murderers to justice."

Colston told the dark story in the most careless of tones between the puffs of his after-breakfast cigarette. Arnold stifled his horror as well as he was able, but he could not help saying, when his host had done—

"This Brotherhood of yours is well named the Terror; but was not that rather a murder than an execution?"

"By no means," replied Colston, a trifle coldly. "Society hangs or beheads a man who kills another. Ainsworth knew as well as we did that if the man he tried to betray by false evidence had once set foot in Russia, the torments of a hundred deaths would have been his before he had been allowed to die.

"He betrayed his office and his faith to his English masters in order to commit this vile crime, and so he was killed as a murderous and treacherous reptile that was not fit to live. We of the Terror are not lawyers, and so we make no distinctions between deliberate plotting for money to kill and the act of killing itself. Our law is closer akin to justice than the hair-splitting fraud that is tolerated by Society."

Either from emotional or logical reasons Arnold made no reply to this reasoning, and, seeing he remained silent, Colston resumed his ordinary nonchalant, good-humoured tone, and went on—

"But come, that will be horrors enough for to-day. We have other business in hand, and we may as well get to it at once. About this wonderful invention of yours. Of course I believe all you have told me about it, but you must remember that I am only an agent, and that I am inexorably bound by certain rules, in accordance with which I must act.

"Now, to be perfectly plain with you, and in order that we may thoroughly understand each other before either of us commits himself to anything, I must tell you that I want to see this model flying ship of yours in order to be able to report on it to-night to the Executive of the Inner Circle, to whom I shall also want to introduce you. If you will not allow me to do that say so at once, and, for the present at least, our negotiations must come to a sudden stop."

"Go on," said Arnold quietly; "so far I consent. For the rest I would rather hear you to the end."

"Very well. Then if the Executive approve of the invention, you will be asked to join the Inner Circle at once, and to devote yourself body and soul to the Society and the accomplishment of the objects that will be explained to you. If you refuse there will be an end of the matter, and you will simply be asked to give your word of honour to reveal nothing that you have seen or heard, and then allowed to depart in peace.

"If, on the other hand, you consent, in consideration of the immense importance of your secret—which there is no need to disguise from you—to the Brotherhood, the usual condition of passing through the Outer Circle will be dispensed with, and you will be trusted as absolutely as we shall expect you to trust us.

"Whatever funds you then require to manufacture an airship on the plan of your model will be placed at your disposal, and a suitable place will be selected for the works that you will have to build. When the ship is ready to take the air you will, of course, be appointed to the command of her, and you will pick your crew from among the workmen who will act under your orders in the building of the vessel.

"They will all be members of the Outer Circle, who will not understand your orders, but simply obey them blindly, even to the death. One member of the Inner Circle will act as your second in command, and he will be as perfectly trusted as you will be, so that in unforeseen emergencies you will be able to consult with him with perfect confidence. Now I think I have told you all. What do you say?"

Arnold was silent for a few minutes, too busy for speech with the rush of thoughts that had crowded through his brain as Colston was speaking. Then he looked up at his host and said—

"May I make conditions?"

"You may state them," replied he, with a smile, "but, of course, I don't undertake to accept them without consultation with my—I mean with the Executive."

"Of course not," said Arnold. "Well, the conditions that I should feel myself obliged to make with your Executive would be, briefly speaking, these: I would not reveal to any one the composition of the gases from which I derive my motive force. I should manufacture them myself in given quantities, and keep them always under my own charge.

"At the first attempt to break faith with me in this respect I would blow the air-ship and all her crew, including myself, into such fragments as it would be difficult to find one of them. I have and wish for no life apart from my invention, and I would not survive it."

"Good!" interrupted Colston. "There spoke the true enthusiast. Go on."

"Secondly, I would use the machine only in open warfare— when the Brotherhood is fighting openly for the attainment of a definite end. Once the appeal to force has been made I will employ a force such as no nation on earth can use without me, and I will use it as unsparingly as the armies and fleets engaged will employ their own engines of destruction on one another. But I will be no party to the destruction of defenceless towns and people who are not in arms against us. If I am ordered to do that I tell you candidly that I will not do it. I will blow the air-ship itself up first."

"The conditions are somewhat stringent, although the sentiments are excellent," replied Colston; "still, of myself I can neither accept nor reject them. That will be for the Executive to do. For my own part I think that you will be able to arrive at a basis of agreement on them. And now I think we have said all we can say for the present, and so if you are ready we'll be off and satisfy my longing to see the invention that is to make us the arbiters of war—when war comes, which I fancy will not be long now."

Something in the tone in which these last words were spoken struck Arnold with a kind of cold chill, and he shivered slightly as he said in answer to Colston—

"I am ready when you are, and no less anxious than you to set eyes on my model. I hope to goodness it is all safe! Do you know, when I am away from it I feel just like a woman away from her first baby."

A few minutes later two of the most dangerous enemies of Society alive were walking quietly along the Embankment towards Blackfriars, smoking their cigars and chatting as conventionally as though there were no such things on earth as tyranny and oppression, and their necessarily ever-present enemies conspiracy and brooding revolution.

CHAPTER IV.

THE HOUSE ON CLAPHAM COMMON.

TWENTY minutes' walk took Arnold and Colston to the door of the tenement-house in which the former had lived since his fast-dwindling store of money had convinced him of the necessity of bringing his expenses down to the lowest possible limit if he wished to keep up the struggle with fate very much longer.

As they mounted the dirty, evil-smelling staircase, Colston said—

"Phew! Verily you are a hero of science if you have brought yourself to live in a hole like this for a couple of years rather than give up your dream, and grow fat on the loaves and fishes of conventionality."

"This is a palace compared with some of the rookeries about here," replied Arnold, with a laugh. "The march of progress seems to have left this half of London behind as hopeless. Ten years ago there were a good many thousands of highly respectable mediocrities living on this side of the river, but now I am told that the glory has departed from the very best of its localities, and given them up to various degrees of squalor. Vice, poverty, and misery seem to gravitate naturally southward in London. I don't know why, but they do. Well, here is the door of my humble den."

As he spoke he put the key in the lock, and opened the door, bidding his companion enter as he did so.

Arnold's anxiety was soon relieved by finding the precious model untouched in its resting-place, and it was at once brought out. Colston was delighted beyond his powers of expression with the marvellous ingenuity with which the miracle of mechanical skill was contrived and put together; and when Arnold, after showing and explaining to him all the various parts of the mechanism and the external structure, at length set the engine working, and the air-ship rose gracefully from the floor and began to sail round the room in the wide circle to which it was confined by its mooring-line, he stared at it for several minutes in wondering silence, following it round and round with his eyes, and then he said in a voice from which he vainly strove to banish the signs of the emotion that possessed him—

"It is the last miracle of science! With a few such ships as that one could conquer the world in a month!"

"Yes, that would not be a very difficult task, seeing that neither an army nor a fleet could exist for twelve hours with two or three of them hovering above it," replied Arnold.

The trial over, Arnold set to work and took the model partly to pieces for packing up; and while he was putting it away in the old sea-chest, Colston counted out ten sovereigns and laid them on the table. Hearing the clink of the gold, Arnold looked up and said—

"What is that for? A sovereign will be quite enough to get me out of my present scrape, and then if we come to any terms to-night it will be time enough to talk about payment."

"The Brotherhood does not do business in that way," was the reply. "At present your only connection with it is a commercial one, and ten pounds is a very moderate fee for the privilege of inspecting such an invention as this. Anyhow, that is what I am ordered to hand over to you in payment for your trouble now and to-night, so you must accept it as it is given—as a matter of business."

"Very well," said Arnold, closing and locking the chest as he spoke, "if you think it worth ten pounds, the money will not come amiss to me. Now, if you will remain and guard the household gods for a minute, I will go and pay my rent and get a cab."

Half an hour later his few but priceless possessions were loaded on a four-wheeler and Arnold had bidden farewell for ever to the dingy room in which he had passed so many hours of toil and dreaming, suffering and disappointment. Before lunch time they were safely bestowed in a couple of rooms which Colston had engaged for him in the same building in which his own rooms were.

In the afternoon, among other purchases, a more convenient case was bought for the model, and in this it was packed with the plans and papers which explained its construction, ready for the evening journey.

The two friends dined together at six in Colston's rooms, and at seven sharp his servant announced that the cab was at the door. Within ten minutes they were bowling along the Embankment towards Westminster Bridge in a luxuriously appointed hansom of the newest type, with the precious case lying across their knees.

"This is a comfortable cab," said Arnold, when they had gone a hundred yards or so. "By the way, how does the man know where to go? I didn't hear you give him any directions."

"None were necessary," was the reply. "This cab, like a good many others in London, belongs to the Brotherhood, and the man who is driving is one of the Outer Circle. Our Jehus are the most useful spies that we have. Many is the secret of the enemy that we have learnt from, and many is the secret police agent who has been driven to his rendezvous by a Terrorist who has heard every word that has been spoken on the journey."

"How on earth is that managed?"

"Every one of the cabs is fitted with a telephonic arrangement communicating with the roof. The driver has only to button the wire of the transmitter up inside his coat so that the transmitter itself lies near to his ear, and he can hear even a whisper inside the cab.

"The man who is driving us, for instance, has a sort of retainer from the Russian Embassy to be on hand at certain hours on certain nights in the week. Our cabs are all better horsed, better appointed, and better driven than any others in London, and, consequently, they are favourites, especially among the young attachés, and are nearly always employed by them on their secret missions or love affairs, which, by the way, are very often the same thing. Our own Jehu has a job on to-night, from which we expect some results that will mystify the enemy not a little. We got our first suspicions of

Ainsworth from a few incautious words that he spoke in one of our cabs."

"It's a splendid system, I should think, for discovering the movements of your enemies," said Arnold, not without an uncomfortable reflection on the fact that he was himself now completely in the power of this terrible organisation, which had keen eyes and ready hands in every capital of the civilised world. "But how do you guard against treachery? It is well known that all the Governments of Europe are spending money like water to unearth this mystery of the Terror. Surely all your men cannot be incorruptible."

"Practically they are so. The very mystery which enshrouds all our actions makes them so. We have had a few traitors, of course; but as none of them has ever survived his treachery by twenty-four hours, a bribe has lost its attraction for the rest."

In such conversation as this the time was passed, while the cab crossed the river and made its way rapidly and easily along Kennington Road and Clapham Road to Clapham Common. At length it turned into the drive of one of those solid abodes of pretentious respectability which front the Common, and pulled up before a big stucco portico.

"Here we are!" exclaimed Colston, as the doors of the cab automatically opened. He got out first, and Arnold handed the case to him, and then followed him.

Without a word the driver turned his horse into the road again and drove off towards town, and as they ascended the steps the front door opened, and they went in, Colston saying as they did so—

"Is Mr. Smith at home?"

"Yes, sir; you are expected, I believe. Will you step into the drawing-room?" replied the clean-shaven and immaculately respectable man-servant, in evening dress, who had opened the door for them.

They were shown into a handsomely furnished room lit with electric light. As soon as the footman had closed the door behind him, Colston said—

"Well, now, here you are in the conspirators' den, in the very headquarters of those Terrorists for whom Europe is being ransacked constantly without the slightest success. I have often wondered what the rigid respectability of Clapham Common would think if it knew the true character of this harmless-looking house. I hardly think an earthquake in Clapham Road would produce much more sensation that such a discovery would.

"And now," he continued, his tone becoming suddenly much more serious, "in a few minutes you will be in the presence of the Inner Circle of the Terrorists, that is to say, of those who practically hold the fate of Europe in their hands. You know pretty clearly what they want with you. If you have thought better of the business that we have discussed you are still at perfect liberty to retire from it, on giving your word of honour not to disclose anything that I have said to you."

"I have not the slightest intention of doing anything of the sort," replied Arnold. "You know the conditions on which I came here. I shall put them before your Council, and if they are accepted your Brotherhood will, within their limits, have no more faithful adherent than I. If not, the business will simply come to an end as far as I am concerned, and your secret will be as safe with me as though I had taken the oath of membership."

"Well said!" replied Colston, "and just what I expected you to say. Now listen to me for a minute. Whatever you may see or hear for the next few minutes say nothing till you are asked to speak. I will say all that is necessary at first. Ask no questions, but trust to anything that may seem strange being explained in due course—as it will be. A single indiscretion on your part might raise suspicions which would be as dangerous as they would be unfounded. When you are asked to speak do so without the slightest fear, and speak your mind as openly as you have done to me."

"You need have no fear for me," replied Arnold. "I think I am sensible enough to be prudent, and I am quite sure that I am desperate enough to be fearless. Little worse can happen to me than the fate that I was contemplating last night."

As he ceased speaking there was a knock at the door. It opened and the footman reappeared, saying in the most commonplace fashion—

"Mr. Smith will be happy to see you now, gentlemen. Will you kindly walk this way?"

They followed him out into the hall, and then, somewhat to Arnold's surprise, down the stairs at the back, which apparently led to the basement of the house.

The footman preceded them to the basement floor and halted before a door in a little passage that looked like the entrance to a coal cellar. On this he knocked in peculiar fashion with the knuckles of one hand, while with the other he pressed the button of an electric bell concealed under the paper on the wall. The bell sounded faintly as though some distance off, and as it rang the footman said abruptly to Colston—

"Das Wort ist Freiheit."

Arnold knew German enough to know that this meant "The word is 'Freedom,'" but why it should have been spoken in a foreign language mystified him not a little.

While he was thinking about this the door opened, as if by a released spring, and he saw before him a long, narrow passage, lit by four electric arcs, and closed at the other end by a door, guarded by a sentry armed with a magazine rifle.

He followed Colston down the passage, and when within a dozen feet of the sentry, he brought his rifle to the "ready," and the following strange dialogue ensued between him and Colston—

"Quien va?"

"Zwei Freunde der Bruderschaft."

"Por la libertad?"

"Für Freiheit über alles!"

"Pass, friends."

The rifle grounded as the words were spoken, and the sentry stepped back to the wall of the passage.

At the same moment another bell rang beyond the door, and then the door itself opened as the other had done.

They passed through, and it closed instantly behind them, leaving them in total darkness.

Colston caught Arnold by the arm, and drew him towards him, saying as he did so—

"What do you think of our system of passwords?"

"Pretty hard to get through unless one knew them, I should think. Why the different languages?"

"To make assurance doubly sure every member of the Inner Circle must be conversant with four European languages. On these the changes are rung, and even I did not know what the two languages were to be to-night before I entered the house, and if I had asked for 'Mr. Brown' instead of 'Mr. Smith,' we should never have got beyond the drawing-room.

"When the footman told me in German that the word was 'Freedom,' I knew that I should have to answer the challenge of the sentry in German. I did not know that he would challenge in Spanish, and if I had not understood him, or had replied in any other language but German, he would have shot us both down without saying another word, and no one would ever have known what had become of us. You will be exempt from this condition, because you will always come with me. I am, in fact, responsible for you."

"H'm, there doesn't seem much chance of any one getting through on false pretences," replied Arnold, with an irrepressible shudder. "Has any one ever tried?"

"Yes, once. The two gentlemen whose disappearance made the famous 'Clapham Mystery' of about twelve months ago. They were two of the smartest detectives in the French service, and the only two men who ever guessed the true nature of this house. They are buried under the floor on which you are standing at this moment."

The words were spoken with a cruel inflexible coldness, which struck Arnold like a blast of frozen air. He shivered, and was about to reply when Colston caught him by the arm again, and said hurriedly—

"H'st! We are going in. Remember what I said, and don't speak again till some one asks you to do so."

As he spoke a door opened in the wall of the dark chamber in which they had been standing for the last few minutes, and a flood of soft light flowed in upon their dazzled eyes. At the same moment a man's voice said from the room beyond in Russian—

"Who stands there?"

"Maurice Colston and the Master of the Air," replied Colston in the same language.

"You are welcome," was the reply, and then Colston, taking Arnold by the arm, led him into the room.

CHAPTER V.

THE INNER CIRCLE.

S soon as Arnold's eyes got accustomed to the light, he saw that he was in a large, lofty room with panelled walls adorned with a number of fine paintings. As he looked at these his gaze was fascinated by them, even more than by the strange company which was assembled round the long table that occupied the middle of the room.

Though they were all manifestly the products of the highest form of art, their subjects were dreary and repulsive beyond description. There was a horrible realism about them which reminded him irresistibly of the awful collection of pictorial horrors in the Musée Wiertz, in Brussels—those works of the brilliant but unhappy genius who was driven into insanity by the sheer exuberance of his own morbid imagination.

Here was a long line of men and women in chains staggering across a wilderness of snow that melted away into the horizon without a break. Beside them rode Cossacks armed with long whips that they used on men and women alike when their fainting limbs gave way beneath them, and they were like to fall by the wayside to seek the welcome rest that only death could give them.

There was a picture of a woman naked to the waist, and tied up to a triangle in a prison yard, being flogged by a soldier with willow wands, while a group of officers stood by, apparently greatly interested in the performance. Another painting showed a poor wretch being knouted to death in the market-place of a Russian town, and yet another showed a young and beautiful woman in a prison cell with her face distorted by the horrible leer of madness, and her little white hands clawing nervously at her long dishevelled hair.

Arnold stood for several minutes fascinated by the hideous realism of the pictures, and burning with rage and shame at the thought that they were all too terribly true to life, when he was startled out of his reverie by the same voice that had called them from the dark room saying to him in English—

"Well, Richard Arnold, what do you think of our little picture gallery? The paintings are good in themselves, but it may make them more interesting to you if you know that they are all faithful reproductions of scenes that have really taken place within the limits of the so-called civilised and Christian world. There are some here in this room now who have suffered the torments depicted on those canvases, and who could tell of worse horrors than even they portray. We should like to know what you think of our paintings?"

Arnold glanced towards the table in search of Colston, but he had vanished. Around the long table sat fourteen masked and shrouded forms that were absolutely indistinguishable one from the other. He could not even tell whether they were men or women, so closely were their forms and faces concealed. Seeing that he was left to his own discretion, he laid the case containing the model, which he had so far kept under his arm, down on the floor, and, facing the strange assembly, said as steadily as he could—

"My own reading tells me that they are only too true to the dreadful reality. I think that the civilised and Christian Society which permits such crimes to be committed against humanity, when it has the power to stop them by force of arms, is neither truly civilised nor truly Christian."

"And would *you* stop them if you could?"

"Yes, if it cost the lives of millions to do it! They would be better spent than the thirty million lives that were lost last century over a few bits of territory."

"That is true, and augurs well for our future agreement. Be kind enough to come to the table and take a seat."

The masked man who spoke was sitting in the chair at the foot of the table, and as he said this one of those sitting at the side got up and motioned to Arnold to take his place. As soon as he had done so the speaker continued—

"We are glad to see that your sentiments are so far in accord with our own, for that fact will make our negotiations all the easier.

"As you are aware, you are now in the Inner Circle of the Terrorists. Yonder empty chair at the head of the table is that of our Chief, who, though not with us in person, is ever present as a guiding influence in our councils. We act as he directs, and it was from him that we received news of you and your marvellous invention. It is also by his direction that you have been invited here to-night with an object that you are already aware of.

"I see from your face that you are about to ask how this can be, seeing that you have never confided your secret to any one until last night. It will be useless to ask me, for I myself do not know. We who sit here simply execute the Master's will. We ask no questions, and therefore we can answer none concerning him."

"I have none to ask," said Arnold, seeing that the speaker paused as though expecting him to say something. "I came at the invitation of one of your Brotherhood to lay certain terms before you, for you to accept or reject as seems good to you. How you got to know of me and my invention is, after all, a matter of indifference to me. With your perfect system of espionage you might well find out more secret things than that."

"Quite so," was the reply. "And the question that we have to settle with you is how far you will consent to assist the work of the Brotherhood with this invention of yours, and on what conditions you will do so."

"I must first know as exactly as possible what the work of the Brotherhood is."

"Under the circumstances there is no objection to your knowing that. In the first place, that which is known to the outside world as the Terror is an international secret society underlying and directing the operations of the various bodies known as Nihilists, Anarchists, Socialists—in fact, all those organisations which have for their object the reform or destruction, by peaceful or violent means, of Society as it is at present constituted.

"Its influence reaches beyond these into the various trade

unions and political clubs, the moving spirits of which are all members of our Outer Circle. On the other side of Society we have agents and adherents in all the Courts of Europe, all the diplomatic bodies, and all the parliamentary assemblies throughout the world.

"We believe that Society as at present constituted is hopeless for any good thing. All kinds of nameless brutalities are practised without reproof in the names of law and order, and commercial economics. On one side human life is a splendid fabric of cloth of gold embroidered with priceless gems, and on the other it is a mass of filthy, festering rags, swarming with vermin.

"We think that such a Society—a Society which permits considerably more than the half of humanity to be sunk in poverty and misery while a very small portion of it fools away its life in perfectly ridiculous luxury—does not deserve to exist, and ought to be destroyed.

"We also know that sooner or later it will destroy itself, as every similar Society has done before it. For nearly forty years there has now been almost perfect peace in Europe. At the same time, over twenty millions of men are standing ready to take the field in a week.

"War — universal war that will shake the world to its foundations—is only a matter of a little more delay and a few diplomatic hitches. Russia and England are within rifleshot of each other in Afghanistan, and France and Germany are flinging defiances at each other across the Rhine.

"Some one must soon fire the shot that will set the world in a blaze, and meanwhile the toilers of the earth are weary of these dreadful military and naval burdens, and would care very little if the inevitable happened to-morrow.

"It is in the power of the Terrorists to delay or precipitate that war to a certain extent. Hitherto all our efforts have been devoted to the preservation of peace, and many of the so-called outrages which have taken place in different parts of Europe, and especially in Russia, during the last few years, have been accomplished simply for the purpose of forcing the attention of the administrations to internal affairs for the time, and so putting off what would have led to a declaration of war.

"This policy has not been dictated by any hope of avoiding war altogether, for that would have been sheer insanity. We have simply delayed war as long as possible, because we have not felt that we have been strong enough to turn the tide of battle at the right moment in favour of the oppressed ones of the earth and against their oppressors.

"But this invention of yours puts a completely different aspect on the European situation. Armed with such a tremendous engine of destruction as a navigable air-ship must necessarily be, when used in conjunction with the explosives already at our disposal, we could make war impossible to our enemies by bringing into the field a force with which no army or fleet could contend without the certainty of destruction. By these means we should ultimately compel peace and enforce a general disarmament on land and sea.

"The vast majority of those who make the wealth of the world are sick of seeing that wealth wasted in the destruction of human life, and the ruin of peaceful industries. As soon, therefore, as we are in a position to dictate terms under such tremendous penalties, all the innumerable organisations with which we are in touch all over the world will rise in arms and enforce them at all costs.

"Of course, it goes without saying that the powers that are now enthroned in the high places of the world will fight bitterly and desperately to retain the rule that they have held for so long, but in the end we shall be victorious, and then on the ruins of this civilisation a new and a better shall arise.

"That is a rough, brief outline of the policy of the Brotherhood, which we are going to ask you to-night to join. Of course, in the eyes of the world we are only a set of fiends, whose sole object is the destruction of Society, and the inauguration of a state of universal anarchy. That, however, has no concern for us. What is called popular opinion is merely manufactured by the Press according to order, and does not count in serious concerns. What I have described to you are the true objects of the Brotherhood; and now it remains for you to say, yes or no, whether you will devote yourself and your invention to carrying them out or not."

For two or three minutes after the masked spokesman of the Inner Circle had ceased speaking, there was absolute silence in the room. The calmly spoken words which deliberately sketched out the ruin of a civilisation and the establishment of a new order of things made a deep impression on Arnold's mind. He saw clearly that he was standing at the parting of the ways, and facing the most tremendous crisis that could occur in the life of a human being.

It was only natural that he should look back, as he did, to the life from which a single step would now part him for ever, without the possibility of going back. He knew that if he once put his hands to the plough, and looked back, death, swift and inevitable, would be the penalty of his wavering. This, however, he had already weighed and decided.

Most of what he had heard had found an echo in his own convictions. Moreover, the life that he had left had no charms for him, while to be one of the chief factors in a world-revolution was a destiny worthy both of himself and his invention. So the fatal resolution was taken, and he spoke the words that bound him for ever to the Brotherhood.

"As I have already told Mr. Colston," he began by saying, "I will join and faithfully serve the Brotherhood if the conditions that I feel compelled to make are granted"—

"We know them already," interrupted the spokesman, "and they are freely granted. Indeed, you can hardly fail to see that we are trusting you to a far greater extent than it is possible for us to make you trust us, unless you choose to do so. The air-ship once built and afloat under your command, the game of war would to a great extent be in your own hands. True, you would not survive treachery very long; but, on the other hand, if it became necessary to kill you, the air-ship would be useless, that is, if you took your secret of the motive power with you into the next world."

"As I undoubtedly should," added Arnold quietly.

"We have no doubt that you would," was the equally quiet rejoinder. "And now I will read to you the oath of membership that you will be required to sign. Even when you have heard it, if you feel any hesitation in subscribing to it, there will still be time to withdraw, for we tolerate no unwilling or half-hearted recruits."

Arnold bowed his acquiescence, and the spokesman took a piece of paper from the table and read aloud—

"I, Richard Arnold, sign this paper in **the full knowledge that in doing so I devote myself absolutely for the rest of my life to the service of the Brotherhood of Freedom, known to the world as the Terrorists. As long as I live its ends shall be my ends, and no human considerations shall weigh with me where those ends are concerned. I will take life without mercy, and yield my own without hesitation at its bidding. I will break all other laws to obey those which it obeys, and if I disobey these I shall expect death as the just penalty of my perjury."**

As he finished reading the oath, he handed the paper to Arnold, saying as he did so—

"There are no theatrical formalities to be gone through. Simply sign the paper and give it back to me, or else tear it up and go in peace."

Arnold read it through slowly, and then glanced round the table. He saw the eyes of the silent figures sitting about him shining at him through the holes in their masks. He laid the paper down on the table in front of him, dipped a pen in an inkstand that stood near, and signed the oath in a firm, unfaltering hand. Then—committed for ever, for good or evil, to the new life that he had adopted—he gave the paper back again.

The President took it and read it, and then passed it to the mask on his right hand. It went from one to the other round the table, each one reading it before passing it on, until it got back to the President. When it reached him he rose from his seat, and, going to the fireplace, dropped it into the flames, and watched it until it was consumed to ashes. Then, crossing the room to where Arnold was sitting, he removed his mask with one hand, and held the other out to him in greeting, saying as he did so—

"Welcome to the Brotherhood! Thrice welcome! for your coming has brought the day of redemption nearer!"

CHAPTER VI.

NEW FRIENDS.

S Arnold returned the greeting of the President, all the other members of the Circle rose from their seats and took off their masks and the black shapeless cloaks which had so far completely covered them from head to foot.

Then, one after the other, they came forward and were formally introduced to him by the President. Nine of the fourteen were men, and five were women of ages varying from middle age almost to girlhood. The men were apparently all between twenty-five and thirty-five, and included some half-dozen nationalities among them.

All, both men and women, evidently belonged to the educated, or rather to the cultured class. Their speech, which seemed to change with perfect ease from one language to another in the course of their somewhat polyglot converse, was the easy flowing speech of men and women accustomed to the best society, not only in the social but the intellectual sense of the word.

All were keen, alert, and swift of thought, and on the face of each one there was the dignifying expression of a deep and settled purpose which at once differentiated them in Arnold's eyes from the ordinary idle or merely money-making citizens of the world.

As each one came and shook hands with the new member of the Brotherhood, he or she had some pleasant word of welcome and greeting for him ; and so well were the words chosen, and so manifestly sincerely were they spoken, that by the time he had shaken hands all round Arnold felt as much at home among them as though he were in the midst of a circle of old friends.

Among the women there were two who had attracted his attention and roused his interest far more than any of the other members of the Circle. One of these was a tall and beautifully-shaped woman, whose face and figure were those of a woman in the early twenties, but whose long, thick hair was as white as though the snows of seventy winters had drifted over it. As he returned her warm, firm hand-clasp, and looked upon her dark, resolute, and yet perfectly womanly features, the young engineer gave a slight start of recognition. She noticed this at once and said, with a smile and a quick flash from her splendid grey eyes—

"Ah! I see you recognise me. No, I am not ashamed of my portrait. I am proud of the wounds that I have received in the war with tyranny, so you need not fear to confess your recognition."

It was true that Arnold had recognised her. She was the original of the central figure of the painting which depicted the woman being flogged by the Russian soldiers.

Arnold flushed hotly at the words with the sudden passionate anger that they roused within him, and replied in a low, steady voice—

"Those who would sanction such a crime as that are not fit to live. I will not leave one stone of that prison standing upon another. It is a blot on the face of the earth, and I will wipe it out utterly!"

"There are thousands of blots as black as that on earth, and I think you will find nobler game than an obscure Russian provincial prison. Russia has cities and palaces and fortresses that will make far grander ruins than that—ruins that will be worthy monuments of fallen despotism," replied the girl, who had been introduced by the President as Radna Michaelis. " But here is some one else waiting to make your acquaintance. This is Natasha. She has no other name among us, but you will soon learn why she needs none."

Natasha was the other woman who had so keenly roused Arnold's interest. Woman, however, she hardly was, for she was seemingly still in her teens, and certainly could not have been more than twenty.

He had mixed but little with women, and during the past few years not at all, and therefore the marvellous beauty of the girl who came forward as Radna spoke seemed almost unearthly to him, and confused his senses for the moment as some potent drug might have done. He took her outstretched hand in awkward silence, and for an instant so far forgot himself as to gaze blankly at her in speechless admiration.

She could not help noticing it, for she was a woman, and for the same reason she saw that it was so absolutely honest and involuntary that it was impossible for any woman to take offence at it. A quick bright flush swept up her lovely face as his hand closed upon hers, her darkly-fringed lids fell for an instant over the most wonderful pair of sapphire-blue eyes that Arnold had ever even dreamed of, and when she raised them again the flush had gone, and she said in a sweet, frank voice—

"I am the daughter of Natas, and he has desired me to bid you welcome in his name, and I hope you will let me do so in my own as well. We are all dying to see this wonderful invention of yours. I suppose you are going to satisfy our feminine curiosity, are you not?"

The daughter of Natas! This lovely girl, in the first sweet flush of her pure and innocent womanhood, the daughter of the unknown and mysterious being whose ill-omened name caused a shudder if it was only whispered in the homes of the rich and powerful; the name with which the death-sentences of the Terrorists were invariably signed, and which had come to be an infallible guarantee that they would be carried out to the letter.

No death-warrants of the most powerful sovereigns of Europe were more certain harbingers of inevitable doom than were those which bore this dreaded name. Whether he were high or low, the man who received one of them made ready for his end. He knew not where or when the fatal blow would be struck. He only knew that the invisible hand of the Terror would strike him as surely in the uttermost ends of the earth as it would in the palace or the fortress. Never once had it missed its aim, and never once had the slightest clue been obtained to the identity of the hand that held the knife or pistol.

Some such thoughts as these flashed one after another through Arnold's brain as he stood talking with Natasha. He saw at once why she had only that one name. It was enough, and it was not long before he learnt that it was the symbol of an authority in the Circle that admitted of no question.

She was the envoy of him whose word was law, absolute and irrevocable, to every member of the Brotherhood; to disobey whom was death; and to obey whom had, so far at least, meant swift and invariable success, even where it seemed least to be hoped for.

Of course, Natasha's almost girlish question about the airship was really a command, which would have been none the less binding had she only had her own beauty to enforce it. As she spoke the President and Colston—who had only lost himself for the time behind a mask and cloak—came up to Arnold and asked him if he was prepared to give an exhibition of the powers of his model, and to explain its working and construction to the Circle at once.

He replied that everything was perfectly ready for the trial, and that he would set the model working for them in a few minutes. The President then told him that the exhibition should take place in another room, where there would be much more space than where they were, and bade him bring the box and follow him.

A door was now opened in the wall of the room remote from that by which he and Colston had entered, and through this the whole party went down a short passage, and through another door at the end which opened into a very large apartment, which, from the fact of its being windowless, Arnold rightly judged to be underground, like the Council-chamber that they had just left.

A single glance was enough to show him the chief purpose to which the chamber was devoted. The wall at one end was covered with arm-racks containing all the newest and most perfect makes of rifles and pistols; while at the other end, about twenty paces distant, were three electric signalling targets, graded, as was afterwards explained to him, to one, three, and five hundred yards range.

In a word, the chamber was an underground range for rifle and pistol practice, in which a volley could have been fired without a sound being heard ten yards away. It was here that the accuracy of the various weapons invented from time to time was tested; and here, too, every member of the Circle, man and woman, practised with rifle and pistol until an infallible aim was acquired. A register of scores was kept, and at the head of it stood the name of Radna Michaelis.

A long table ran across the end at which the arm-racks were, and on this Arnold laid the case containing the model, he standing on one side of the table, and the members of the Circle on the other, watching his movements with a curiosity that they took no trouble to disguise.

He opened the case, feeling something like a scientific demonstrator, with an advanced and critical class before him. In a moment the man disappeared, and the mechanician and the enthusiast took his place. As each part was taken out and laid upon the table, he briefly explained its use; and then, last of all, came the hull of the air-ship.

This was three feet long and six inches broad in its midships diameter. It was made in two longitudinal sections of polished aluminium, which shone like burnished silver. It would have been cigar-shaped but for the fact that the forward end was drawn out into a long sharp ram, the point of which was on a level with the floor of the hull amidships as it lay upon the table. Two deep bilge-plates, running nearly the whole length of the hull, kept it in an upright position and prevented the blades of the propellors from touching the table. For about half its whole length the upper part of the hull was flattened and formed a deck from which rose three short strong masts, each of which carried a wheel of thin metal whose spokes were six inclined fans something like the blades of a screw.

A little lower than this deck there projected on each side a broad, oblong, slightly curved sheet of metal, very thin, but strengthened by means of wire braces, till it was as rigid as a plate of solid steel, although it only weighed a few ounces. These air-planes worked on an axis amidships, and could be inclined either way through an angle of thirty degrees. At the pointed stern there revolved a powerful four-bladed propeller, and from each quarter, inclined slightly outwards from the middle line of the vessel, projected a somewhat smaller screw working underneath the after end of the air-planes.

The hull contained four small double-cylinder engines, one of which actuated the stern-propeller, and the other three the fan-wheels and side-propellers. There were, of course, no furnaces, boilers, or condensers. Two slender pipes ran into each cylinder from suitably placed gas reservoirs, or power-cylinders, as the engineer called them, and that was all.

Arnold deftly and rapidly put the parts together, continuing his running description as he did so, and in a few minutes the beautiful miracle of ingenuity stood complete before the wondering eyes of the Circle, and a murmur of admiration ran from lip to lip, bringing a flush of pleasure to the cheek of its creator.

"There," said he, as he put the finishing touches to the apparatus, " you see that she is a combination of two principles —those of the Aëronef and the Aëroplane. The first reached its highest development in Jules Verne's imaginary "Clipper of the Clouds," and the second in Hiram Maxim's Aëroplane. Of course, Jules Verne's Aëronef was merely an idea, and one that could never be realised while Robur's mysterious source of electrical energy remained unknown—as it still does.

"Maxim's Aëroplane is, as you all know, also an unrealised ideal so far as any practical use is concerned. He has succeeded in making it fly, but only under the most favourable conditions, and practically without cargo. Its two fatal defects have been shown by experience to be the comparatively overwhelming weight of the engine and the fuel that he has to carry to develop sufficient power to rise from the ground and progress against the wind, and the inability of the machine to ascend perpendicularly to any required height.

"Without the power to do this no air-ship can be of any use save under very limited conditions. You cannot carry a railway about with you, or a station to get a start from every time you want to rise, and you cannot always choose a nice level plain in which to come down. Even if you could the Aëroplane would not rise again without its rails and carriage. For purposes of warfare, then, it may be dismissed as totally useless.

"In this machine, as you see, I have combined the two principles. These helices on the masts will lift the dead weight of the ship perpendicularly without the slightest help from the side-planes, which are used to regulate the vessel's flight when afloat. I will set the engines that work them in motion independently of the others which move the propellers, and then you will see what I mean."

As he spoke, he set one part of the mechanism working. Those watching saw the three helices begin to spin round, the centre one revolving in an opposite direction to the other two, with a soft whirring sound that gradually rose to a high-pitched note.

When they attained their full speed they looked like solid wheels, and then the air-ship rose, at first slowly, and then more and more swiftly, straight up from the table, until it strained hard at the piece of cord which prevented it from reaching the roof.

A universal chorus of "bravas" greeted it as it rose, and every eye became fixed on it as it hung motionless in the air, sustained by its whirling helices. After letting it remain aloft for a few minutes Arnold pulled it down again, saying as he did so—

"That, I think, proves that the machine can rise from any position where the upward road is open, and without the slightest assistance of any apparatus. Now it shall take a voyage round the room.

"You see it is steered by this rudder-fan under the stern propeller. In the real ship it will be worked by a wheel, like the rudder of a sea-going vessel; but in the model it is done by this lever, so that I can control it by a couple of strings from the ground."

He went round to the other side of the table while he was speaking, and adjusted the steering gear, stopping the engines meanwhile. Then he put the model down on the floor, set all four engines to work, and stood behind with the guiding-strings in his hands. The spectators heard a louder and somewhat shriller whirring noise than before, and the beautiful fabric, with its shining, silvery hull and side-planes, rose slantingly from the ground and darted forward down the room, keeping Arnold at a quick run with the rudder-strings tightly strained.

Like an obedient steed, it instantly obeyed the slightest pull upon either of them, and twice made the circuit of the room before its creator pulled it down and stopped the machinery.

The experiment was a perfect and undeniable success in

every respect, and not one of those who saw it had the slightest doubt as to Arnold's air-ship having at last solved the problem of aërial navigation, and made the Brotherhood lords of a realm as wide as the atmospheric ocean that encircles the globe.

As soon as the model was once more resting on the table, the President came forward and, grasping the engineer by both hands, said in a voice from which he made but little effort to banish the emotion that he felt—

"Bravo, brother! Henceforth you shall be known to the Brotherhood as the Master of the Air, for truly you have been the first among the sons of men to fairly conquer it. Come, let us go back and talk, for there is much to be said about this, and we cannot begin too soon to make arrangements for building the first of our aërial fleet. You can leave your model where it is in perfect safety, for no one ever enters this room save ourselves."

So saying the President led the way to the Council-chamber, and there, after the *Ariel*—as it had already been decided to name the first air-ship—had been christened in anticipation in twenty-year old champagne, the Circle settled down at once to business, and for a good three hours discussed the engineer's estimate and plans for building the first vessel of the aërial fleet.

At length all the practical details were settled, and the President rose in token of the end of the conference. As he did so he said somewhat abruptly to Arnold—

"So far so good. Now there is nothing more to be done but to lay those plans before the Chief and get his authority for withdrawing out of the treasury sufficient money to commence operations. I presume you could reproduce them from memory if necessary—at any rate, in sufficient outline to make them perfectly intelligible?"

"Certainly," was the reply. "I could reproduce them in *fac simile* without the slightest difficulty. Why do you ask?"

"Because the Chief is in Russia, and you must go to him and place them before him from memory. They are far too precious to be trusted to any keeping, however trustworthy. There are such things as railway accidents, and other forms of sudden death, to say nothing of the Russian customs, false arrests, personal searches, and imprisonments on mere suspicion.

"We can risk none of these, and so there is nothing for it but your going to Petersburg and verbally explaining them to the Chief. You can be ready in three days, I suppose?"

"Yes, in two, if you like," replied Arnold, not a little taken aback at the unexpected suddenness of what he knew at once to be the first order that was to test his obedience to the Brotherhood. "But as I am absolutely ignorant of Russia and the Russians, I suppose you will make such arrangements as will prevent my making any innocent but possibly awkward mistakes."

"Oh yes," replied the President, with a smile, "all arrangements have been made already, and I expect you will find them anything but unpleasant. Natasha goes to Petersburg in company with another lady member of the Circle whom you have not yet seen.

"You will go with them, and they will explain everything to you *en route*, if they have no opportunity of doing so before you start. Now let us go upstairs and have some supper. I am famished, and I suppose every one else is too."

Arnold simply bowed in answer to the President; but one pair of eyes at least in the room caught the quick, faint flush that rose in his cheek as he was told in whose company he was to travel. As for himself, if the journey had been to Siberia instead of Russia, he would have felt nothing but pleasure at the prospect after that.

They left the Council-chamber by the passage and the ante-room, the sentry standing to attention as they passed him, each giving the word in turn, till the President came last and closed the doors behind him. Then the sentry brought up the rear and extinguished the lights as he left the passage.

Fifteen minutes later there sat down to supper, in the solidly comfortable dining-room of the upper house, a party of ladies and gentlemen who chatted through the meal as merrily and innocently as though there were no such things as tyranny or suffering in the world, and whom not the most acute observer would have taken for the most dangerous and desperately earnest body of conspirators that ever plotted the destruction, not of an empire, but of a civilisation and a social order that it had taken twenty centuries to build up.

CHAPTER VII.

THE DAUGHTER OF NATAS.

UPPER was over about eleven, and then the party adjourned to the drawing-room, where for an hour or so Arnold sat and listened to such music and singing as he had never heard in his life before. The songs seemed to be in every language in Europe, and he did not understand anything like half of them, so far, at least, as the words were concerned.

They were, however, so far removed from the average drawing-room medley of twaddle and rattle that the music interpreted the words into its own universal language, and made them almost superfluous.

For the most part they were sad and passionate, and once or twice, especially when Radna Michaelis was singing, Arnold saw tears well up into the eyes of the women, and the brows of the men contract and their hands clench with sudden passion at the recollection of some terrible scene or story that was recalled by the song.

At last, close on midnight, the President rose from his seat and asked Natasha to sing the "Hymn of Freedom." She acknowledged the request with an inclination of her head, and then as Radna sat down to the piano, and she took her place beside it, all the rest rose to their feet like worshippers in a chuch.

The prelude was rather longer than usual, and as Radna played it Arnold heard running through it, as it were, echoes of all the patriotic songs of Europe from "Scots Wha Hae" and "The Shan van Voght" to the forbidden Polish National Hymn and the Swiss Republican song, which is known in

England as "God Save the Queen." The prelude ended with a few bars of the "Marseillaise," and then Natasha began.

It was a marvellous performance. As the air changed from nation to nation the singer changed the language, and at the end of each verse the others took up the strain in perfect harmony, till it sounded like a chorus of the nations in miniature, each language coming in its turn until the last verse was reached.

Then there was silence for a moment, and then the opening chords of the "Marseillaise" rang out from the piano, slow and stately at first, and then quickening like the tread of an army going into battle.

Suddenly Natasha's voice soared up, as it were, out of the music, and a moment later the Song of the Revolution rolled forth in a flood of triumphant melody, above which Natasha's pure contralto thrilled sweet and strong, till to Arnold's intoxicated senses it seemed like the voice of some angel singing from the sky in the ears of men, and it was not until the hymn had been ended for some moments that he was recalled to earth by the President saying to him—

"Some day, perhaps, you will be floating in the clouds, and you will hear that hymn rising from the throats of millions gathered together from the ends of the earth, and when you hear that you will know that our work is done, and that there is peace on earth at last."

"I hope so," replied the engineer quietly, "and, what is more, I believe that some day I shall hear it."

"I believe so too," suddenly interrupted Radna, turning round on her seat at the piano, "but there will be many a battle-song sung to the accompaniment of battle-music before that happens. I wish"—

"That all Russia were a haystack, and that you were beside it with a lighted torch," said Natasha, half in jest and half in earnest.

"Yes, truly!" replied Radna, turning round and dashing fiercely into the "Marseillaise" again.

"I have no doubt of it. But, come, it is after midnight, and we have to get back to Cheyne Walk. The princess will think we have been arrested or something equally dreadful. Ah, Mr. Colston, we have a couple of seats to spare in the brougham. Will you and our Admiral of the Air condescend to accept a lift as far as Chelsea?"

"The condescension is in the offer, Natasha," replied Colston, flushing with pleasure and glancing towards Radna the while. Radna answered with an almost imperceptible sign of consent, and Colston went on: "If it were in an utterly opposite direction"—

"You would not be asked to come, sir. So don't try to pay compliments at the expense of common sense," laughed Natasha before he could finish. "If you do you shall sit beside me instead of Radna all the way."

There was a general smile at this retort, for Colston's avowed devotion to Radna and the terrible circumstances out of which it had sprung was one of the romances of the Circle.

As for Arnold, he could scarcely believe his ears when he heard that he was to ride from Clapham Common to Chelsea sitting beside this radiantly beautiful girl, behind whose innocence and gaiety there lay the shadow of her mysterious and terrible parentage.

Lovely and gentle as she seemed, he knew even now how awful a power she held in the slender little hand whose nervous clasp he could still feel upon his own, and this knowledge seemed to raise an invisible yet impassable barrier between him and the possibility of looking upon her as under other circumstances it would have been natural for a man to look upon so fair a woman.

Natasha's brougham was so far an improvement on those of the present day that it had two equally comfortable seats, and on these the four were cosily seated a few minutes after the party broke up. To Arnold, and, doubtless, to Colston also, the miles flew past at an unheard-of speed; but for all that, long before the carriage stopped at the house in Cheyne Walk, he had come to the conviction that, for good or evil, he was now bound to the Brotherhood by far stronger ties than any social or political opinions could have formed.

After they had said good-night at the door, and received an invitation to lunch for the next day to talk over the journey to Russia, he and Colston decided to walk to the Savoy, for it was a clear moonlit night, and each had a good deal to say to the other, which could be better and more safely said in the open air than in a cab. So they lit their cigars, buttoned up their coats, and started off eastward along the Embankment to Vauxhall.

"Well, my friend, tell me how you have enjoyed your evening, and what you think of the company," said Colston, by way of opening the conversation.

"Until supper I had a very pleasant time of it. I enjoyed the business part of the proceedings intensely, as any other mechanical enthusiast would have done, I suppose. But I frankly confess that after that my mind is in a state of complete chaos, in the midst of which only one figure stands out at all distinctly."

"And that figure is?"

"Natasha. Tell me—who is she?"

"I know no more as to her true identity than you do, or else I would answer you with pleasure."

"What! Do you mean to say"—

"I mean to say just what I have said. Not only do I not know who she is, but I do not believe that more than two or three members of the Circle, at the outside, know any more than I do. Those are, probably, Nicholas Roburoff, the President of the Executive, and his wife, and Radna Michaelis."

"Then, if Radna knows, how comes it that you do not know? You must forgive me if I am presuming on a too short acquaintance; but it certainly struck me to-night that you had very few secrets from each other."

"There is no presumption about it, my dear fellow," replied Colston, with a laugh. "It is no secret that Radna and I are lovers, and that she will be my wife when I have earned her."

"Now you have raised my curiosity again," interrupted Arnold, in an inquiring tone.

"And will very soon satisfy it. You saw that horrible picture in the Council-chamber? Yes. Well, I will tell you the whole story of that some day when we have more time; but for the present it will be enough for me to tell you that I have sworn not to ask Radna to come with me to the altar while a single person who was concerned in that nameless crime remains alive.

"There were five persons responsible for it to begin with—the governor of the prison, the prefect of police for the district, a spy, who informed against her, and the two soldiers who executed the infernal sentence. It happened nearly three years ago, and there are two of them alive still—the governor and the prefect of police.

"Of course the Brotherhood would have removed them long ago had it decided to do so; but I got the circumstances laid before Natas, by the help of Natasha, and received permission to execute the sentences myself. So far I have killed three with my own hand, and the other two have not much longer to live.

"The governor has been transferred to Siberia, and will probably be the last that I shall reach. The prefect is now in command of the Russian secret police in London, and unless an accident happens he will never leave England."

Colston spoke in a cold, passionless, merciless tone, just as a lawyer might speak of a criminal condemned to die by the ordinary process of the law, and as Arnold heard him he shuddered. But at the same time the picture in the Council-chamber came up before his mental vision, and he was forced to confess that men who could so far forget their manhood as to lash a helpless woman up to a triangle and flog her till her flesh was cut to ribbons, were no longer men but wild beasts, whose very existence was a crime. So he merely said—

"They were justly slain. Now tell me more about Natasha."

"There is very little more that I can tell you, I'm afraid. All I know is that the Brotherhood of the Terror is the conception and creation of a single man, and that that man is Natas, the father of Natasha, as she is known to us. His orders come to us either directly in writing through Natasha, or indirectly through him you have heard spoken of as the Chief."

"Oh, then the Chief is not Natas?"

"No, we have all of us seen him. In fact, when he is in London he always presides at the Circle meetings. You would hardly believe it, but he is an English nobleman, and Secretary to the English Embassy at Petersburg."

"Then he is Lord Alanmere, and an old college friend of mine!" exclaimed Arnold. "I saw his name in the paper the night before last. It was mentioned in the account of the murder"—

"We don't call those murders, my friend," drily interrupted Colston; "we call them what they really are—executions."

"I beg your pardon; I was using the phraseology of the newspaper. What was his crime?"

"I don't know. But the fact that the Chief was there when he died is quite enough for me. Well, as I was saying, the Chief, as we call him, is the visible and supreme head of the Brotherhood so far as we are concerned. We know that Natas exists, and that he and the Chief admit no one save Natasha to their councils.

"They control the treasury absolutely, and apart from the contributions of those of the members who can afford to make them, they appear to provide the whole of the funds. Of course, Lord Alanmere, as you know, is enormously wealthy, and probably Natas is also rich. At any rate, there is never any want of money where the work of the Brotherhood is concerned.

"The estimates are given to Natasha when the Chief is not present, and at the next meeting she brings the money in English gold and notes, or in foreign currency as may be required, and that is all we know about the finances.

"Perhaps I ought to tell you that there is also a very considerable mystery about the Chief himself. When he presides at the Council meetings he displays a perfectly marvellous knowledge of both the members and the working of the Brotherhood.

"It would seem that nothing, however trifling, is hidden from him; and yet when any of us happen to meet him, as we often do, in Society, he treats us all as the most perfect strangers, unless we have been regularly introduced to him as ordinary acquaintances. Even then he seems utterly ignorant of his connection with the Brotherhood.

"The first time I met him outside the Circle was at a ball at the Russian Embassy. I went and spoke to him, giving the sign of the Inner Circle as I did so. To my utter amazement, he stared at me without a sign of recognition, and calmly informed me, in the usual way, that I had the advantage of him.

"Of course I apologised, and he accepted the apology with perfect good humour, but as an utter stranger would have done. A little later Natasha came in with the Princess Ornovski, whom you are going to Russia with, and who is there one of the most trusted agents of the Petersburg police. I told her what had happened.

"She looked at me for a moment rather curiously with those wonderful eyes of hers; then she laughed softly, and said, 'Come, I will set that at rest by introducing you; but mind, not a word about politics or those horrible secret societies, as you value my good opinion.'

"I understood from this that there was something behind which could not be explained there, where every other one you danced with might be a spy, and I was introduced to his Lordship, and we became very good friends in the ordinary social way; but I failed to gather the slightest hint from his conversation that he even knew of the existence of the Brotherhood.

"When we left I drove home with Natasha and the Princess to supper, and on the way Natasha told me that his Lordship found it necessary to lead two entirely distinct lives, and that he adhered so rigidly to this rule that he never broke it even with her. Since then I have been most careful to respect what, after all, is a very wise, if not an absolutely necessary, precaution on his part."

"And, now," said Arnold, speaking in a tone that betrayed not a little hesitation and embarrassment, "if you can do so, answer me one more question, and do so as shortly and directly as you can. Is Natasha in love with, or betrothed to, any member of the Brotherhood as far as you know?"

Colston stopped and looked at him with a laugh in his eyes. Then he put his hand on his shoulder and said—

"As I thought, and feared! You have not escaped the common lot of all heart-whole men upon whom those terrible eyes of hers have looked. The Angel of the Revolution, as we call her among ourselves, is peerless among the daughters of men. What more natural, then, that all the sons of men should fall speedy victims to her fatal charms? So far as I know, every man who has ever seen her is more or less in love with her—and mostly more!

"As for the rest, I am as much in the dark as you are, save for the fact that I know, on the authority of Radna, that she is not betrothed to any one, and, so far as *she* knows, still in the blissful state of maiden fancy-freedom."

"Thank God for that!" said Arnold, with an audible sigh of relief. Then he went on in somewhat hurried confusion, "But there, of course, you think me a presumptuous ass, and so I am; wherefore"—

"There is no need for you to talk nonsense, my dear fellow. There never can be presumption in an honest man's love, no matter how exalted the object of it may be. Besides, are you not now the central hope of the Revolution, and is not yours the hand that shall hurl destruction on its enemies?

"As for Natasha, peerless and all as she is, has not the poet of the ages said of just such as her—

> She's beautiful, and therefore to be woo'd;
> She is a woman: therefore to be won?

"And who, too, has a better chance of winning her than you will have when you are commanding the aërial fleet of the Brotherhood, and, like a very Jove, hurling your destroying bolts from the clouds, and deciding the hazard of war when the nations of Europe are locked in the death-struggle? Why, you see such a prospect makes even me poetical.

"Seriously, though, you must not consider the distance between you too great. Remember that you are a very different person now to what you were a couple of days ago. Without any offence, I may say that you were then nameless, while now you have the chance of making a name that will go down to all time as that of the solver of the greatest problem of this or any other age.

"Added to this, remember that Natasha, after all, is a woman, and, more than that, a woman devoted heart and soul to a great cause, in which great deeds are soon to be done. Great deeds are still the shortest way to a woman's heart, and that is the way you must take if you are to hope for success."

"I will!" simply replied Arnold, and the tone in which the two words were said convinced Colston that he meant all that they implied to its fullest extent.

CHAPTER VIII.

LEARNING THE PART.

IT was nearly eleven the next morning by the time Arnold and Colston had finished breakfast. This was mostly due to the fact that Arnold had passed an almost entirely sleepless night, and had only begun to doze off towards morning. The events of the previous evening kept on repeating themselves in various sequences time after time, until his brain reeled in the whirl of emotions that they gave rise to.

Although of a strongly mathematical and even mechanical turn of mind, the young engineer was also an enthusiast, and therefore there was a strong colouring of romance in his nature which lifted him far above the level upon which his mere intellect was accustomed to work

Where intellect alone was concerned—as, for instance, in the working out of a problem in engineering or mechanics— he was cool, calculating, and absolutely unemotional. His highly-disciplined mind was capable of banishing every other subject from consideration save the one which claimed the attention of the hour, and of incorporating itself wholly with the work in hand until it was finished.

These qualities would have been quite sufficient to assure his success in life on conventional lines. They would have made him rich, and perhaps famous, but they would never have made him a great inventor; for no one can do anything really great who is not a dreamer as well as a worker.

It was because he was a dreamer that he had sacrificed everything to the working out of his ideal, and risked his life on the chance of success, and it was for just the same reason that the tremendous purposes of the Brotherhood had been able to fire his imagination with luridly brilliant dreams of a gigantic world-tragedy in which he, armed with almost supernatural powers, should play the central part.

This of itself would have been enough to make all other considerations of trivial moment in his eyes, and to bind him irrevocably to the Brotherhood. He saw, it is true, that a frightful amount of slaughter and suffering would be the price either of success or failure in so terrific a struggle; but he also knew that that struggle was inevitable in some form or other, and whether he took a part in it or not.

But since the last sun had set a new element had come into his life, and was working in line with both his imagination and his ambition. So far he had lived his life without any other human love than what was bound up with his recollections of his home and his boyhood. As a man he had never loved any human being. Science had been his only mistress, and had claimed his undivided devotion, engrossing his mind and intellect completely, but leaving his heart free.

And now, as it were in an instant, a new mistress had come forward out of the unknown. She had put her hand upon his heart, and, though no words of human speech had passed between them, save the merest commonplaces, her soul had said to his, "This is mine. I have called it into life, and for me it shall live until the end."

He had heard this as plainly as though it had been said to him with the lips of flesh, and he had acquiesced in the imperious claim with a glad submission which had yet to be tinged with the hope that it might some day become a mastery.

Thus, as the silent, sleepless hours went by, did he review over and over again the position in which he found himself on the threshold of his strange new life, until at last physical exhaustion brought sleep to his eyes if not to his brain, and he found himself flying over the hills and vales of dreamland in his air-ship, with the roar of battle and the smoke of ruined towns far beneath him, and Natasha at his side, sharing with him the dominion of the air that his genius had won.

At length Colston came in to tell him that the breakfast was spoiling, and that it was high time to get up if they intended to be in time for their appointment at Chelsea. This brought him out of bed with effective suddenness, and he made a hasty toilet for breakfast, leaving more important preparations until afterwards.

During the meal their conversation naturally turned chiefly on the visit that they were to pay, and Colston took the opportunity of explaining one or two things that it was necessary for him to know with regard to the new acquaintance that he was about to make at Chelsea.

"So far as the outside world is concerned," said he, "Natasha is the niece of the Princess Ornovski. She is the daughter of a sister of hers, who married an English gentleman, named Darrel, who was drowned with his wife about twelve years ago, when the *Albania* was wrecked off the coast of Portugal. The Princess had a sister, who was drowned with her husband in the *Albania*, and she left a daughter about Natasha's then age, but who died of consumption shortly after in Nice.

"Under these circumstances, it was, of course, perfectly easy for the Princess to adopt Natasha, and introduce her into Society as her niece as soon as she reached the age of coming out.

"This has been of immense service to the Brotherhood, as the Princess is, as I told you, one of the most implicitly trusted allies of the Petersburg police. She is received at the Russian Court, and is therefore able to take Natasha into the best Russian Society, where her extraordinary beauty naturally enables her to break as many hearts as she likes, and to learn secrets which are of the greatest importance to the Brotherhood.

"Her Society name is Fedora Darrel, and it will scarcely be necessary to tell you that outside our own Circle no such being as Natasha has any existence."

"I perfectly understand," replied Arnold. "The name shall never pass my lips save in privacy, and indeed it is hardly likely that it will ever do so even then, for your habit of calling each other by your Christian names is too foreign to my British insularity."

"It is a Russian habit, as you, of course, know, and added to that, we are, so far as the Cause is concerned, all brothers and sisters together, and so it comes natural to us. Anyhow, you will have to use it with Natasha, for in the Circle she has no other name, and to call her Miss Darrel there would be to produce something like an earthquake."

"Oh, in that case, I daresay I shall be able to avoid the calamity, though there will seem to be a presumption about it that will not make me very comfortable at first."

"Too much like addressing one's sweetheart, eh?"

This brought the conversation to a sudden stop, for Arnold's only reply to it was a quick flush, and a lapse into silence that was a good deal more eloquent than any verbal reply could have been. Colston noticed it with a smile, and got up and lit a pipe.

For the first time for a good few years Arnold took considerable pains with his toilet that morning. A new fit-out had just been delivered by a tailor who had promised the things within twenty-four hours, and had kept his word. The consequences were that he was able to array himself in perfect morning costume, from his hat to his boots, and that was what it had not been his to do since he left college.

Colston had recommended him in his easy friendly way to pay scrupulous attention to externals in the part that he would henceforth have to play before the world. He fully saw the wisdom of this advice, for he knew that, however well a part may be played, if it is not dressed to perfection, some sharp eyes will see that it is a part and not a reality.

The playing of his part was to begin that day, and he recognised that at least one of the purposes of his visit to Natasha was the determining of what that part was to be. He thus looked forward with no little curiosity to the events of the afternoon, quite apart from the supreme interest that centred in his hostess.

They started out nearly a couple of hours before they were due at Cheyne Walk, as they had several orders to give with regard to Arnold's outfit for the journey that was before him; and this done, they reached the house about a quarter of an hour before lunch time.

They were received in the most delightful of sitting-rooms by a very handsome, aristocratic-looking woman, who might have been anywhere between forty and fifty. She shook hands very cordially with Arnold, saying as she did so—

"Welcome, Richard Arnold! The friends of the Cause are

mine, and I have heard much about you already from Natasha, so that I already seem to know you. I am very sorry that I was not able to be at the Circle last night to see what you had to show. Natasha tells me that it is quite a miracle of genius."

"She is too generous in her praise," replied Arnold, speaking as quietly as he could in spite of the delight that the words gave him. "It is no miracle, but only the logical result of thought and work. Still, I hope that it will be found to realise its promise when the time of trial comes."

"Of that I have no doubt, from all that I hear," said the Princess. "Before long I shall hope to see it for myself. Ah, here is Natasha. Come, I must introduce you afresh, for you do not know her yet as the world knows her."

Arnold heard the door open behind him as the Princess spoke, and, turning round, saw Natasha coming towards him with her hand outstretched and a smile of welcome on her beautiful face. Before their hands met the Princess moved quietly between them and said, half in jest and half in earnest—

"Fedora, permit me to present to you Mr. Richard Arnold, who is to accompany us to Russia to inspect the war-balloon offered to our Little Father the Tsar. Mr. Arnold, my niece, Fedora Darrel. There, now you know each other."

"I am delighted to make your acquaintance, Mr. Arnold," said Natasha, with mock gravity as they shook hands. "I have heard much already of your skill in connection with aërial navigation, and I have no doubt but that your advice will be of the greatest service to his Majesty."

"That is as it may be," answered Arnold, at once entering into the somewhat grim humour of the situation. "But if it is possible I should like to hear something a little definite as to this mission with which I have been, I fear, undeservingly honoured. I have been very greatly interested in the problem of aërial navigation for some years past, but I must confess that this is the first I have heard of these particular war-balloons."

"It is for the purpose of enlightening you on that subject that this little party has been arranged," said the Princess, turning for the moment away from Colston, with whom she was talking earnestly in a low tone. "Ha! There goes the lunch-bell. Mr. Colston, your arm. Fedora, will you show Mr. Arnold the way?"

Arnold opened the door for the Princess to go out, and then followed with Natasha on his arm. As they went out, she said in a low tone to him—

"I think, if you don't mind, you had better begin at once to call me Miss Darrel, so as to get into the way of it. A slip might be serious, you know."

"Your wishes are my laws, Miss Darrel," replied he, the name slipping as easily off his tongue as if he had known her by it for months. It may have been only fancy on his part, he thought he felt just the lightest imaginable pressure on his arm as he spoke. At any rate, he was vain enough or audacious enough to take the impression for a reality, and walked the rest of the way to the dining-room on air.

The meal was dainty and perfectly served, but there were no servants present, for obvious reasons, and so they waited on themselves. Colston sat opposite the Princess and carved the partridges, while Arnold was *vis-à-vis* to Natasha, a fact which had a perceptible effect upon his appetite.

"Now," said the Princess, as soon as every one was helped, "I will enlighten you, Mr. Arnold, as to your mission to Russia. One part of the business, I presume, you are already familiar with?"

Arnold bowed his assent, and she went on—

"Then the other is easily explained. Interested as you are in the question, I suppose there is no need to tell you that for several years past the Tsar has had an offer open to all the world of a million sterling for a vessel that will float in the air, and be capable of being directed in its course as a ship at sea can be directed."

"Yes, I am well aware of the fact. Pray proceed." As he said this Arnold glanced across the table at Natasha, and a swift smile and a flash from her suddenly unveiled eyes told him that she, too, was thinking of how the world's history might have been altered had the Tsar's million been paid for his invention. Then the Princess went on—

"Well, through a friend at the Russian Embassy, I have learnt that a French engineer has, as he says, perfected a balloon constructed on a new principle, which he claims will meet the conditions of the Tsar's offer.

"My friend also told me that his Majesty had decided to take an entirely disinterested opinion with regard to this invention, and asked me if I could recommend any English engineer who had made a study of aërial navigation, and who would be willing to go to Russia, superintend the trials of the war-balloon, and report as to their success or otherwise.

"This happened a few days ago only, and as I had happened to read an article that you will remember you wrote about six months ago in the *Nineteenth*, or, as it is now called, the *Twentieth Century*, I thought of your name, and said I would try to find some one. Two days later I got news from the Circle of your invention—never mind how; you will learn that later on—and called at the Embassy to say I had found some one whose judgment could be absolutely relied upon. Now, wasn't that kind of me, to give you such a testimonial as that to his Omnipotence the Tsar of All the Russias?"

Once more Arnold bowed his acknowledgments—this time somewhat ironically, and Natasha interrupted the narrative by saying with a spice of malice in her voice—

"No doubt the Little Father will duly recognise your kindness, Princess, when he gets quite to the bottom of the matter."

"I hope he will," replied the Princess, "but that is a matter of the future—and of considerable doubt as well." Then, turning to Arnold again, she continued—

'You will now, of course, see the immense advantage there appeared to be in getting you to examine these war-balloons. They are evidently the only possible rivals to your own invention in the field, and therefore it is of the utmost importance that you should know their strength or their weakness, as the case may be.

"Well, that is all I have to say, so far. It has been decided that you shall go, if you are willing, with us to Petersburg the day after to-morrow to see the balloon, and make your report. All your expenses will be paid on the most liberal scale, for the Tsar is no niggard in spending either his own or other people's money, and you will have a handsome fee into the bargain for your trouble."

"So far as the work is concerned, of course, I undertake it willingly," said Arnold, as the Princess stopped speaking. "But it hardly seems to me to be right that I should take even the Tsar's money under such circumstances. To tell you the truth, it looks to me rather uncomfortably like false pretences."

Again Natasha's eyes flashed approval across the table, but nevertheless she said—

"You seem to forget, my friend, that we are at war with the Tsar, and all's fair in—in love and war. Besides, if you have any scruples about keeping the fee for your professional services—which, after all, you will render as honestly as though it were the merest matter of business—you can put it into the treasury, and so ease your conscience. Remember, too," she went on more seriously, "how the enormous wealth of this same Tsar has swollen by the confiscation of fortunes whose possessors had committed no other crime than becoming obnoxious to the corrupt bureaucracy."

"I will take the fee if I fairly earn it, Miss Darrel," replied Arnold, returning the glance as he spoke, "and it shall be my first contribution to the treasury of the Brotherhood."

"Spoken like a sensible man," chimed in the Princess. "After all, it is no worse than spoiling the Egyptians, and you have scriptural authority for that. However, you can do as you like with his Majesty's money when you get it. The main fact is that you have the opportunity of going to earn it, and that Colonel Martinov is coming here to tea this afternoon to bring our passports, specially authorising us to travel without customs examination or any kind of questioning to any part of the Tsar's dominions, and that, I can assure you, is a very exceptional honour indeed."

"Who did you say? Martinov? Is that the Colonel Martinov who is the director of the secret police here?" asked Colston hurriedly.

"Yes," replied the Princess, "the same. Why do you ask?"

"Because," said Colston quietly, "he received the sentence of death nearly a month ago, and to-morrow night he will be executed, unless there is some accident. It was he who stood with the governor of Brovno in the prison-yard and watched

Radna Michaelis flogged by the soldiers. I received news this morning that the arrangements are complete, and that the sentence will be carried out to-morrow night."

"Yes, that is so," added Natasha, as Colston ceased speaking. "Everything is settled. It is therefore well that he should do something useful before he meets his fate."

"How curious that it should just happen so!" said the Princess calmly, as she rose from the table and moved towards the door followed by Natasha.

As soon as the ladies had left the room, Colston and Arnold lit their cigarettes and chatted while they smoked over their last glass of claret. Arnold would have liked to have asked more about the coming tragedy, but something in Colston's manner restrained him; and so the conversation remained on the subject of the Russian journey until they returned to the sitting-room.

CHAPTER IX.

THE BEGINNING OF SORROWS.

ON the 6th of March 1904, just six months after Arnold's journey to Russia, a special meeting of the Inner Circle of the Terrorists took place in the Council-chamber, at the house on Clapham Common.

Although it was only attended by twelve persons all told, and those men and women whose names were unknown outside the circle of their own Society and the records of the Russian police, it was the most momentous conference that had taken place in the history of the world since the council of war that Abdurrhaman the Moslem had held with his chieftains eleven hundred and seventy-two years before, and, by taking their advice, spared the remnants of Christendom from the sword of Islam.

Then the fate of the world hung in the balance of a council of war, and the supremacy of the Cross or the Crescent depended, humanly speaking, upon the decision of a dozen warriors. Now the fate of the civilisation that was made possible by that decision, lay at the mercy of a handful of outlaws and exiles who had laboriously brought to perfection the secret schemes of a single man.

The work of the Terrorists was finally complete. Under the whole fabric of Society lay the mines which a single spark would now explode, and above this slumbering volcano the earth was trembling with the tread of millions of armed men, divided into huge hostile camps, and only waiting until Diplomacy had finished its work in the dark, and gave the long-awaited signal of inevitable and universal war.

To-night that spark was to be shaken from the torch of Revolution, and to-morrow the first of the mines would explode. After that, if the course to be determined on by the Terrorist Council failed to arrive at the results which it was designed to reach, the armies of Europe would fight their way through the greatest war that the world had ever seen, the Fates would once more decide in favour of the strongest battalions, the fittest would triumph, and a new era of military despotism would begin—perhaps neither much better nor much worse than the one it would succeed.

If, on the other hand, the plans of the Terrorists were successfully worked out to their logical conclusion, it would not be war only, but utter destruction that Society would have to face. And then with dissolution would come anarchy. The thrones of the world would be overthrown, the fabric of Society would be dissolved, commerce would come to an end, the structure that it had taken twenty centuries of the discipline of war and the patient toil of peace to build up, would crumble into ruins in a few short months, and then—well, after that no man could tell what would befall the remains of the human race that had survived the deluge. The means of destruction were at hand, and they would be used without mercy, but for the rest no man could speak.

When Nicholas Roburoff, the President of the Executive, rose in his place at eight o'clock to explain the business in hand, every member present saw at a glance, by the gravity of his demeanour, that the communication that he had to make was of no ordinary nature, but even they were not prepared for the catastrophe that he announced in the first sentence that he uttered.

"Friends," he said, in a voice that was rendered deeply impressive by the emotion that he vainly tried to conceal, "it is my mournful duty to tell you that she whom any one of us would willingly shed our blood to serve or save from the slightest evil, our beautiful and beloved Angel of the Revolution, as we so fondly call her, Natasha, the daughter of the Master, has, in the performance of her duty to the Cause, fallen into the hands of Russia."

Save for a low, murmuring groan that ran round the table, the news was received in silence. It was too terrible, too hideous in the awful meaning that its few words conveyed, for any exclamations of grief, or any outburst of anger, to express the emotions that it raised.

Not one of those who heard it but had good reason to know what it meant for a revolutionist to fall into the hands of Russia. For a man it meant the last extremity of human misery that flesh and blood could bear, but for a young and beautiful woman it was a fate that no words could describe— a doom that could only be thought of in silence and despair; and so the friends of Natasha were silent, though they did not yet despair. Roburoff bowed his head in acknowledgment of the inarticulate but eloquent endorsement of his words, and went on—

"You already know the outcome of Richard Arnold's visit to Russia; how he was present at the trial of the Tsar's war-balloon, and was compelled to pronounce it such a complete success, that the Autocrat at once gave orders for the construction of a fleet of fifty aërostats of the same pattern; and how, thanks to the warning conveyed by Anna Ornovski, he was able to prevent his special passport being stolen by a police agent, and so to foil the designs of the chief of the Third Section to stop him taking the secret of the construction of the war-balloon out of Russia. You also know that he brought back the Chief's authority to build an air-ship after the model which was exhibited to us here, and that since his return he has been prosecuting that work on Drumcraig Island, one of the possessions of the Chief in the Outer Hebrides, which he placed at his disposal for the purpose.

"You know, also, that Natasha and Anna Ornovski went to Russia partly to discover the terms of the secret treaty that we believed to exist between France and Russia, and partly to warn, and, if possible, remove from Russian soil a large number of our most valuable allies, whose names had been revealed to the Minister of the Interior, chiefly through the agency of the spy Martinov, who was executed in this room six months ago.

"The first part of the task was achieved, not without difficulty, but with complete success, and of that more anon. The second part was almost finished when Natasha and Anna Ornovski were surprised in the house of Alexei Kassatkin, a member of the Moscow Nihilist Circle, in the Bolshoi

Dmitrietka. He had been betrayed by one of his own servants, and a police visit was the result.

"Added to this there is reason to believe that she had, quite apart from this, become acquainted with enough official secrets to make her removal desirable in high quarters. I need not tell you that that is the usual way in which the Tsar rewards those of his secret servants who get to know too much.

"The fact of her being found in the house of a betrayed Nihilist was taken as sufficient proof of sympathy or complicity, and she was arrested. Natasha, as Fedora Darrel, claimed to be a British subject, and, as such, to be allowed to go free in virtue of the Tsar's safe conduct, which she exhibited. Instead of that she was taken before the chief of the Moscow police, rudely interrogated, and then brutally searched. Unhappily, in the bosom of her dress was found a piece of paper bearing some of the new police cypher. That was enough. That night they were thrown into prison, and three days later taken to the convict depot under sentence of exile by administrative process to Sakhalin for life.

"You know what that means for a beautiful woman like Natasha. She will not go to Sakhalin. They do not bury beauty like hers in such an abode of desolation as that. If she cannot be rescued, she will only have two alternatives before her. She will become the slave and plaything of some brutal governor or commandant at one of the stations, or else she will kill herself. Of course, of these two she would choose the latter—if she could and when she could. Should she be driven to that last resort of despair, she shall be avenged as woman never yet was avenged; but rescue must, if possible, come before revenge.

"The information that we have received from the Moscow agent tells us that the convict train to which Natasha and Anna Ornovski are attached left the depot nearly a fortnight ago; they were to be taken by train in the usual way to Nizhni Novgorod, thence by barge on the Volga and Kama to Perm, and on by rail to Tiumen, the forwarding station for the east. Until they reach Tiumen they will be safe from anything worse than what the Russians are pleased to call 'discipline,' but once they disappear into the wilderness of Siberia they will be lost to the world, and far from all law but the will of their official slave-drivers.

"It has, therefore, been decided that the rescue shall be attempted before the chain-gang leaves Tiumen, if it can be reached in time. As nearly as we can calculate, the march will begin on the morning of Friday the 9th, that is to say, in three nights and one day from now. Happily we possess the means of making the rescue, if it can be accomplished by human means. I have received a report from Richard Arnold saying that the *Ariel* is complete, and that she has made a perfectly satisfactory trial trip to the clouds. The *Ariel* is the only vehicle in existence that could possibly reach the frontier of Siberia in the given time, and it is fitting that her first duty should be the rescue of the Angel of the Revolution from the clutches of the Tyrant of the North.

"Alexis Mazanoff, it is the will of the Master that you shall take these instructions to Richard Arnold and accompany him on the voyage in order to show him what course to steer, and assist him in every way possible. You will find the Chief's yacht at Port Patrick ready to convey you to Drumcraig Island. When you have heard what is further necessary for you to hear, you will take the midnight express from Euston. Have you any preparations to make?"

"No," replied Mazanoff, or Colston, to call him by a name more familiar to the reader. "I can start in half an hour if necessary, and on such an errand you may, of course, depend on me not to lose much time. I presume there are full instructions here?"

"Yes, both for the rescue and for your conduct afterwards, whether you are successful or unsuccessful," said the President. Then turning to the others he continued—

"You may now rest assured that all that can be done to rescue Natasha will be done, and we must therefore turn to other matters. I said a short time ago that the conditions of the secret treaty between France and Russia had been discovered by the two brave women who are now suffering for their devotion to the cause of the Revolution. A full copy of them is in the hands of the Chief, who arrives in London to-day, and will at once lay the documents before Mr. Balfour, the Premier.

"It is extremely hostile to England, and amounts, in fact, to a compact on the part of France to declare war and seize the

Suez Canal, as soon as the first shot is fired between Great Britain and Russia. In return for this, Russia is to invade Germany and Austria, destroy the eastern frontier fortresses with her fleet of war-balloons, and then cross over and do the same on the Rhine, while France at last throws herself upon her ancient foe.

"Meanwhile, the French fleet is to concentrate in the Mediterranean as quietly and rapidly as possible, before war actually breaks out, so as to be able to hold the British and Italians in check, and shut the Suez Canal, while Russia, who is pushing her troops forward to the Hindu Kush, gets ready for a dash at the passes, and a rush upon Cashmere, before Britain can get sufficient men out to India by the Cape to give her very much trouble.

"As there also exists a secret compact between Britain and the Triple Alliance, binding all four powers to declare war the moment one is threatened, the disclosure of this treaty must infallibly lead to war in a few weeks. In addition to this, measures have been taken to detach Italy from the Triple Alliance at the last moment, if possible. Success in this respect is, however, somewhat uncertain.

"To make assurance doubly sure, the Chief informs me that he has ordered Ivan Brassoff, who is in command of a large reconnoitring party on the Afghan side of the Hindu Kush, to provoke reprisals from a similar party of Indian troops who have been told off to watch their movements. Captain Brassoff is one of us, and can be depended upon to obey at all costs. He will do this in a fortnight from now, and therefore we may feel confident that Great Britain and Russia will be at war within a month.

"With the first outbreak of war our work for the present ceases, so far as active interference goes. We shall therefore withdraw from the scene of action until the arrival of the supreme moment when the nations of Europe shall be locked in the death-struggle, and the fate of the world will rest in our hands. The will of the Master now is that all the members of the Brotherhood shall at once wind up their businesses, and turn all of their possessions that are not portable and useful into money.

"A large steamer has been purchased and manned with

members of the Outer Circle who are sailors by profession. She is now being loaded at Liverpool with all the machinery and materials necessary for the construction of twelve air-ships like the *Ariel*. "This steamer, when ready for sea, will sail, ostensibly, for Rio de Janeiro with a cargo of machinery, but in reality for Drumcraig, where she will embark the workmen who will be left there by the *Ariel* with all the working plant on the island, and from there she will proceed to a lonely island off the West Coast of Africa, between Cape Blanco and Cape Verde, where new works will be set up and the fleet of air-ships put together as rapidly as possible.

"The position of this island is in the instructions which Alexis Mazanoff takes to Drumcraig to-night, and the *Ariel* will rendezvous there when the work that is in hand for her is done. The members of the Brotherhood will, of course, go in the steamer as passengers for Rio, so that no suspicions may be aroused, and every one must be ready to embark in ten days from now.

"That is all I have to say at present in the name of the Master. And now, Alexis Mazanoff, it is time you set out. We shall remain here and discuss every detail fully so that nothing may be overlooked. You will find that everything has been provided for in the instructions you have, so go, and may the Master of Destiny be with you!"

As he spoke he held out his hand, which the young man grasped heartily, saying—

"Farewell! I will obey to the death, and if success can be earned we will earn it. If not, you shall hear of the *Ariel's* work in Russia before the week is out."

He then took leave of the other members of the Council, coming last to Radna. As their hands clasped she said—

"I wish I could come with you, but that is impossible. But bring Natasha back to us safe and sound, and there is nothing that you can ask of me that I will not say 'yes' to. Go, and God speed your good work. Farewell!"

For all answer he took her in his arms before them all. Their lips met in one long silent kiss, and a moment later he had gone to strike the first blow in the coming world-war, and to bring the beginning of sorrows on the Tyrant of the North.

CHAPTER X.

THE "ARIEL."

N the sixth stroke of twelve that night the Scotch express drew out of Euston Station. At half-past nine the next morning, the *Lurline*, Lord Alanmere's yacht, steamed out of Port Patrick Harbour, and at one o'clock precisely she dropped her anchor in the little inlet that served for a harbour at Drumcraig.

Colston had the quarter-boat lowered and pulled ashore without a moment's delay, and as his foot touched the shore Arnold grasped his hand, and, after the first words of welcome, asked for the latest news of Natasha.

Without immediately answering, Colston put his arm through his, drew him away from the men who were standing about, and told him as briefly and gently as he could the terrible news of the calamity that had befallen the Brotherhood, and the errand upon which he had come.

Arnold received the blow as a brave man should—in silence. His now bronzed face turned pale, his brows contracted, and his teeth clenched till Colston could hear them gritting upon each other. Then a great wave of agony swept over his soul as a picture too horrible for contemplation rose before his eyes, and after that came calm, the calm of rapid thought and desperate resolve.

He remembered the words that Natasha had used in a letter that she had given him when she took leave of him in Russia. "We shall trust to you to rescue us, and, if that is no longer possible, to avenge us."

Yes, and now the time had come to justify that trust and

prove his own devotion. It should be proved to the letter, and if there was cause for vengeance, the proof should be written in blood and flame over all the wide dominions of the Tsar. Grief might come after, when there was time for it; but this was the hour of action, and a strange savage joy seemed to come with the knowledge that the safety of the woman he loved now depended mainly upon his own skill and daring.

Colston respected his silence, and waited until he spoke. When he did he was astonished at the difference that those few minutes had made in the young engineer. The dreamer and the enthusiast had become the man of action, prompt, stern, and decided. Colston had never before heard from his lips the voice in which he at length said to him—

"Where is this place? How far is it as the crow flies from here?"

"At a rough guess I should say about two thousand two hundred miles, almost due east, and rather less than two hundred miles on the other side of the Ourals."

"Good! That will be twenty hours' flight for us, or less if this south-west wind holds good."

"What!" exclaimed Colston. "Twenty hours, did you say? You must surely be making some mistake. Don't you mean forty hours? Think of the enormous distance. Why, even then we should have to travel over sixty miles an hour through the air."

"My dear fellow, I don't make mistakes where figures are concerned. The paradox of aërial navigation is 'the greater the speed the less the resistance.'

"In virtue of that paradox I am able to tell you that the speed of the *Ariel* in moderate weather is a hundred and twenty miles an hour, and a hundred and twenty into two thousand two hundred goes eighteen times and one-third. This is Wednesday, and we have to be on the Asiatic frontier at daybreak on Friday. We shall start at dusk to-night, and you shall see to-morrow's sun set over the Ourals."

"That means from the eastern side of the range!"

"Of course. There will be no harm in being a few hours too soon. In case we may have a long cruise, I must have additional stores, and power-cylinders put on board. Come, you have not seen the *Ariel* yet.

"I have made several improvements on the model, as I

expected to do when I came to the actual building of the ship, and, what is more important than that, I have immensely increased the motive power and economised space and weight at the same time. In fact, I don't despair now of two hundred miles an hour before very long. Come!"

The engineer and the enthusiast had now come to the fore again, and the man and the lover had receded, put back, as it were, until the time for love, or perchance for sorrow, had come.

He put his arm through Colston's, and led him up a hill-path and through a little gorge which opened into a deep valley, completely screened on all sides by heather-clad hills. Sprinkled about the bottom of this valley were a few wooden dwelling-houses and workshops, and in the centre was a huge shed, or rather an enclosure now, for its roof had been taken off.

In this lay, like a ship in a graving-dock, a long, narrow, grey-painted vessel almost exactly like a sea-going ship, save for the fact that she had no funnel, and that her three masts, instead of yards, each carried a horizontal fan-wheel, while from each of her sides projected, level with the deck, a plane twice the width of the deck and nearly as long as the vessel herself.

They entered the enclosure and walked round the hull. This was seventy feet long and twelve wide amidships, and save for size it was the exact counterpart of the model already described.

As soon as he had taken Colston round the hull, and roughly explained its principal features, reserving more detailed description and the inspection of the interior for the voyage, he gave the necessary orders for preparing for a lengthy journey, and the two went on board the *Lurline* to dinner, which Colston had deferred in order to eat it in Arnold's company.

After dinner they carefully discussed the situation in order that every possible accident might be foreseen, argued the pros and cons of the venture in all their bearings, and even went so far as to plan the vengeance they would take should, by any chance, the rescue fail or come too late.

The instructions, signed by Natas himself, were very precise on certain essential points, and in their broad outlines, but, like all wisely planned instructions to such men as these, they left ample margin for individual initiative in case of emergency.

Some of the stores of the *Lurline* had to be transferred to the *Ariel*, and these were taken ashore after dinner, and at the same time Colston made his first inspection of the interior of the air-ship, under the guidance of her creator. What struck him most at first sight was the apparent inadequacy of the machinery to the attainment of the tremendous speed at which Arnold had promised they should travel.

There were four somewhat insignificant-looking engines in all. Of these, one drove the stern propeller, one the side propellers, and two the fan-wheels on the masts. He learnt as soon as the voyage began, that, by a very simple switch arrangement, the power of the whole four engines could be concentrated on the propellers; for, once in the air, the lifting wheels were dispensed with and lowered on deck, and the ship was entirely sustained by the pressure of the air under her planes.

There was not an ounce of superfluous wood or metal about the beautifully constructed craft, but for all that she was complete in every detail, and the accommodation she had for crew and passengers was perfectly comfortable, and in some respects cosy in the extreme. Forward there was a spacious cabin with berths for six men, and aft there were separate cabins for six people, and a central saloon for common use.

On deck there were three structures, a sort of little conning tower forward, a wheel-house aft, and a deck saloon amidships. All these were, of course, so constructed as to offer the least possible resistance to the wind, or rather the current created by the vessel herself when flying through the air at a speed greater than that of the hurricane itself.

All were closely windowed with toughened glass, for it is hardly necessary to say that, but for such a protection, every one who appeared above the level of the deck would be almost instantly suffocated, if not whirled overboard, by the rush of air when the ship was going at full speed. Her armament consisted of four long, slender cannon, two pointing over the bows, and two over the stern.

The crew that Arnold had chosen for the voyage consisted, curiously enough, of men belonging to the four nationalities which would be principally concerned in the **Titanic** struggle which a few weeks would now see raging over Europe. Their names were Andrew Smith, Englishman, and coxswain; Ivan Petrovitch, Russian; Franz Meyer, German; and Jean Guichard, Frenchman. Diverse as they were, there never were four better workers, or four better friends.

They had no country but the world, and no law save those which governed their Brotherhood. They conversed in assorted but perfectly intelligible English, for the very simple reason that Mr. Andrew Smith consistently refused to attempt even the rudiments of any other tongue.

While the stores were being put on board, Arnold made a careful examination of every part of the machinery, and then of the whole vessel, in order to assure himself that everything was in perfect order. This done, he gave his final instructions to those of the little community who were left behind to await the arrival of the steamer, and as the sun sank behind the western ridges of the island, he went on board the *Ariel* with Colston, took his place at the wheel, and ordered the fan-wheels to be set in motion.

Colston was standing by the open door of the wheel-house as Arnold communicated his order to the engine-room by pressing an electric button, one of four in a little square of mahogany in front of the wheel.

There was no vibration or grinding, as would have been the case in starting a steamer, but only a soft whirring, humming sound, that rose several degrees in pitch as the engines gained speed, and the fan-wheels revolved faster and faster until they sang in the air, and the *Ariel* rose without a jar or a tremor from the ground, slowly at first, and then more and more swiftly, until Colston saw the ground sinking rapidly beneath him, and the island growing smaller and smaller, until it looked like a little patch on the dark grey water of the sea.

Away to the north and west he could see the innumerable islands of the Hebrides, while to the east the huge mountainous mass of the mainland of Scotland loomed dark upon the horizon.

When the barometer marked eight hundred feet above the sea-level, the *Ariel* passed through a stratum of light clouds, and on the upper side of this the sun was still shining, shooting his almost level rays across it as though over some illimitable sea of white fleecy billows, whose crests were tipped with rosy, golden light.

Above the surface of this fairy sea rose north-eastward the black mass of Ben More on the Island of Mull, and to the southward, the lesser peaks of Jura and Islay.

While he was still wrapped in admiration of the strange beauty of this, to him, marvellous scene, the *Ariel* had risen to a thousand feet, still almost in a vertical line from the island. Arnold now pressed another button, and the stern propeller began to revolve swiftly and noiselessly, and Colston saw the waves of the cloud-sea begin to slip behind, although so smooth was the working of the machinery, and the motion of the airship, that, but for this, he could hardly have guessed that he was in motion.

Arnold now turned a few spokes of the wheel, and headed the *Ariel* due east by the compass. Then he touched a third button. The side propellers began to turn swiftly on their axes, and, at the same time the speed of the fan-wheels slackened, and gradually stopped.

Colston now began to feel the air rushing by him in a stream so rapid and strong, that he had to take hold of the side of the wheel-house doorway to steady himself.

"I think you had better come inside and shut the door," said Arnold. "We are getting up speed now, and in a few minutes you won't be able to hold yourself there. You'll be able to see just as well inside."

Colston did as he was bidden, and as soon as he was safely inside Arnold pulled a lever beside the wheel, and slightly inclined the planes from forward aft. At the same time the fan-wheels began to slide down the masts until they rested upon the deck.

"Now, you shall see her fly," said Arnold, taking a speaking-tube from the wall and whistling thrice into it.

Colston felt a slight tremor in the deck beneath his feet, and then a lifting movement. He staggered a little, and said to Arnold—

"What's that? Are we going higher still?"

"Yes," replied the engineer. "She is feeling the air-planes now under the increased speed. I am going up to fifteen hundred feet, so that we shall only have the highest peaks to steer clear of in crossing Scotland. Now, use your eyes, and you will see something worth looking at."

The upper part of the wheel-house was constructed almost entirely of glass, and so Colston could see just as well as if he had been on deck outside. He did use his eyes. In fact, for some time to come, all his other senses seemed to be merged in that of sight, for the scene was one of such rare and marvellous beauty, and the sensations that it called up were of so completely novel a nature, that, for the time being, he felt as though he had been suddenly transported into fairyland.

The cloud-sea now lay about seven hundred feet beneath them. The sun had sunk quite below the horizon, even at that elevation; but his absence was more than made up for by the nearly full moon, which had risen to the southward, as though to greet the conqueror of the air, and was spreading a flood of silvery radiance over the snowy plain beneath, through the great gaps in which they could see the darker sheen of the moving sea-waves.

Their course lay almost exactly along the fifty-sixth parallel of latitude, and took them across Argyle, Dumbarton, and Stirlingshire to the head of the Firth of Forth. As they approached the mainland, Colston saw one or two peaks rise up out of the clouds, and soon they were sweeping along in the midst of a score or so of these. To the left Ben Lomond towered into the clear sky above his attendant peaks, and to the right the lower summits of the Campsie Fells soon rose a few miles ahead.

The rapidity with which these mountain-tops rose up on either side, and were left behind, proved to Colston that the *Ariel* must be travelling at a tremendous speed, and yet, but for a very slight quivering of the deck, there was no motion perceptible, so smoothly did the air-ship glide through the elastic medium in which she floated.

So engrossed was he with the unearthly beauty of the new world into which he had risen, that for nearly two hours he stood without speaking a word. Arnold, wrapped in his own thoughts, maintained a like silence, and so they sped on amidst a stillness that was only broken by the soft whirring of the propellers, and the singing of the wind past the masts and stays.

At length a faint sound like the dashing of breakers on a rocky coast roused Colston from his reverie, and he turned to Arnold and said—

"What is that? Not the sea, surely!"

"Yes, those are the waves of the Firth of Forth breaking on the shores of Fife."

"What! Do you mean to tell me that we have crossed Scotland already? Why, we have not been an hour on the way yet!"

"Oh yes, we have," replied the engineer. "We have been nearly two. You have been so busy looking about you that you have not noticed how the time has passed. We have travelled a little over two hundred and forty miles. We are over the German Ocean now, and as there will be no more hills until we reach the Ourals we can go down a little."

As he spoke he moved the lever beside him about an inch, and instantly the clouds seemed to rise up toward them as the *Ariel* swept downwards in her flight. A hundred feet above them Arnold touched the lever again, and the air-ship at once resumed her horizontal course.

Then he put her head a little more to the northward, and called down the speaking tube for Andrew Smith to come and relieve him. A minute later Smith's head appeared at the top of the companion-ladder which led from the saloon to the wheel-house, and Arnold gave him the wheel and the course, saying at the same time to Colston—

"Now, come down and have something to eat, and then we will have a smoke and a chat and go to bed. There is nothing more to be seen until the morning, and then I will show you Petersburg as it looks from the clouds."

"If you told me you would show me the Ourals themselves, I should believe you after what I have seen," replied Colston, as together they descended the companion-way from the wheel-house to the saloon.

"Ah, I'm afraid that would be too much even for the *Ariel* to accomplish in the time," said Arnold. "Still, I think I can guarantee that you shall cross Europe in such time as no man ever crossed it before."

CHAPTER XI.

FIRST BLOOD.

AFTER supper the two friends ascended to the deck saloon for a smoke, and to continue their discussion of the tremendous events in which they were so soon to be taking part. They found the *Ariel* flying through a cloudless sky over the German Ocean, whose white-crested billows, silvered by the moonlight, were travelling towards the northeast under the influence of the south-west breeze from which the engineer had promised himself assistance when they started.

"We seem to be going at a most frightful speed," said Colston, looking down at the water. "There's a strong southwest breeze blowing, and yet those white horses seem to be travelling quite the other way."

"Yes," replied Arnold, looking down. "This wind will be travelling about twenty miles an hour, and that means that we are making nearly a hundred and fifty. The German Ocean here is five hundred miles across, and we shall cross it at this rate in about three hours and a half, and if the wind holds over the land we shall sight Petersburg soon after sunrise.

"The sun will rise to-morrow morning a few minutes after five by Greenwich time, which is about two hours behind Petersburg time. Altogether we shall make, I expect, from two to two and a half hours' gain on time."

The two men talked until a few minutes after ten, and then went to bed. Colston, who had been travelling all the previous night, began to feel drowsy in spite of the excitement of the novel voyage, and almost as soon as he lay down in his berth dropped off into a sound, dreamless sleep, and knew nothing more until Arnold knocked at his door and said—

"If you want to see the sun rise, you had better get up. Coffee will be ready in a quarter of an hour."

Colston pulled back the slide which covered the large oblong pane of toughened glass which was let into the side of his cabin and looked out. There was just light enough in the grey dawn to enable him to see that the *Ariel* was passing over a sea dotted in the distance with an immense number of islands.

"The Baltic," he said to himself as he jumped out of bed. "This is travelling with a vengeance! Why, we must have travelled a good deal over a thousand miles during the night. I suppose those islands will be off the coast of Finland. If so, we are not far from Petersburg, as the *Ariel* seems to count distance."

The most magnificent spectacle that Colston had ever seen in his life, or, for the matter of that, ever dreamed of, was the one that he saw from the conning-tower of the *Ariel* while the sun was rising over the vast plain of mingled land and water which stretched away to the eastward until it melted away into the haze of early morning.

The sky was perfectly clear and cloudless, save for a few light clouds that hung about the eastern horizon, and were blazing gold and red in the light of the newly-risen sun. The air-ship was flying at an elevation of about two thousand feet, which appeared to be her normal height for ordinary travelling. There was land upon both sides of them, but in front opened a wide bay, the northern shores of which were still fringed with ice and snow.

"That is the Gulf of Finland," said Arnold. "The winter must have been very late this year, and that probably means that we shall find the eastern side of the Ourals still snow-bound."

"So much the better," replied Colston. "They will have a much better chance of escape if there is good travelling for a sleigh."

"Yes," replied Arnold, his brows contracting as he spoke. "Do you know, if it were not for the Master's explicit orders, I should be inclined to smash up the station at Ekaterinburg a few hours beforehand, and then demand the release of the whole convict train, under penalty of laying the town in ruins."

Colston shook his head, saying—

"No, no, my friend, we must have a little more diplomacy than that. Your thirst for the life of the enemy will, no doubt, be fully gratified later on. Besides, you must remember that you would probably blow some hundreds of perfectly innocent people to pieces, and very possibly a good many friends of the Cause among them."

"True," replied Arnold; "I didn't think of that; but I'll tell you what we can do, if you like, without transgressing our instructions or hurting any one except the soldiers of the Tsar, who, of course, are paid to slaughter and be slaughtered, and so don't count."

"What is that?" asked Colston.

"We shall be passing over Kronstadt in a little over an hour, and we might take the opportunity of showing his Majesty the Tsar what the *Ariel* can do with the strongest fortress in Europe. How would you like to fire the first shot in the war of the Revolution?"

Colston was silent for a few moments, and then he looked up and said—

"There is not the slightest reason why we should not take a shot at Kronstadt, if only to give the Russians a foretaste of favours to come. Still, I won't fire the first shot on any account, simply because that honour belongs to you. I'll fire the second with pleasure."

"Very good," replied Arnold. "We'll have two shots apiece, one each as we approach the fortress, and one each as we leave it. Now come and take a preparatory lesson in the new gunnery."

They went down into the chief saloon, and there Arnold showed Colston a model of the new weapon with which the *Ariel* was armed, and thoroughly explained the working of it. After this they went to the wheel-house, where Arnold inclined the planes at a sharper angle, and sent the *Ariel* flying up into the sky, until the barometer showed an elevation of three thousand feet.

Then he signalled to the engine-room, the fan-wheels rose from the deck, as if by their own volition, and, as soon as they reached their places, began to spin round faster and faster, until Colston could again hear the high-pitched singing sound that he had heard as the *Ariel* rose from Drumcraig Island.

At the same time the speed of the vessel rapidly decreased; the side propellers ceased working, and the stern-screw revolved more and more slowly, until the speed came down to about thirty miles an hour.

By this time the great fortress of Kronstadt could be distinctly seen lying upon its island, like some huge watch-dog crouched at the entrance to his master's house, guarding the way to St. Petersburg.

"Now," said Arnold, "we can go outside without any fear of being blown off into space."

They went out and walked forward to the bow. Arrived there they found two of the men, each with a curious-looking shell in his arms. The projectiles were about two feet long and six inches in diameter, and were, as Arnold told Colston, constructed of *papier-maché*. There were three blades projecting from the outside, and running spirally from the point to the butt. These fitted into grooves in the inside of the cannon, which were really huge air-guns twenty feet long, including the air-chamber at the breech.

The projectiles were placed in position, the breeches of the guns closed, and a minute later the air-chambers were filled with air at a pressure of two hundred atmospheres, pumped from the forward engines through pipes leading up to the guns for the purpose.

"Now," said Arnold, "we're ready! Meanwhile you two can go and load the two after guns."

The men saluted and retired, and Arnold continued—

"Just take a look down with your glasses and see if they see us. I expect they do by this time."

Colston put his field-glass to his eyes, and looked down at the fortress, which was now only six or seven miles ahead.

"Yes," he said, "at any rate I can see a lot of little figures running about on the roof of one of the ramparts, which I suppose are soldiers. What's the range of your gun? I should say the fortress is about six miles off now."

"We can hit it from here, if you like," replied Arnold, "and if we were a thousand feet higher I could send a shell into Petersburg. See! there is the City of Palaces. Away yonder in the distance you can just see the sun shining on the houses. We could see it quite plainly if it wasn't for the haze that seems to be lying over the Neva."

While he was speaking, Arnold trained the gun according to a scale on a curved steel rod which passed through a screw socket in the breech of the piece.

"Now," he said. "Watch!"

He pressed a button on the top of the breech. There was a sharp but not very loud sound as the compressed air was released; something rushed out of the muzzle of the gun, and a few seconds later, Colston could see the missile boring its way through the air, and pursuing a slanting but perfectly direct path for the centre of the fortress.

A second later it struck. He could see a bright greenish flash as it smote the steel roof of the central fort. Then the fort seemed to crumble up and dissolve into fragments, and a few moments later a dull report floated up into the sky mingled, as he thought, with screams of human agony.

For a moment he stared in silence through the glasses, then he turned to Arnold and said in a voice that trembled with violent emotion—

"Good God, that is awful! The whole of the centre citadel is gone as though it had been swept off the face of the earth. I can hardly see even the ruins of it. Surely that's murder rather than war!"

"No more murder than the use of torpedoes in naval warfare, as far as I can see," replied Arnold coolly. "Remember, too," he continued in a sterner tone, "that fortress belongs to the power that flogged Radna and has captured Natasha. Come, let's see what execution you can do."

He crossed the deck and set the other gun by its scale, saying as he did so—

"Put your finger on the button and press when I tell you."

Colston did as he was bid, and as his finger touched the little knob his hand was as firm as though he had been making a shot at billiards.

"Now!"

He pressed the button down hard. There was the same sharp sound, and a second messenger of destruction sped on its way towards the doomed fortress.

"Good God, that is awful."

See page 82.

First Blood.

They saw it strike, and then came the flash, and after that a huge cloud of dust mingled with flying objects that might have been blocks of masonry, guns, or human bodies, rose into the air, and then fell back again to the earth.

"There goes one of the angles of the fortification into the sea," said Arnold, as he saw the effects of the shot. "Kronstadt won't be much good when the war breaks out, it strikes me. I suppose they'll be replying soon with a few rifle shots. We'd better quicken up a bit."

He went aft to the wheel-house, followed by Colston, and signalled for the three propellers to work at their utmost speed. The order was instantly obeyed; the fan-wheels ceased revolving, and under the impetus of her propellers the *Ariel* leapt forwards and upwards like an eagle on its upward swoop, rose five hundred feet in the air, and then swept over Kronstadt at a speed of more than a hundred miles an hour.

As they passed over they saw a series of flashes rise from one of the untouched portions of the fortress, but no bullets came anywhere near them. In fact, they must have passed through the air two or three miles astern of the flying *Ariel*. No soldier who ever carried a rifle could have sent a bullet within a thousand yards of an object seventy feet long travelling over a hundred miles an hour at a height of nearly four thousand feet, and so the Russians wasted their ammunition.

As soon as they had passed over the fortress, Arnold signalled for the propellers to stop, and the fan-wheels to revolve again at half speed. The air-ship stopped within three miles, and remained suspended in air over the opening mouth of the Neva. Then the two after guns were trained upon the fortress, and Colston and Arnold fired them together.

The two shells struck at the same moment, one in each of two angles of the ramparts. Their impact was followed by a tremendous explosion, far greater than could be accounted for by the shells themselves.

"There goes one, if not two, of his powder magazines. Look! half the fortress is a wreck. I wonder which fired the lucky shot."

The man who a year before had been an inoffensive student of mechanics and an enthusiast dreaming of an unsolved problem, spoke of the frightful destruction of life and the havoc that he had caused by just pressing a button with his finger, as coolly and quietly as a veteran officer of artillery might have spoken of shelling a fort.

There were two reasons for this almost miraculous change. One was to be found in the bitter hatred of Russian tyranny which he had imbibed during the last six months, and the other was the fact that the woman for whom he would have himself died a thousand deaths if necessary, was a captive in Russian chains, being led at that moment to slavery and degradation.

As soon as they had seen the effects of the last two shots, Arnold said with a grim, half-smile on his lips—

"I think it will be better if we don't show ourselves too plainly to Petersburg. It will take some time for the news of the destruction of Kronstadt to reach the city, and, of course, there will be the wildest rumours as to the agency by which it was done, so we may as well leave them to argue the matter out among themselves."

He signalled again to the engine-room, and with the united aid of her planes and fan-wheels the *Ariel* mounted up and up into the sky, driven only by the stern-propeller and with the force of the other engines concentrated on the lifting wheels, until a height of five thousand feet was reached.

At that height she would have looked, if she could have been seen at all, nothing more than a little grey spot against the blue of the sky, and as they heard afterwards she passed over St. Petersburg without being noticed.

From St. Petersburg to Tiumen, as the crow flies, the distance is 1150 English miles, and nine hours after she had passed over the Capital of the North, the *Ariel* had winged her way over the Ourals and the still snow-clad forests of the eastern slopes, past the tear-washed Pillar of Farewells, and had come to a rest after her voyage of two thousand two hundred miles, including the delay at Kronstadt, in twenty hours almost to the minute, as her captain had predicted.

CHAPTER XII.

IN THE MASTER'S NAME.

HE *Ariel*, in order to avoid being seen from the town, had made a wide circuit to the northward at a considerable elevation, and as soon as a suitable spot had been sought out by means of the field-glasses, she dropped suddenly and swiftly from the clouds into the depths of the dense forest through which the Tobolsk road runs from Tiumen to the banks of the Tobol.

From Tiumen to the Tobol is about twenty-five miles by road. The railway, which was then finished as far as Tomsk, ran to Tobolsk by a more northerly and direct route than the road, but convicts were still marched on foot along the great post road after the gangs had been divided at Tiumen according to their destinations.

The spot which had been selected for the resting-place of the *Ariel* was a little glade formed by the bend of a frozen stream about five miles east of the town, and at a safe distance from the road.

Painted a light whitish-grey all over, she would have been invisible even from a short distance as she lay amid the snow-laden trees, and Arnold gave strict orders that all the window-slides were to be kept closed, and no light shown on any account.

Every precaution possible was taken to obviate a discovery which should seriously endanger the success of the rescue, but, nevertheless, the fan-wheels were kept aloft, and everything was in readiness to rise into the air at a moment's notice should any emergency require them to do so.

It was a little after three o'clock on the Thursday afternoon when the *Ariel* settled down in her resting-place, and half an hour later Colston and Ivan Petrovitch appeared on deck completely disguised, the former as a Russian fur trader, and the latter as his servant.

All the arrangements for the rescue had been once more gone over in every detail, and just before he swung himself over the side Colston shook hands for the last time with Arnold, saying as he did so—

"Well, good-bye again, old fellow! Ivan shall come back and bring you the news, if necessary; but if he doesn't come, don't be uneasy, but possess your soul in patience till you hear the whistle from the road in the morning. I expect the train will get in sometime during the night, and in that case we shall have everything ready to make the attempt soon after daybreak, if not before.

"If we can get as far as this without being pursued we shall come right on board. If not we must trust to our horses and our pistols to keep the Cossacks at a distance till you can help us. In any case, rest assured that once clear of Tiumen, we shall never be taken alive. Those are the Master's orders, and I will shoot Natasha myself before she goes back to captivity."

"Yes, do so," replied Arnold. His lips quivered as he spoke, but there was no tremor in the hand with which he gripped Colston's in farewell. "She will prefer death to slavery, and I shall prefer it for her. But if you have to do it you will at least have the consolation of knowing that within twelve hours of your death the Tsar shall be lying buried beneath the ruins of the Peterhof Palace. I will have his life for hers if only I live to take it."

"I will tell her," said Colston simply, "and if die she must, she will die content."

So saying, he descended the little rope-ladder, followed by Ivan, and in a few moments the two were lost in the deep shadow of the trees, while Arnold went down into the saloon to await with what patience he might the moment that would decide the fate of the daughter of Natas and the man who had gone, as he would so gladly have done, to risk his life to restore her to liberty.

Rather more than half an hour's tramp through the forest

brought Colston and Ivan out on the road at a point a little less than five miles from Tiumen.

Colston was provided with passports and permits to travel for himself and Ivan. These, of course, were forged on genuine forms which the Terrorists had no difficulty in obtaining through their agents in high places, who were as implicitly trusted as the Princess Ornovski had been but a few months before.

So skilfully were they executed, however, that it would have been a very keen official eye that had discovered anything wrong with them. They described him as "Stepan Bakuinin, fur merchant of Nizhni Novgorod, travelling in pursuit of his business, with his servant, Peter Petrovitch, also of Nizhni Novgorod."

Instead of going straight into the town by the main road they made a considerable detour and entered it by a lane that led them through a collection of miserable huts occupied by the poorest class of Siberian mujiks, half peasants, half townsfolk, who cultivate their patches of ground during the brief spring and summer, and struggle through the long dreary winter as best they can on their scanty savings and what work they can get to do from the Government or their richer neighbours.

Colston had never been in Tiumen before, but Ivan had, for ten years before he had voluntarily accompanied his father, who had been condemned to five years' forced labour on the new railway works from Tiumen to Tobolsk, for giving a political fugitive shelter in his house. He had died of hard labour and hard usage, and that was one reason why Ivan was a member of the Outer Circle of the Terrorists.

He led his master through the squalid suburb to the business part of the town, which had considerably developed since the through line to Tobolsk and Tomsk had been constructed, and at length they stopped before a comfortable-looking house in the street that ends at the railway station.

They knocked, gave their names, and were at once admitted. The servant who opened the door to them led them to a room in which they found a man of about fifty in the uniform of a sub-commissioner of police. As Colston held out his hand to him he said—

mystified him with the apparent miracle of his presence in Tiumen after so short an absence from London, in order to command his more complete obedience in the momentous work that was on hand.

He allowed the official a few moments to absorb the full wonder of the seeming marvel, and then he replied—

"Yes, we are all his servants *to the death*. At least I know of none who have even thought of treason to him and lived to put their thoughts into action. But tell me, are all the arrangements complete as far as you can make them? Much depends upon how you carry them out, you know, to say nothing of the two thousand roubles that I shall hand to you as soon as the two ladies are delivered into my charge."

"All is arranged, Nobleness," replied the official, bowing involuntarily at the mention of the money. "Such of the prisoners, that is to say the politicals, who can afford to pay for the privilege, may, by the new regulations, be lodged in the houses of approved persons during their sojourn in Tiumen, if it be only for a night, and so escape the common prison.

"We knew at the police bureau of the arrest of the Princess Ornovski some days ago, and I have obtained permission from the chief of police to lodge her Highness and her companion in misfortune—if they are prepared to pay what I shall ask. It has come to be looked upon as a sort of perquisite of diligent officials, and as I have been very diligent here I had no difficulty in getting the permission—which I shall have to pay for in due course."

"Just so! Nothing for nothing in Russian official circles. Very good. Now listen. If this escape is successfully accomplished you will be degraded and probably punished into the bargain for letting the prisoners slip through your fingers. But that must not happen if it can be prevented.

"Now this has been foreseen, as everything is with the Master; and his orders are that you shall take this passport —which you will find in perfect order, save for the fact that the date has been slightly altered—from me as soon as I have got the ladies safely in the troika out on the Tobolsk road, put off the livery of the Tsar, disguise yourself as effectually as may be, and take the first train back to Perm and Nizhni Novgorod as Stepan Bakuinin, fur merchant.

"In the Master's name!"

The official took his hand, and, bending over it, replied in a low tone—

"I am his servant. What is his will?"

"That Anna Ornovski and Fedora Darrel, the English girl who was taken with her, be released as soon as may be," replied Colston. "Is the train from Ekaterinburg in yet?"

"Not yet. The snow is still deep between here and the mountains. The winter has been very severe and long. We have almost starved in Tiumen in spite of the railway. There has been a telegram from Ekaterinburg to say that the train descended the mountain safely, and one from Kannishlov to say that we expect it soon after ten to-night."

"Good! That is sooner than we expected in London. We thought it would not reach here till to-morrow morning."

"In London! What do you mean? You cannot have come from London, for there has been no train for two days."

"Nevertheless I have come from London. I left England yesterday evening."

"Yesterday evening! But, with all submission, that is impossible. If there were a railway the whole distance it could not be done."

"To the Master there is nothing impossible. Look! I received that the evening I left London."

As he spoke, Colston held out an envelope. The Russian examined it closely. It bore the Ludgate Hill post-mark, which was dated "March 7."

Colston's host bent over it with almost superstitious reverence, and handed it back, saying humbly—

"Forgive my doubts, Nobleness! It is a miracle! I ask no more. The Tsar himself could not have done it. The Master is all powerful, and I am proud to be his servant, even to the death."

Although the twentieth century had dawned, the Siberian Russians were still inclined to look even upon the railway as a miracle. This man, although he occupied a post of very considerable responsibility and authority under the Russian Government, was only a member of the Outer Circle of the Terrorists, as most of the officials were, and therefore he knew nothing of the existence of the *Ariel*, and Colston purposely

"The servant you can leave behind on any excuse. From Novgorod you can travel viâ Moscow to Königsberg, and, if you will take my advice, you will get out of Russia as soon as the Fates will let you."

"It shall be done, Nobleness. But how will the disappearance of Dmitri Soudeikin, sub-commissioner of police, be accounted for?"

"That also has been provided for. Before you go you will pin this with a dagger to your sitting-room table."

The official took the little piece of paper which Colston held out to him as he spoke. It read thus—

Dmitri Soudeikin, sub-commissioner of police at Tiumen, has been removed for over-zeal in the service of the Tsar. NATAS.

Soudeikin bowed almost to the ground as the dreaded name of the Master of the Terror met his eyes, and then he said, as he handed the paper back—

"It is so! The Master sees all, and cares for the least of his servants. My life shall be forfeited if the ladies are not released as I have said."

"It probably will be," returned Colston drily. "None of us expect to get out of this business alive if it does not succeed. Now that is all I have to say for the present. It is for you to bring the ladies here as your prisoners, to see us out of the town before daybreak, and to have the troika in readiness for us on the Tobolsk road. Then see to yourself and I will be responsible for the rest."

As it still wanted more than two hours to the expected arrival of the train, Soudeikin had the samovar, or tea-urn, brought in, and Colston and Ivan made a hearty meal after their five-mile walk through the snow. Then they and their host lit their pipes, and smoked and chatted until a distant whistle warned Soudeikin that the train was at last approaching the station, and that it was time for him to be on duty to receive his convict-lodgers.

CHAPTER XIII.

FOR LIFE OR DEATH.

NO time had ever seemed so long to Colston as did the hour and a half which passed after the departure of Soudeikin until his return. He would have given anything to have accompanied him to the station, but it would have been so very unwise to have incurred the risk of being questioned, and perhaps obliged to show the passport that Soudeikin was to use, that he controlled his impatience as best he could, and let events take their course.

At length, when he had looked at his watch for the fiftieth time, and found that it indicated nearly half-past eleven, there was a heavy knock at the door. As it opened, Colston heard a rattle of arms and a clinking of chains. Then there was a sound of gruff guttural voices in the entrance-hall, and the next moment the door of the room was thrown open, and Soudeikin walked in, followed by a young man in the uniform of a lieutenant of the line, and after them came two soldiers, to one of whom was handcuffed the Princess Ornovski, and to the other Natasha.

Shocked as he was at the pitiable change that had taken place in the appearance of the two prisoners since he had last seen them in freedom, Colston was far too well trained in the school of conspiracy to let the slightest sign of surprise or recognition escape him.

He and Ivan rose as the party entered, greeted Soudeikin and saluted the officer, hardly glancing at the two pale, haggard women in their rough grey shapeless gowns and hoods as they stood beside the men to whom they were chained.

As the officer returned Colston's salute he turned to Soudeikin and said civilly enough—

"I did not know you had another guest. I hope we shall not overcrowd you."

"By no means," replied the commissioner, waving his hand toward Colston as he spoke. "This is only my nephew, Ernst Vronski, who is staying with me for a day or two on his way through to Nizhni Novgorod with his furs, and that is his servant, Ivan Arkavitch. You need not be uneasy. I have plenty of rooms, as I live almost alone, and I have set apart one for the prisoners which I think will satisfy you in every way. Would it please you to come and see it?"

"Yes, we will go now and get them put in safety for the night, if you will lead the way."

As the party left the room Colston caught one swift glance from Natasha which told him that she understood his presence in the house fully, and he felt that, despite her miserable position, he had an ally in her who could be depended upon.

The officer carefully examined the room which had been provided for the two prisoners, tried the heavy shutters with which the windows were closed, and took from Soudeikin the keys of the padlocks to the bars which ran across them. He then directed the prisoners to be released from their handcuffs and locked them in the room, stationing one of the soldiers at the door and sending the other to patrol the back of the house from which the two windows of the room looked out.

At the end of two hours the sentries were to change places, and in two hours more they were to be relieved by a detachment from the night patrol. This arrangement had been foreseen by Soudeikin, and it had been settled that the rescue was to be attempted as soon as the guard had been changed.

This would give the prisoners time to get a brief but much needed rest after their long and miserable journey from Perm, penned up like sheep in iron-barred cattle trucks, and it would leave the drowsiest part of the night, from four o'clock to sunrise, for the hazardous work in hand.

"That is a pretty girl you have there, captain," said Colston, as the officer returned to the sitting-room. "Is she for the mines or Sakhalin?"

"For Sakhalin by sentence, but as a matter of fact for neither, as far as I can see."

"You mean that the Little Father will pardon her or give her a lighter sentence, I suppose."

The officer grinned meaningly as he replied—

"*Nu vot!* That is hardly likely. What I mean is that Captain Kharkov, who is in command of the convict train from here, has had instructions to convey her as comfortably as possible, and with no more fatigue than is necessary, to Tchit, in the Trans-Baikal, and that he is also charged with a letter from the Governor of Perm to the Governor of Tchit.

"You know these gentlemen like to do each other a good turn when they can, and so, putting two and two together, I should say that his Excellency of Perm has concluded that our pretty prisoner will serve to beguile the dulness of that Godforsaken hole in which his Excellency of Tchit is probably dying of *ennui*. She will be more comfortable there than at Sakhalin, and it is a lucky thing for her that she has found favour in his Excellency's eyes."

Colston could have shot the fellow where he sat leering across the table; but though his blood was at boiling point, he controlled himself sufficiently to make a reply after the same fashion, and soon after took his leave and retired for the night.

At four o'clock the guard was changed. The new officer, after taking the keys, unlocked the door of the room in which Natasha and the Princess were confined, and roused them up to satisfy himself that they were still in safe keeping. It was a brutal formality, but perfectly characteristic of Siberian officialism.

The man who had been on guard so far joined the patrol and returned to the barracks, while the new officer made himself comfortable with a bottle of brandy, with which Soudeikin had obligingly provided him, in the sitting-room. It was a bitterly cold night, and he drank a couple of glasses of it in quick succession. Ten minutes after he had swallowed the second he rolled backwards on the couch on which he was sitting and went fast asleep. A few moments later he had ceased to breathe.

Then the door opened softly and Soudeikin and Colston slipped into the room. The former shook him by the shoulder.

His eyes remained half closed, his head lolled loosely from side to side, and his arms hung heavily downwards.

"He's gone," whispered Soudeikin; and, without another word, they set to work to strip the uniform off the lifeless body. Then Colston dressed himself in it and gave his own clothes to Soudeikin.

As soon as the change was effected, Colston took the keys and went to the door at which the sentry was keeping guard. The man was already half asleep, and blinked at him with drowsy eyes as he challenged him. For all answer the Terrorist levelled his pistol at his head and fired. There was a sharp crack that could hardly have been heard on the other side of the wall, and the man tumbled down with a bullet through his brain.

Colston stepped over the corpse, unlocked the door, and found Natasha and the Princess already dressed in male attire as two peasant boys, with sheepskin coats and shapkas, and wide trousers tucked into their half boots. These disguises had been provided beforehand by Soudeikin, and hidden in the bed in which they were to sleep.

Colston grasped their hands in silence, and the three left the room. In the passage they found Ivan and Soudeikin, the former dressed in the uniform of the soldier who had been on guard outside the house, and whose half-stripped corpse was now lying buried in the snow.

"Ready?" whispered Soudeikin.

"Have you finished in there?" asked Colston, jerking his thumb towards the sitting-room.

Soudeikin nodded in reply, and the five left the house by the back door.

It was then after half-past four. Fortunately it was a dark cloudy morning, and the streets of the town were utterly deserted. By ones and twos they stole through the by-streets and lanes without meeting a soul, until Soudeikin at length stopped at a house on the eastern edge of the town about a mile from the Tobolsk road.

He tapped at one of the windows. The door was softly opened by an invisible hand, and they entered and passed through a dark passage and out into a stable-yard behind the house. Under a shed they found a troika, or three-horse sleigh, with the horses ready harnessed, in charge of a man dressed as a mujik.

They got in without a word, all but Soudeikin, who went to the horses' heads, while the other man went and opened the gates of the yard. The bells had been removed from the harness, and the horses' feet made no sound as Soudeikin led them out through the gate. Ivan took the reins, and Colston held out his hand from the sleigh. There was a roll of notes in it, and as he gave it to Soudeikin he whispered—

"Farewell! If we succeed, the Master shall know how well you have done your part."

Soudeikin took the money with a salute and a whispered farewell, and Ivan trotted his horses quietly down the lane and swung round into the road at the end of it.

So far all had gone well, but the supreme moment of peril had yet to come. A mile away down the road was the guard-house on the Tobolsk road leading out of the town, and this had to be passed before there was even a chance of safety.

As there was no hope of getting the sleigh past unobserved, Colston had determined to trust to a rush when the moment came. He had given Natasha and the Princess a magazine pistol apiece, and held a brace in his own hands; so among them they had a hundred shots.

Ivan kept his horses at an easy trot till they were within a hundred yards of the guard-house. Then, at a sign from Colston, he suddenly lashed them into a gallop, and the sleigh dashed forward at a headlong speed, swept round the curve past the guard-house, hurling one of the sentries on guard to the earth, and away out on to the Tobolsk road.

The next instant the notes of a bugle rang out clear and shrill just as another sounded from the other end of the town. Colston at once guessed what had happened. The inspector of the patrols, in going his rounds, had called at Soudeikin's house to see if all was right, and had discovered the tragedy that had taken place. He looked back and saw a body of Cossacks galloping down the main street towards the guard-house, waving their lanterns and brandishing their spears above their heads.

"Whip up, Ivan, they will be on us in a couple of minutes!" he cried and Ivan swung his long whip out over his horses'

ears, and shouted at them till they put their **heads down and**
tore **over** the smooth snow in gallant style.

By the time the race for life or death really began they had
a good **mile start, and as they had only four more to go** Ivan
did **not spare his cattle, but plied whip and voice with** a will
till the trees whirled **past in a continuous dark line,** and the
sleigh seemed to **fly over the snow almost without** touching it.

Still the **Cossacks gained on them yard by yard,** till at the
end of the **fourth mile they were less than three** hundred
yards behind. Then Colston leant over the back of the sleigh,
and taking the best aim he could, sent **half a dozen** shots
among them. He saw a couple of the flying figures reel and
fall, but their comrades galloped heedlessly over them, yelling
wildly at the tops of their voices, and every moment lessening
the distance between themselves and the sleigh.

Colston fired a dozen more shots into them, and had **the**
satisfaction of seeing three or four of them roll into the snow.
At the same time he put a whistle to his lips, and blew a long
shrill call that sounded **high and clear** above the hoarse yells
of the Cossacks.

Their **pursuers were now within a hundred yards of them,**
and Natasha, **speaking for the first time since the race had**
begun, said—

"I think I can do something now."

As she spoke **she leaned out of the** sleigh sideways, and
began firing rapidly **at the Cossacks.** Shot after shot told
either upon man or beast, **for the** daughter of Natas was one
of the best shots in the Brotherhood; but before she had fired a
dozen times a bright gleam **of** white light shot downwards over
the trees, apparently from the clouds, full in the faces of their
pursuers.

Involuntarily they **reined** up like one man, and **their** yells
of fury changed in an instant into a general cry of terror. The
Cossacks are as brave as any soldiers on earth, and they can
fight any mortal **foe** like the fiends that **they** are, but here was
an enemy they had never **seen** before, a strange, white, ghostly-
looking thing **that** floated in the **clouds** and glared at them
with **a** great blazing, blinding eye, **dazzling** them and making
their horses plunge and rear like things possessed.

They were not long left **in doubt** as to the intentions of their new enemy. Something came rushing through the air and struck the ground almost at the feet of their first rank. Then there was a flash of green light, a stunning report, and men and horses were rent into fragments and hurled into the air like dead leaves before a hurricane.

Only three or four who had turned tail at once were left alive; and these, without daring to look behind them, drove their spurs into their horses' flanks and galloped back to Tiumen, half mad with terror, to tell how a demon had come down from the skies, annihilated their comrades, and carried the fugitives away into the clouds upon its back.

When they reached the town it was a scene of the utmost panic. Soldiers were galloping and running hither and thither, bugles were sounding, and the whole population were turning out into the snow-covered streets. On every lip there were only two words—"Natas!" "The Terrorists!"

The death sentence on Soudeikin, the sub-commissioner of police, had been found pinned with a dagger to the table in the room in which lay the body of the lieutenant, with the bloody T on his forehead. Soudeikin had vanished utterly, leaving only his uniform behind him; so had the two prisoners for whom he had made himself responsible, and at the door of their room lay the corpse of the sentry with a bullet-hole clean through his head from front to back, while in the snow under one of the windows of the room lay the body of the other sentry, stabbed through the heart.

From the very midst of one of the strongholds of Russian tyranny in Siberia, two important prisoners and a police official had been spirited away as though by magic, and now upon the top of all the wonder and dismay came the fugitive Cossacks with their wild tale about the air-demon that had swooped down and destroyed their troop at a single blow. To crown all, half an hour later three horses, mad with fear, came galloping up the Tobolsk road, dragging behind them an empty sleigh, to one of the seats of which was pinned a scrap of paper on which was written—

"The daughter of Natas sends greeting to the Governor of Tiumen, and thanks him for his hospitality."

7

CHAPTER XIV.

THE PSYCHOLOGICAL MOMENT.

ON the morning of Tuesday, the 9th of March 1904, the *Times* published the following telegram at the head of its Foreign Intelligence:—

ASTOUNDING OCCURRENCE IN RUSSIA.

Destruction of Kronstadt by an unknown Air-Ship.

(From our own Correspondent.)

St. Petersburg, *March 8th*, 4 P.M.

Between six and seven this morning, the fortress of Kronstadt was partially destroyed by an unknown air-ship, which was first sighted approaching from the westward at a tremendous speed.

Four shots in all were fired upon the fortress, and produced the most appalling destruction. There was no smoke or flame visible from the guns of the air-ship, and the explosives with which the missiles were charged must have been far more powerful than anything hitherto used in warfare, as in the focus of the explosion masses of iron and steel and solid masonry were instantly reduced to powder.

Two shots were fired as the strange vessel approached, and two as she left the fortress. The two latter exploded over one of the powder magazines, dissolved the steel roof to dust, and ignited the whole contents of the magazine, blowing that portion of the fortification bodily into the sea. At least half the garrison has disappeared, most of the unfortunate men having been practically annihilated by the terrific force of the explosions.

The air-ship was not of the navigable balloon type, and is described by the survivors as looking more like a flying torpedo-boat than anything else. She flew no flag, and there is no clue to her origin.

After destroying the fortress, she ascended several thousand feet, and continued her eastward course at such a prodigious speed, that in less than five minutes she was lost to sight.

The excitement in St. Petersburg almost reaches the point of panic. All efforts to keep the news of the disaster secret have completely failed, and I have therefore received permission to send this telegram, which has been revised by the Censorship, and may therefore be accepted as authentic.

Within an hour of the appearance of this telegram, which appeared only in the *Times*, the Russian Censorship having refused to allow any more to be despatched, the astounding news was flying over the wires to every corner of the world.

The *Times* had a lengthy and very able article on the subject, which, although by no means alarmist in tone, told the world, in grave and weighty sentences, that there could now be no doubt but that the problem of aërial navigation had been completely solved, and that therefore mankind stood confronted by a power that was practically irresistible, and which changed the whole aspect of warfare by land and sea.

In the face of this power, the fortresses, armies, and fleets of the world were useless and helpless. The destruction of Kronstadt had proved that to demonstration. From a height of several thousand feet, and a distance of nearly seven miles, the unknown air-vessel had practically destroyed, with four shots from her mysterious, smokeless, and flameless guns, the strongest fortress in Europe. If it could do that, and there was not the slightest doubt but that it had done so, it could destroy armies wholesale without a chance of reprisals, sink fleets, and lay cities in ruins, at the leisure of those who commanded it.

And here arose the supreme question of the hour—a question beside which all other questions of national or international policy sank instantly into insignificance—Who were those who held this new and appalling power in their hands? It was hardly to be believed that they were representatives of any regularly-constituted national Power, for, although the air was full of rumours of war, there was at present unbroken peace all over the world.

Even in the hands of a recognised Power, the possession of such a frightful engine of destruction could not be viewed by the rest of the world with anything but the gravest apprehension, for that Power, however insignificant otherwise, would now be in a position to terrorise any other nation, or league of nations, however great. Manifestly those who had built the one air-vessel that had been seen, and had given such conclusive proof of her terrible powers, could construct a fleet if they chose to do so, and then the world would be at their mercy.

If, however, as seemed only too probable, the machine was in the hands of a few irresponsible individuals, or, still worse, in those of such enemies of humanity as the Nihilists, or that yet more mysterious and terrible society who were popularly known as the Terrorists, then indeed the outlook was serious beyond forecast or description. At any moment the forces of destruction and anarchy might be let loose upon the world, in such fashion that little less than the collapse of the whole fabric of Society might be expected as the result.

The above necessarily brief and imperfect digest gives only the headings of an article which filled nearly two columns of the *Times*, and it is needless to say that such an article in the leading columns of the most serious and respectable newspaper in the world produced an intense impression wherever it was read.

Of course the telegram was instantly copied by the evening papers, which ran out special editions for the sole purpose of reproducing it, with their own comments upon it, which, after all, were not much more original than the telegram. Meanwhile the *Berliner Tageblatt*, the *Newe Freie Presse*, the *Kölnische Zeitung*, and the *Journal des Débats* had received later and somewhat similar telegrams, and had given their respective views of the catastrophe to the world.

By noon all the capitals of Europe were in a fever of expectation and apprehension. The cables had carried the news to America and India; and when the evening of the same day brought the telegraphic account of the extraordinary occurrence at Tiumen in the grey dusk of the early morning, proving almost conclusively that the rescue had been effected by the same agency that had destroyed Kronstadt, and that, worse than all, the air-vessel was at the command of Natas, the unknown Chief of the mysterious Terrorists, excitement rose almost to frenzy, and everywhere the wildest rumours were accepted as truth.

In a word, the "psychological moment" had come all over Europe, the moment in which all men were thinking of the same thing, discussing the same event, and dreading the same results. To have found a parallel state of affairs, it would have been necessary to go back more than a hundred years, to the hour when the head of Louis XVI. fell into the basket of the guillotine, and the monarchies of Europe sprang to arms to avenge his death.

Meanwhile other and not less momentous events had, unknown to the newspapers or the public, been taking place in three very different parts of the world.

On the evening of Saturday, the 6th, Lord Alanmere had called upon Mr. Balfour in Downing Street, and laid the duplicates of the secret treaty between France and Russia, and copies of all the memoranda appertaining to it, before him, and had convinced him of their authenticity. At the same time he showed him plans of the war-balloons, of which a fleet of fifty would within a few days be at the command of the Tsar.

The result of this interview was a meeting of a Cabinet Council, and the immediate despatch of secret orders to mobilise the fleet and the army, to put every available ship into commission, and to double the strength of the Mediterranean Squadron at once. That evening three Queen's messengers left Charing Cross by the night mail, one for Berlin, one for Vienna, and one for Rome, each of them bearing a copy of the secret treaty.

On Monday morning a Council of Ministers was held at the Peterhof Palace in St. Petersburg, presided over by the Tsar, and convened to discuss the destruction of Kronstadt.

At this Council it was announced that the fleet of war-balloons would be ready to take the air in a week's time from then, and that the concentration of troops on the Afghan frontier was as complete as it could be without provoking immediate hostilities with Britain. In fact, so close were the Cossacks and the Indian troops to each other, both on the Pamirs and on the western slopes of the Hindu Kush, that a collision might be expected at any moment.

The Council of the Tsar decided to let matters take their course in the East, and to make all arrangements with France to simultaneously attack the Triple Alliance as soon as the war-balloons had been satisfactorily tested.

Soon after daybreak on Wednesday, the 10th, an affair of outposts took place near the northern end of the Sir Ulang Pass of the Hindu Kush, between two considerable bodies of

Cossacks and Ghoorkhas, in which, after a stubborn fight, the Russians gave way before the magazine fire of the Indian troops, and fled, leaving nearly a fourth of their number on the field.

The news of this encounter reached London on Wednesday night, and was published in the papers on Thursday morning, together with the intelligence that the fight had been watched from a height of nearly three thousand feet by a small party of men and women in an air-ship, evidently a vessel of war, from the fact that she carried four long guns. She took no part in the fight, and as soon as it was over went off to the south-west at a speed which carried her out of sight in a few minutes.

CHAPTER XV.

A VOYAGE OF DISCOVERY.

HILE all Europe was thrilling with the apprehension of approaching war, and the excitement caused by the appearance of the strange air-ship and the news of its terrible exploits at Kronstadt and Tiumen, the *Ariel* herself was quietly pursuing her way in mid-air south-westerly from the scene of the skirmish outside the Sir Ulang Pass.

She was bound for a region in the midst of Africa, which, even in the first decade of the twentieth century, was still unknown to the geographer and untrodden by the explorer.

Fenced in by huge and precipitous mountains, round whose bases lay vast forests and impenetrable swamps and jungles, from whose deadly areas the boldest pioneers had turned aside as being too hopelessly inhospitable to repay the cost and toil of exploration, it had remained undiscovered and unknown save by two men, who had reached it by the only path by which it was accessible—through the air and over the mountains which shut it in on every side from the external world.

These two adventurous travellers were a wealthy and eccentric Englishman, named Louis Holt, and Thomas Jackson, his devoted retainer, and these two had taken it into their heads—or rather Louis Holt had taken it into his head—to achieve in fact the feat which Jules Verne had so graphically described in fiction, and to cross Africa in a balloon.

They had set out from Zanzibar towards the end of the last year of the nineteenth century, and, with the exception of one or two vague reports from the interior, nothing more had been heard of them until, nearly a year later, a collapsed miniature balloon had been picked up in the Gulf of Guinea by the captain of a trading steamer, who had found in the little car attached to it, a hermetically sealed meat-tin, which contained a manuscript, the contents of which will become apparent in due course.

The captain of the steamer was a practical and somewhat stupid man, who read the manuscript with considerable scepticism, and then put it away, having come to the conclusion that it was no business of his, and that there was no money in it anyhow. He thought nothing more of it until he got back to Liverpool, and then he gave it to a friend of his, who was a Fellow of the Royal Geographical Society, and who duly laid it before that body.

It was published in the *Transactions*, and there was some talk of sending out an expedition under the command of an eminent explorer to rescue Louis Holt and his servant; but when that personage was approached on the subject, it was found that the glory would not be at all commensurate with the expense and risk, and so, after being the usual nine days' wonder, and being duly elaborated by several able editors in the daily and weekly press, the strange adventures of Louis Holt had been dismissed, as of doubtful authenticity, into the limbo of exhausted sensations.

One man, however, had laid the story to heart somewhat more seriously, and that was Richard Arnold, who, on reading it, had formed the resolve that, if ever his dream of aërial navigation were realised, the first use he would make of his air-ship would be to discover and rescue the lonely travellers who were isolated from the rest of the world in the strange, inaccessible region of which the manuscript had given a brief but graphic and fascinating account. He was now carrying out that resolve, and at the same time working out a portion of a plan that was not his own, and which he had been very far from foreseeing when he made the resolution.

Louis Holt's original MS. had been purchased by the President of the Inner Circle, and the *Ariel* was now, in fact, on a voyage of exploration, the object of which was the discovery of this unknown region, with a view to making it the seat of a settlement from which the members of the Executive could watch in security and peace the course of the tremendous struggle which would, ere long, be shaking the world to its foundations.

In such a citadel as this, fenced in by a series of vast natural obstacles, impassable to all who did not possess the means of aërial locomotion, they would be secure from molestation, though all the armies of Europe sought to attack them; and the *Ariel* could, if necessary, traverse in twenty-five hours the three thousand odd miles which separated it from the centre of Europe.

After the rescue of Natasha and the Princess on the Tobolsk road, the *Ariel*, in obedience to the orders of the Council, had shaped her course southward to the western slopes of the Hindu Kush, in order to be present at the prearranged attack of the Cossacks on the British reconnoitring force.

Arnold's orders were simply to wait for the engagement, and only to watch it, unless the British were attacked in overwhelming numbers. In that case he was to have dispersed the Russian force, as the plan of the Terrorists did not allow of any advantage being gained by the soldiers of the Tsar in that part of the world just then.

As the British had defeated them unaided, the *Ariel* had taken no part in the affair, and, after vanishing from the sight of the astonished combatants, had proceeded upon her voyage of discovery.

As a good month would have to elapse before she could keep her rendezvous with the steamer that was to bring out the materials for the construction of the new air-ships from England, there was plenty of time to make the voyage in a leisurely and comfortable fashion. As soon, therefore, as he was out of sight of the skirmishers, he had reduced the speed of the *Ariel* to about forty miles an hour, using only the stern-propeller driven by one engine, and supporting the ship on the air-planes and two fan-wheels.

At this speed he would traverse the three thousand odd miles which lay between the Hindu Kush and "Aeria"—as Louis Holt had somewhat fancifully named the region that could be reached only through the air—in a little over seventy-five hours, or rather more than three days.

Those three days were the happiest that his life had so far

contained. The complete success of his invention, and the absolute fulfilment of his promises to the Brotherhood, had made him a power in the world, and a power which, as he honestly believed, would be used for the highest good of mankind when the time came to finally confront and confound the warring forces of rival despotisms.

But far more than this in his eyes was the fact that he had been able to use the unique power which his invention had placed in his hands, to rescue the woman that he loved so dearly from a fate which, even now that it was past, he could not bring himself to contemplate.

When she had first greeted him in the Council-chamber of the Inner Circle, the distance that had separated her from him had seemed immeasurable, and she—the daughter of Natas and the idol of the most powerful society in the world—might well have looked down upon him—the nameless dreamer of an unrealised dream, and a pauper, who would not have known where to have looked for his next meal, had the Brotherhood not had faith in him and his invention.

But now all that was changed. The dream had become the reality, and the creation of his genius was bearing her with him swiftly and smoothly through a calm atmosphere, and under a cloudless sky, over sea and land, with more ease than a bird wings its flight through space. He had accomplished the greatest triumph in the history of human discovery. He had revolutionised the world, and ere long he would make war impossible. Surely this entitled him to approach even her on terms of equality, and to win her for his own if he could.

Natasha saw this too as clearly as he did—more clearly, perhaps; for, while he only arrived at the conclusion by a process of reasoning, she reached it intuitively at a single step. She knew that he loved her, that he had loved her from the moment that their hands had first met in greeting, and, peerless as she was among women, she was still a woman, and the homage of such a man as this was sweet to her, albeit it was still unspoken.

She knew, too, that the hopes of the Revolution, which, before all things human, claimed her whole-souled devotion, now depended mainly upon him, and the use that he might make of the power that lay in his hands, and this of itself was no light bond between them, though not necessarily having anything to do with affection.

So far she was heart-whole, and though many had attempted the task, no man had yet made her pulses beat a stroke faster for his sake. Ever since she had been old enough to know what tyranny meant, she had been trained to hate it, and prepared to work against it, and, if necessary, to sacrifice herself body and soul to destroy it.

Thus hatred rather than love had been the creed of her life and the mainspring of her actions, and, save her father and her one friend Radna, she stood aloof from mankind and its loves and friendships, rather the beautiful incarnation of an abstract principle than a woman, to whom love and motherhood were the highest aims of existence.

More than this, she was the daughter of a Jew, and therefore held herself absolutely at her father's disposal as far as marriage was concerned, and if he had given her in wedlock even to a Russian official, telling her that the Cause demanded the sacrifice, she would have obeyed, though her heart had broken in the same hour.

Although he had never hinted directly at such a thing, the conviction had been growing upon her for the last two or three years that Natas really intended her to marry Tremayne, and so, in the case of his own death, form a bond that should hold him to the Brotherhood when the chain of his own control was snapped. Though she instinctively shrank from such a union of mere policy, she would enter it without hesitation at her father's bidding, and for the sake of the Cause to which her life was devoted.

How great such a sacrifice would be, should it ever be asked of her, no one but herself could ever know, for she was perfectly well aware that in Tremayne's strange double life there were two loves, one of which, and that not the real and natural one, was hers.

Had she felt that she had the disposal of herself in her own hands, she would not, perhaps, have waited with such painful apprehension the avowal which hour after hour, now that they were brought into such close and constant relationships on board this little vessel high in mid-air, she saw trembling on the lips of her rescuer.

Arnold's life of hard, honest work, **and his** constant habit of facing truth in **its most** uncompromising forms, had made dissimulation almost impossible to **him; and** added to that, situated as he **was,** there was **no necessity for** it. Colston knew of his love, and the Princess **had guessed it long ago.** Did **Natasha know his** open secret? **Of that he hardly dared to be sure, though** something told him that the inevitable **moment of knowledge was** near at hand.

For the first twenty-four hours **of the** voyage he had **seen very little of either** her or the **Princess,** as they had mostly **remained in their** cabins, enjoying a complete rest after the **terrible** fatigue and suffering they had gone through since their capture in Moscow, but on the Thursday morning they had had breakfast in the saloon with him and Colston, and had afterwards spent a portion of the morning **on** deck, deeply interested in watching the fight between **the** British and Russians. Thanks to Radna's foresight, they had each found a trunk full of suitable clothing on board the *Ariel*. These had been taken to Drumcraig by Colston, and placed in the cabins intended for their use, and so they were able to discard the uncouth but **useful** costumes in **which** they had made their escape.

In the afternoon Arnold had had to **perform the** pleasant task of showing them over the *Ariel*, explaining the working of the machinery, and putting the wonderful vessel through **various evolutions** to show what she was capable of doing.

He rushed her at full speed through the air, took flying leaps over **outlying spurs** of mountain ranges that lay in their path, **swooped down into** valleys, and flew over level plains fifty **yards from the** ground, like an albatross over the surface of a smooth tropic sea. Then he soared up from the earth again, until the horizon **widened** out to vast extent, and they could see the mighty buttresses of "the Roof of the World" stretching out below them in an endless succession of **ranges as** far as the eye could reach.

Neither Natasha nor the Princess **could find** words to at all adequately express all that they **saw and** learnt during that day of wonders, and all night Natasha could hardly sleep for waking dreams of universal empire, **and a** world at peace equitably ruled by a power **that had no** need of aggression, because all the realms of earth and air belonged to those who wielded it.

When at last she did go to sleep, it was to dream again, and this time of herself, the Angel of the Revolution, sharing the aërial throne of the world-empire with the man who had made revolutions impossible by striking the sword from the hand of the tyrants of earth for ever.

CHAPTER XVI.

A WOOING IN MID AIR.

AFTER breakfast on the Friday morning, Natasha and Arnold were standing in the bows of the *Ariel*, admiring the magnificent panorama that lay stretched out five thousand feet below them.

The air-ship had by this time covered a little over 2000 miles of her voyage, and was now speeding smoothly and swiftly along over the south-western shore of the Red Sea, a few miles southward of the sixteenth parallel of latitude. Eastward the bright blue waves of the sea were flashing behind them in the cloudless morning sun; the high mountains of the African coast rose to right and left and in front of them; and through the breaks in the chain they could see the huge masses of Abyssinia to the southward, and the vast plains that stretched away westward across the Blue and White Niles, away to the confines of the Libyan Desert.

"What a glorious world!" exclaimed Natasha, after gazing for many silent minutes with entranced eyes over the limitless landscape. "And to think that, after all, all this is but a little corner of it!"

"It is yours, Natasha, if you will have it," replied Arnold quietly, yet with a note in his voice that warned her that the moment which she had expected and yet dreaded, had already come. There was no use in avoiding the inevitable for a time. It would be better if they understood each other at once; and so she looked round at him with eyebrows elevated in well-simulated surprise, and said—

"Mine! What do you mean, my friend?"

There was an almost imperceptible emphasis on the last word that brought the blood to Arnold's cheek, and he answered, with a ring in his voice that gave unmistakable evidence of the effort that he was making to restrain the passion that inspired his words—

"I mean just what I say. All the kingdoms of the world, and the glory of them, from pole to pole, and from east to west, shall be yours, and shall obey your lightest wish. I have conquered the air, and therefore the earth and sea. In two months from now I shall have an aërial navy afloat that will command the world, and I — is it not needless to tell you, Natasha, why I glory in the possession of that power? Surely you must know that it is because I love you more than all that a subject world can give me, and because it makes it possible for me, if not to win you, at least not to be unworthy to attempt the task?"

It was a distinctly unconventional declaration—such a one, indeed, as no woman had ever heard since Alexander the Great had whispered in the ears of Lais his dreams of universal empire, but there was a straightforward earnestness about it which convinced her beyond question that it came from no ordinary man, but from one who saw the task before him clearly, and had made up his mind to achieve it.

For a moment her heart beat faster than it had ever yet done at the bidding of a man's voice, and there was a bright flush on her cheeks, and a softer light in her eyes, as she replied in a more serious tone than Arnold had ever heard her use—

"My friend, you have forgotten something. You and I are not a man and a woman in the relationship that exists between us. We are two factors in a work such as has never been undertaken since the world began; two units in a mighty problem whose solution is the happiness or the ruin of the whole human race. It is not for us to speak of individual love while these tremendous issues hang undecided in the balance.

"One does not speak of love in the heat of war, and you and I and those who are with us are at war with the powers of the earth, and higher things than the happiness of individuals are at stake. You know my training has been one of hate and not of love, and till the hate is quenched I must not know what love is.

"Remember your oath—the oath which I have taken as well as you—'As long as I live those ends shall be my ends, and no human considerations shall weigh with me where those ends are concerned.' Is not this love of which you speak a human consideration that might clash with the purposes of the Brotherhood whose ends you and I have solemnly sworn to hold supreme above all earthly things?

"My father has told me that when love takes possession of a human soul, reason abdicates her throne, and great aims become impossible. No, no; that great power which you hold in your hands was not given you just to win the love of a woman, and I tell you frankly that you will never win mine with it.

"More than this, if I saw you using it for such an end, I would take care that you did not use it for long. No man ever had such an awful responsibility laid upon him as the possession of this power lays upon you. It is yours to make or mar the future of the human race, of which I am but a unit. It is not the power that will ever win either my respect or my love, but the wisdom and the justice with which it may be used."

"Ah! I see you distrust me. You think that because I have the power to be a despot, that therefore I may forget my oath and become one. I forgive you for the thought, unworthy of you as it is, and also, I hope, of me. No, Natasha; I am no skilled hand at love-making, for I have never wooed any mistress but one before to-day, and she is won only by plain honesty and hard service; just what I will devote to the winning of you, whether you are to be won or not—but I must have expressed myself clumsily indeed for you to have even thought of treason to the Cause.

"You are no more devoted adherent of it than I am. You have suffered in one way and I in another from the falsehood and rottenness of present-day Society, but you do not hate it more utterly than I do, and you would not go to greater lengths than I would to destroy it. Yours is a hatred of emotion, and mine is a hatred of reason. I have proved that, as Society is constituted, it is the worst and not the best qualities of humanity that win wealth and power, and such respect as the vulgar of all classes can give. But it is not such power as this that I would lay at your feet, when I ask you to share the world-empire with me. It is an empire of peace and not of war that I shall offer to you."

"Then," said Natasha, taking a step towards him, and laying her hand on his arm as she spoke, "when you have made war impossible to the rivalry of nations and races, and have proclaimed peace on earth, then I will give myself to you, body and soul, to do with as you please, to kill or to keep alive, for then truly you will have done that which all the generations of men before you have failed to do, and it will be yours to ask and to have."

As she spoke these last words Natasha bowed her proudly-carried head as though in submission to the dictum that her own lips had pronounced; and Arnold, laying his hand on hers and holding it for a moment unresisting in his own, said—

"I accept the condition, and as you have said so shall it be. You shall hear no more words of love from my lips until the day that peace shall be proclaimed on earth and war shall be no more; and when that day comes, as it shall do, I will hold you to your words, and I will claim you and take you, body and soul, as you have said, though I break every other human tie save man's love for woman to possess you."

Natasha looked him full in the eyes as he spoke these last words. She had never heard such words before, and by their very strength and audacity they compelled her respect and even her submission. Her heart was still untamed and unconquered, and no man was its lord, yet her eyes sank before the steady gaze of his, and in a low sweet voice she answered—

"So be it! There never was a true woman yet who did not love to meet her master. When that day comes I shall have met my master, and I will do his bidding. Till then we are friends and comrades in a common Cause to which both our lives are devoted. Is it not better that it should be so?"

"Yes, I am content. I would not take the prize before I have won it. Only answer me one question frankly, and then I have done till I may speak again."

"What is that."

"Have I a rival—not among men, for of that I am careless—but in your own heart?"

8

"No, none. I am heart-whole and heart-free. Win me if you can. It is a fair challenge, and I will abide by the result, be it what it may."

"That is all I ask for. If I do not win you, may Heaven do so to me that I shall have no want of the love of woman for ever!"

So saying, he raised her hand to his lips and kissed it, in token of the compact that was made between them. Then, intuitively divining that she wished to be alone, he turned away without another word, and walked to the after end of the vessel.

Natasha remained where she was for a good half-hour, leaning on the rail that surrounded the deck, and gazing out dreamily over the splendid and ever-changing scene that lay spread out beneath her. Truly it was a glorious world, as she had said, even now, cursed as it was with war and the hateful atrocities of human selfishness, and the sordid ambition of its despots.

What would it be like in the day when the sword should lie rusting on the forgotten battle-field, and the cannon's mouth be choked with the desert dust for ever? What was now a hell of warring passions would then be a paradise of peaceful industry, and he who had the power, if any man had, to turn that hell into the paradise that it might be, had just told her that he loved her, and would create that paradise for her sake.

Could he do it? Was not this marvellous creation of his genius, that was bearing her in mid-air over land and sea, as woman had never travelled before, a sufficient earnest of his power? Truly it was. And to be won by such a man was no mean destiny, even for her, the daughter of Natas, and the peerless Angel of the Revolution.

Situated as they were, it would of course have been impossible, even if it had been in any way desirable, for Arnold and Natasha to have kept their compact secret from their fellow-travellers, who were at the same time their most intimate friends.

There was not, however, the remotest reason for attempting to do so. Although with regard to the rest of the world the members of the Brotherhood were necessarily obliged to live lives of constant dissimulation, among themselves they had no secrets from each other.

Thus, for instance, it was perfectly well known that Tremayne, during those periods of his double life in which he acted as Chief of the Inner Circle, regarded the daughter of Natas with feelings much warmer than those of friendship or brotherhood in a common cause, and until Arnold and his wonderful creation appeared on the scene, he was looked upon as the man who, if any man could, would some day win the heart of their idolised Angel.

Of the other love that was the passion of his other life, no one save Natasha, and perhaps Natas himself, knew anything; and even if they had known, they would not have considered it possible for any other woman to have held a man's heart against the peerless charms of Natasha. In fact they would have looked upon such rivalry as mere presumption that it was not at all necessary for their incomparable young Queen of the Terror to take into serious account.

In Arnold, however, they saw a worthy rival even to the Chief himself, for there was a sort of halo of romance, even in their eyes, about this serious, quiet-spoken young genius, who had come suddenly forth from the unknown obscurity of his past life to arm the Brotherhood with a power which revolutionised their tactics and virtually placed the world at their mercy. In a few months he had become alike their hero and their supreme hope, so far as all active operations went; and now that with his own hand he had snatched Natasha from a fate of unutterable misery, and so signally punished her persecutors, it seemed to be only in the fitness of things that he should love her, win her for his own, if won she was to be by any man.

This, at any rate, was the line of thought which led the Princess and Colston each to express their unqualified satisfaction with the state of affairs arrived at in the compact that had been made between Natasha and Arnold—"armed neutrality," as the former smilingly described to the Princess while she was telling her of the strange wooing of her now avowed lover. Natasha was no woman to be wooed and won in the ordinary way, and it was fitting that she should be the guerdon of such an achievement as no man had ever undertaken before, since the world began.

The voyage across Africa progressed pleasantly and almost uneventfully for the thirty-six hours after the crossing of the Red Sea. After passing over the mountains of the coast, the *Ariel* had travelled at a uniform height of about 3000 feet over a magnificent country of hill and valley, forest and prairie, occasionally being obliged to rise another thousand feet or so to cross some of the ridges of mountain chains which rose into peaks and mountain knots, some of which touched the snow-line.

Several times the air-ship was sighted by the people of the various countries over which she passed, and crowds swarmed out of the villages and towns, gesticulating wildly, and firing guns and beating drums to scare the flying demon away.

Once or twice they heard bullets singing through the air, but of these they took little heed, beyond quickening the speed of the air-ship for the time, knowing that there was not a chance in a hundred thousand of the *Ariel* being hit, and that even if she were the bullet would glance harmlessly off her smooth hull of hardened aluminium.

Once only they descended in a delightful little valley among the mountains, which appeared to be totally uninhabited, and here they renewed their store of fresh water, and laid in one of fruit, as well as taking advantage of the opportunity to stretch their legs on *terra firma*.

This was on the Saturday morning; and when they again rose into the air to continue their voyage, they saw that they had crossed the great mountain mass that divides the Sahara from the little-known regions of Equatorial Africa, and that in front of them to the south-west lay, as far as the eye could reach, a boundless expanse of dense forest and jungle and swamp, a gloomy and forbidding-looking region which it would be well-nigh impossible to traverse on foot.

Early in the afternoon the four voyagers were gathered in the deck-saloon, closely examining a somewhat rudely-drawn chart that was spread out on the table. It was the map that formed part of the manuscript which had been found in the car of Louis Holt's miniature balloon, and sketched out his route from Zanzibar to Aeria, and the country lying round so far as he had been able to observe it.

"This gives us, after all, very little idea of the distance we have yet to go," said Arnold; "for though Holt has got his latitude presumably right, we have very little clue to his longitude, for he says himself that his watch was stopped in a thunder-storm, and that in the same storm he lost all count of the distance he had travelled. Added to that, he admits that he was blown about for twelve days in one direction and another, so that all we really know is that somewhere across this fearful wilderness beneath us we shall find Aeria, but where is still a problem."

"What is your own idea?" asked Colston.

"Not a very clear one, I must confess. At this elevation we can see about sixty miles as the atmosphere is now, and as far as we can see to the south-west there is nothing but the same kind of country that we have under us. We have travelled rather more than 2700 miles since we left the Hindu Kush, and according to my reckoning Aeria lies somewhere between 3000 and 3200 miles south-west of where we started from on Thursday morning. That means that we are within between three and five hundred miles of Aeria, unless, indeed, our calculations are wholly at fault, and at that rate, as we only have about four and a half hours' daylight left, we shall not get there to-day at our present speed."

"Couldn't we go a bit faster?" put in Natasha. "You know I and the Princess are dying to see this mysterious unknown country that only two other people have ever seen."

"You have but to say so, Natasha, and it is already done," replied Arnold, signalling at the same moment to the engine-room by means of a similar arrangement of electric buttons to that which was in the wheel-house. "Only you must remember that you must not go out on deck now, or you will be blown away like a feather into space."

While he was speaking the three propellers had begun to revolve at full speed, and the *Ariel* darted forward with a velocity that caused the mountains she had just crossed to sink rapidly on the horizon.

All the afternoon the *Ariel* flew at full speed over the seemingly interminable wilderness of swamp and jungle, until, when the equatorial sun was within a few degrees of the horizon, one of the crew, who had been stationed in the conning tower at the bows, signalled to call the attention of the man in the

wheel-house. Arnold, who was in the after-saloon at the time, heard the signal, and hurried forward to the look-out. He gave one quick glance ahead, signalled "half-speed" to the engine-room, and then went aft again to the saloon, and said—
"Aeria is in sight!"

Immediately everyone hastened to the deck saloon, from the windows of which could be seen a huge mass of mountains looming dark and distinct against the crimsoning western sky.

It rose like some vast precipitous island out of the sea of forest that lay about its base; and above the mighty rock-walls that seemed to rise sheer from the surrounding plain at least a dozen peaks towered into the sky, two of their summits covered with eternal snow, and shining like points of rosy fire in the almost level rays of the sun.

As nearly as Arnold could judge in the deceptive state of the atmosphere, they were still between thirty and forty miles from it, and as it would not be safe to approach its lofty cliffs at a high rate of speed in the half light that would so soon merge into darkness, he said to his companions—

"We shall have to find a resting-place up among the cliffs on this side to-night, for we have lost the moon, and unless it were absolutely necessary to cross the mountains in the dark, I should not care to do so with the ladies on board. Besides, there is no hurry now that we are here, and we shall get a much finer first impression of our new kingdom if we cross at sunrise. What do you think?"

All agreed that this would be the best plan, and so the *Ariel* ran up to within a mile of the rocks, and then the forward engine was connected with the dynamo, and the searchlight, which had so disconcerted the Cossacks on the Tobolsk road, was turned on to the cliffs, which they carefully explored, until they found a little plateau covered with luxuriant vegetation and well watered, about two thousand feet above the plain below.

Here it was decided to come to a halt for the night, and to reserve the exploration of Aeria for the morning, and so the fan-wheels were sent aloft, and the *Ariel*, after hovering for a few minutes over the verdant little plain seeking for a suitable spot to alight in, sank gently to the earth after her flight of more than three thousand miles.

CHAPTER XVII.

AERIA FELIX.

EVERY one on board the *Ariel* was astir the next morning as soon as the first rays of dawn were shooting across the vast plain that stretched away to the eastward, and by the time it was fairly daylight breakfast was over and all were anxiously speculating as to what they would find on the other side of the tremendous cliffs, on an eyrie in which they had found a resting-place for the night.

As soon as all was ready for a start, Arnold said to Natasha, who was standing alone with him on the after part of the deck—

"If you would like to steer the *Ariel* into your new kingdom, I shall be delighted to give you the lesson in steering that I promised you yesterday."

Natasha saw the inner meaning of the offer at a glance, and replied with a smile that made his blood tingle—

"That would be altogether too great a responsibility for a beginner. I might run on to some of these fearful rocks. But if you will take the helm when the dangerous part comes, I will learn all I can by watching you."

"As long as you are with me in the wheel-house for the next hour or so," said Arnold, with almost boyish frankness, "I shall be content. I need scarcely tell you why I want to be alone with you when we first sight this new home of our future empire."

"I have half a mind not to come after that very injudicious speech. Still, if only for the sake of its delightful innocence, I will forgive you this time. You really must practise the worldly art of dissimulation a little, or I shall have to get the Princess to play chaperon."

Natasha spoke these words in a bantering tone, and with a flush on her lovely cheeks, that forced Arnold to cut short the conversation for the moment, by giving an order to Andrew Smith, who at that instant put his head out of the wheel-house door to say—

"All ready, sir!"

"Very well," replied Arnold. "I will take the wheel, and do you tell every one to keep under cover."

Smith saluted, and disappeared, and then Natasha and Arnold went into the wheel-house, while Colston and the Princess took their places in the deck-saloon, the two men off duty going into the conning tower forward.

"Why every one under cover, Captain Arnold?" asked Natasha, as soon as the two were ensconced in the wheel-house and the door shut.

"Because I am going to put the *Ariel* through her paces, and enter Aeria in style," replied he, signalling for the fan-wheels to revolve. "The fact is that, so far as I can see, these mountains are too high for us to rise over them by means of the lifting-wheels, which are only calculated to carry the ship to a height of about five thousand feet. After that the air gets too rarefied for them to get a solid grip. Now, these mountains look to me more like seven thousand feet high."

"Then how will you get over them?"

"I shall first take a cruise and see if I can find a negotiable gap, and then leap it."

"What! Leap seven thousand feet?"

"No; you forget that we shall be over five thousand up when we take the jump, and I have no doubt that we shall find a place where a thousand feet or so more will take us over. That we shall rise easily with the planes and propellers, and you will see such a leap as man never made in the world before."

While he was speaking the *Ariel* had risen from the ground, and was hanging a few hundred feet above the little plateau. He gave the signal for the wheels to be lowered, and the propellers to set to work at half-speed. Then he pulled the lever which moved the air-planes, and the vessel sped away forwards and upwards at about sixty miles an hour.

Arnold headed her away from the mountains until he had got an offing of a couple of miles, and then he swung her round and skirted the cliffs, rising ever higher and higher, and keeping a sharp look-out for a depression among the ridges that still towered nearly three thousand feet above them.

When he had explored some twenty miles of the mountain wall, Arnold suddenly pointed towards it, and said—

"There is a place that I think will do. Look yonder, between those two high peaks away to the southward. That ridge is not more than six thousand feet from the earth, and the *Ariel* can leap that as easily as an Irish hunter would take a five-barred gate."

"It looks dreadfully high from here," said Natasha, in spite of herself turning a shade paler at the idea of taking a six thousand foot ridge at a flying leap. She had splendid nerves, but this was her first aërial voyage, and it was also the first time that she had ever been brought so closely face to face with the awful grandeur of Nature in her own secret and solitary places.

She would have faced a levelled rifle without flinching, but as she looked at that frowning mass of rocks towering up into the sky, and then down into the fearful depths below, where huge trees looked like tiny shrubs, and vast forests like black patches of heather on the earth, her heart stood still in her breast when she thought of the frightful fate that would overwhelm the *Ariel* and her crew should she fail to rise high enough to clear the ridge, or if anything went wrong with her machinery at the critical moment.

"Are you sure you can do it?" she asked almost involuntarily.

"Perfectly sure," replied Arnold quietly, "otherwise I should not attempt it with you on board. The *Ariel* contains enough explosives to reduce her and us to dust and ashes, and if we hit that ridge going over, she would go off like a dynamite shell. No, I know what she can do, and you need not have the slightest fear!"

"I am not exactly afraid, but it *looks* a fearful thing to attempt."

"If there were any danger I should tell you—with my usual lack of dissimulation. But really there is none, and all you have to do is to hold tight when I tell you, and keep your eyes open for the first glimpse of Aeria."

By this time the Ariel was more than ten miles away from the mountains. Arnold, having now got offing enough, swung her round again, headed her straight for the ridge between the two peaks, and signalled "full speed" to the engine-room.

In an instant the propellers redoubled their revolutions, and the *Ariel* gathered way until the wind sang and screamed past her masts and stays. She covered eight miles in less than four minutes, and it seemed to Natasha as though the rock-wall were rushing towards them at an appalling speed, still frowning down a thousand feet above them. For the instant she was all eyes. She could neither open her lips nor move a limb for sheer, irresistible, physical terror. Then she heard Arnold say sharply—

"Now, hold on tight!"

The nearest thing to her was his own arm, the hand of which grasped one of the spokes of the steering wheel. Instinctively she passed her own arm under it, and then clasped it with both her hands. As she did so she felt the muscles tighten and harden. Then with his other hand he pulled the lever back to the full, and inclined the planes to their utmost.

Suddenly, as though some Titan had overthrown it, the huge black wall of rock in front seemed to sink down into the earth, the horizon widened out beyond it, and the *Ariel* soared upwards and swept over it nearly a thousand feet to the good.

"Ah!"

The exclamation was forced from her white lips by an impulse that Natasha had no power to resist. All the pride of her nature was conquered and humbled for the moment by the marvel that she had seen, and by the something greater and stranger than all, that she saw in the man beside her who had worked this miracle with a single touch of his hand. A moment later she had recovered her self-possession. She unclasped her hands from his arm, and as the colour came back to her cheeks she said, as he thought, more sweetly than she had ever spoken to him before—

"My friend, you have glorious nerves where physical danger is concerned, and now I freely forgive you for fainting in the Council-chamber when Martinov was executed. But don't try mine again like that if you can help it. For the moment I thought that the end of all things had come. Oh, look! What

a paradise! Truly this is a lovely kingdom that you have brought me to!"

"And one that you and I will yet reign over together," replied Arnold quietly, as he moved the lever again and allowed the *Ariel* to sink smoothly down the other side of the ridge over which she had taken her tremendous leap.

When she had called it a paradise, Natasha had used almost the only word that would fitly describe the scene that opened out before them as the *Ariel* sank down after her leap across the ridge. The interior of the mountain mass took the form of an oval valley, as nearly as they could guess about fifty miles long by perhaps thirty wide. All round it the mountains seemed to rise unbroken by a single gap or chasm to between three and four thousand feet above the lowest part of the valley, and above this again the peaks rose high into the sky, two of them to the snow-line, which in this latitude was over 15,000 feet above the sea.

Of the two peaks which reached to this altitude, one was at either end of a line drawn through the greater length of the valley, that is to say, from north to south. At least ten other peaks all round the walls of the valley rose to heights varying from eight to twelve thousand feet.

The centre of the valley was occupied by an irregularly shaped lake, plentifully dotted with islands about its shores, but quite clear of them in the middle. In its greatest length it would be about twelve miles long, while its breadth varied from five miles to a few hundred yards. Its sloping shores were covered with the most luxuriant vegetation, which reached upwards almost unbroken, but changing in character with the altitude, until there was a regular series of transitions, from the palms and bananas on the shores of the lake, to the sparse and scanty pines and firs that clung to the upper slopes of the mountains.

The lake received about a score of streams, many of which began as waterfalls far up the mountains, while two of them at least had their origin in the eternal snows of the northern and southern peaks. So far as they could see from the air-ship, the lake had no outlet, and they were therefore obliged to conclude that its surplus waters escaped by some subterranean channel, probably to reappear again as a river

The second comer, if he felt any astonishment at the apparition that had invaded his solitude, certainly betrayed none. On the contrary, he walked deliberately from the hut to the bit of sward over which the *Ariel* hung motionless, and, seeing two ladies leaning on the rail that ran round the deck, he doffed his goatskin cap with a well-bred gesture, and said, in a voice that betrayed not the slightest symptom of surprise—

"Good morning, ladies and gentlemen! Good morning, and welcome to Aeria! I see that the problem of aërial navigation has been solved; I always said it would be in the first ten years of the twentieth century, though I often got laughed at by the wiseacres who know nothing until they see a thing before their noses. May I ask whether that little message that I sent to the outside world some years ago has procured me the pleasure of this visit?"

"Yes, Mr. Holt. Your little balloon was picked up about three years ago in the Gulf of Guinea, and, after various adventures and much discussion, has led to our present voyage."

"I am delighted to hear it. I suppose there were plenty of noodles who put it down to a practical joke or something of that sort? What's become of Stanley? Why didn't he come out and rescue me, as he did Emin? Not glory enough, I suppose? It would bother him, too, to get over these mountains, unless he flew over. By the way, has he got an air-ship?"

"No," replied Arnold, with a laugh. "This is the only one in existence, and she has not been a week afloat. But if you'll allow us, we'll come down and get generally acquainted, and after that we can explain things at our leisure."

"Quite so, quite so; do so by all means. Most happy, I'm sure. Ah! beautiful model. Comes down as easily as a bird. Capital mechanism. What's your motive-power? Gas, electricity—no, not steam, no funnels! Humph! Very ingenious. Always said it would be done some day. Build flying navies next, and be fighting in the clouds. Then there'll be general smash. Serve 'em right. Fools to fight. Why can't they live in peace?"

While Louis Holt was running along in this style, jerking his words out in little short snappy sentences, and fussing welling from the earth, it might be, hundreds of miles away.

Of inhabitants there were absolutely no traces to be seen, from the direction in which the *Ariel* was approaching. Animals and birds there seemed to be in plenty, but of man no trace was visible, until in her flight along the valley the *Ariel* opened up one of the many smaller valleys formed by the ribs of the encircling mountains.

There, close by a clump of magnificent tree-ferns, and nestling under a precipitous ridge, covered from base to summit with dark-green foliage and brilliantly-coloured flowers, was a well-built log-hut surrounded by an ample verandah, also almost smothered in flowers, and surmounted by a flagstaff from which fluttered the tattered remains of a Union-Jack.

In a little clearing to one side of the hut, a man, who might very well have passed for a modern edition of Robinson Crusoe, so far as his attire was concerned, was busily skinning an antelope which hung from a pole suspended from two trees. His back was turned towards them, and so swift and silent had been their approach that he did not hear the soft whirring of the propellers until they were within some three hundred yards of him.

Then, just as he looked round to see whence the sound came, Andrew Smith, who was standing in the bows near the conning tower, put his hands to his mouth and roared out a regular sailor's hail—

"Thomas Jackson, ahoy!"

The man straightened himself up, stared open-mouthed for a moment at the strange apparition, and then, with a yell either of terror or astonishment, bolted into the house as hard as he could run.

As soon as he was able to speak for laughing at the queer incident, Arnold sent the fan-wheels aloft and lowered the *Ariel* to within about twenty feet of the ground over a level patch of sward, across which meandered a little stream on its way to the lake. While she was hanging motionless over this, the man who had fled into the house reappeared, almost dragging another man, somewhat similarly attired, after him, and pointing excitedly towards the *Ariel*.

about round the air-ship, she had sunk gently to the earth, and her passengers had disembarked.

Arnold for the time being took no notice of the questions with regard to the motive-power, but introduced first himself, then the ladies, and then Colston, to Louis Holt, who may be described here, as elsewhere, as a little, bronzed, grizzled man, anywhere between fifty-five and seventy, with a lean, wiry, active body, a good square head, an ugly but kindly face, and keen, twinkling little grey eyes, that looked straight into those of any one he might be addressing.

The introductions over, he was invited on board the *Ariel*, and a few minutes later, in the deck-saloon, he was chattering away thirteen to the dozen, and drinking with unspeakable gusto the first glass of champagne he had tasted for nearly five years.

CHAPTER XVIII.

A NAVY OF THE FUTURE.

RNOLD'S instructions from the Council had been to remain in Aeria, and make a thorough exploration of the wonderful region described in Louis Holt's manuscript, until the time came for him to meet the *Avondale*, the steamer which was to bring out the materials for constructing the Terrorists' aërial navy.

Louis Holt and his faithful retainer, during the three years and a half that they had been shut up in it from the rest of the world, had made themselves so fully acquainted with its geography that very little of its surface was represented by blanks on the map which the former had spent several months in constructing, and so no better or more willing guides could have been placed at their service than they were.

Holt was an enthusiastic naturalist, and he descanted at great length on the strangeness of the flora and fauna that it had been his privilege to discover and classify in this isolated and hitherto unvisited region. It appeared that neither its animals nor its plants were quite like those of the rest of the continent, but seemed rather to belong to an anterior geological age.

From this fact he had come to the conclusion that at some very remote period, while the greater portion of Northern Africa was yet submerged by the waters of that ocean of which what is now the Sahara was probably the deepest part, Aeria was one of the many islands that had risen above its surface; and that, as the land rose and the waters subsided, its peculiar shape had prevented the forms of life which it contained from migrating or becoming modified in the struggle for existence with other forms, just as the flora and fauna of Australia have been shut off from those of the rest of the world.

There were no traces of human inhabitants to be found; but there were apparently two or three families of anthropoid apes, that seemed, so far as Holt had been able to judge—for they were extremely shy and cunning, and therefore difficult of approach—to be several degrees nearer to man, both in structure and intelligence, than any other members of the Simian family that had been discovered in other parts of the world.

As may well be imagined, a month passed rapidly and pleasantly away, what with exploring excursions by land and air, in the latter of which by no means the least diverting element was the keen and quaintly-expressed delight of Louis Holt at the new method of travel. Two or three times Arnold had, for his satisfaction, sent the *Ariel* flying over the ridge across which she had entered Aeria, but he had always been content with a glimpse of the outside world, and was always glad to get back again to the "happy valley," as he invariably called his isolated paradise.

The brief sojourn in this delightful land had brought back all the roses to Natasha's lovely cheeks, and had completely restored both her and the Princess to the perfect health that they had lost during their short but terrible experience of Russian convict life; but towards the end of the month they both began to get restless and anxious to get away to the rendezvous with the steamer that was bringing their friends and comrades out from England.

So it came about that an hour or so after sunrise on Friday, the 20th of May, the company of the *Ariel* bade farewell for a time to Louis Holt and his companion, leaving with them a good supply of the creature comforts of civilisation which alone were lacking in Aeria, rose into the air, and disappeared over the ridge to the north-west.

They had rather more than 2500 miles of plain and mountain and desert to cross, before they reached the sea-coast on which they expected to meet the steamer, and Arnold regulated the speed of the *Ariel* so that they would reach it about daybreak on the following morning.

The voyage was quite uneventful, and the course that they pursued led them westward through the Zegzeb and Nyli countries, then **north-westward** along the valley of the Niger, and then westward across **the desert to** the desolate sandy shores of **the** Western Sahara, which they crossed at sunrise on the Sunday morning, in **the** latitude of the island which was to form their rendezvous with the steamer.

They sighted the island **about an hour** later, but there **was no sign** of any vessel **for** fifty **miles** round it. The ocean **appeared** totally deserted, as, indeed, it usually is, for there is **no trade** with this barren and **savage** coast, and ships going **to and from** the southward portions of the continent give its **treacherous** sandbanks as wide a berth **as** possible. This, in fact, was **the** principal reason **why this** rocky islet, some sixty miles **from the** coast, had been **chosen by** the Terrorists for their temporary dockyard.

According to their calculations, **the** steamer **would not be due** for another twenty-four **hours** at the least, **and at that moment would be** about three hundred miles to the **northward.** The *Ariel* was therefore headed **in** that direction, at a hundred **miles an hour,** with a view to meeting her **and convoying her for the rest** of her voyage, and obviating such **a disaster as** Natasha's apprehensions pointed **to.**

The air-ship was kept at **a height** of two thousand **feet** above the water, and a man was **stationed in** the forward conning tower to keep a bright look-out **ahead.** For more than three hours she sped on her way without interruption, and then, a few minutes before twelve, the **man** in the conning tower signalled to the wheel-house—"Steamer in sight."

The signal was at once **transmitted to** the saloon, where Arnold was sitting with the **rest of the** party; he immediately signalled "half-speed" in reply **to** it, and went to the conning tower to see the steamer **for** himself.

She was then about twelve miles to the northward. At the speed at which the *Ariel* was travelling a very few minutes sufficed **to bring her within** view **of** the ocean voyagers. A red flag flying from **the stern of** the air-ship was answered by a similar one from **the mainmast of** the steamer. The *Ariel's* engines were at once slowed **down, the** fan-wheels **went aloft, and she sank gently down to within** twenty feet **of the water,** and swung round the steamer's stern.

As **soon** as they were within hailing distance, those on board the air-ship recognised Nicholas Roburoff and his wife, Radna Michaelis, and several other members of the Inner Circle, standing on the bridge of the steamer. Handkerchiefs were waved, and cries of welcome and greeting passed and re-passed from the air to the sea, until Arnold raised his hand for silence, and, hailing Roburoff, said—

"Are you all well on board?"

"Yes, all well," was the reply, "though we have had rather a risky time of it, for war was generally declared a fortnight ago, and we have had to run the blockade for a good part of the way. That is why we are a little before our time. Can you come nearer? We have some letters for you."

"Yes," replied Arnold. "I'll come alongside. You go ahead, I'll do the rest."

So saying, he ran the *Ariel* up close to the quarter of the *Avondale* as easily as though she had been lying at anchor instead of going twenty miles an hour through the water, and went forward and shook hands with Roburoff over the rail, taking a packet of letters from him at the same time. Meanwhile Colston, who had grasped the situation at a glance, had swung himself on to the steamer's deck, and was already engaged in an animated conversation with Radna.

The first advantage that Arnold took of the leisure that was now at his disposal, was to read the letter directed to himself that was among those for Natasha, the Princess, and Colston, which had been brought out by the *Avondale*. He recognised the writing as Tremayne's, and when he opened the envelope he found that it contained a somewhat lengthy letter from him, and an enclosure in an unfamiliar hand, which consisted of only a few lines, and was signed "Natas."

He started as his eye fell on the terrible name, which now meant so much to him, and he naturally read the note to which it was appended first. There was neither date nor formal address, and it ran as follows:—

You have done well, and fulfilled your promises as a true man should. For the personal service that you have rendered to me I will not thank you in words, for the time may come when I shall be able to do so in deeds. What you have done for the Cause was your duty, and for that I know that you desire no thanks. You have proved that you hold in your hands such power as no single man ever wielded before. Use it well, and in the ages to come men shall remember your name with blessings, and you, if the Master of Destiny permits, shall attain to your heart's desire. NATAS.

Arnold laid the little slip of paper down almost reverently, for, few as the words were, they were those of a man who was not only Natas, the Master of the Terror, but also the father of the woman whose love, in spite of his oath, was the object to the attainment of which he held all things else as secondary, and who therefore had the power to crown his life-work with the supreme blessing without which it would be worthless, however glorious, for he knew full well that, though he might win Natasha's heart, she herself could never be his unless Natas gave her to him.

The other letter was from Tremayne, dated more than a fortnight previously, and gave him a brief résumé of the course of events in Europe since his voyage of exploration had begun. It also urged him to push on the construction of the aërial navy as fast as possible, as there was now no telling where or how soon its presence might be required to determine the issue of the world-war, the first skirmishes of which had already taken place in Eastern Europe. Natas and the Chief were both in London, making the final arrangements for the direction of the various diplomatic and military agents of the Brotherhood throughout Europe. From London they were to go to Alanmere, where they would remain until all arrangements were completed. As soon as the fleet was built and the crews and commanders of the air-ships had thoroughly learned their duties, the flagship was to go to Plymouth, where the *Lurline* would be lying. The news of her arrival would be telegraphed to Alanmere, and Natas and Tremayne would at once come south and put to sea in her. The air-ship was to wait for them at a point two hundred miles due south-west of the Land's End, and pick them up. The yacht was then to be sunk, and the Executive of the Terrorists would for the time being vanish from the sight of men.

It is unnecessary to say that Arnold carried out the plans laid down in this letter in every detail, and with the utmost possible expedition. The *Avondale* arrived the next day at the island which had been chosen as a dockyard, and the shipbuilding was at once commenced.

All the material for constructing the air-ships had been brought out completely finished as far as each individual part was concerned, and so there was nothing to do but to put them together. The crew and passengers of the steamer included the members of the Executive of the Inner Circle, and sixty picked members of the Outer Circle, chiefly mechanics and sailors, destined to be first the builders and then the crews of the new vessels.

These, under Arnold's direction, worked almost day and night at the task before them. Three of the air-ships were put together at a time, twenty men working at each, and within a month from the time that the *Avondale* discharged her cargo, the twelve new vessels were ready to take the air.

They were all built on the same plan as the *Ariel*, and eleven of them were practically identical with her as regards size and speed; but the twelfth, the flagship of the aërial fleet, had been designed by Arnold on a more ambitious scale.

This vessel was larger and much more powerful than any of the others. She was a hundred feet long, with a beam of fifteen feet amidships. On her five masts she carried five fan-wheels, capable of raising her vertically to a height of ten thousand feet without the assistance of her air-planes, and her three propellers, each worked by duplex engines, were able to drive her through the air at a speed of two hundred miles an hour in a calm atmosphere.

She was armed with two pneumatic guns forward and two aft, each twenty-five feet long and with a range of twelve miles at an altitude of four thousand feet; and in addition to these she carried two shorter ones on each broadside, with a range of six miles at the same elevation. She also carried a sufficient supply of power-cylinders to give her an effective range of operations of twenty thousand miles without replenishing them.

In addition to the building materials and the necessary tools and appliances for putting them together, the cargo of the *Avondale* had included an ample supply of stores of all kinds, not the least important part of which consisted of a quantity of power-cylinders sufficient to provide the whole fleet three times over.

The necessary chemicals and apparatus for charging them were also on board, and the last use that Arnold made of the engines of the steamer, which he had disconnected from the propeller and turned to all kinds of uses during the building operations, was to connect them with his storage pumps and charge every available cylinder to its utmost capacity.

At length, when everything that could be carried in the airships had been taken out of the steamer, she was towed out into deep water, and then a shot from one of the flagship's broadside guns sent her to the bottom of the sea, so severing the last link which had connected the now isolated band of revolutionists with the world on which they were ere long to declare war.

The naming of the fleet was by common consent left to Natasha, and her half-oriental genius naturally led her to appropriately name the air-ships after the winged angels and air-spirits of Moslem and other Eastern mythologies. The flagship she named the *Ithuriel*, after the angel who was sent to seek out and confound the Powers of Darkness in that terrific conflict between the upper and nether worlds, which was a fitting antetype to the colossal struggle which was now to be waged for the empire of the earth.

Arnold's first task, as soon as the fleet finally took the air, was to put the captains and crews of the vessels through a thorough drilling in management and evolution. A regular code of signals had been arranged, by means of which orders as to formation, speed, altitude, and direction could be at once transmitted from the flagship. During the day flags were used, and at night flashes from electric reflectors.

The scene of these evolutions was practically the course taken by the *Ariel* from Aeria to the island; and as the captains and lieutenants of the different vessels were all men of high intelligence, and carefully selected for the work, and as the mechanism of the air-ships was extremely simple, the whole fleet was well in hand by the time the mountain mass of Aeria was sighted a week after leaving the island.

Arnold in the *Ithuriel* led the way to a narrow defile on the south-western side, which had been discovered during his first visit, and which admitted of entrance to the valley at an elevation of about 3000 feet. Through this the fleet passed in single file soon after sunrise one lovely morning in the middle of June, and within an hour the thirteen vessels had come to rest on the shores of the lake.

Then for the first time, probably, since the beginning of the world, the beautiful valley became the scene of a busy activity, in the midst of which the lean wiry figure of Louis Holt seemed to be here, there, and everywhere at once, doing the honours of Aeria as though it were a private estate to which the Terrorists had come by his special invitation.

He was more than ever delighted with the air-ships, and especially with the splendid proportions of the *Ithuriel*, and the brilliant lustre of her polished hull, which had been left unpainted, and shone as though her plates had been of burnished silver. Altogether he was well pleased with this invasion of a solitude which, in spite of its great beauty and his professed contempt for the world in general, had for the last few months been getting a good deal more tedious than he would have cared to admit.

In the absence of Natas and the Chief, the command of the new colony devolved, in accordance with the latter's directions, upon Nicholas Roburoff, who was a man of great administrative powers, and who set to work without an hour's delay to set his new kingdom in order, marking out sites for houses and gardens, and preparing materials for building them and the factories for which the water-power of the valley was to be utilised.

Arnold, as admiral of the fleet, had transferred the command of the *Ariel* to Colston, but he retained him as his lieutenant in the *Ithuriel* for the next voyage, partly because he wanted to have him with him on what might prove to be a momentous expedition, and partly because Natasha, who was naturally anxious to rejoin her father as soon as possible, wished to have Radna for a companion in place of the Princess, who had elected to remain in the valley. As another separation of the lovers, who, according to the laws of the Brotherhood, now only waited for the formal consent of Natas to their marriage, was not to be thought of, this arrangement gave everybody the most perfect satisfaction.

Three days sufficed to get everything into working order in the new colony, and on the morning of the fourth the *Ithuriel*, having on board the original crew of the *Ariel*, reinforced by two engineers and a couple of sailors, rose into the air amidst the cheers of the assembled colonists, crossed the northern ridge, and vanished like a silver arrow into space.

CHAPTER XIX.

THE EVE OF BATTLE.

T will now be necessary to go back about six weeks from the day that the *Ithuriel* started on her northward voyage, and to lay before the reader a brief outline of the events which had transpired in Europe subsequently to the date of Tremayne's letter to Arnold.

On the evening of that day he went down to the House of Lords, to make his speech in favour of the Italian Loan. He had previously spoken some half dozen times since he had taken his seat, and, young as he was, had always commanded a respectful hearing by his sound common sense and his intimate knowledge of foreign policy, but none of his brother peers had been prepared for the magnificent speech that he had made on this momentous night.

He had never given his allegiance to any of the political parties of the day, but he was one of the foremost advocates of what was then known as the Imperial policy, and which had grown up out of what is known in the present day as Imperial Federation. To this he subordinated everything else, and held as his highest, and indeed almost his only political ideal, the consolidation of Britain and her colonies into an empire commercially and politically intact and apart from the rest of the world, self-governing in all its parts as regards local affairs, but governed as a whole by a representative Imperial Parliament, sitting in London, and composed of delegates from all portions of the empire.

This ideal—which, it is scarcely necessary to say, was still considered as " beyond the range of practical politics "—formed the keynote of such a speech as had never before been heard in the British House of Lords. He commenced by giving a rapid but minute survey of foreign policy, which astounded the most experienced of his hearers. Not only was it absolutely accurate as far as they could follow it, but it displayed an intimate knowledge of involutions of policy at which British diplomacy had only guessed.

More than this, members of the Government and the Privy Council saw, to their amazement, that the speaker knew the inmost secrets of their own policy even better than they did themselves. How he had become possessed of them was a mystery, and all that they could do was to sit and listen in silent wonder.

He drew a graphic word-picture of the nations of the earth standing full-armed on the threshold of such a war as the world had never seen before,—a veritable Armageddon, which would shake the fabric of society to its foundations, even if it did not dissolve it finally in the blood of countless battlefields.

He estimated with marvellous accuracy the exact amount of force which each combatant would be able to put on to the field, and summed up the appalling mass of potential destruction that was ready to burst upon the world at a moment's notice. He showed the position of Italy, and proved to demonstration that if the loan were not immediately granted, it would be necessary either for Britain to seize her fleet, as she did that of Denmark a century before—an act which the Italians would themselves resist at all hazards—or else to finance her through the war, as she had financed Germany during the Napoleonic struggle.

To grant the loan would be to save the Italian fleet and army for the Triple Alliance; to refuse it would be to detach Italy from the Alliance, and to drive her into the arms of their foes, for not only could she not stand alone amidst the shock of the contending Powers, but without an immediate supply of ready money she would not be able to keep the sea for a month.

Thus, he said in conclusion, the fate of Europe, and perhaps of the world, lay for the time being in their Lordships' hands. The Double Alliance was already numerically stronger than the Triple, and, moreover, they had at their command a new means of destruction, for the dreadful effectiveness of which he could vouch from personal experience.

The trials of the Russian war-balloons had been secret, it was true, but he had nevertheless witnessed them, no matter how, and he knew what they could accomplish. It was true that there were in existence even more formidable engines than these, but they belonged to no nation, and were in the hands of those whose hands were against every man's, and whose designs were still wrapped in the deepest mystery.

He therefore besought his hearers not to trust too implicitly to that hitherto unconquerable valour and resource which had so far rendered Britain impregnable to her enemies. These were not the days of personal valour. They were the days of warfare by machinery, of wholesale destruction by means which men had never before been called upon to face, and which annihilated from a distance before mere valour had time to strike its blow.

If ever the Fates were on the side of the biggest battalions, they were now, and, so far as human foresight could predict the issue of the colossal struggle, the greatest and the most perfectly equipped armaments would infallibly insure the ultimate victory, quite apart from considerations of personal heroism and devotion.

No such speech had been heard in either House since Edmund Burke had fulminated against the miserable policy which severed America from Britain, and split the Anglo-Saxon race in two; but now, as then, personal feeling and class prejudice proved too strong for eloquence and logic.

Italy was the most intensely Radical State in Europe, and she was bankrupt to boot; and, added to this, there was a very strong party in the Upper House which believed that Britain needed no such ally, that with Germany and Austria at her side she could fight the world, in spite of the Tsar's new-fangled balloons, which would probably prove failures in actual war as similar inventions had done before, and even if her allies succumbed, had she not stood alone before, and could she not do it again if necessary?

She would fulfil her engagement with the Triple Alliance, and declare war the moment that one of the Powers was attacked, but she would not pour British gold in millions into the bottomless gulf of Italian bankruptcy.

Such were the main points in the speech of the Duke of Argyle, who followed Lord Alanmere, and spoke just before the division. When the figures were announced, it was found that the Loan Guarantee Bill had been negatived by a majority of seven votes.

The excitement in London that night was tremendous. The two Houses of Parliament had come into direct collision on a question which the Premier had plainly stated to be of vital importance, and a deadlock seemed inevitable. The evening papers brought out special editions giving Tremayne's speech *verbatim*, and the next morning the whole press of the country was talking of nothing else.

The "leading journals," according to their party bias, discussed it pro and con, and rent each other in a furious war of words, the prelude to the sterner struggle that was to come.

Unhappily the parties in Parliament were very evenly balanced, and a very strong section of the Radical Opposition was, as it always had been, bitterly opposed to the arrangement with the Triple Alliance, which every one suspected and no one admitted until Tremayne astounded the Lords by reciting its conditions in the course of his speech.

It was the avowed object of this section of the Opposition to stand out of the war at any price till the last minute, and not to fight at all if it could possibly be avoided. The immediate consequence was that, when the Government on the following day asked for an urgency vote of ten millions for the mobilisation of the Volunteers and the Naval Reserve, the Opposition, led by Mr. John Morley, mustered to its last man, and defeated the motion by a majority of eleven.

The next day a Cabinet Council was held, and in the afternoon Mr. Balfour rose in a densely-crowded House, and, after a dignified allusion to the adverse vote of the previous day, told the House that in view of the grave crisis which was now inevitable in European affairs, a crisis in which the fate, not only of Britain, but of the whole Western world, would probably be involved, the Ministry felt it impossible to remain in office without the hearty and unequivocal support of both Houses— a support which the two adverse votes in Lords and Commons had made it hopeless to look for as those Houses were at present constituted.

He had therefore to inform the House that, after consultation with his colleagues, he had decided to place the resignations of the Ministry in the hands of his Majesty,[1] and appeal to the country on the plain issue of Intervention or Non-intervention. Under the circumstances, there was nothing else to be done. The deplorable crisis which immediately followed was the logical consequence of the inherently vicious system of party government.

While the fate of the world was practically trembling in the balance, Europe, armed to the teeth in readiness for the Titanic struggle that a few weeks would now see shaking the world, was amused by the spectacle of what was really the most powerful nation on earth losing its head amidst the excitement of a general election, and frittering away on the petty issues of party strife the energies that should have been devoted with single-hearted unanimity to preparation for the conflict whose issue would involve its very existence.

For a month the nations held their hand, why, no one exactly knew, except, perhaps, two men who were now in daily consultation in a country house in Yorkshire. It may have been that the final preparations were not yet complete, or that the combatants were taking a brief breathing-space before entering the arena, or that Europe was waiting to see the decision of Britain at the ballot-boxes, or possibly the French fleet of war-balloons was not quite ready to take the air,—any of these reasons might have been sufficient to explain the strange calm before the storm; but meanwhile the British nation was busy listening to the conflicting eloquence of partisan orators from a thousand platforms throughout the land, and trying to make up its mind whether it should return a Conservative or a Radical Ministry to power.

In the end, Mr. Balfour came back with a solid hundred majority behind him, and at once set to work to, if possible, make up for lost time. The moment of Fate had, however, gone by for ever. During the precious days that had been

---

[1] At the period in which the action of the narrative takes place, her Majesty Queen Victoria had abdicated in favour of the present Prince of Wales, and was living in comparative retirement at Balmoral, retaining Osborne as an alternative residence.

fooled away in party strife, **French** gold and **Russian** diplomacy had done their work.

The day **after the** Conservative Ministry **returned** to power, France declared **war, and Russia, who** had been nominally at **war with Britain for over a month,** suddenly took the offensive, **and poured her Asiatic troops into the passes of the Hindu Kush.** Two days later, the defection of Italy from the Triple Alliance told Europe how accurately Tremayne had gauged the situation in his now historic speech, and how the month of strange quietude had been spent by the controllers of the Double Alliance.

The spell was **broken at last.** After forty years of peace, Europe plunged into the abyss of war; and from one end of the Continent to the other nothing was heard but the tramp **of** vast armies as they marshalled themselves along the threatened frontiers, and concentrated at the points of attack and defence.

On all the lines of ocean traffic, **steamers** were hurrying homeward or to neutral ports, in the hope of reaching a place of safety before hostilities actually broke out. Great liners **were** racing across **the** Atlantic either to Britain or America with their precious freights, while those flying **the French flag** on the westward voyage prepared to run the gauntlet of the British cruisers as best they might.

All along the routes to India and **the East** the same thing **was** happening, and not a day passed but saw desperate races **between** fleet ocean greyhounds **and** hostile cruisers, which, as **a rule, terminated** in favour of the former, thanks to **the superiority of** private enterprise **over** Government contract-work **in turning** out ships and engines.

In Britain the excitement was indescribable. **The result** of the general election had cast the final die **in favour** of immediate war in concert with the Triple **Alliance.** The defection of Italy had thoroughly awakened **the** popular **mind** to the extreme gravity **of the** situation, and **the** declaration of war by France had raised the blood of the **nation to** fever heat. **The magic of** battle had instantly quelled **all party** differences **so far as** the bulk of the people **was** concerned, and no one talked of anything **but** the war and **its immediate** issues. Men forgot that they belonged **to parties, and only** remembered that **they** were citizens of the **same nation.**

CHAPTER XX.

BETWEEN TWO LIVES.

SIX weeks after he had made his speech in the House of Lords, Tremayne was sitting in his oak-panelled library at Alanmere, in deep and earnest converse with a man who was sitting in an invalid chair by a window looking out upon the lawn. The face of this man exhibited a contrast so striking and at the same time terrible, that the most careless glance cast upon it would have revealed the fact that it was the face of a man of extraordinary character, and that the story of some strange fate was indelibly stamped upon it.

The upper part of it, as far down as the mouth, was cast in a mould of the highest and most intellectual manly beauty. The forehead was high and broad and smooth, the eyebrows dark and firm but finely arched, the nose somewhat prominently aquiline, but well shaped, and with delicate, sensitive nostrils. The eyes were deep-set, large and soft, and dark as the sky of a moonless night, yet shining in the firelight with a strange magnetic glint that seemed to fasten Tremayne's gaze and hold it at will.

But the lower portion of the face was as repulsive as the upper part was attractive. The mouth was the mouth of a wild beast, and the lips and cheeks and chin were seared and seamed as though with fire, and what looked like the remains of a moustache and beard stood in black ragged patches about the heavy unsightly jaws.

When the thick, shapeless lips parted, they did so in a hideous grin, which made visible long, sharp white teeth, more like those of a wolf than those of a human being.

His body, too, exhibited no less strange a contrast than his face did. To the hips it was that of a man of well-knit, muscular frame, not massive, but strong and well-proportioned. The arms were long and muscular, and the hands white and small, but firm, well-shaped, and nervous.

But from his hips downwards, this strange being was a dwarf and a cripple. His hips were narrow and shrunken, one of his legs was some inches shorter than the other, and both were twisted and distorted, and hung helplessly down from the chair as he sat.

Such was Natas, the Master of the Terror, and the man whose wrongs, whatever they might have been, had caused him to devote his life to a work of colossal vengeance, and his incomparable powers to the overthrow of a whole civilisation.

The tremendous task to which he had addressed himself with all the force of his mighty nature for twenty years, was now at length approaching completion. The mine that he had so patiently laid, year after year, beneath the foundations of Society, was complete in every detail, the first spark had been applied, and the first rumbling of the explosion was already sounding in the ears of men, though they little knew how much it imported. The work of the master-intellect was almost done. The long days and nights of plotting and planning were over, and the hour for action had arrived at last.

For him there was little more to do, and the time was very near when he could retire from the strife, and watch in peace and confidence the reaping of the harvest of ruin and desolation that his hands had sown. Henceforth, the central figure in the world-revolution must be the young English engineer, whose genius had brought him forth out of his obscurity to take command of the subjugated powers of the air, and to arbitrate the destinies of the world.

This was why he was sitting here, in the long twilight of the June evening, talking so earnestly with the man who, under the spell of his mysterious power and master-will, had been his second self in completing the work that he had designed, and had thought and spoken and acted as he had inspired him against all the traditions of his race and station, in that strange double life that he had lived, in each portion of which he had been unconscious of all that he had been and had done in the other. The time had now come to draw aside the veil which had so far divided these two lives from each other, to show him each as it was in very truth, and to leave him free to deliberately choose between them.

Natas had been speaking without any interruption from Tremayne for nearly an hour, drawing the parallel of the two lives before him with absolute fidelity, neither omitting nor justifying anything, and his wondering hearer had listened to him in silence, unable to speak for the crowding emotions which were swarming through his brain. At length Natas concluded by saying—

"And now, Alan Tremayne, I have shown you faithfully the two paths which you have trodden since first I had need of you. So far you have been as clay in the hands of the potter. Now the spell is removed, and you are free to choose which of them you will follow to the end,—that of the English gentleman of fortune and high position, whose country is on the brink of a war that will tax her vast resources to the utmost, and may end in her ruin; or that of the visible and controlling head of the only organisation which can at the supreme moment be the arbiter of peace or war, order or anarchy, and which alone, if any earthly power can, will evolve order out of chaos, and bring peace on earth at last."

As Natas ceased, Tremayne passed his hand slowly over his eyes and brows, as though to clear away the mists which obscured his mental vision. Then he rose from his chair, and paced the floor with quick, uneven strides for several minutes. At length he replied, speaking as one might who was just waking from some evil dream—

"You have made a conspirator and a murderer of me. How is it possible that, knowing this, I can again become what I was before your infernal influence was cast about me?"

"What you have done at my command is nothing to you, and leaves no stain upon your honour, if you choose to put it so, for it was not your will that was working within you, but mine. As for the killing of Dornovitch, it was necessary, and you were the only instrument by which it could have been accomplished before irretrievable harm had been done.

"He alone of the outside world possessed the secret of the Terror. A woman of the Outer Circle in Paris had allowed her love for him to overcome her duty to the Brotherhood, and had betrayed what she could, in order, as she vainly thought, to shield him from its vengence for the executive murders of the year before. He too had on him the draft of the secret treaty, the possession of which has enabled us to control the drift of European politics at the most crucial time.

"Had he escaped, not only would hundreds of lives have been sacrificed on suspicion to Russian official vengeance, but Russia and France would now be masters of the British line of communication to the East, for it would not have been possible for Mr. Balfour to have been forewarned, and therefore forearmed, in time to double the Mediterranean Squadron as he has done. Surely one Russian's life is not too great a price to pay for all that."

"I do not care for the man's life, for he was an enemy, and even then plotting the ruin of my own country in the dark. It is not the killing, but the manner of it. England does not fight her battles with the assassin's knife, and his blood is on my hands"—

"On your hands, perhaps, but not on your soul. It is on mine, and I will answer for it when we stand face to face at the Bar where all secrets are laid bare. The man deserved death, for he was plotting the death of thousands. What matter then how or by whose hands he died?

"It is time the world had done with these miserable sophistries, and these spurious distinctions between murder by wholesale and by retail, and it soon will have done with them. I, by your hand, killed Dornovitch in his sleep. That was murder, says the legal casuist. You read this morning in the *Times* how one of the Russian war-balloons went the night before last and hung in the darkness over a sleeping town on the Austrian frontier, and dropped dynamite shells upon it, killing and maiming hundreds who had no personal quarrel with Russia. That is war, and therefore lawful!

"Nonsense, my friend, nonsense! There is no difference. All violence is crime, if you will, but it is a question of degree only. The world is mad on this subject of war. It considers the horrible thing honourable, and gives its highest distinctions to those who shed blood most skilfully on the battlefield, and the triumphs that are won by superior force or cunning are called glorious, and those who achieve them the nations fall down and worship.

"The nations must be taught wisdom, for war has had victims enough. But men are still foolish, and to cure them a terrible lesson will be necessary. But that lesson shall be taught, even though the whole earth be turned into a battle-field, and all the dwellings of men into charnel-houses, in order to teach it to them."

"In other words, Society is to be dissolved in order that anarchy and lawlessness may take its place. Society may not be perfect,—nay, I will grant that its sins are many and grievous, that it has forgotten its duty both to God and man in its worship of Mammon and its slavery to externals,—but you who have plotted its destruction, have you anything better to put in its place? You can destroy, perhaps, but can you build up?"

"The jungle must be cleared and the swamp drained before the habitations of men can be built in their place. It has been mine to destroy, and I will pursue the work of destruction to the end, as I have sworn to do by that Name which a Jew holds too sacred for speech. I believe myself to be the instrument of vengeance upon this generation, even as Joshua was upon Canaan, and as Khalid the Sword of God was upon Byzantium in the days of her corruption. You may hold this for an old man's fancy if you will, but it shall surely come to pass in the fulness of time, which is now at hand; and then, where I have destroyed, may you, if you will, build up again!"

"What do you mean? You are speaking in parables."

"Which shall soon be made plain. You read in your newspaper this morning of a mysterious movement that is taking place throughout the Buddhist peoples of the East. They believe that Buddha has returned to earth, reincarnated, to lead them to the conquest of the world. Now, as you know, every fourth man, woman, and child in the whole human race is a Buddhist, and the meaning of this movement is that that mighty mass of humanity, pent up and stagnant for centuries, is about to burst its bounds and overflow the earth in a flood of desolation and destruction.

"The nations of the West know nothing of this, and are unsheathing the sword to destroy each other. Like a house divided against itself, their power shall be brought to confusion, and their empire be made as a wilderness. And over the starving and war-smitten lands of Europe these Eastern swarms shall sweep, innumerable as the locusts, resistless as the pestilence, and what fire and sword have spared they shall devour, and nothing shall be left of all the glory of Christendom but its name and the memory of its fall!"

Natas spoke his frightful prophecy like one entranced, and when he had finished he let his head fall forward for a moment on his breast, as though he were exhausted. Then he raised it again, and went on in a calmer voice—

"There is but one power under heaven that can stand between the Western world and this destruction, and that is the race to which you belong. It is the conquering race of earth, and the choicest fruit of all the ages until now. It is nearly two hundred million strong, and it is united by the ties of kindred blood and speech the wide world over.

"But it is also divided by petty jealousies, and mean commercial interests. But for these the world might be an Anglo-Saxon planet. Would it not be a glorious task for you, who are the flower of this splendid race, so to unite it that it should stand as a solid barrier of invincible manhood before which this impending flood of yellow barbarism should dash itself to pieces like the cloud-waves against the granite summits of the eternal hills?"

"A glorious task, truly!" exclaimed Tremayne, once more springing from his chair and beginning to pace the room again; "but the man is not yet born who could accomplish it."

"There are fifty men on earth at this moment who can accomplish it, and of them the two chief are Englishmen,— yourself and this Richard Arnold, whose genius has given the Terrorists the command of the air.

"Come, Alan Tremayne! here is a destiny such as no man ever had before revealed to him. It is not for a man of your nation and lineage to shrink from it. You have reproached me for using you to unworthy ends, as you thought them, and with pulling down where I am not able to build up again. Obey me still, this time of your own free will and with your eyes open, and, as I have pulled down by your hand, so by it will I build up again, if the Master of Destiny shall permit me; and if not, then shall you achieve the task without me. Now give me your ears, for the words that I have to say are weighty ones.

"No human power can stop the war that has now begun, nor can any curtail it until it has run its appointed course. But we have at our command a power which, if skilfully applied at the right moment, will turn the tide of conflict in favour of Britain, and if at that moment the Mother of Nations can gather her children about her in obedience to the call of common kindred, all shall be well, and the world shall be hers.

"But before that is made possible she must pass through the fire, and be purged of that corruption which is even now poisoning her blood and clouding her eyes in the presence of her enemies. The overweening lust of gold must be burnt out of her soul in the fiery crucible of war, and she must learn to hold honour once more higher than wealth, and rich and poor and gentle and simple must be as one family, and not as master and servant.

"East and west, north and south, wherever the English tongue is spoken, men must clasp hands and forget all other things save that they are brothers of blood and speech, and that the world is theirs if they choose to take it. This is a work that cannot be done by any nation, but only by a whole race, which with millions of hands and a single heart devotes itself to achieve success or perish."

"Brave words, brave words!" cried Tremayne, pausing in his walk in front of the chair in which Natas sat; "and if you could make me believe them true, I would follow you blindly to the end, no matter what the path might be. But I cannot believe them. I cannot think that you or I and a few followers, even aided by Arnold and his aërial fleet, could accomplish such a stupendous task as that. It is too great. It is superhuman! And yet it would be glorious even to fail worthily in such a task, even to fall fighting in such a Titanic conflict!"

He paused, and stood silent and irresolute, as though appalled by the prospect with which he was confronted here at the parting of the ways. He glanced at the extraordinary being sitting near him, and saw his deep, dark eyes fixed upon him, as though they were reading his very soul within him. Then he took a step towards the cripple's chair, took his right hand in his, and said slowly and steadily and solemnly—

"It is a worthy destiny! I will essay it for good or evil, for life or death. I am with you to the end!"

As Tremayne spoke the fatal words which once more bound him, and this time for life and of his own free will, to Natas the Jew, this cripple who, chained to his chair, yet aspired to the throne of a world, he fancied he saw his shapeless lips move in a smile, and into his eyes there came a proud look of mingled joy and triumph as he returned the handclasp, and said in a softer, kinder voice than Tremayne had ever heard him use before—

"Well spoken! Those words were worthy of you and of your race! As your faith is, so shall your reward be. Now wheel my chair to yonder window that looks out towards the east, and you shall look past the shadows into the day which is beyond. So! that will do. Now get another chair and sit beside me. Fix your eyes on that bright star that shows above the trees, and do not speak, but think only of that star and its brightness."

Tremayne did as he was bidden in silence, and when he was seated Natas swept his hands gently downwards over his open eyes again and again, till the lids grew heavy and fell, shutting out the brightness of the star, and the dim beauty of the landscape which lay sleeping in the twilight and the June night.

Then suddenly it seemed as though they opened again of their own accord, and were endowed with an infinite power of vision. The trees and lawns of the home park of Alanmere and the dark rolling hills of heather beyond were gone, and in their place lay stretched out a continent which he saw as though from some enormous height, with its plains and lowlands and rivers, vast steppes and snowclad hills, forests and tablelands, huge mountain masses rearing lonely peaks of everlasting ice to a sunlight that had no heat; and then beyond these again more plains and forests, that stretched away southward until they merged in the all-surrounding sea.

Then he seemed to be carried forward towards the scene until he could distinguish the smallest objects upon the earth, and he saw, swarming southward and westward, vast hordes of men, that divided into long streams, and poured through

mountain passes and defiles, and spread themselves again over fertile lands, like locusts over green fields of young corn. And wherever those hordes swept forward, a long line of fire and smoke went in front of them, and where they had passed the earth was a blackened wilderness.

Then, too, from the coasts and islands vast fleets of war-ships put out, pouring their clouds of smoke to the sky, and making swiftly for the southward and westward, where from other coasts and islands other vessels put out to meet them, and, meeting them, were lost with them under great clouds of grey smoke, through which flashed incessantly long livid tongues of flame.

Then, like a panorama rolled away from him, the mighty picture receded and new lands came into view, familiar lands which he had traversed often. They too were black and wasted with the tempest of war from east to west, but nevertheless those swarming streams came on, countless and undiminished, up out of the south and east, while on the western verge vast armies and fleets battled desperately with each other on sea and land, as though they heeded not those locust swarms of dusky millions coming ever nearer and nearer.

Once more the scene rolled backwards, and he saw a mighty city closely beleaguered by two vast hosts of men, who slowly pushed their batteries forward until they planted them on all the surrounding heights, and poured a hail of shot and shell upon the swarming, helpless millions that were crowded within the impassable ring of fire and smoke. Above the devoted city swam in mid-air strange shapes like monstrous birds of prey, and beneath where they floated the earth seemed ever and anon to open and belch forth smoke and flame into which the crumbling houses fell and burnt in heaps of shapeless ruins. Then——

He felt a cool hand laid almost caressingly on his brow, and the voice of Natas said beside him—

"That is enough. You have seen the Field of Armageddon, and when the day of battle comes you shall be there and play the part allotted to you from the beginning. Do you believe?"

"Yes," replied Tremayne, rising wearily from his chair, "I believe; and as the task is, so may Heaven make my strength in the stress of battle!"

"You have seen the Field of Armageddon."

"Amen!" said Natas very solemnly.

That night the young Lord of Alanmere went sleepless to bed, and lay awake till dawn, revolving over and over again in his mind the marvellous things that he had seen and heard, and the tremendous task to which he had now irrevocably committed himself for good or evil. In all these waking dreams there was ever present before his mental vision the face of a woman whose beauty was like and yet unlike that of the daughter of Natas. It lacked the brilliance and subtle charm which in Natasha so wondrously blended the dusky beauty of the daughters of the South with the fairer loveliness of the daughters of the North; but it atoned for this by that softer grace and sweetness which is the highest charm of purely English beauty.

It was the face of the woman whom, in that portion of his strange double life which had been free from the mysterious influence of Natas, he had loved with well-assured hope that she would one day rule his house and broad domains with him. She was now Lady Muriel Penarth, the daughter of Lord Marazion, a Cornish nobleman, whose estates abutted on those which belonged to Lord Alanmere as Baron Tremayne, of Tremayne, in the county of Cornwall, as the *Peerage* had it. Noble alike by lineage and nature, no fairer mistress could have been found for the lands of Tremayne and Alanmere, but —what seas of blood and flame now lay between him and the realisation of his love-ideal!

He must forsake his own, and become a revolutionary and an outcast from Society. He must draw the sword upon the world and his own race, and, armed with the most awful means of destruction that the wit of man had ever devised, he must fight his way through universal war to that peace which alone he could ask her to share with him. Still much could be done before he took the final step of severance which might be perpetual, and he would lose no time in doing it.

As soon as it was fairly light, he rose and took a long, rapid walk over the home park, and when he returned to breakfast at nine he had resolved to execute forthwith a deed of gift, transferring the whole of his vast property, which was unentailed and therefore entirely at his own disposal, to the woman who was to have shared it with him in a few months as his wife. If the Fates were kind, he would come back from the world-war and reclaim both the lands and their mistress, and if not he would have the satisfaction of knowing that his broad acres at least had a worthy mistress.

At breakfast he met Natas again, and during the meal one of his footmen entered, bringing the letters that had come by the morning post.

There were several letters for each of them, those for Natas being addressed to "Herr F. Niemand," and for some time they were both employed in looking through their correspondence. Suddenly Natas looked up, and said—

"When do you expect to hear that Arnold is off the south coast?"

"Almost any day now; in fact, within the week, if everything has gone right. Here is a letter from Johnston to say that the *Lurline* has arrived at Plymouth, and that a bright look-out is being kept for him. He will telegraph here and to the club in London as soon as the air-ship is sighted. Twenty-four hours will then see us on board the *Ariel*, or whichever of the ships he comes in."

"I hope the news will come soon, for Michael Roburoff, the President's brother, who has been in command of the American Section, cables to say that he sails from New York the day after to-morrow with detailed accounts. That means that he will come with full reports of what the Section has done and will be ready to do when the time comes, and also what the enemy are doing.

"He sails in the *Aurania*, and as the Atlantic routes are swarming with war-ships and torpedo-boats, she will probably have to run the gauntlet, and it is of the last importance that Michael and his reports reach us safely. It will therefore be necessary for the air-ship to meet the *Aurania* as soon as possible on her passage, and take him off her before any harm happens to him. If he and his reports fell into the hands of the enemy, there is no telling what might happen."

"As nearly as I can calculate," said Tremayne, the air-ship should be sighted in three days from now, perhaps in two. It will take the *Aurania* over four days to cross the Atlantic, and so we ought to be able to meet her somewhere in mid-ocean if she is able to get so far without being overhauled.

Unfortunately she is known to be a British ship and subsidised by the British Government, so there will be very little chance of her getting through under the American flag. Still she's about the fastest steamer afloat, and will take a lot of catching."

"And if the worst comes and she falls into the hands of the enemy, we must fight our first naval battle and retake her, even if we have to sink a few cruisers to do so," added Natas; "for, come what may, Michael must not be captured."

"Arnold will almost certainly come in his flagship, and if she is what he promised, she should be more than a match for a whole fleet, so I don't think there is much to fear unless the *Aurania* gets sunk before we reach her," said Tremayne.

Natas and his host devoted the rest of the forenoon to their correspondence, and to making the final arrangements for leaving Alanmere. Tremayne wrote full instructions to his lawyers for the drawing up of the deed, and directed them to have it ready for his signature by two o'clock on the following day. After lunch he rode over to Knaresborough himself with the post-bag, telegraphed an abstract of his instructions in advance, and ordered his private saloon carriage to be attached to the up express which passed through at eight the next morning.

CHAPTER XXI.

JUST IN TIME.

S the train drew up in King's Cross station at twelve the next day, almost the first words that Tremayne heard were—
"Special *Pall Mall*, sir! Appearance of the mysterious air-ship over Plymouth this morning! Great battle in Austria yesterday, defeat of the Austrians—awful slaughter with war-balloons! Special!"

The boy was selling the papers as fast as he could hand them out to the eager passengers. Tremayne secured one, shut the door of the saloon again, and, turning to the middle page, read aloud to Natas—

"We have just received a telegram from our Plymouth correspondent, to say that soon after daybreak this morning torpedo-boat No. 157 steamed into the Sound, bringing the news that she had sighted a large five-masted air-ship about ten miles from the coast, when in company with the cruiser *Ariadne*, whose commander had despatched her with the news. Hardly had the report been received when the air-ship herself passed over Mount Edgcumbe and came towards the town.

"The news spread like wildfire, and in a few minutes the streets were filled with crowds of people, who had thrown on a few clothes and rushed out to get a look at the strange visitant. At first it was thought that an attack on the arsenal was intended by the mysterious vessel, and the excitement had risen almost to the pitch of panic, when it was observed that she was flying a plain white flag, and that her intentions were apparently peaceful.

"Panic then gave place to curiosity. The air-ship crossed the town at an elevation of about 3000 feet, described a complete circle round it in the space of a few minutes, and then suddenly shot up into the air and vanished to the south-westward at an inconceivable speed. The vessel is described as being about a hundred feet long, and was apparently armed with eight guns. Her hull was of white polished metal, probably aluminium, and shone like silver in the sunlight.

"The wildest rumours are current as to the object of her visit, but of course no credence can be attached to any of them. The vessel is plainly of the same type as that which destroyed Kronstadt two months ago, but larger and more powerful. The inference is that she is one of a fleet in the hands of the Terrorists, and the profoundest uncertainty and anxiety prevail throughout naval and military circles everywhere as to the use that they may make of these appalling means of destruction should they take any share in the war."

"Humph!" said Tremayne, as he finished reading. "Johnston's telegram must have crossed us on the way, but I shall find one at the club. Well, we have no time to lose, for we ought to start for Plymouth this evening. Your men will take you straight to the Great Western Hotel, and I will hurry my business through as fast as possible, and meet you there in time to catch the 6.30. At this rate we shall meet the *Aurania* soon after she leaves New York."

Within the next six hours Tremayne transferred the whole of his vast property in a single instrument to his promised wife, thus making her the richest woman in England; handed the precious deeds to her astonished father; obtained his promise to take his wife and daughter to Alanmere at the end of the London season, and to remain there with her until he returned to reclaim her and his estates together; and said good-bye to Lady Muriel herself in an interview which was a good deal longer than that which he had with his bewildered and somewhat scandalised lawyers, who had never before been forced to rush any transaction through at such an indecent speed. Had Lord Alanmere not been the best client in the kingdom, they might have rebelled against such an outrage on the law's time-honoured delays; but he was not a man to be trifled with, and so the work was done and an unbeatable record in legal despatch accomplished, albeit very unwillingly, by the men of law.

By midnight the *Lurline*, ostensibly bound for Queenstown, had cleared the Sound, and, with the Eddystone Light on her port bow, headed away at full-speed to the westward. She was about the fastest yacht afloat, and at a pinch could be driven a good twenty-seven miles an hour through the water. As both Natas and Tremayne were anxious to join the air-ship as soon as possible, every ounce of steam that her boilers would stand was put on, and she slipped along in splendid style through the long, dark seas that came rolling smoothly up Channel from the westward.

In an hour and a half after passing the Eddystone she sighted the Lizard Light, and by the time she had brought it well abeam the first interruption of her voyage occurred. A huge, dark mass loomed suddenly up out of the darkness of the moonless night, then a blinding, dazzling ray of light shot across the water from the searchlight of a battleship that was patrolling the coast, attended by a couple of cruisers and four torpedo-boats. One of these last came flying towards the yacht down the white path of the beam of light, and Tremayne, seeing that he would have to give an account of himself, stopped his engines and waited for the torpedo-boat to come within hail.

"Steamer ahoy! Who are you? and where are you going to at that speed?"

"This is the *Lurline*, the Earl of Alanmere's yacht, from Plymouth to Queenstown. We're only going at our usual speed."

'Oh, if it's the *Lurline*, you needn't say that," answered the officer who had hailed from the torpedo-boat, with a laugh. "Is Lord Alanmere on board?"

"Yes, here I am," said Tremayne, replying instead of his sailing-master. "Is that you, Selwyn? I thought I recognised your voice."

"Yes, it's I, or rather all that's left of me after two months in this buck-jumping little brute of a craft. She bobs twice in the same hole every time, and if it's a fairly deep hole she just dives right through and out on the other side; and there are such a lot of Frenchmen about that we get no rest day or night on this patrolling business."

"Very sorry for you, old man; but if you will seek glory in

a torpedo-boat, I don't see that you can expect anything else. Will you come on board and have a drink?"

"No, thanks. Very sorry, but I can't stop. By the way, have you heard of that air-ship that was over this way this morning? I wonder what the deuce it really is, and what it's up to?"

"I've heard of it; it was in the London papers this morning. Have you seen any more of it?"

"Oh yes; the thing was cruising about in mid-air all this morning, taking stock of us and the Frenchmen too, I suppose. She vanished during the afternoon. Where to, I don't know. It's awfully humiliating, you know, to be obliged to crawl about here on the water, at twenty-five knots at the utmost, while that fellow is flying a hundred miles an hour or so through the clouds without turning a hair, or I ought to say without as much as a puff of smoke. He seems to move of his own mere volition. I wonder what on earth he is."

"Not much on earth apparently, but something very considerable in the air, where I hope he'll stop out of sight until I get to Queenstown; and as I want to get there pretty early in the morning, perhaps you'll excuse me saying good-night and getting along, if you won't come on board."

"No, very sorry I can't. Good-night, and keep well in to the coast till you have to cross to Ireland. Good-bye?"

"Good-bye!" shouted Tremayne in reply, as the torpedo-boat swung round and headed back to the battleship, and he gave the order to go ahead again at full-speed.

In another hour they were off the Land's End, and from there they headed out due south-west into the Atlantic. They had hardly made another hundred miles before it began to grow light, and then it became necessary to keep a bright look-out for the air-ship, for according to what they had heard from the commander of the torpedo-boat she might be sighted at any moment as soon as it was light enough to see her.

Another hour passed, but there was still no sign of the air-ship. This of course was to be expected, for they had still another seventy-five miles or so to go before the rendezvous was reached.

"Steamer to the south'ard!" sang out the man on the forecastle, just as Tremayne came on deck after an attempt at a brief nap. He picked up his glass, and took a good look at the thin cloud of smoke away on the southern horizon.

From what he could see it was a large steamer, and was coming up very fast, almost at right angles to the course of the *Lurline.* Fifteen minutes later he was able to see that the stranger was a warship, and that she was heading for Queenstown. She was therefore either a British ship attached to the Irish Squadron, or else she was an enemy with designs on the liners bound for Liverpool.

In either case it was most undesirable that the yacht should be overhauled again. Any mishap to her, even a lengthy delay, might have the most serious consequences. A single unlucky shell exploding in her engine-room would disable her, and perhaps change the future history of the world.

Tremayne therefore altered her course a little more to the northward, thus increasing the distance between her and the stranger, and at the same time ordered the engineer to keep up the utmost head of steam, and get the last possible yard out of her.

The alteration in her course appeared to be instantly detected by the warship, for she at once swerved off more to the westward, and brought herself dead astern of the *Lurline.* She was now near enough for Tremayne to see that she was a large cruiser, and attended by a brace of torpedo-boats, which were running along one under each of her quarters, like a couple of dogs following a hunter.

There was now no doubt but that, whatever her nationality, she was bent on overhauling the yacht, if possible, and the dense volumes of smoke that were pouring out of her funnels told Tremayne that she was stoking up vigorously for the chase.

By this time she was about seven miles away, and the *Lurline,* her twin screws beating the water at their utmost speed, and every plate in her trembling under the vibration of her engines, rushed through the water faster than she had ever done since the day she was launched. As far as could be seen, she was holding her own well in what had now become a dead-on stern chase.

Still the stranger showed no flag, and though Tremayne could hardly believe that a hostile cruiser and a couple of torpedo-boats would venture so near to the ground occupied by the British battle-ships, the fact that she showed no colours looked at the best suspicious. Determined to settle the question, if possible, one way or the other, he ran up the ensign of the Royal Yacht Squadron.

This brought no reply from the cruiser, but a column of bluish-white smoke shot up a moment later from the funnels of one of the torpedo-boats, telling that she had put on the forced draught, and, like a greyhound slipped from the leash, she began to draw away from the big ship, plunging through the long rollers, and half-burying herself in the foam that she threw up from her bows.

Tremayne knew that there were some of these viperish little craft in the French navy that could be driven thirty miles an hour through the water, and if this was one of them, capture was only a matter of time, unless the air-ship sighted them and came to the rescue.

Happily, although there was a considerable swell on, the water was smooth and free from short waves, and this was to the advantage of the *Lurline*; for she went along "as dry as a bone," while the torpedo-boat, lying much lower in the water, rammed her nose into every roller, and so lost a certain amount of way. The yacht was making a good twenty-eight miles an hour under the heroic efforts of the engineers; and at this rate it would be nearly two hours before she was overhauled, provided that the torpedo-boat was not able to use the gun that she carried forward of her funnels with any dangerous effect.

There could now be no doubt as to the hostility of the pursuers. Had they been British, they would have answered the flag flying at the peak of the yacht.

"Steamer coming down from the nor'ard, sir!" suddenly sang out a man whom Tremayne had just stationed in the fore cross-trees to look out for the air-ship that was now so anxiously expected.

A dense volume of smoke was seen rising in the direction indicated, and a few minutes later a second big steamer came into view, bearing down directly on the yacht, and so approaching the torpedo-boat almost stem on. There was no doubt about her nationality. A glance through the glass showed Tremayne the white ensign floating above the horizontal stream of smoke that stretched behind her. She was a British cruiser, no doubt a scout of the Irish Squadron, and had sighted the smoke of the yacht and her pursuers, and had come to investigate.

Tremayne breathed more freely now, for he knew that his flag would procure the assistance of the new-comer in case it was wanted, as indeed it very soon was.

Hardly had the British cruiser come well in sight than a puff of smoke rose from the deck of the other warship, and a shell came whistling through the air, and burst within a hundred yards of the *Lurline*. Twenty-four hours ago Tremayne had been one of the richest men in England, and just now he would have willingly given all that he had possessed to be twenty-five miles further to the south-westward than he was.

Another shell from the Frenchman passed clear over the *Lurline*, and plunged into the water and burst, throwing a cloud of spray high into the air. Then came one from the torpedo-boat, but she was still too far off for her light gun to do any damage, and the projectile fell spent into the sea nearly five hundred yards short.

Immediately after this came a third shell from the French cruiser, and this, by an unlucky chance, struck the forecastle of the yacht, burst, and tore away several feet of the bulwarks, and, worse than all, killed four of her crew instantly.

"First blood!" said Tremayne to himself through his clenched teeth. "That shall be an unlucky shot for you, my friend, if we reach the air-ship before you sink us."

Meanwhile the two cruisers, each approaching the other at a speed of more than twenty miles an hour, had got within shot. A puff of smoke spurted out from the side of the latest comer. The well-aimed projectile passed fifty yards astern of the *Lurline*, and struck the advancing torpedo-boat square on the bow.

The next instant it was plainly apparent that there was nothing more to be feared from her. The solid shot had passed clean through her two sides. Her nose went down and her stern came up. Then bang went another gun from the British cruiser. This time the messenger of death was a shell. It struck the inclined deck amidships, there was a flash of flame, a cloud of steam rose up from her bursting boilers, and then she broke in two and vanished beneath the smooth-rolling waves.

Two minutes later the duel began in deadly earnest. The tricolor ran up to the masthead of the French cruiser, and jets of mingled smoke and flame spurted one after the other from her sides, and shells began bursting in quick succession round the rapidly-advancing Englishman. Evidently the Frenchman, with his remaining torpedo-boat, thought himself a good match for the British cruiser, for he showed no disposition to shirk the combat, despite the fact that he was so near to the cruising ground of a powerful squadron.

As the two cruisers approached each other, the fire from their heavy guns was supplemented by that of their light quick-firing armament, until each of them became a floating volcano, vomiting continuous jets of smoke and flame, and hurling showers of shot and shell across the rapidly-lessening space between them.

The din of the hideous concert became little short of appalling, even to the most hardened nerves. The continuous deep booming of the heavy guns, as they belched forth their three-hundred-pound projectiles, mingled with the sharp ringing reports of the thirty and forty pound quick-firers, and the horrible grinding rattle of the machine guns in the tops that sounded clearly above all, and every few seconds came the scream and the bang of bursting shells, and the dull, crashing sound of rending and breaking steel, as the terrible missiles of death and destruction found their destined mark.

Happily the *Lurline* was out of the line of fire, or she would have been torn to fragments and sent to the bottom in a few seconds. She continued on her course at her utmost speed, and the French cruiser was, of course, too busy to pay any further attention to her. Not so the remaining torpedo-boat, however, which, leaving the two big ships to fight out their duel for the present, was pursuing the yacht at the utmost speed of her forced draught.

Capture or destruction soon only became a matter of a few minutes. Tremayne, determined to hold on till he was sunk or sighted the air-ship, kept his flag flying and his engines working to the last ounce that the quivering boilers would stand, and the Frenchman, seeing that he was determined to escape if he could, opened fire on him with his twenty-pounder.

Owing to the high speed of the two vessels, and the rolling of the torpedo-boat, not much execution was done at first; but, as the distance diminished, shell after shell crashed through the bulwarks of the *Lurline*, ripping them longitudinally, and tearing up the deck-planks with their jagged fragments. The wheel-house and the funnel escaped by a miracle, and the yacht being end on to her pursuer, the engines and boilers were comparatively safe.

One boat had also escaped, and that was hanging ready to be lowered at a moment's notice.

At last a shell struck the funnel, burst, and shattered it to fragments. Almost at the same moment the man in the fore-cross-trees, who had stuck to his post in defiance of the cannonade, sang out with a triumphant shout—

"The air-ship! The air-ship!"

Hardly had the words left his lips when a shell from the torpedo-boat struck the *Lurline* under the quarter, and ripped one of her plates out like a sheet of paper. The next instant the engineer rushed up on deck, crying—

"The bottom's out of her! She'll go down in five minutes!"

Tremayne, who was the only man on deck save the look-out, ran out of the wheel-house, dived into the cabin, and a moment later reappeared with Natas in his arms, and followed by his two attendants. Then, without the loss of a second, but in perfect order, the quarter-boat was manned and lowered, and pulled clear of the ill-fated *Lurline* just as she pitched backwards into the sea and went down with a run, stern foremost.

The air-ship, coming up at a tremendous speed, swooped suddenly down from a height of two thousand feet, and slowed up within a thousand yards of the torpedo-boat. A projectile rushed through the air and landed on the deck of the Frenchman. There was a flash of greenish flame, a cloud of mingled smoke and steam, and when this had drifted away there was not a vestige of the torpedo-boat to be seen. Then a few fragments of iron splashed into the water here and there, and that was all that betokened her fate.

CHAPTER XXII.

ARMED NEUTRALITY.

HARDLY had the *Lurline* disappeared than the air-ship was lying alongside the boat, floating on the water as easily and lightly as a seagull, and Natas and his two attendants, Tremayne, and the three men who had been saved from the yacht, were at once taken on board.

It would be useless to interrupt the progress of the narrative to describe the welcoming greetings which passed between the rescued party and the crew of the *Ithuriel*, or the amazement of Arnold and his companions when Natasha threw her arms round the neck of the almost helpless cripple, who was lifted over the rail by Tremayne and his two attendants, kissed him on the brow, and said so that all could hear her—

"We were in time! Thank God we were in time, my father!"

Her father! This paralytic creature, who could not move a yard without the assistance of some one else—this was Natas, the father of Natasha, and the Master of the Terror, the man who had planned the ruin of a civilisation, and for all they knew might aspire to the empire of the world!

It was marvellous, inconceivable, but there was no time to think about it now, for the two cruisers were still blazing away at each other, and Tremayne had determined to punish the Frenchman for his discourtesy in not answering his flag, and his inhumanity in firing on an unarmed vessel which was well known as a private pleasure-yacht all round the western and southern shores of Europe.

As soon as Natas had been conveyed into the saloon, Tremayne, after returning Arnold's hearty handclasp, said to him—

"That rascally Frenchman chased and fired on us, and then sent his torpedo-boat after us, without the slightest provocation. I purposely hoisted the Yacht Squadron flag to show that we were non-combatants, and still he sank us. I suppose he took the *Lurline* for a fast despatch boat, but still he ought to have had the sense and the politeness to let her alone when he saw she was a yacht, so I want you to teach him better manners."

"Certainly," replies Arnold. "I'll sink him for you in five seconds as soon as we get aloft again."

"I don't want you to do that if you can help it. She has five or six hundred men on board, who are only doing as they are told, and we have not declared war on the world yet. Can't you disable her, and force her to surrender to the British cruiser that came to our rescue? You know we must have been sunk or captured half an hour ago if she had not turned up so opportunely, in spite of your so happily coming fifty miles this side of the rendezvous. I should like to return the compliment by delivering his enemy into his hand."

"I quite see what you mean, but I'm afraid I can't guarantee success. You see, our artillery is intended for destruction, and not for disablement. Still I'll have a try with pleasure. I'll see if I can't disable his screws, only you mustn't blame me if he goes to the bottom by accident."

"Certainly not, you most capable destroyer of life and property," laughed Tremayne. "Only let him off as lightly as you can. Ah, Natasha! Good morning again! I suppose Natas has taken no harm from the unceremonious way in which I had to almost throw him on board the boat. Aërial voyaging seems to agree with you, you"—

"Must not talk nonsense, my Lord of Alanmere, especially when there is sterner work in hand," interrupted Natasha, with a laugh. "What are you going to do with those two cruisers that are battering each other to pieces down there? Sink them both, or leave them to fight it out?"

"Neither, with your permission, fair lady. The British cruiser saved us by coming on the scene at the right moment, and as the Frenchman fired upon us without due cause, I want Captain Arnold to disable her in some way and hand her over a prisoner to our rescuer."

"Ah, that would be better, of course. One good turn deserves another. What are you going to do, Captain Arnold?"

"Drop a small shell under his stern and disable his propellers, if I can do so without sinking him, which I am afraid is rather doubtful," replied Arnold.

While they were talking, the *Ithuriel* had risen a thousand feet or so from the water, and had advanced to within about half a mile of the two cruisers, which were now manœuvring round each other at a distance of about a thousand yards, blazing away without cessation, and waiting for some lucky shot to partially disable one or the other, and so give an opportunity for boarding, or ramming.

In the old days, when France and Britain had last grappled in the struggle for the mastery of the sea, the two ships would have been laid alongside each other long before this. But that was not to be thought of while those terrible machine guns were able to rain their hail of death down from the tops, and the quick-firing cannon were hurling their thirty shots a minute across the intervening space of water.

The French cruiser had so far taken no notice of the sudden annihilation of her second torpedo-boat by the air-ship, but as soon as the latter made her way astern of her she seemed to scent mischief, and turned one of her three-barrelled Nordenfeldts on to her. The shots soon came singing about the *Ithuriel* in somewhat unpleasant proximity, and Arnold said—

"Monsieur seems to take us for a natural enemy, and if he wants fight he shall have it. If I don't disable him with this shot I'll sink him with the next."

So saying he trained one of the broadside guns on the stern of the French cruiser, and at the right moment pressed the button. The shell bored its way through the air and down into the water until it struck and exploded against the submerged rudder.

A huge column of foam rose up under the cruiser's stern;

half lifted out of the water, she plunged forward with a mighty lurch, burying her forecastle in the green water, and then she righted and lay helpless upon the sea, deprived of the power of motion and steering, and with the useless steam roaring in great clouds from her pipes. A moment later she began to settle by the stern, showing that her after plates had been badly injured, if not torn away by the explosion.

Meanwhile the *Ithuriel* had shot away out of range until the two cruisers looked like little toy-ships spitting fire at each other, and Arnold said to Tremayne, who was with him in the wheel-house—

"I think that has settled her, as far as any more real fighting is concerned. Look! She can't stand that sort of thing very long."

He handed Tremayne the glasses as he spoke. The French cruiser was lying motionless upon the water, with her after compartments full, and very much down by the stern. She was still blazing away gamely with all her available guns, but it was obvious at a glance that she was now no match for her antagonist, who had taken full advantage of the help rendered by her unknown ally, and was pouring a perfect hail of shot and shell point-blank into her half-disabled adversary, battering her deck-works into ruins, and piercing her hull again and again.

At length, when the splendid fabric had been reduced to little better than a floating wreck by the terrible cannonade, the fire from the British cruiser stopped, and the signal " Will you surrender ?" flew from her masthead.

A few moments later the tricolor, for the first time in the war, dipped to the White Ensign, and the naval duel was over.

"Now we will leave them to talk it over," said Tremayne, shutting the glasses. "I should like to hear what they have to say about us, I must confess, but there is something more important to be done, and the sooner we are on the other side of the Atlantic the better. The *Aurania* started from New York this morning. How soon can you get across?"

"In about sixteen hours if we had to go all the way," replied Arnold. "It is, say, three thousand miles from here to New York, and the *Ithuriel* can fly two hundred miles an hour if necessary. But the *Aurania*, if she starts in good time, will make between four and five hundred miles during the day, and so we ought to meet her soon after sundown this evening if we are lucky."

As Arnold ceased speaking, the report of a single gun came up from the water, and a string of signal flags floated out from the masthead of the British cruiser.

"Hullo!" said Tremayne, once more turning the glasses on the two vessels, "that was a blank cartridge, and as far as I can make out that signal reads, 'We want to speak you.' And look: there goes a white flag to the fore. His intentions are evidently peaceful. What do you say, shall we go down?"

"I see no objection to it. It will only make a difference of half an hour or so, and perhaps we may learn something worth knowing from the captain about the naval force afloat in the Atlantic. I think it would be worth while. We have no need for concealment now; and besides, all Europe is talking about us, so there can be no harm in showing ourselves a bit more closely."

"Very well, then, we will go down and hear what he has to say," replied Tremayne. "But I don't think it would be well for me to show myself just now, and so I will go below."

Arnold at once signalled the necessary order from the conning tower to the engine-room. The fan-wheels revolved more slowly, and the *Ithuriel* sank swiftly downwards towards the two cruisers, now lying side by side.

As soon as she came to a standstill within speaking distance of the British man-of-war, discipline was for the moment forgotten on board of both victor and vanquished, under the influence of the intense excitement and curiosity aroused by seeing the mysterious and much-talked-of air-ship at such close quarters.

The French and British captains were both standing on the quarter-deck eagerly scanning the strange craft through their glasses till she came near enough to dispense with them, and every man and officer on board the two cruisers who was able to be on deck, crowded to points of 'vantage, and stared at her with all their eyes. The whole company of the *Ithuriel*, with the exception of Natas, Tremayne, and those whose duties kept them in the engine-room, were also on deck, and Arnold stood close by the wheel-house and the after gun, ready to give any orders that might be necessary in case the conversation took an unfriendly turn.

"May I ask the name of that wonderful craft, and to what I am indebted for the assistance you have given me?" hailed the British captain.

"Certainly. This is the Terrorist air-ship *Ithuriel*, and we disabled the French cruiser because her captain had the bad manners to fire upon and sink an unarmed yacht that had no quarrel with him. But for that we should have left you to fight it out."

"The Terrorists, are you? If I had known that, I confess I should not have asked to speak you, and I tell you candidly that I am sorry you did not leave us to fight it out, as you say. As I cannot look upon you as an ally or a friend, I can only regret the advantage you have given me over an honourable foe."

There was an emphasis on the word "honourable" which brought a flush to Arnold's cheek, as he replied—

"What I did to the French cruiser I should have done whether you had been on the scene or not. We are as much your foes as we are those of France, that is to say, we are totally indifferent to both of you. As for *honourable* foes, I may say that I only disabled the French cruiser because I thought she had acted both unfairly and dishonourably. But we are wasting time. Did you merely wish to speak us in order to find out who we were?"

"Yes, that was my first object, I confess. I also wished to know whether this is the same air-ship which crossed the Mediterranean yesterday, and if not, how many of these vessels there are in existence, and what you mean to do with them?"

"Before I answer, may I ask how you know that an air-ship crossed the Mediterranean yesterday?" asked Arnold, thoroughly mystified by this astounding piece of news.

"We had it by telegraph at Queenstown during the night. She was going northward, when observed, by Larnaka"—

"Oh yes, that was one of our despatch boats, replied Arnold, forcing himself to speak with a calmness that he by no means felt. "I'm afraid my orders will hardly allow me to answer your other questions very fully, but I may tell you that we have a fleet of air-ships at our command, all constructed in England under the noses of your intelligent authorities, and that we mean to use them as it seems best to us, should we at any time consider it worth our while to interfere in the game that the European Powers are playing with each other. Meanwhile we keep a position of armed neutrality. When we think the war has gone far enough we shall probably stop it when a good opportunity offers."

This was too much for a British sailor to listen to quietly on his own quarter-deck, whoever said it, and so the captain of the *Andromeda* forgot his prudence for the moment, and said somewhat hotly—

"Confound it, sir! you talk as if you were omnipotent and arbiters of peace and war. Don't go too far with your insolence, or I shall haul that flag of truce down and give you five minutes to get out of range of my guns or take your chance"—

For all answer there came a contemptuous laugh from the deck of the *Ithuriel*, the rapid ringing of an electric bell, and the disappearance of her company under cover. Then with one mighty leap she rose two thousand feet into the air, and before the astounded and disgusted captain of H.M. cruiser *Andromeda* very well knew what had become of her, she was a mere speck of light in the sky, speeding away at two hundred miles an hour to the westward.

As soon as she was fairly on her course, Arnold gave up the wheel to one of the crew, and went into the saloon to disscuss with Tremayne and Natas the all-important scrap of news that had fallen from the lips of the captain of the British cruiser. What was the other air-ship that had been seen crossing the Mediterranean?

Surely it must be one of the Terrorist fleet, for there were no others in existence. And yet strict orders had been given that none of the fleet were to take the air until the *Ithuriel* returned. Was it possible that there were traitors, even in Aeria, and that the air-ship seen from Larnaka was a deserter going northward to the enemy, the worst enemy of all, the Russians?

CHAPTER XXIII.

A BATTLE IN THE NIGHT.

AT half-past five on the morning of the 23rd of June, the Cunard liner *Aurania* left New York for Queenstown and Liverpool. She was the largest and swiftest passenger steamer afloat, and on her maiden voyage she had lowered the Atlantic record by no less than twelve hours; that is to say, she had performed the journey from Sandy Hook to Queenstown in four days and a half exactly. Her measurement was forty-five thousand tons, and her twin screws, driven by quadruple engines, developing sixty thousand horse-power, forced her through the water at the unparalleled speed of thirty knots, or thirty-four and a half statute miles an hour.

Since the outbreak of the war it had been found necessary to take all but the most powerful vessels off the Atlantic route, for, as had long been foreseen, the enemies of the Anglo-German Alliance were making the most determined efforts to cripple the Transatlantic trade of Britain and Germany, and swift, heavily-armed French and Italian cruisers, attended by torpedo-boats and gun-boats, and supported by battle-ships and depôt vessels for coaling purposes, were swarming along the great ocean highway.

These, of course, had to be opposed by an equal or greater force of British warships. In fact, the burden of keeping the Atlantic route open fell entirely on Britain, for the German and Austrian fleets had all the work they were capable of doing nearer home in the Baltic and Mediterranean.

The terrible mistake that had been made by the House of Lords in negativing the Italian Loan had already become disastrously apparent, for though the Anglo-Teutonic Alliance was putting forth every effort, its available ships were only just sufficient to keep the home waters clear and the ocean routes practically open, even for the fastest steamers.

The task, therefore, which lay before the *Aurania* when she cleared American waters was little less than running the gauntlet for nearly three thousand miles. The French cruiser which had been captured by the *Andromeda*, thanks to the assistance of the *Ithuriel*, had left Brest with the express purpose of helping to intercept the great Cunarder, for she had crossed the Atlantic five times already without a scratch since the war had begun, showing a very clean pair of heels to everything that had attempted to overhaul her, and now on her sixth passage a grand effort was to be made to capture or cripple the famous ocean greyhound.

It was by far her most important voyage in more senses than one. In the first place, her incomparable speed and good luck had made her out of sight the prime favourite with those passengers who were obliged to cross the Atlantic, war or no war, and for the same reasons she also carried more mails and specie than any other liner, and this voyage she had an enormously valuable consignment of both on board. As for passengers, every available foot of space was taken for months in advance.

Enterprising agents on both sides of the water had bought up every berth from stem to stern, and had put them up to auction, realising fabulous prices, which had little chance of being abated, even when her sister ship the *Sidonia*, the construction of which was being pushed forward on the Clyde with all possible speed, was ready to take the water.

But the chief importance of this particular passage lay, though barely half a dozen persons were aware of it, in the fact that among her passengers was Michael Roburoff, chief of the American Section of the Terrorists, who was bringing to the Council his report of the work of the Brotherhood in the United States, together with the information which he had collected, by means of an army of spies, as to the true intentions of the American Government with regard to the war.

These, so far as the rest of the world was concerned, were a profound secret, and he was the only man outside the

President's Cabinet and the Tsar's Privy Council who had accurate information with regard to them. The *Aurania* was therefore not only carrying mails, treasure, and passengers, but, in the person of Michael Roburoff, she was carrying secrets on the revelation of which the whole issue of the war and the destiny of the world might turn.

America was the one great Power not involved in the tremendous struggle that was being waged. The most astute diplomatist in Europe had no idea what her real policy was, but every one knew that the side on which she threw the weight of her boundless wealth and vast resources must infallibly win in the long run.

The plan that had been adopted by Britain for keeping the Atlantic route open was briefly as follows:—All along the 3000 miles of the steamer track a battleship was stationed at the end of every day's run, that is to say, at intervals of about 500 miles, and patrolled within a radius of 100 miles. Each of these was attended by two heavily-armed cruisers and four torpedo-boats, while between these points swifter cruisers were constantly running to and fro convoying the liners.

Thus, when the *Aurania* left New York, she was picked up on the limit of the American water by two cruisers, which would keep pace with her as well as they could until she reached the first battleship. As she passed the ironclad these two would leave her, and the next two would take up the running, and so on until she reached the range of operations of the Irish Squadron.

No other Power in the world could have maintained such a system of ocean police, but Britain was putting forth the whole of her mighty naval strength, and so she spared neither ships nor money to keep open the American and Canadian routes, for on them nearly half her food-supply depended, as well as her chief line of communication with the far East.

On the other hand, her enemies were making desperate efforts to break the chain of steel that was thus stretched across the hemisphere, for they well knew that, this once broken, the first real triumph of the war would have been won.

Five hundred miles out from New York the *Aurania* was joined by the *Oceana*, the largest vessel on the Canadian Pacific line from Halifax to Liverpool. **So far no enemy had** been seen. The two great liners reached **the first** battleship together, and were joined by the second pair of cruisers. Before sunset the Cunarder had drawn ahead **of** her companions, **and** by nightfall **was racing away** alone **over** the water with every light **carefully concealed, and keeping** an **eager look-out for** friend **or foe.**

There was no moon, and **the** sky was **so** heavily overcast with **clouds, that, under** any other circumstances, it would **have been the height of** rashness to go rushing through the darkness at such **a** headlong speed. But the captain of the *Aurania* was aware of the state of the road, and he knew that **in** speed and secrecy lay his only chances of getting his magnificent vessel through in safety.

Soon after ten o'clock lights **were** sighted dead ahead. **The** course was slightly altered, and the great liner swept past **one** of the North German Lloyd boats in company with a **cruiser.** The private signal was made and answered, and **in** half **an hour** she was again alone amidst the darkness.

It **was** nearly eleven o'clock, when Michael Roburoff, who was standing under the lee of one of the ventilators amidships, smoking a last **pipe** before turning in, saw **a** figure muffled in a **huge** grey **ulster** creeping into the deeper shadows under the **bridge.** It was so dark that he could only **just** make out the **outline of** the figure, but he could see enough to rouse his ever **ready** suspicions in the **furtive movements that** the man **was making.**

He stole out on the **starboard,** that is the southward, **rail of the** spar-deck, and Michael, straining his eyes to the utmost, saw him take a round flat object from under his coat, and then look round stealthily to see if he was observed. As **he** did so Michael whipped a pistol **out of** his pocket, **levelled it** at the man, and said in a low, distinct tone—

"Put that back, **or** I'll shoot!"

For all answer the **man raised his arm to** throw the object overboard. Michael, taking the **best aim he** could in the darkness, fired. The bullet struck the elbow **of the** raised arm, the man lurched forward with **a** low cry **of** rage and pain, grasped **the** object with his other hand, and, as he fell to the deck, flung **it into the sea.**

Scarcely had it touched the water when it burst into flame, and an intensely bright blaze of bluish-white light shot up, shattering the darkness, and illuminating the great ship from the waterline to the trucks of her masts. Instantly the deck of the liner was a scene of wild excitement. In a moment the man whom Roburoff had wounded was secured in the act of trying to throw himself overboard. Michael himself was rapidly questioned by the captain, who was immediately on the spot.

He told his story in a dozen words, and explained that he had fired to disable the man and prevent the fire-signal falling into the sea. There was no doubt about the guilt of the traitor, for he himself cut the captain's interrogation short by saying defiantly, in broken English that at once betrayed him as a Frenchman—

"Yees, I do it! I give signal to ze fleet down there. If I succeeded, I got half million francs. I fail, so shoot! C'est la fortune de la guerre! Voilà, look! They come!'

As the spy said this he pointed to the south-eastern horizon. A brief bright flash of white light went up through the night and vanished. It was the answering signal from the French or Italian cruisers, which were making all speed up from the south-east to head off the *Aurania* before she reached the next station and gained the protection of the British battleship.

The spy's words were only too true. He had gone to America for the sole purpose of returning in the *Aurania* and giving the signal at this particular point on the passage. Within ten miles were four of the fleetest French and Italian cruisers, six torpedo-boats, and two battleships, which, by keeping well to the southward during the day, and then putting on all steam as soon as night fell, had managed to head off the ocean greyhound at last.

Two cruisers and a battleship with two torpedo-boats were coming up from the south-east; one cruiser, the other battleship, and two torpedo-boats were bearing down from the south-west, and the remaining cruiser and brace of torpedo-boats had managed to slip through the British line and gain a position to the northward.

This large force had not been brought up without good reason. The *Aurania* was the biggest prize afloat, and well worth fighting for, if it came to blows, as it very probably would do; added to which there was a very good chance of one or two other liners falling victims to a well-planned and successful raid.

The French spy was at once sent below and put into safe keeping, and the signal to "stoke up" was sent to the engine-rooms. The firemen responded with a will, extra hands were put on in the stokeholes, and the furnaces taxed to their utmost capacity. The boilers palpitated under the tremendous head of steam, the engines throbbed and groaned like labouring giants, and the great ship, trembling like some live animal under the lash, rushed faster and faster over the long dark rollers under the impulse of her whirling screws.

There was no longer any need for concealment even if it had been possible. Speed and speed only afforded the sole chance of escape. Of course the captain of the *Aurania* had no idea of the strength or disposition of the force that had undertaken his capture. Had he known the true state of the case, his anxiety would have been a good deal greater than it was. He fully believed that he could outsteam the vessels to the south-east, and, once past these, he knew that he would be in touch with the British ships at the next station before any harm could come to him. He therefore headed a little more to the northward, and trusted with perfect confidence to his heels.

Michael Roburoff was the hero of the moment, and the captain cordially thanked him for his prompt attempt to frustrate the atrocious act of the spy which deliberately endangered the liberty and perhaps the lives of more than a thousand non-combatants. Michael, however, cut his thanks short by taking him aside and asking him what he thought of the position of affairs. He spoke so seriously that the captain thought he was frightened, and by way of reassuring him replied cheerily—

"Don't have any fear for the *Aurania*, Mr. Roburoff. That's only a cruiser, or perhaps a couple, down there, and the enemy haven't a ship that I can't give a good five knots and a beating to. We shall sight the British ships soon after daybreak, and by that time those fellows will be fifty miles behind us.

"I have as much confidence in the *Aurania's* speed as you have, Captain Frazer," replied Michael. "but I'm afraid you are underrating the enemy's strength. Do you know that within the last few days it has been almost doubled, and that a determined effort is to be made, not only to catch or sink the *Aurania*, but also to break the British line of posts, and cut the line of American and Canadian communication altogether?"

"No, sir," replied the captain, looking sharply at Michael. "I don't know anything of the sort, neither do the commanders of the British warships on this side. If your information is correct, I should like to know how you came by it. You are a Russian by name"—

"But not a subject of the Tsar," quickly interrupted Michael. "I am an American citizen, and I have come by this information not as the friend of Russia, as you seem to suspect, but as her enemy, or rather as the enemy of her ruler. How I got it is my business. It is enough for you to know that it is correct, and that you are in far greater danger than you think you are. The signal given by that French spy was evidently part of a prearranged plan, and for all you know you may even now be surrounded, or steaming straight into a trap that has been laid for you. If I may advise, I would earnestly counsel you to double on your course and make every effort to rejoin the other liner and the cruisers we have passed."

"Nonsense, sir, nonsense!" answered the captain testily. "Our watch-dogs are far too wide awake to be caught napping like that. You have been deceived by one of the rumours that are filling the air just now. You can go to your berth and sleep in peace, and to-morrow you shall be half-way across the Atlantic without an enemy's ship in sight."

"Captain Frazer," said Michael very seriously, "with your leave I shall not go to my berth; and what is more, I can tell you that very few of us will get much sleep to-night, and that if you do not back I hardly think you will be flying the British flag to-morrow. Ha! look there—and there!"

Michael seized the captain's arm suddenly, and pointed rapidly to the south-east and north-east. Two thin rays of light flashed up into the sky one after the other. Then came a third from the south-west, and then darkness again. At the same instant came the hails from the look-outs announcing the lights.

Captain Frazer was wrong, and he saw that he was at a

glance. The flash in the north-east could not be from a friend, for it was a plain answer to the known enemy in the south-east, and so too in all probability was the third. If so, the *Aurania* was almost surrounded.

The captain wasted no words in confessing his error, but ran up on to the bridge to rectify it as far as he could at once. The helm was put hard over, the port screw was reversed, and the steamer swung round in a wide sweep, and was soon speeding back westward over her own tracks. An hour's run brought her in sight of the lights of the *North German* and her escort. She slowed as she passed them, and told the news. Then she sped on again at full-speed to meet the *Oceana* and the two cruisers, which were about fifty miles behind.

By one A.M. the three cruisers and the three liners had joined forces, and were steaming westward at twenty knots an hour, the liners in single file led by a cruiser, and having one on each beam. Soon the flashes on the horizon grew more frequent, always drawing closer together.

Then those in the westward dropped from the perpendicular to the horizontal, and swept the water as though seeking something. It was not long before the darting rays of one of the searchlights fell across the track of the British flotilla. Instantly from all three points converging flashes were concentrated upon it, revealing the outline of every ship with the most perfect distinctness.

The last hope of running through the hostile fleet unperceived had now vanished. There was nothing for it but to go ahead full-speed, and trust to the chances of a running fight to get clear. With a view of finding out the strength of the enemy, the British cruisers now turned their searchlights on and swept the horizon.

A very few moments sufficed to show that an overwhelming force was closing in on them from three sides. They were completely caught in a trap, from which there was no escape save by running the gauntlet. Whichever way they headed they would have to pass through the converging fire of the enemy.

The weakest point, so far as they could see, was the one cruiser and two torpedo-boats to the northward, and so towards them they headed. At the speed at which they were travelling it needed but a few minutes to bring them within range, and the British commanders rightly decided to concentrate their fire for the present on the single cruiser and her two attendants, in the hope of sinking them before the others could get into action.

At three thousand yards the heavy guns came into play, and a storm of shell was hurled upon the advancing foe, who lost no time in replying in the same terms. As the vessels approached each other the shooting became closer and terribly effective.

The searchlights of the British cruisers were kept full ahead, and every attempt of the torpedo-boats to get round on the flank was foiled by a hail of shot from the quick-firing guns. Within fifteen minutes of opening fire one of these was sunk and the other disabled. The French cruiser, too, suffered fearfully from the tempest of shot and shell that was rained upon her.

Had the British got within range of her half an hour sooner the plan would have been completely foiled. As it was, her fate was sealed, but it was too late. The three British warships rushed at her together, vomiting flame and smoke and iron across the rapidly-decreasing distance, until within five hundred yards of her. Then the fire from the two on either flank suddenly stopped.

The centre one, still blazing away, put on her forced draught, swerved sharply round, and then darted in on her with the ram. There was a terrific shock, a heavy, grinding crunch, and then the mighty mass of the charging vessel, hurled at nearly thirty miles an hour upon her victim, bored and ground her resistless way into her side.

Then she suddenly reversed her engines and backed out. In less than thirty seconds it was all over. The Frenchman, almost cut in half by the frightful blow, reeled once, and once only, and then went down like a stone.

But by this time the other two divisions of the enemy were within range, and through the roar of the lighter artillery now came the deep, sullen boom of the big guns on the battleships, and the great thousand-pound projectiles began to scream through the air and fling the water up into mountains of foam where they pitched.

Where one of them struck, death and destruction would follow as surely as though it were a thunderbolt from Heaven. The three liners scattered and steamed away to the northward as fast as their propellers would drive them. But what was their utmost speed to that of the projectiles cleaving through the air at more than two thousand feet a second?

See! one at length strikes the German liner square amidships, and bursts. There is a horrible explosion. The searchlight thrown on her shows a cloud of steam and smoke and flame rising up from her riven decks. Where her funnels were is a huge ragged black hole. This is visible for an instant, then her back breaks, and in two halves she follows the French cruiser to the bottom of the Atlantic.

The sinking of the German liner was the signal for the appearance of a new actor on the scene, and the commencement of a work of destruction more appalling than anything that human warfare had so far known.

Michael Roburoff, standing on the spar-deck of the flying *Aurania*, suddenly saw a bright stream of light shoot down from the clouds, and flash hither and thither, till it hovered over the advancing French and Italian squadron. For the moment the combat ceased, so astounded were the combatants on both sides at this mysterious apparition.

Then, without the slightest warning, with no flash or roar of guns, there came a series of frightful explosions among the ships of the pursuers. They followed each other so quickly that the darkness behind the electric lights seemed lit with a continuous blaze of livid green flame for three or four minutes.

Then there was darkness and silence. Black darkness and absolute silence. The searchlights were extinguished, and the roar of the artillery was still. The British waited in dazed silence for it to begin again, but it never did. The whole of the pursuing squadron had been annihilated.

CHAPTER XXIV.

THE NEW WARFARE.

IT will now be necessary, in order to insure the continuity of the narrative, to lay before the reader a brief sketch of the course of events in Europe from the actual commencement of hostilities on a general scale between the two immense forces which may be most conveniently designated as the Anglo-Teutonic Alliance and the Franco-Slavonian League.

In order that these two terms may be fully understood, it will be well to explain their general constitution. When the two forces, into which the declaration of war ultimately divided the nations of Europe, faced each other for the struggle which was to decide the mastery of the Western world, the Anglo-Teutonic Alliance consisted primarily of Britain, Germany, and Austria, and, ranged under its banner, whether from choice or necessity, stood Holland, Belgium, and Denmark in the north-west, with Bulgaria, Greece, and Turkey in the south-west.

Egypt was strongly garrisoned for the land defence of the Suez Canal and the high road to the East by British, Indian, and Turkish troops. British and Belgian troops held Antwerp and the fortresses of the Belgian Quadrilateral in force.

A powerful combined fleet of British, Danish, and Dutch war vessels of all classes held the approaches by the Sound and Kattegat to the Baltic Sea, and co-operated in touch with the German fleet; the Dutch and the German having, at any rate for the time being, and under the pressure of irresistible circumstances, laid aside their hereditary national hatred, and consented to act as allies under suitable guarantees to Holland.

The co-operation of Denmark had been secured, in spite of the family connections existing between the Danish and the Russian Courts, and the rancour still remaining from the old Schleswig-Holstein quarrel, by very much the same means that had been taken in the historic days of the Battle of the Baltic. It is true that matters had not gone so far as they went when Nelson disobeyed orders by putting his telescope to his blind eye, and engaged the Danish fleet in spite of the signals; but a demonstration of such overwhelming force had been made by sea and land on the part of Britain and Germany, that the House of Dagmar had bowed to the inevitable, and ranged itself on the side of the Anglo-Teutonic Alliance.

Marshalled against this imposing array of naval and military force stood the Franco-Slavonian League, consisting primarily of France, Russia, and Italy, supported—whether by consent or necessity—by Spain, Portugal, and Servia. The co-operation of Spain had been purchased by the promise of Gibraltar at the conclusion of the war, and that of Portugal by the guarantee of a largely increased sphere of influence on the West Coast of Africa, plus the Belgian States of the Congo.

Roumania and Switzerland remained neutral, the former to be a battlefield for the neighbouring Powers, and the latter for the present safe behind her ramparts of everlasting snow and ice. Scandinavia also remained neutral, the sport of the rival diplomacies of East and West, but not counted of sufficient importance to materially influence the colossal struggle one way or the other.

In round numbers the Anglo-Teutonic Alliance had seven millions of men on the war footing, including, of course, the Indian and Colonial forces of the British Empire, while in case of necessity urgent levies were expected to produce between two and three millions more. Opposed to these, the Franco-Slavonian League had about ten millions under arms, with nearly three millions in reserve.

As regards naval strength, the Alliance was able to pit rather more than a thousand warships of all classes, and about the same number of torpedo-boats, against nearly nine hundred warships and about seven hundred torpedo-boats at the disposal of the League.

In addition to this latter armament, it is very necessary to name a fleet of a hundred war-balloons of the type mentioned in an earlier chapter, fifty of which belonged to Russia and fifty to France. No other European Power possessed any engine of destruction that was capable of being efficiently matched against the invention of M. Riboult, who was now occupying the position of Director of the aërial fleet in the service of the League.

It would be both a tedious repetition of sickening descriptions of scenes of bloodshed and a useless waste of space, to enumerate in detail all the series of conflicts by sea and land which resulted from the collision of the tremendous forces which were thus arrayed against each other in a conflict that was destined to be unparalleled in the history of the human race.

To do so would be to occupy pages filled with more or less technical descriptions of strategic movements, marches, and countermarches, skirmishes, reconnaissances, and battles, which followed each other with such unparalleled rapidity that the combined efforts of the war correspondents of the European press proved entirely inadequate to keep pace with them in the form of anything like a continuous narrative.

It will therefore be necessary to ask the reader to remain content with such brief summary as has been given, supplemented with the following extracts from a very lengthy *résumé* of the leading events of the war up to date, which were published in a special War Supplement issued by the *Daily Telegraph* on the morning of Tuesday the 28th of June 1904:—

"Although little more than a period of six weeks has elapsed since the actual outbreak of hostilities which marked the commencement of what, be its issue what it may, must indubitably prove the most colossal struggle in the history of human warfare, changes have already occurred which must infallibly mark their effect upon the future destiny of the world. Almost as soon as the first shot was fired the nations of Europe, as if by instinct or under the influence of some power higher than that of international diplomacy, automatically marshalled themselves into the two most mighty hosts that have ever trod the field of battle since man first fought with man.

"Not less than twenty millions of men are at this moment facing each other under arms throughout the area of the war. These are almost equally divided; for, although what is now known as the Franco-Slavonian League has some three millions of men more on land, it may be safely stated that the preponderance of naval strength possessed by the Anglo-Teutonic Alliance fully counterbalances this advantage.

"There is, however, another most important element which has now for the first time been introduced into warfare, and which, although it is most unhappily arrayed amongst the forces opposed to our own country and her gallant allies, it would be both idle and most imprudent to ignore. We refer, of course, to the two fleets of war-balloons, or, as it would be more correct to call them, navigable aerostats, possessed by France and Russia.

"So tremendous has been the influence which these terrible inventions have exercised upon the course of the war, that we are not transgressing the bounds of sober truth when we say that they have utterly disconcerted and brought to nought the highest strategy and the most skilfully devised plans of the brilliant array of masters of the military art whose presence adorns the ranks and enlightens the councils of the Alliance.

"Since the day when the Russians crossed the German and Austrian frontiers, and the troops of France and Italy simultaneously flung themselves across the western frontiers of Germany and through the passes of the Tyrol, their progress, unparalleled in rapidity even by the marvellous marches of Napoleon, has been marked, not by what we have hitherto been accustomed to call battles, but rather by a series of colossal butcheries.

"In every case of any moment the method of procedure on the part of the attacking forces has been the same, and, with the deepest regret we confess it, it has been marked with the same unvarying success. Whenever a large army has been set in motion upon a predetermined point of attack, whether a fortress, an entrenched camp, or a strongly occupied position in the field, a squadron of aerostats has winged its way through the air under cover of the darkness of night, and silently and unperceived has marked the disposition of forces, the approximate strength of the army or the position to be attacked, and, as far as they were observable, the points upon which the attack could be most favourably delivered. Then they have returned with their priceless information, and, according to it, the assailants have been able, in every case so far, to make their assault where least expected, and to make it, moreover, upon an already partially demoralised force.

"From the detailed descriptions which we have already published of battles and sieges, or rather of the storming of great fortresses, it will be remembered that every assault on the part of the troops of the League has been preceded by a preliminary and irresistible attack from the clouds.

"The aerostats have stationed themselves at great elevations over the ramparts of fortresses and the bivouacs of armies, and have rained down a hail of dynamite, melinite, fire-shells and cyanogen poison-grenades, which have at once put guns out of action, blown up magazines, rendered fortifications untenable, and rent masses of infantry and squadrons of cavalry into demoralised fragments, before they had the time or the opportunity to strike a blow in reply. Then upon these silenced batteries, these wrecked fortifications, and these demoralised brigades, there has been poured a storm of artillery fire from the untouched enemy, advancing in perfect order, and inspired with high-spirited confidence, which has been irresistibly opposed to the demoralisation of their enemies.

"Is it any wonder, or any disgrace, to the defeated, that under such novel and appalling conditions the orderly and disciplined onslaughts of the legions of the League have in almost every case been completely successful? The sober truth is that the invention and employment of these devastating appliances have completely altered the face of the field of battle and the conditions of modern warfare. It is not in human valour, no matter how heroic or self-devoted it may be, to oppose itself with anything like confidence to an enemy which strikes from the skies, and cannot be struck in return.

"It was thus that the battles of Alexandrovo, Kalisz, and Czernowicz were won in the early stages of the war upon the Austro-German frontier. So, too, in the Rhine Provinces, were the battles of Treves, Mulhausen, and Freiburg turned by the aid of the French aerostats from battles into butcheries. It was under the assault of these irresistible engines that the great fortresses of Königsberg, Thorn, Breslau, Strasburg, and Metz, to say nothing of many minor, but strongly fortified, places, were first reduced to a state of impotence for defence, and then battered into ruins by the siege-guns of the assailants.

"All these terrible events, forming a series of catastrophes unparalleled in the annals of war, are still fresh in the minds of our readers, for they have followed one upon the other with almost stupefying rapidity, and it is yet hardly six weeks since the Cossacks and Uhlans were engaged in their first skirmish near Gnesen.

"This is an amazingly brief space of time for the fate of empires to be decided, and yet we are forced, with the utmost sorrow and reluctance, to admit that what were two months ago the magnificently disciplined and equipped armies of Germany and Austria, are now completely shattered and broken up into fragmentary and isolated army corps, decimated as to numbers and demoralised as to discipline, gathered in and about such strong places as are left to them, and awaiting only with the courage of desperation the moment, we fear the inevitable moment, when they shall be finally crushed between the rapidly converging hosts of the victorious League.

"Within the next few days, Berlin, Hanover, Prague, Munich, and Vienna must be invested, and may possibly be destroyed or compelled to ignominious and unconditional surrender by the irresistible forces that will be arrayed against them.

"Meanwhile, with still deeper regret, we are forced to confess that those operations in the Low Countries and the east of Europe and Asia Minor in which our own gallant troops have been engaged in conjunction with their several allies, have been, if not equally disastrous, at least void of any tangible success.

"Erzeroum, Trebizond, and Scutari have fallen; the passes of the Balkans have been forced, although at immense cost to the enemy; Belgrade has been stormed; Adrianople is invested, and Constantinople is therefore most seriously threatened.

"By heroic efforts the French attack upon the Quadrilateral has been rolled back at a fearful expense of human life. Antwerp is still untouched, and the command of the Baltic is still ours. In our own waters, as well as in the Atlantic and the Mediterranean, we have won victories which prove that Great Britain is still the unconquered, and we trust unconquerable, mistress of the seas. We have kept the Dardanelles open, and the Suez Canal is still inviolate.

"Two combined attacks, delivered by the allied French and Italian squadrons on Malta and Gibraltar, have been repulsed by Admiral Beresford with heavy loss to the enemy, thanks to the timely warning delivered to Mr. Balfour by the Earl of Alanmere—upon whose mysterious disappearance we comment in another column—and the Prime Minister's prompt and statesmanlike action in doubling the strength of the Mediterranean fleet before the outbreak of hostilities.

"Thanks to the tireless activity and splendid handling of the Channel fleet, the North Sea Division, and the Irish Squadron, the enemy's flag has been practically swept from the home waters, and the shores of our beloved country are as inviolate as they have been for more than seven centuries. These brilliant achievements go far to compensate us as an individual nation for the disasters which have befallen our allies on the Continent, and, in addition, we have the satisfaction of knowing that, so far, the most complete success has attended our arms in the East, and that the repeated and determined assaults of our Russian foes have been triumphantly hurled back from the impregnable bulwarks of our Indian Empire.

"It has been pointed out, and it would be vain to ignore the fact, that not only have all our victories been won in the absence of the aërial fleets of the League; but that we, in common with our allies, have been worsted in each of the happily few cases in which even one of these terrible aerostats has delivered its assaults upon us. Against this, however, we take leave to set our belief that these machines do not yet inspire sufficient confidence in their possessors to warrant them in undertaking operations above the sea, or at any considerable distance from their bases of manœuvring. It is true that we are entirely ignorant of the essentials of their construction; but the fact that no attempt has yet been made to send them into action over blue water inspires us with the hope and belief that their effective range of operations is confined to the land. . . .

"It would be superfluous to say that the British Empire is now involved in a struggle in comparison with which all our former wars sink into absolute insignificance, a struggle which will tax its immense resources to the very utmost. Nothing, however, has yet occurred to warrant the belief that those resources will not prove equal to the strain, or that the greatest empire on earth will not emerge from this combat of the giants with her ancient glory enhanced by new and hitherto unequalled triumphs.

"Certainly at no period in our history have we been so splendidly prepared to face our enemies both at home and abroad. All arms of the Services are in the highest state of efficiency, and the Government dockyards and arsenals, as well as private firms, are working day and night to still further strengthen them, and provide ample supplies of munitions of war. The hearts of all the nations united under our flag are beating as that of one man, and from the highest to the lowest ranks of Society all are inspired by a spirit of whole-souled patriotism which, if necessary, will make any sacrifice to preserve the flag untarnished, and the honour of Britain without a spot.

"At the head of affairs stands the man who of all others has proved himself to be the most fitted to direct the destinies of the empire in this tremendous crisis of her history. Party feeling for the time being has almost entirely disappeared, save amongst the few scattered bands of isolated Revolutionaries and malcontents, and Mr. Balfour possesses the absolute confidence of his Majesty on the one hand, and the undivided support of an impregnable majority in both Houses of Parliament on the other. He is admirably seconded by such lieutenants as Lord Randolph Churchill, Sir Joseph Chamberlain, and Sir George J. Goschen on his own side of the House, and by the Earls of Rosebery and Morley, Lord Brassey, and Sir Charles Dilke in what, previous to the outbreak of the war, was the opposing political camp, but which is now a party as loyal as that of the Government to the best interests of the Empire, and fully determined to give the utmost possible moral support consistent with fair and impartial criticism.

"The disastrous mistake which was made by a very small majority of the Upper House in rejecting the Government guarantee for the ill-fated Italian loan is now, of course, past repair; for Italy, as events have proved, exasperated by what her spokesmen termed her selfish betrayal by Britain, has passionately thrown herself into the arms of the League, and the Alliance has now no more bitter enemy than she is. It is, however, only justice to those who defeated the loan to add that they have now clearly seen and frankly owned their grievous mistake, and rallied as one man to the support of the Government."

CHAPTER XXV.

THE HERALDS OF DISASTER.

NOTHER column in the same issue contained an account of the "Mysterious Disappearance of Lord Alanmere" and the doings of the *Ithuriel* in the Atlantic. The account concluded as follows:—

"As the enemy's squadron came up in chase it was annihilated without warning and with appalling suddenness by the air-ship, which must have crossed the Atlantic in something like sixteen hours. After this fearful achievement it descended to the *Aurania*, took off a saloon passenger named Michael Roburoff, evidently, from his reception, a Terrorist himself, and then vanished through the clouds. For the present, and until we have fuller information, we attempt no detailed analysis of these astounding events. We merely content ourselves with saying in the most solemn words that we can use, that, awful and disastrous as is the war that is now raging throughout the greatest part of the old world, it is our firm belief that, behind the smoke-clouds of battle, and beneath the surface of visible events, there is working a secret power, possibly greater than any which has yet been called into action, and which at an unexpected moment may suddenly put forth its strength, upheave the foundations of Society, and bury existing institutions in the ruins of Civilisation.

"One fact is quite manifest, and that is, that although the League possesses a weapon of fearful efficiency for destruction in their fleet of aerostats, the Terrorists, controlled by no law save their own, and hampered by no traditions or limitations of civilised warfare, are in command of another fleet of unknown strength, the air-ships of which are apparently as superior to the aerostats of the League as a modern battleship would be to a three-decker of the time of Nelson.

"The power represented by such a fleet as this is absolutely inconceivable. The aerostats are large, clumsy, and comparatively slow. They do not carry guns, and can only drop their projectiles vertically downwards. Moreover, their sphere of operations has so far been entirely confined to the land.

"Very different, however, would seem to be the powers of the Terrorist air-ships. They have proved conclusively that they are swift almost beyond imagination. They have crossed oceans and continents in a few hours; they can ascend to enormous heights, and they carry artillery of unknown design and tremendous range, whose projectiles excel in destructiveness the very lightnings of heaven itself.

"In the presence of such an awful and mysterious power as this even the quarrels of nations seem to shrink into unimportance, and almost to pettiness. Where and when it may strike, no man knows save those who wield it, and therefore there is nothing for the peoples of the earth, however mighty they may be, to do but to await the blow in humiliating impotence, but still with a humble trust in that Higher Power which alone can save it from accomplishing the destruction of Society and the enslavement of the human race."

It may well be imagined with what interest, and it may fairly be added with what intense anxiety, these words were read by hundreds of thousands of people throughout the British Islands. Even the news from the Seat of War began to pall in interest before such tidings as these, invested as they were with the irresistible if terrible charm of the unknown and the mysterious.

By noon it was almost impossible to get any one in London or any of the large towns to talk of anything but the disappearance of Lord Alanmere, the Terrorists, and their marvellous aërial fleet. But it goes without saying that nowhere did the news produce greater distress or more utter bewilderment than it did among the occupants of Alanmere Castle, and especially in the breast of her who had been so quickly and so strangely installed as its new owner and mistress.

Everywhere the wildest rumours passed from lip to lip, growing in sensation and absurdity as they went. A report, telegraphed by an anonymous idiot from Liverpool, to the effect that six air-ships had appeared over the Mersey, and demanded a ransom of £10,000,000 from the town, was eagerly seized on by the cheaper evening papers, which rushed out edition after edition on the strength of it, until the *St. James's Gazette* put an end to the excitement by publishing a telegram from the Mayor of Liverpool denouncing the report as an insane and criminal hoax.

The next edition of the *St. James's*, however, contained a telegram from Hiorring, in Denmark, *viâ* Newcastle, which was of almost, if not quite, as startling and disquieting a nature, and which, moreover, contained a very considerable measure of truth. The telegram ran as follows:—

NAVAL DISASTER IN THE BALTIC.

The Sound forced by a Russian Squadron, assisted by a Terrorist Air-Ship.

(*From our own Correspondent.*)

Hiorring, June 28th, 8 A.M.

With the deepest regret I have to record the first naval disaster to the British arms during the present war. As soon as it became dark last night heavy firing was heard from Copenhagen to the southward, and before long the sound deepened into an almost continuous roar of light and heavy guns.

Our naval force in the Baltic was so strong that it was deemed incredible that the Russian fleet, which we have held imprisoned here since the commencement of hostilities, should dream even of making an attempt to escape. The cannonade, however, was the beginning of such an attempt, and it is useless disguising the fact that it has been completely successful. That this would have been the case, or, indeed, that the attempt would ever have been made by the Russian fleet alone, cannot be for a moment credited. But, incredible as it seems, it is nevertheless true that it was assisted, and that in a practically irresistible fashion, by one of those air-ships which have hitherto been believed to belong exclusively to the Terrorists, that is to say, to the deadliest enemies that Russia possesses.

As nearly as is known the Russian fleet consisted of twelve battleships, twenty-five armoured and unarmoured cruisers, and about forty torpedo-boats. These came charging ahead at full speed into the entrance to the Sound in spite of the overwhelming force of the Allied fleets, supported by the fortresses of Copenhagen and Elsinore. The attack was so sudden and so completely unexpected, that it must be confessed the defenders were to a certain extent taken

"On the water the results of the air-ship's attack were destructive almost beyond description."   *See page* 191.

unawares. The Russians came on in the form of an elongated wedge, their most powerful vessels being at the apex and external sides.

The firing was furious and sustained from beginning to end of the rush, but the damage inflicted by the cannonade of the Russian fleet and the torpedo-boats, which every now and then darted out from between the warships as opportunity offered to employ their silent and deadly weapons, was as nothing in comparison with the frightful havoc achieved by the air-ship.

This extraordinary craft hovered over the attacking force, darting hither and thither with bewildering rapidity, and raining down shells charged with an unknown explosive of fearful power among the crowded ships of the great force which was blocking the Sound. Half a dozen of these shells were fired upon the seaward fortifications of Copenhagen in passing, and produced a perfectly paralysing effect.

On the water the results of the air-ship's attack were destructive almost beyond description, particularly when she stationed herself over the Allied fleet and began firing her four guns right and left, ahead and astern. Every time a shell struck either a battleship or a cruiser, the terrific explosion which resulted either sank the ship in a few minutes, or so far disabled it that it fell an easy prey to the guns and rams of the Russians. As for the torpedo-boats which were struck, they were simply scattered over the water in indistinguishable fragments.

Under these conditions maintenance of formation and effective fighting were practically impossible, and the huge iron wedge of the Russian squadron was driven almost without a check through the demoralised ranks of the Allied fleet. The Gut of Elsinore was reached in a little more than three hours after the first sounds of the cannonade were heard. Shortly before this the air-ship had stationed itself about a thousand feet above the water, and a mile from the fortifications.

From this position it commenced a brief, rapid cannonade from its smokeless and flameless guns, the effects of which on the fortress are said to have been indescribably awful. Great blocks of steel-sheathed masonry were dislodged from the ramparts and hurled bodily into the sea, carrying with them guns and men to irretrievable destruction. In less than half an hour the once impregnable fortress of Elsinore was little better than a heap of ruins. The last shell blew up the central magazine; the tremendous explosion was heard for miles along the coast, and proved to be the closing act of the briefest but most deadly great naval action in the history of war.

The Russian fleet steamed triumphantly past the silenced Cerberus of the Sound with flashing searchlights, blazing rockets, and jubilant salvos of blank cartridge in honour of their really brilliant victory.

The losses of the Allied fleet, so far as they are at present known, are distressingly heavy. We have lost the battleships *Neptune*, *Hotspur*, *Anson*, *Superb*, *Black Prince*, and *Rodney*, the armoured cruisers *Narcissus*, *Beatrice*, and *Mersey*, the unarmoured cruisers *Arethusa*, *Barossa*, *Clyde*, *Lais*, *Seagull*, *Grasshopper*, and *Nautilus*, and not less than nineteen torpedo-boats of the first and second classes.

The Germans and Danes have lost the battleships *Kaiser Wilhelm*, *Friedrich der Grosse*, *Dantzig*, *Viborg*, and *Funen*, five German and three Danish cruisers, and about a dozen torpedo-boats.

Under whatever circumstances the Russians have obtained the assistance of the air-ship, which rendered them services that have proved so disastrous to the Allies, there can be no doubt but that her arrival on the scene puts a completely different aspect on the face of affairs at sea.

I have written this telegram on board first-class torpedo-boat, No. 87, which followed the Russian fleet from the Sound round the Skawe. They passed through the Kattegat in two columns of line ahead, with the air-ship apparently resting after her flight on board one of the largest steamers. We could see her quite distinctly by the glare of the rockets and the electric light. She is a small three-masted vessel almost exactly resembling the one which partially destroyed Kronstadt in the middle of March.

After rounding the Skawe, the Russian fleet steamed away westward into the German Ocean, and we put in here to send off our despatches. This telegram has, of course, been officially revised, and my information, as far as it goes, can therefore be relied upon.

CHAPTER XXVI.

AN INTERLUDE.

AT noon on the 26th, as the tropical sun was pouring down its vertical rays upon the lovely valley of Aeria, the *Ithuriel* crossed the Ridge which divided it from the outer world, and came to rest on the level stretch of sward on the northern shore of the lake.

Before she touched the earth Arnold glanced rapidly round and discovered his aërial fleet resting under a series of large palm-thatched sheds which had already been erected to protect them from the burning sun, and the rare but violent tropical rain-storms. He counted them. There were only eleven, and therefore the evil tidings that they had heard from the captain of the *Andromeda* was true.

Even before greetings were exchanged with the colonists Natas ordered Nicholas Roburoff to be summoned on board alone. He received him in the lower saloon, on either side of which, as he went in, he found a member of the crew armed with a magazine rifle and fixed bayonet.

Seated at the cabin table were Natas, Tremayne, and Arnold. The President was received in cold and ominous silence, not even a glance of recognition was vouchsafed to him. He stood at the other end of the table with bowed head, a prisoner before his judges. Natas looked at him for some moments in dead silence, and there was a dark gleam of anger in his eyes which made Arnold tremble for the man whose life hung upon a word of a judge from whose sentence there could be no appeal.

At length Natas spoke; his voice was hard and even; there were no modulations in it that displayed the slightest feeling, whether of anger or any other emotion. It was like the voice of an impassive machine speaking the very words of Fate itself.

"You know why we have returned, and why you have been sent for?"

"Yes, Master."

Roburoff's voice was low and respectful, but there was no quaver of fear in it.

"You were left here in command of the settlement and in charge of the fleet. You were ordered to permit no vessel to leave the valley till the flagship returned. One of them was seen crossing the Mediterranean in a northerly direction three days ago. Either you are a traitor, or that vessel is in the hands of traitors. Explain."

Nicholas Roburoff remained silent for a few moments. His breast heaved once or twice convulsively, as though he were striving hard to repress some violent emotion. Then he drew himself up like a soldier coming to attention, and, looking straight in front of him, told his story briefly and calmly, though he knew that, according to the laws of the Order, its sequel might, and probably would, be his own death.

"The night of the day on which the flagship left the valley was visited by a violent storm, which raged for about four hours without cessation. We had no proper shelter but the air-ships, and so I distributed the company among them.

"When nearly all had been provided for, there was one vessel left unoccupied, and four of the unmarried men had not been accommodated. They therefore took their places in the spare vessel. They were Peter Tamboff, Amos Vornjeh, Ivan Tscheszco, and Paul Oreloff, all Russians.

"We closed the hatches of the vessels, and remained inside till the storm ceased. When we were able to open the hatches again, it was pitch dark—so dark that it was impossible to see even a yard from one's face. Suspecting no evil, we retired to rest again till sunrise. When day dawned it was found that the vessel in which the four men I have named had taken shelter had disappeared.

"I at once ordered three vessels to rise and pass through the defile. On the outside we separated and made the entire circuit of Aeria, rising as high as the fan-wheels would take us, and examining the horizon in all directions for the missing vessel.

"We failed to discover her, and were forced to the conclusion that the deserters had taken her away early in the night at full speed, and would, therefore, be far beyond the possibility of capture, as we possessed no faster vessel than the missing one. So we returned. That is all."

"Go to the forward cabin and remain there till you're sent for," said Natas.

The President instantly turned and walked mechanically through the door that was opened for him by one of the sentinels. The other went in front of him, the second behind, closing the door as he left the saloon.

A brief discussion took place between Natas and his two lieutenants, and within a quarter of an hour Nicholas Roburoff was again standing at the end of the table to hear the decision of his judges. Without any preamble it was delivered by Natas in these words—

"We have heard your story, and believe it. You have been guilty of a serious mistake, for these four men were all ordinary members of the Outer Circle, who had only been brought here on account of their mechanical skill to occupy subordinate positions. You therefore committed a grave error, amounting almost to a breach of the rule which states that no members of the Outer Circle shall be entrusted with any charge, or work, save under the supervision of a member of the Inner Circle responsible for them.

"Had such a breach been even technically committed your life would have been forfeited, and you would have been executed for breach of trust. We have considered the circumstances, and find you guilty of indiscretion and want of forethought.

"You will cease from now to be President of the Inner Circle. Your place will be taken for the time by Alan Tremayne as Chief of the Executive. You will cease also to share the Councils of the Order for a space of twelve months, during which time you will be incapable of any responsible charge or authority. Your restoration will, of course, depend upon your behaviour. I have said."

As he finished speaking Natas waved his hand towards the

door. It was opened, the sentries stepped aside, and Nicholas Roburoff walked out in silence, with bowed head and a heart heavy with shame. The penalty was really the most severe that could be inflicted on him, for he found himself suddenly deprived both of authority and the confidence of his chiefs at the very hour when the work of the Brotherhood was culminating to its fruition.

Yet, heavy as the punishment seemed in comparison with the fault, it was justified by the necessities of the case. Without the strictest safeguards, not only against treachery or disobedience, but even mere carelessness, it would have been impossible to have carried on the tremendous work which the Brotherhood had silently and secretly accomplished, and which was soon to produce results as momentous as they would be unexpected. No one knew this better than the late President himself, who frankly acknowledged the justice and the necessity of his punishment, and prepared to devote himself heart and soul to regaining his lost credit in the eyes of the Master.

No sooner was the sentence pronounced than the matter was instantly dismissed and never alluded to again, so far as Roburoff was concerned, by any one. No one presumed even to comment upon a word or deed of the Master. The disgraced President fell naturally, and apparently without observation, into his humbler sphere of duties, and the members of the colony treated him with exactly the same friendliness and fraternity as they had done before. Natas had decided, and there was nothing more for any one to say or do in the matter.

Arnold, as soon as he had exchanged greetings with the Princess, now known simply as Anna Ornovski, and his other friends and acquaintances in the colony, not, of course, forgetting Louis Holt, at once shut himself up in his laboratory by the turbine, and for the next four hours remained invisible, preparing a large supply of his motor gases, and pumping them into the exhausted cylinders of the *Ithuriel*, and all the others that were available, by means of his hydraulic machinery.

Soon after four he had finished his task, and come out to take his part in a ceremony of a very different character to that at which he had been obliged to assist earlier in the day. This was the fulfilment of the promise which Radna Michaelis had made to Colston in the Council-chamber of the house on Clapham Common on the evening of his departure on the expedition which had so brilliantly proved the powers of the *Ariel*, and brought such confusion on the enemies of the Brotherhood.

Almost the first words that Colston had said to Radna when he boarded the *Avondale* were—

"Natasha is yonder, safe and sound, and you are mine at last!"

And she had replied very quietly, yet with a thrill in her voice that told her lover how gladly she accepted her own condition—

"What you have fairly won is yours to take when you will have it. Besides, you cannot do justice on Kastovitch now, for it has already been done. We had news before we left England that he had been shot through the heart by the brother of a girl whom he treated worse than he treated me."

But, as has been stated before, the laws of the Brotherhood did not permit of the marriage of any of its members without the direct sanction of Natas, and therefore it had been necessary to wait until now.

As Radna and Colston were two of the most trusted and prominent members of the Inner Circle, it was fitting that their wedding should be honoured by the presence of the Master in person. An added solemnity was also given to it by the fact that, in all human probability, it was the first time since the world began that the mighty hills which looked down upon Aeria had witnessed the plighting of the troth of a man and a woman.

Like all other formal acts of the Brotherhood, the ceremony was simple in the extreme; but, in this case at least, it was none the less impressive on that account. In a lovely glade, through which a crystal stream ran laughing on its way to the lake, Natas sat under the shade of a spreading tree-fern. In front of him was a small table covered with a white cloth, on which lay a roll of parchment and a copy of the Hebrew Scriptures.

At this table, facing Natas, stood the betrothed pair with their witnesses, Natasha for Radna, and Arnold for Colston, or Alexis Mazanoff, to give him his true name, which must, of course, be used on such an occasion. In a wide semicircle some four yards off stood all the members of the little community, Louis Holt and his faithful servitor not excepted.

In the midst of a silence broken only by the whispering of the warm, scented wind in the tree-tops, the Master of the Terror spoke in a kindly yet solemn tone—

"Alexis Mazanoff and Radna Michaelis, you stand here before Heaven, and in the presence of your comrades, to take each other for wedded wife and husband, till death shall part the hands that now are joined!

"Your mutual vows have long ago been pledged, and what you are about to do is good earnest of their fulfilment. But above the duty that you owe to each other stands your duty to that great Cause to which you have already irrevocably devoted your lives. You have already sworn that as long as you shall live its ends shall be your ends, and that no human considerations shall weigh with you where those ends are concerned. Do you take each other for husband and wife subject to that condition and all that it implies?"

"We do!" replied the lovers with one voice, and then Natas went on—

"Then by the laws of our Order, the only laws that we are permitted to obey, I pronounce you man and wife before Heaven and this company. Be faithful to each other and the Cause in the days to come as you have been in the days that are past, and if it shall please the Master of Destiny that you shall be blessed with children, see to it that you train them up in the love of truth, freedom, and justice, and in the hatred of tyranny and wrong.

"May the blessings of life be yours as you shall deserve them, and when the appointed hour shall come, may you be found ready to pass from the mystery of the things that are into the deeper mystery of the things that are to be!"

So saying, the Master raised his hands as though in blessing, and as Alexis and Radna bent their heads the slanting sunrays fell upon the thickly coiled white hair of the new-made wife, crowning her shapely head like a diadem of silver.

All that remained to do now was to sign the Marriage Roll

of the Brotherhood, and when they had done this the entry stood as follows:—

"Married on the tenth day of the Month Tamuz, in the Year of the World five thousand six hundred and sixty-four, in the presence of me, Natas, and those of the Brotherhood now resident in the Colony of Aeria:—

{ALEXIS MAZANOFF,
{RADNA MICHAELIS MAZANOFF.

Witnesses {RICHARD ARNOLD,
{NATASHA.

As Natasha laid down the pen after signing she looked up quickly, as though moved by some sudden impulse, her eyes met Arnold's, and an instant later the happy flush on Radna's cheek was rivalled by that which rose to her own. Her lips half parted in a smile, and then she turned suddenly away to be the first to offer her congratulations to the newly-wedded wife, while Arnold, his heart beating as it had never done since the model of the *Ariel* first rose from the floor of his room in the Southwark tenement-house, grasped Mazanoff by the hand and said simply—

"God bless you both, old man!"

The whole ceremony had not taken more than fifteen minutes from beginning to end. After Arnold came Tremayne with his good wishes, and then Anna Ornovski and the rest of the friends and comrades of the newly-wedded lovers.

One usually conspicuous feature in similar ceremonies was entirely wanting. There were no wedding presents. For this there was a very sufficient reason. All the property of the members of the Inner Circle, saving only articles of personal necessity, were held in common. Articles of mere convenience or luxury were looked upon with indifference, if not with absolute contempt, and so no one had anything to give.

After all, this was not a very serious matter for a company of men and women who held in their hands the power of levying indemnities to any amount upon the wealth-centres of the world under pain of immediate destruction.

That evening the supper of the colonists took the shape of

a sylvan marriage feast, eaten in the open air under the palms and tree ferns, as the sun was sinking down behind the western peaks of Aeria, and the full moon was rising over those to the eastward.

The whole earth might have been searched in vain for a happier company of men and women than that which sat down to the marriage feast of Radna Michaelis and Alexis Mazanoff in the virgin groves of Aeria. For the time being the world-war and all its horrors were forgotten, and they allowed their thoughts to turn without restraint to the promise of the days when the work of the Brotherhood should be accomplished, and there should be peace on earth at last.

It had been decided that three of the air-ships would be sufficient for the chase and capture or destruction, as the case might be, of the deserters. These were the *Ithuriel*, under the command of Arnold; the *Ariel*, commanded by Mazanoff, who, of course, did not sail alone; and the *Orion*, in charge of Tremayne, who had already mastered the details of aërial navigation under Arnold's tuition.

To the unspeakable satisfaction of the latter, Natas had signified his intention of accompanying him in the *Ithuriel*. As Natasha utterly refused to be parted so soon from her father again, one of his attendants was dispensed with and she took his place. This fact had, of course, something to do with the Admiral's satisfaction with the arrangement.

By nine o'clock the moon was high in the heavens. At that hour the fan-wheels of the little squadron rose from the decks, and at a signal from Arnold began to revolve. The three vessels ascended quietly into the air amidst the cheers and farewells of the colonists, and in single file passed slowly down the beautiful valley bathed in the brilliant moonlight. One by one they disappeared through the defile that led to the outer world, and, once clear of the mountains, the *Ithuriel*, with one of her consorts on either side, headed away due north at the speed of a hundred miles an hour.

CHAPTER XXVII.

ON THE TRACK OF TREASON.

THE *Ithuriel* and her consorts crossed the northern coast of Africa soon after daybreak on the 27th, in the longitude of Alexandria, at an elevation of nearly 4000 feet. From thence they pursued almost the same course as that steered by the deserters, as Natas had rightly judged that they would first make for Russia, probably St. Petersburg, and there hand the air-ship over to the representatives of the Tsar.

There was, of course, another alternative, and that was the supposition that they had stolen the *Lucifer*—the "fallen Angel," as Natasha had now re-named her—for purposes of piracy and private revenge; but that was negatived by the fact that Tamboff knew that he only had a certain supply of motive power which he could not renew, and which, once exhausted, left his air-ship as useless as a steamer without coal. His only reasonable course, therefore, would be to sell the vessel to the Tsar, and leave his Majesty's chemists to discover and renew the motive power if they could.

These conclusions once arrived at, it was an easy matter for the keen and subtle intellect of Natas to deduce from them almost the exact sequence of events that had actually taken place. The *Lucifer* had a sufficient supply of power-cylinders and shells for present use, and these would doubtless be employed at once by the Tsar, who would trust to his chemists and engineers to discover the nature of the agents employed.

For this purpose it would be absolutely necessary for him to give them one or two of the shells, and at least two of the spare power-cylinders as subjects for their experiments.

Now Natas knew that if there was one man in Russia who could discover the composition of the explosives, that man was Professor Volnow of the Imperial Arsenal Laboratory, and therefore the shells and cylinders would be sent to him at the Arsenal for examination. The whereabouts of the deserters for the present mattered nothing in comparison with the possible discovery of the secret on which the whole power of the Terrorists depended.

That once revealed, the sole empire of the air was theirs no longer. The Tsar, with millions of money at his command, could very soon build an aërial fleet, not only equal, but, numerically at least, vastly superior to their own, and this would practically give him the command of the world.

Natas therefore came to the conclusion that no measures could be too extreme to be justified by such a danger as this, and so, after a consultation with the commanders of the three vessels, it was decided to, if necessary, destroy the Arsenal at St. Petersburg, on the strength of the reasoning that had led to the logical conclusion that within its precincts the priceless secret either might be or had already been discovered.

As the crow flies, St. Petersburg is thirty degrees of latitude, or eighteen hundred geographical miles, north of Alexandria, and this distance the *Ithuriel* and her consorts, flying at a speed of a hundred and twenty miles an hour, traversed in fifteen hours, reaching the Russian capital a few minutes after seven on the evening of the 27th.

The Rome of the North, basking in the soft evening sunlight of the incomparable Russian summer, lay vast and white and beautiful on the islands formed by the Neva and its ten tributaries; its innumerable palaces, churches, and theatres, and long straight streets of stately houses, its parks and gardens, and its green shady suburbs, making up a picture which forced an exclamation of wonder from Arnold's lips as the air-ships slowed down and he left the conning-tower of the *Ithuriel* to admire the magnificent view from the bows. They passed over the city at a height of four thousand feet, and so were quite near enough to see and enjoy the excitement and consternation which their sudden appearance instantly caused among the inhabitants. The streets and squares filled in an inconceivably short space of time with crowds of people, who ran about like tiny ants upon the ground, gesticulating and pointing upwards, evidently in terror lest the fate of Kronstadt was about to fall upon St. Petersburg.

The experimental department of the Arsenal had within the last two or three years been rebuilt on a large space of waste ground outside the northern suburbs, and to this the three air-ships directed their course after passing over the city. It was a massive three-storey building, built in the form of a quadrangle. The three air-ships stopped within a mile of it at an elevation of two thousand feet. It had been decided that, before proceeding to extremities, which, after all, might still leave them in doubt as to whether or not they had really destroyed all means of analysing the explosives, they should make an effort to discover whether Professor Volnow had received them for experiment, and, if so, what success he had had.

Mazanoff had undertaken this delicate and dangerous task, and so, as soon as the *Ithuriel* and the *Orion* came to a standstill, and hung motionless in the air, with all their guns ready trained on different parts of the building, the *Ariel* sank suddenly and swiftly down, and stopped within forty feet of the heads of a crowd of soldiers and mechanics, who had rushed pell-mell out of the building, under the impression that it was about to be destroyed.

The bold manœuvre of the *Ariel* took officers and men completely by surprise. So intense was the terror in which these mysterious air-ships were held, and so absolute was the belief that they were armed with perfectly irresistible means of destruction, that the sight of one of them at such close quarters paralysed all thought and action for the time being. The first shock over, the majority of the crowd took to their heels and fled incontinently. Of the remainder a few of the bolder spirits handled their rifles and looked inquiringly at their officers. Mazanoff saw this, and at once raised his hand towards the sky and shouted—

"Ground arms! If a shot is fired the Arsenal will be destroyed as Kronstadt was, and then we shall attack Petersburg."

The threat was sufficient. A grey-haired officer in undress uniform glanced up at the *Ithuriel* and her consort, and then at the guns of the *Ariel*, all four of which had been swung round and brought to bear on the side of the building near which she had descended. He was no coward, but he saw that Mazanoff had the power to do what he said, and that even if this one air-ship were captured or destroyed, the other two would take a frightful vengeance. He thought of Kronstadt, and decided to parley. The rifle butts had come to the ground before Mazanoff had done speaking.

"Order arms, and keep silence!" said the officer, and then he advanced alone from the crowd and said—

"Who are you, and what is your errand?"

"Alexis Mazanoff, late prisoner of the Tsar, and now commander of the Terrorist air-ship *Ariel*. I have not come to destroy you unless you force me to do so, but to ask certain questions, and demand the giving up of certain property delivered into your hands by deserters and traitors."

"What are your questions?"

"First, is Professor Volnow in the building?"

"He is."

"Then I must ask you to send for him at once."

It went sorely against the grain of the servant of the Tsar to acquiesce in the demand of an outlaw, but there was nothing else for it. The outlaw could blow him and all his subordinates into space with a pressure of his finger; and so he sent an orderly with a request for the presence of the professor. Meanwhile Mazanoff continued—

"An air-ship similar to this arrived here three days ago, I believe?"

The officer bit his lips with rage at his helpless position, and bowed affirmatively.

"And certain articles were taken out of her for examination here—two gas cylinders and a projectile, I believe?"

Again the officer bowed, wondering how on earth the Terrorist could have come by such accurate information.

"And the air-ship has been sent on to the seat of war, while the Professor is trying to discover the composition of the gases and the explosive used in the shell?" went on Mazanoff, risking a last shot at the truth.

The officer did not bow this time. Giving way at last to his rising fury, he stamped on the ground and almost screamed—

"Great God! you insolent scoundrel! Why do you ask me questions when you know the answers as well as I do, and better? Yes, we have got one of your diabolical ships of the air, and we will build a fleet like it and hunt you from the world!"

"All in good time, my dear sir," replied Mazanoff ironically. "When you have found a place in which to build them that we cannot blow off the face of the earth before you get one finished. Meanwhile, let me beg of you to keep your temper, and to remember that there is a lady present. That girl standing yonder by the gun was once stripped and flogged by Russians calling themselves men and soldiers. Her fingers are itching to make the movement that would annihilate you and every one standing near you, so pray try keep your temper; for if we fire a shot the air-ships up yonder will at once open fire, and not stop while there is a stone of that building left upon another. Ah! here comes the Professor."

As he spoke the man of science advanced, looking wonderingly at the air-ship. Mazanoff made a sign to the old officer to keep silence, and continued in the same polite tone that he had used all along—

"Good evening, Professor! I have come to ask you whether you have yet made any experiments on the contents of the shell and the two cylinders that were given to you for examination?"

"I must first ask for your authority to put such an inquiry to me on a confidential subject," replied the Professor stiffly.

"On the authority given me by the power to enforce an answer, sir," returned the Terrorist quietly. "I know that Professor Volnow will not lie to me, even at the order of the Tsar, and when I tell you that your refusal to reply will cost the lives of every one here, and possibly involve the destruction of Petersburg itself, I feel sure that, as a mere matter of humanity, you will comply with my request."

"Sir, the orders of my master are absolute secrecy on this subject, and I will obey them to the death. I have analysed the contents of one of the cylinders, but what they are I will tell to no one save by the direct command of his Majesty. That is all I have done."

"Then in that case, Professor, I must ask you to surrender

yourself prisoner of war, and to come on board this vessel at once."

As Mazanoff said this the *Ariel* dropped to within ten feet of the ground, and a rope-ladder fell over the side.

"Come, Professor, there is no time to be lost. I shall give the order to fire in one minute from now."

He took out his watch, and began to count the seconds. Ten, twenty, thirty passed and the Professor stood irresolute. Two of the *Ariel's* guns pointed at the gables of the Arsenal, and two swept the crowded space in front.

Konstantin Volnow knew enough to see clearly the frightful slaughter and destruction that twenty seconds more would bring if he refused to give himself up. As Mazanoff counted "forty" he threw up his hands with a gesture of despair, and cried—

"Stop! I will come. The Tsar has as good servants as I am! Colonel, tell his Majesty that I gave myself up to save the lives of better men."

Then the Professor mounted the ladder amidst a murmur of relief and applause from the crowd, and, gaining the deck of the *Ariel*, bowed coldly to Mazanoff and said—

"I am your prisoner, sir!"

The captain of the *Ariel* bowed in reply, and stamped thrice on the deck. The fan-wheels whirled round, and the air-ship rapidly ascended, at the same time moving diagonally across the quadrangle of the Arsenal.

Scarcely had she reached the other side when there was a tremendous explosion in the north-eastern angle of the building. A sheet of flame shot up through the roof, the walls split asunder, and masses of stone, wood, and iron went flying in all directions, leaving only a fiercely burning mass of ruins where the gable had been.

The Professor turned ashy pale, staggered backwards with both his hands clasped to his head, and gasped out brokenly as he stared at the conflagration—

"God have mercy on me! My laboratory! My assistant— I told him"—

"What did you tell him, Professor?" said Mazanoff sternly, grasping him suddenly by the arm.

"I told him not to open the other cylinder."

"And he has done so, and paid for his disobedience with his life," said Mazanoff calmly. "Console yourself, my dear sir! He has only saved me the trouble of destroying your laboratory. I serve a sterner and more powerful master than yours. He ordered me to make your experiments impossible if it cost a thousand lives to do so, and I would have done it if necessary. Rest content with the knowledge that you have saved, not only the rest of the Arsenal, but also Petersburg, by your surrender; for sooner than that secret had been revealed, we should have laid the city in ruins to slay the man who had discovered it."

The prisoner of the Terrorists made no reply, but turned away in silence to watch the rapidly receding building, in the angle of which the flames were still raging furiously. A few minutes later the *Ariel* had rejoined her consorts. Her captain at once went on board the flagship to make his report and deliver up his prisoner to Natas, who looked sharply at him and said—

"Professor, will you give me your word of honour to attempt no communication with the earth while it may be found necessary to detain you? If not, I shall be compelled to keep you in strict confinement till it is beyond your power to do so."

"Sir, I give you my word that I will not do so," said the Professor, who had now somewhat regained his composure.

"Very well," replied Natas. "Then on that condition you will be made free of the vessel, and we will make you as comfortable as we can. Captain Arnold, full speed to the south-westward, if you please."

CHAPTER XXVIII.

A SKIRMISH IN THE CLOUDS.

A FEW minutes after two on the following morning, that is to say on the 28th, the electric signal leading from the conning-tower of the *Ithuriel* to the wall of Arnold's cabin, just above his berth, sounded. As it was only permitted to be used on occasions of urgency, he knew that his presence was immediately required forward for some good reason, and so he turned out at once, threw a dressing-gown over his sleeping suit, and within three minutes was standing in the conning-tower beside Andrew Smith, whose watch it then happened to be.

"Well, Smith, what's the matter?"

"Fleet of war-balloons coming up from the south'ard, sir. You can just see 'em, sir, coming on in line under that long bank of cloud."

The captain of the *Ithuriel* took the night-glasses, and looked eagerly in the direction pointed out by his keen-eyed coxswain. As soon as he picked them up he had no difficulty in making out twelve small dark spots in line at regular intervals sharply defined against a band of light that lay between the earth and a long dark bank of clouds.

It was a division of the Tsar's aërial fleet, returning from some work of death and destruction in the south to rejoin the main force before Berlin. Arnold's course was decided on in an instant. He saw a chance of turning the tables on his Majesty in a fashion that he would find as unpleasant as it would be unexpected. He turned to his coxswain and said—

"How is the wind, Smith?"

"Nor'-nor'-west, with perhaps half a point more north in it, sir. About a ten-knot breeze—at least that's the drift that Mr. Marston's allowing for."

"Yes, that's near enough. Then those fellows, if they are going full speed, are coming up at about twenty miles an hour, or not quite that. They're nearly twenty miles off, as nearly as I can judge in this light. What do you make it?"

"That's about it, sir; rather less than more, if anything, to my mind."

"Very well, then. Now signal to stop, and send up the fan-wheels; and tell the *Ariel* and the *Orion* to close up and speak."

"Ay, ay, sir," said the coxswain, as he saluted and disappeared. Arnold at once went back to his cabin and dressed, telling his second officer, Frank Marston, a young Englishman, whom he had chosen to take Mazanoff's place, to do the same as quietly as possible, as he did not wish to awaken any of his three passengers just at present.

By the time he got on deck the three air-ships had slowed down considerably, and the two consorts of the *Ithuriel* were within easy speaking distance. Mazanoff and Tremayne were both on deck, and to them he explained his plans as follows—

"There are a dozen of the Tsar's war-balloons coming up yonder to the southward, and I am going to head them off and capture the lot if I can. If we can do that, we can make what terms we like for the surrender of the *Lucifer*.

"You two take your ships and get to windward of them as fast as you can. Keep a little higher than they are, but not much. On no account let one of them get above you. If they try to descend, give each one that does so a No. 1 shell, and blow her up. If one tries to pass you, ram her in the upper part of the gas-holder, and let her down with a smash.

"I am going up above them to prevent any of them from rising too far. They can outfly us in that one direction, so I shall blow any that attempt it into little pieces. If you have to fire on any of them, don't use more than No. 1; you'll find that more than enough.

"Keep an eye on me for signals, and remember that the whole fleet must be destroyed rather than one allowed to escape. I want to give the Tsar a nice little surprise. He

seems to be getting a good deal too cock-sure about these old gas-bags of his, and it's time to give him a lesson in real aërial warfare."

There was not a great newspaper in the world that would not have given a very long price to have had the privilege of putting a special correspondent on the deck of the *Ithuriel* for the two hours which followed the giving of Arnold's directions to his brother commanders of the little squadron. The journal which could have published an exclusive account of the first aërial skirmish in the history of the world would have scored a triumph which would have left its competitors a long way behind in the struggle to be "up to date."

As soon as Arnold had given his orders, the three air-ships at once separated. The *Ariel* and the *Orion* shot away to the southward on only a slightly upward course, while the *Ithuriel* soared up beyond the stratum of clouds which lay in thin broken masses rather more than four thousand feet above the earth.

It was still rather more than an hour before sunrise, and, as the moon had gone down, and the clouds intercepted most of the starlight, it was just "the darkest hour before the dawn," and therefore the most favourable for the carrying out of the plan that Arnold had in view.

Shortly after half-past two he knocked at Natasha's cabin-door, and said—

"If you would like to see an aërial battle, get up and come into the conning-tower at once. We have overtaken a squadron of Russian war-balloons, and we are going either to capture or destroy them."

"Glorious!" exclaimed Natasha, wide awake in an instant at such startling news. "I'll be with you in five minutes. Tell my father, and please don't begin till I come."

"I shouldn't think of opening the ball without your ladyship's presence," laughed Arnold in reply, and then he went and called Natas and his attendant and the Professor before going to the conning-tower, where in a very few minutes he was joined by Natasha. The first words she said were—

"I have told Ivan to send us some coffee as soon as he has attended to my father. You see how thoughtful I am for your creature comforts. Now, where are the war-balloons?"

"Come now, and fire the first shot in the warfare of the future."

See page 211.

"On the other side of those clouds. There, look down through that big rift, and you will see one of them."

"Why, what a height we must be from the earth! The balloon looks like a little toy thing, but it must be a great clumsy contrivance for all that."

"The barometer gives five thousand three hundred feet. You will soon see why I have come up so high. The balloons can rise to fifteen or twenty thousand feet, if they wish to, and in that way they could easily escape us; therefore, if one of them attempts to rise through those clouds, I shall send him back to earth in little bits."

"And what are the other two air-ships doing?"

"They are below the clouds, heading the balloons off from the Russian camp, which is about fifty miles to the north-westward. Ha! look, there go the searchlights!"

As he spoke, two long converging beams of light darted across a broad space of sky that was free from cloud. They came from the *Ariel* and the *Orion*, which thus suddenly revealed themselves to the astonished and disgusted Russians, one at each end of their long line, and only a little more than half a mile ahead of it.

The searchlights flashed to and fro along the line, plainly showing the great masses of the aerostats' gas-holders, with their long slender cars beneath them. A blue light was burnt on the largest of the war-balloons, and at once the whole flotilla began to ascend towards the clouds, followed by the two air-ships.

"Here they come!" said Arnold, as he saw them rising through a cloud-rift. "Come out and watch what happens to the first one that shows herself."

He went out on deck, followed by Natasha, and took his place by one of the broadside guns. At the same time he gave the order for the *Ithuriel's* searchlight to be turned on, and to sweep the cloud-field below her. Presently a black rounded object appeared rising through the clouds like a whale coming to the surface of the sea.

He trained the gun on to it as it came distinctly into view, and said to Natasha—

"Come, now, and fire the first shot in the warfare of the future. Put your finger on the button, and press when I tell you."

Natasha did as he told her, and at the word "Fire!" pressed the little ivory button down. The shell struck the upper envelope of the balloon, passed through, and exploded. A broad sheet of flame shot up, brilliantly illuminating the sea of cloud for an instant, and all was darkness again. A few seconds later there came another blaze, and the report of a much greater explosion from below the clouds.

"What was that?" asked Natasha.

"That was the car full of explosives striking the earth and going off promiscuously," replied Arnold. "There isn't as much of that aerostat left as would make a pocket-handkerchief or a walking-stick."

"And the crew?"

"Never knew what happened to them. In the new warfare people will not be merely killed, they will be annihilated."

"Horrible!" exclaimed Natasha, with a shudder. "I think you may do the rest of the shooting. The effects of that shot will last me for some time. Look, there's another of them coming up!"

The words were hardly out of her mouth before Arnold had crossed to the other side of the deck and sped another missile on its errand of destruction with almost exactly the same result as before. This second shot, as it was afterwards found, threw the Russian squadron into complete panic.

The terrific suddenness with which the two aerostats had been destroyed convinced those in command of the others that there was a large force of air-ships above the clouds ready to destroy them one by one as they ascended. Arnold waited for a few minutes, and then, seeing that no others cared to risk the fate that had overwhelmed the first two that had sought to cross the cloud-zone, sank rapidly through it, and then stopped again.

He found himself about six hundred feet above the rest of the squadron. The *Ithuriel* coming thus suddenly into view, her eight guns pointing in all directions, and her searchlight flashing hither and thither as though seeking new victims, completed the demoralisation of the Russians. For all they knew there were still more air-ships above the clouds. Even this one could not be passed while those mysterious guns of unknown range and infallible aim were sweeping the sky, ready to hurl their silent lightnings in every direction.

Ascend they dare not. To descend was to be destroyed in detail as they lay helpless upon the earth. There was only one chance of escape, and that was to scatter. The commander of the squadron at once signalled for this to be done, and the aerostats headed away to all points of the compass. But here they had reckoned without the incomparable speed of their assailants.

Before they had moved a hundred yards from their common centre the *Ariel* and the *Orion* headed away in different directions, and in an inconceivably short space of time had described a complete circle round them, and then another and another, narrowing each circle that they made. One of the aerostats, watching its opportunity, put on full speed and tried to get outside the narrowing zone. She had almost succeeded, when the *Orion* swerved outwards and dashed at her with the ram.

In ten seconds she was overtaken. The keen steel prow of the air-ship, driven at more than a hundred miles an hour, ripped her gas-holder from end to end as if it had been tissue paper. It collapsed like broken bubble, and the wreck, with its five occupants and its load of explosives, dropped like a stone to the earth, three thousand feet below, exploding like one huge shell as it struck.

This was the last blow struck in the first aërial battle in the history of warfare. The Russians had no stomach for this kind of fighting. It was all very well to sail over armies and fortresses on the earth and drop shells upon them without danger of retaliation; but this was an entirely different matter.

Three of the aerostats had been destroyed in little more than as many minutes, so utterly destroyed that not a vestige of them remained, and the whole squadron had not been able to strike a blow in self-defence. They carried no guns, not even small arms, for they had no use for them in the work that they had to do. There were only two alternatives before them—surrender or piecemeal destruction.

As soon as she had destroyed the third aerostat, the *Orion* swerved round again, and began flying round the squadron as before in an opposite direction to the *Ariel*. None of the aerostats made an attempt to break the strange blockage again. As the circles narrowed they crowded closer and closer together, like a flock of sheep surrounded by wolves.

Meanwhile the *Ithuriel*, floating above the centre of the disordered squadron, descended slowly until she hung a hundred feet above the highest of them. Then Arnold with his searchlight flashed a signal to the *Ariel* which at once slowed down, the *Orion* continuing on her circular course as before.

As soon as the *Ariel* was going slowly enough for him to make himself heard, Mazanoff shouted through a speaking-trumpet—

"Will you surrender, or fight it out?"

"*Nu vot!* how can we fight with those devil-ships of yours? What is your pleasure?"

The answering hail came from one of the aerostats in the centre of the squadron. Mazanoff at once replied—

"Unconditional surrender for the present, under guarantee of safety to every one who surrenders. Who are you?"

"Colonel Alexei Alexandrovitch, in command of the squadron. I surrender on those terms. Who are you?"

"The captain of the Terrorist air-ship *Ariel*. Be good enough to come out here, Colonel Alexei Alexandrovitch."

One of the aerostats moved out of the midst of the Russian squadron and made its way towards the *Ariel*. As she approached Mazanoff swung his bow round and brought it level with the car of the aerostat, at the same time training one of his guns full on it. Then, with his arm resting on the breach of the gun, he said,—

"Come on board, Colonel, and bid your balloon follow me. No nonsense, mind, or I'll blow you into eternity and all your squadron after you."

The Russian did as he was bidden, and the *Ariel*, followed by the aerostat, ascended to the *Ithuriel*, while the *Orion* kept up her patrol round the captive war-balloons.

"Colonel Alexandrovitch, in command of the Tsar's aërial squadron, surrenders unconditionally, save for guarantee of personal safety to himself and his men," reported Mazanoff, as he came within earshot of the flagship.

"Very good," replied Arnold from the deck of the *Ithuriel*.

You will keep Colonel Alexandrovitch as hostage for the good behaviour of the rest, and shoot him the moment one of the balloons attempts to escape. After that destroy the rest without mercy. They will form in line close together. The *Ariel* and the *Orion* will convoy them on either flank, and you will follow me until you have the signal to stop. On the first suspicion of any attempt to escape you will know what to do. You have both handled your ships splendidly."

Mazanoff saluted formally, more for the sake of effect than anything else, and descended again to carry out his orders. The captured flotilla was formed in line, the balloons being closed up until there was only a couple of yards or so between any of them and her next neighbour, with the *Orion* and the *Ariel* to right and left, each with two guns trained on them, and the *Ithuriel* flying a couple of hundred feet above them. In this order captors and captured made their way at twenty miles an hour to the north-west towards the headquarters of the Tsar.

CHAPTER XXIX.

AN EMBASSY FROM THE SKY.

Y the time the captured war-balloons had been formed in order, and the voyage fairly commenced, the eastern sky was bright with the foreglow of the coming dawn, and, as the flotilla was only floating between eight and nine hundred feet above the earth, it was not long before the light was sufficiently strong to render the landscape completely visible.

Far and wide it was a scene of desolation and destruction, of wasted, blackened fields trampled into wildernesses by the tread of countless feet, of forests of trees broken, scorched, and splintered by the iron hail of artillery, and of towns and villages, reduced to heaps of ruins, still smouldering with the fires that had destroyed them.

No more eloquent object-lesson in the horrors of what is called civilised warfare could well have been found than the scene which was visible from the decks of the air-ships. The promised fruits of a whole year of patient industry had been withered in a few hours under the storm-blast of war; homes which but a few days before had sheltered stalwart, well-fed peasants and citizens, were now mere heaps of blackened brick and stone and smoking thatches.

Streets which had been the thoroughfares of peaceful industrious folk, who had no quarrel with the Powers of the earth, or with any of their kind, were now strewn with corpses and encumbered with ruins, and the few survivors, more miserable than those who had died, were crawling, haggard and starving, amidst the wrecks of their vanished prosperity, seeking for some scanty morsels of food to prolong life if only for a few more days of misery and nights of sleepless anxiety.

As the sun rose and shed its midsummer splendour, as if in sublime mockery, over the scene of suffering and desolation, hideous features of the landscape were brought into stronger and more horrifying relief; the scorched and trampled fields were seen to be strewn with unburied corpses of men and horses, and ploughed up with cannon shot and torn into great irregular gashes by shells that had buried themselves in the earth and then exploded.

It was evident that some frightful tragedy must have taken place in this region not many hours before the air-ships had arrived upon the scene. And this, in fact, had been the case. Barely three days previously the advance guard of the Russian army of the North had been met and stubbornly but unsuccessfully opposed by the remnants of the German army of the East, which, driven back from the frontier, was retreating in good order to join the main force which had concentrated about Berlin, under the command of the Emperor, there to fight out the supreme struggle, on the issue of which depended the existence of that German Empire which fifty years before had been so triumphantly built up by the master-geniuses of the last generation.

After a flight of a little over two hours the flotilla came in sight of the Russian army lying between Cüstrin on the right and Frankfort-on-Spree on the left. The distance between these two towns is nearly twelve English miles, and yet the wings of the vast host under the command of the Tsar spread for a couple of miles on either side to north and south of each of them.

In spite of the colossal iniquity which it concealed, the spectacle was one of indescribable grandeur. Almost as far as the eye could reach the beams of the early morning sun were gleaming upon innumerable white tents, and flashing over a sea of glittering metal, of bare bayonets and sword scabbards, of spear points and helmets, of gold-laced uniforms and the polished accoutrements of countless batteries of field artillery.

Far away to the westward the stately city of Berlin could be seen lying upon its intersecting waters, and encircled by its fortifications bristling with guns, and in advance of it were the long serried lines of its defenders gathered to do desperate battle for home and fatherland.

As soon as the Russian army was fairly in sight the *Ithuriel* shot ahead, sank to the level of the flotilla, and then stopped until she was overtaken by the *Orion*. Tremayne was on deck, and Arnold as soon as he came alongside said—

"You must stop here for the present. I want the aerostat commanded by Colonel Alexandrovitch to come with me; meanwhile you and the *Ariel* will rise with the rest of the balloons to a height of four thousand feet; you will keep strict guard over the balloons, and permit no movement to be made until my return. We are going to bring his Majesty the Tsar to book, or else make things pretty lively for him if he won't listen to reason."

"Very well," replied Tremayne. "I will do as you say, and await developments with considerable interest. If there is going to be a fight, I hope you're not going to leave us out in the cold."

"Oh no," replied Arnold. "You needn't be afraid of that. If his Majesty won't come to terms, you will smash up the war-balloons and then come and join us in the general bombardment. I see, by the way, that there are ten or a dozen more of these unwieldy monsters with the Russian force moored to the ground yonder on the outskirts of Cüstrin. It will be a little amusement for us if we have to come to blows to knock them to pieces before we smash up the Tsar's headquarters.

So saying, Arnold increased the speed of the *Ithuriel*, swept round in front of the line, and communicated the same instructions to the captain of the *Ariel*.

A few minutes later the *Ariel* and the *Orion* began to rise with their charges to the higher regions of the air, leaving the *Ithuriel* and the one aerostat to carry out the plan which had been arranged by Natas and Arnold an hour previously.

As the speed of the aerostat was only about twenty miles an hour against the wind, a rope was passed from the stern of the *Ithuriel* to the cordage connecting the car with the gas-holder, and so the aerostat was taken in tow by the air-ship, and dragged through the air at a speed of about forty miles an hour, as a wind-bound sailing vessel might have been towed by a steamer.

On the journey the elevation was increased to more than four thousand feet,—an elevation at which both the *Ithuriel* and her captive, and especially the former, presented practically impossible marks for the Russian riflemen. Almost immediately over Cüstrin they came to a standstill, and then Colonel Alexandrovitch and Professor Volnow were summoned by Natas into the deck saloon.

He explained to them the mission which he desired them to undertake, that is to say, the conveyance of a letter from himself to the Tzar offering terms for the surrender of the *Lucifer*. They accepted the mission; and in order that they might fully understand the gravity of it, Natas read them the letter, which ran as follows:—

> ALEXANDER ROMANOFF,—
> Three days ago one of my fleet of air-ships, named the *Lucifer*, was delivered into your hands by traitors and deserters, whose lives are forfeit in virtue of the oaths which they took of their own free will. I have already taken measures to render abortive the analysis which you ordered to be performed in the chemical department of your Arsenal at St. Petersburg, and I have now come to make terms, if possible, for the restoration of the air-ship. Those terms are as follows—
> An hour before daybreak this morning I captured nine of your war-balloons, after destroying three others which attempted to escape. I have no desire to take any present part in the war which you are now carrying on with the Anglo-Teutonic Alliance, and if you will tell me where the *Lucifer* is now to be found, and will despatch orders both by land and through Professor Volnow, who brings this letter to you, and will return with your answer, for her to be given up to me forthwith with everything she has on board, and will surrender with her the four traitors who delivered her into your hands, I will restore the nine war-balloons to you intact, and when I have recovered the *Lucifer* I will take no further part in the war unless either you or your opponents proceed to unjustifiable extremities.
> If you reject these terms, or if I do not receive an answer to this letter within two hours of the time that the bearer of it descends in the aerostat, I shall give orders for the immediate destruction of the war-balloons now in my hands, and I shall then proceed to destroy Cüstrin and the other aerostats which are moored near the town. That done I shall, for the time being, devote the force at my disposal to the defence of Berlin, and do my utmost to bring about the defeat and dispersal of the army which will then no longer be commanded by yourself.
> In case you may doubt what I say as to the capture of the fleet of war-balloons, Professor Volnow will be accompanied by Colonel Alexei Alexandrovitch, late in command of the squadron, and now my prisoner of war.
> NATAS.

The ambassadors were at once transferred to the aerostat, and with a white flag hoisted on the after stays of the balloon she began to sink rapidly towards the earth, and at the same time Natas gave orders for the *Ithuriel* to ascend to a height of eight thousand feet in order to frustrate any attempts that might be made, whether with or without the orders of the Tzar, to injure her by means of a volley from the earth.

Even from that elevation, those on board the *Ithuriel* were able with the aid of their field-glasses to see with perfect ease the commotion which the appearance of the air-ship with the captured aerostat had produced in the Russian camp. The whole of the vast host, numbering more than four millions of men, turned out into the open to watch their aërial visitors, and everywhere throughout the whole extent of the huge camp the plainest signs of the utmost excitement were visible.

In less than half an hour they saw the aerostat touch the earth near to a large building, above which floated the imperial standard of Russia. An hour had been allowed for the interview and for the Tzar to give his decision, and half an hour for the aerostat to return and meet the air-ship.

In all the history of the world there had probably never been an hour so pregnant with tremendous consequences, not only to Europe, but to the whole civilised world, as that was; and though apparently a perfect calm reigned throughout the air-ship, the issue of the embassy was awaited with the most intense anxiety.

Another half hour passed, and hardly a word was spoken on the deck of the *Ithuriel*, hanging there in mid-air over the mighty Russian host, and in range of the field-glasses of the outposts of the German army of Berlin lying some ten or twelve miles away to the westward.

It was the calm before the threatening storm,—a storm which in less than an hour might break in a hail of death and destruction from the sky, and turn the fields of earth into a volcano of shot and flame. Certainly the fate of an empire, and perhaps of Europe, or indeed the world, hung in the balance over that field of possible carnage.

If the Russians regained their war-balloons and were left to themselves, nothing that the heroic Germans could do would be likely to save Berlin from the fate that had overwhelmed Strassburg and Metz, Breslau and Thorn.

On the other hand, should the aerostat not return in time with a satisfactory answer, the victorious career of the Tsar would be cut short by such a bolt from the skies as had wrecked his fortress at Kronstadt,—a blow which he could neither guard against nor return, for it would come from an unassailable vantage point, a little vessel a hundred feet long floating in the air six thousand feet from the earth, and looking a mere bright speck amidst the sunlight. She formed a mark that the most skilful rifle-shot in his army could not hit once in a thousand shots, and against whose hull of hardened aluminium, bullets, even if they struck, would simply splash and scatter, like raindrops on a rock.

The remaining minutes of the last half hour were slipping away one by one, and still no sign came from the earth. The aerostat remained moored near the building surmounted by the Russian standard, and the white flag, which, according to arrangement, had been hauled down to be re-hoisted if the answer of the Tsar was favourable, was still invisible. When only ten minutes of the allotted time were left, Arnold, moving his glass from his eyes, and looking at his watch, said to Natas—

"Ten minutes more; shall I prepare?"

"Yes," said Natas. "And let the first gun be fired with the first second of the eleventh minute. Destroy the aerostats first and then the batteries of artillery. After that send a shell into Frankfort, if you have a gun that will carry the distance, so that they may see our range of operations; but spare the Tsar's headquarters for the present."

"Very good," replied Arnold. Then, turning to his lieutenant, he said—

"You have the guns loaded with No. 3, I presume, Mr. Marston, and the projectile stands are filled, I see. Very good. Now descend to six thousand feet and go a mile to the westward. Train one broadside gun on that patch of ground where you see those balloons, another to strike in the midst of those field-guns yonder by the ammunition-waggons, and train the starboard after-gun to throw a shell into Frankfort. The distance is a little over twelve miles, so give sufficient elevation."

By the time these orders had been executed, swiftly as the necessary evolution had been performed, only four minutes of the allotted time were left. Arnold took his stand by the broadside gun trained on the aerostats, and, with one hand on the breech of the gun and the other holding his watch, he waited for the appointed moment. Natasha stood by him with her eyes fastened to the eye-pieces of the glasses watching for the white flag in breathless suspense.

"One minute more!" said Arnold.

"Stop, there it goes!" cried Natasha as the words left his lips. "His Majesty has yielded to circumstances!"

Arnold took the glasses from her, and through them saw a tiny white speck shining against the black surface of the gas-holder of the balloon. He handed the glasses back to her, saying—

"We must not be too sure of that. His message may be one of defiance."

"True," said Natasha. "We shall see."

Ten minutes later the aerostat was released from her moorings and rose swiftly and vertically into the air. As soon as it reached her own altitude the *Ithuriel* shot forward to meet it, and stopped within a couple of hundred yards, a gun ready trained upon the car in case of treachery. In the car stood Professor Volnow and Colonel Alexandrovitch. The former held something white in his hand, and across the intervening space came the reassuring hail: "All well!"

In five minutes he was standing on the deck of the *Ithuriel* presenting a folded paper to Natas. He was pale to the lips, and his whole body trembled with violent emotion. As he handed him the paper, he said to Natas in a low, husky voice that was barely recognisable as his—

"Here is the answer of the Tsar. Whether you are man or fiend, I know not, but his Majesty has yielded and accepted your terms. May I never again witness such anger as was his when I presented your letter. It was not till the last moment that he yielded to my entreaties and those of his staff, and ordered the white flag to be hoisted."

"Yes," replied Natas. "He tempted his fate to the last moment. The guns were already trained upon Cüstrin, and thirty seconds more would have seen his headquarters in ruins. He did wisely, if he acted tardily."

So saying, Natas broke the imperial seal. On a sheet of paper bearing the imperial arms were scrawled three or four lines in the Autocrat's own handwriting—

I accept your main terms. The air-ship has joined the Baltic fleet. She will be delivered to you with all on board. The four men are my subjects, and I feel bound to protect them; they will therefore not be delivered up. Do as you like.
ALEXANDER.

"A Royal answer, though it comes from a despot," said Natas as he refolded the paper. "I will waive that point, and let him protect the traitors, if he can. Colonel Alexandrovitch," he continued, turning to the Russian, who had also boarded the air-ship, "you are free. You may return to your war-balloon, and accompany us to give the order for the release of your squadron."

"Free!" suddenly screamed the Russian, his face livid and distorted with passion. "Free, yes, but disgraced! Ruined for life, and degraded to the ranks! I want no freedom from you. I will not even have my life at your hands, but I will have yours, and rid the earth of you if I die a thousand deaths!"

As he spoke he wrenched his sword from its scabbard, thrust the Professor aside, and rushed at Natas with the uplifted blade. Before it had time to descend a stream of pale flame flashed over the back of the Master's chair, accompanied by a long, sharp rattle, and the Russian's body dropped instantly to the deck riddled by a hail of bullets.

"I saw murder in that man's eyes when he began to speak," said Natasha, putting back into her pocket the magazine pistol that she had used with such terrible effect.

"I saw it too, daughter," quietly replied Natas. "But you need not have been afraid; the blow would never have reached me, for I would have paralysed him before he could have made the stroke."

"Impossible! No man could have done it!"

The exclamation burst involuntarily from the lips of Professor Volnow, who had stood by, an amazed and horrified spectator of the rapidly enacted tragedy.

"Professor," said Natas, in quick, stern tones, "I am not accustomed to say what is not true, nor yet to be contradicted by any one in human shape. Stand there till I tell you to move."

As he spoke these last words Natas made a swift, sweeping downward movement with one of his hands, and fixed his eyes upon those of the Professor. In an instant Volnow's muscles stiffened into immovable rigidity, and he stood rooted to the deck powerless to move so much as a finger.

"Captain Arnold," continued Natas, as though nothing had happened. "We will rejoin our consorts, please, and release the aerostats in accordance with the terms. This man's body will be returned in one of them to his master, and the Professor here will write an account of his death in order that it may not be believed that we have murdered him. Konstantin Volnow, go into the saloon and write that letter, and bring it to me when it is done."

Like an automaton the Professor turned and walked mechanically into the deck-saloon. Meanwhile the *Ithuriel* started on her way towards the captive squadron. Before she reached it Volnow returned with a sheet of paper in his hand filled with fresh writing, and signed with his name.

Natas took it from him, read it, and then fixing his eyes on his again, said—

"That will do. I give you back your will. Now, do you believe?"

The Professor's body was suddenly shaken with such a violent trembling that he almost fell to the deck. Then he recovered himself with a violent effort, and cried through his chattering teeth—

"Believe! How can I help it? Whoever and whatever you are, you are well named the Master of the Terror."

CHAPTER XXX.

AT CLOSE QUARTERS.

AS soon as the captive war-balloons had been released, the *Ithuriel* and her consorts, without any further delay or concern for the issue of the decisive battle which would probably prove to be the death-struggle of the German Empire, headed away to the northward at the utmost speed of the two smaller vessels. Their objective point was Copenhagen, and the distance rather more than two hundred and sixty miles in a straight line.

This was covered in under two hours and a half, and by noon they had reached the Danish capital. In crossing the water from Stralsund they had sighted several war-vessels, all flying British, German, or Danish colours, and all making a northerly course like themselves. They had not attempted to speak to any of these, because, as they were all apparently bound for the same point, and, as the speed of the air-ships was more than five times as great as that of the swiftest cruiser, to do so would have been a waste of time, when every moment might be of the utmost consequence.

Off Copenhagen the aërial travellers saw the first signs of the terrible night's work, with the details of which the reader has already been made acquainted. Wrecked fortifications, cruisers and battleships bearing every mark of a heavy engagement, some with their top-works battered into ruins, their military masts gone, and their guns dismounted; some down by the head, and some by the stern, and others evidently run ashore to save them from sinking; and the harbour crowded with others in little better condition—everywhere there were eloquent proofs of the disaster which had overtaken the Allied fleets on the previous night.

"There seems to have been some rough work going on down there within the last few hours," said Arnold to Natas as they came in sight of this scene of destruction. "The Russians could not have done this alone, for when the war began they were shut up in the Baltic by an overwhelming force, of which these seem to be the remains. And those forts yonder were never destroyed by anything but our shells."

"Yes," replied Natas. "It is easy to see what has happened. The *Lucifer* was sent here to help the Russian fleet to break the blockade, and it looks as though it had been done very effectually. We are just a few hours too late, I fear.

"That one victory will have an immense effect on the course of the war, for it is almost certain that the Russians will make for the Atlantic round the north of the Shetland Islands, and co-operate with the French and Italian squadrons along the British line of communication with the West. That once cut, food will go up to famine prices in Britain, and the end will not be far off."

Natas spoke without the slightest apparent personal interest in the subject; but his words brought a flush to Arnold's cheeks, and make him suddenly clench his hands and knit his brows. After all he was an Englishman, and though he owed England nothing but the accident of his birth, the knowledge that one of his own ships should be the means of bringing this disaster upon her made him forget for the moment the gulf that he had placed between himself and his native land, and long to go to her rescue. But it was only a passing emotion. He remembered that his country was now elsewhere, and that all his hopes were now alien to Britain and her fortunes.

If Natas noticed the effect of his words he made no sign that he did, and he went on in the same even tone as before—

"We must overtake the fleet, and either recapture the *Lucifer* or destroy her before she does any more mischief in Russian hands. The first thing to do is to find out what has happened, and what course they have taken. Hoist the Union Jack over a flag of truce on all three ships, and signal to Mazanoff to come alongside. We had better stop here till we get the news."

The Master's orders were at once executed, and as soon as the *Ariel* was floating beside the flagship he said to her captain—

"Go down and speak that cruiser lying at anchor off the harbour, and learn all you can of what has happened. Tell them freely how it happened that the *Lucifer* assisted the Russian, if it turns out that she did so. Say that we have no hostility to Britain at present, but rather the reverse, and that our only purpose just now is to retake the air-ship and prevent her doing any more damage. If you can get any newspapers, do so."

"I understand fully," replied Mazanoff, and a minute later his vessel was sinking rapidly down towards the cruiser.

His reception was evidently friendly, for those on board the *Ithuriel* saw that he ran the *Ariel* close alongside the man-of-war, after the first hails had been exchanged, and conversed for some time with a group of officers across the rails of the two vessels. Then a large roll of newspapers was passed from the cruiser to the air-ship, salutes were exchanged, and the *Ariel* rose gracefully into the air to rejoin her consorts, followed by the envious glances of the crews of the battered warships.

Mazanoff presented his report, the facts of which were substantially those given in the *St. James's Gazette* telegram, and added that the British officers had confessed to him that the damage done was so great, both to the fleet and the shore fortifications, that the Sound was now practically as open as the Atlantic, and that it would be two or three weeks before even half the Allied force would be able to take the sea in fighting trim.

They added that there was not the slightest need to conceal their condition, as the Russians, who had steamed in triumph past their shattered ships and silenced forts, knew it just as well as they did. As regards the Russian fleet, it had been followed past the Skawe, and had headed out westward.

In their opinion it would consider itself strong enough, with the aid of the air-ship, to sweep the North Sea, and would probably attempt to force the Straits of Dover, as it has done the Sound, and effect a junction with the French squadrons at Brest and Cherbourg. This done, a combined attack might possibly be made upon Portsmouth, or the destruction of the Channel fleet attempted. The effects of the air-ship's shells upon both forts and ships had been so appalling that the Russians would no doubt think themselves strong enough for anything as long as they had possession of her.

"They were extremely polite," said Mazanoff, as he concluded his story. "They asked me to go ashore and interview the Admiral, who, they told me, would guarantee any amount of money on behalf of the British Government if we would only co-operate with their fleets for even a month. They said Britain would gladly pay a hundred thousand a month for the hire of each ship and her crew; and they looked quite puzzled when I refused point-blank, and said that a million a month would not do it.

"They evidently take us for a new sort of pirates, corsairs of the air, or something of that kind; for when I said that a few odd millions were no good to people who could levy blackmail on the whole earth if they chose, they stared at me and asked me what we did want if we didn't want money. The idea that we could have any higher aims never seemed to have entered their heads, and, of course, I didn't enlighten them."

"Quite right," said Natas, with a quiet laugh. "They will learn our aims quite soon enough. And now we must overtake the Russian fleet as soon as possible. You say they passed the Skawe soon after five this morning. That gives them nearly six hours' start, and if they are steaming twenty miles an hour, as I daresay they are, they will now be some hundred and twenty miles west of the Skawe. Captain Arnold, if we cut straight across Zeeland and Jutland, about what distance ought we to travel before we meet them?"

Arnold glanced at the chart which lay spread out on the table of the saloon in which they were sitting, and said—

"I should say a course of about two hundred miles due north-west from here ought to take us within sight of them, unless they are making for the Atlantic, and keep very close to the Swedish coast. In that case I should say two hundred and fifty in the same direction."

"Very well, then, let us take that course and make all the speed we can," said Natas; and within ten minutes the three vessels were speeding away to the north-westward at a hundred and twenty miles an hour over the verdant lowlands of the Danish peninsula

The *Ithuriel* kept above five miles ahead of the others, and when the journey had lasted about an hour and three-quarters, the man who had been stationed in the conning-tower signalled, "Fleet in sight" to the saloon. The air-ships were then travelling at an elevation of 3000 feet. A good ten miles to the northward could be seen the Russian fleet steering to the westward, and, judging by the dense clouds of smoke that were pouring out of the funnels of the vessels, making all the speed they could.

Arnold, who had gone forward to the conning-tower as soon as the signal sounded, at once returned to the saloon and made his formal report to Natas.

"The Russian fleet is in sight, heading to the westward, and therefore evidently meaning to reach the Atlantic by the north of the Shetlands. There are twelve large battleships, about twenty-five cruisers of different sizes, eight of them very large, and a small swarm of torpedo-boats being towed by the larger vessels, I suppose to save their coal. I see no signs of the *Lucifer* at present, but from what we have learnt she will be on the deck of one of the large cruisers. What are your orders?"

"Recover the air-ship if you can," replied Natas. "Send Mazanoff with Professor Volnow to convey the Tsar's letter to the Admiral, and demand the surrender of the *Lucifer*. If he refuses, let the *Ariel* return at once, and we will decide what to do. I leave the details with you with the most perfect confidence."

Arnold bowed in silence and retired, catching, as he turned to leave the saloon, a glance from Natasha which, it must be confessed, meant more to him than even the command of the Master. From the expression of his face as he went to the wheel-house to take charge of the ship, it was evident that it would go hard with the Russian fleet if the Admiral refused to recognise the order of the Tsar.

When he got to the wheel-house the *Ithuriel* was almost over the fleet. He signalled "stop" to the engine-room. Immediately the propellers slowed and then ceased their rapid revolutions, and at the same time the fan-wheels went aloft and began to revolve. This was a prearranged signal to the others to do the same, and by the time they had overtaken the flagship they also came to a standstill. As soon as they were within speaking distance Arnold hailed the *Orion* and the *Ariel* to come alongside.

After communicating to Tremayne and Mazanoff the orders of Natas, he said to the latter—

"You will take Professor Volnow to present the Tsar's letter to the Admiral in command of the fleet. Fly the Russian flag over a flag of truce, and if he acknowledges it say that if the *Lucifer* is given up we shall allow the fleet to go on its way unmolested and without asking any question.

"The cruiser that has her on board must separate from the rest of the fleet and allow two of your men to take possession of her and bring her up here. The lives of the four traitors are safe for the present if the air-ship is given up quietly."

"And if they will not recognise the authority of the Tsar's letter, and refuse to give the air-ship up, what then?" asked Mazanoff.

"In that case haul down the Russian flag, and get aloft as quickly as you can. You can leave the rest to us," said Arnold. "Meanwhile, Tremayne, will you go down to two thousand feet or so, and keep your eye on that big cruiser a bit ahead of the rest of the fleet. I fancy I can make out the *Lucifer* on her deck. Train a couple of guns on her, and don't let the air-ship rise without orders. I shall stop up here for the present, and be ready to make things lively for the Admiral if he refuses to obey his master's orders."

The *Ariel* took the Professor on board, and hoisted the Russian colours over the flag of truce, and began to sink down towards the fleet. As she descended, the Admiral in command of the squadron, already not a little puzzled by the appearance of the three air-ships, was still more mystified by seeing the Russian ensign flying from her flagstaff.

Was this only a ruse of the Terrorists, or were they flying the Russian flag for a legitimate reason? As he knew from the experience of the previous night that the air-ships, if their intentions were hostile, could destroy his fleet in detail without troubling to parley with him, he concluded that there was a good reason for the flag of truce, and so he ordered one to be flown from his own masthead in answer to it.

The white flag at once enabled Mazanoff to single out the huge battleship on which it was flying as the Admiral's flagship. The fleet was proceeding in four columns of line abreast. First two long lines of cruisers, each with one or two torpedo boats in tow, and with scouts thrown out on each wing, and then two lines of battleships, in the centre of the first of which was the flagship.

It was a somewhat risky matter for the *Ariel* to descend thus right in the middle of the whole fleet, but Mazanoff had his orders, and they had to be obeyed, and so down he went, running his bow up to within a hundred feet of the hurricane deck, on which stood the Admiral surrounded by several of his officers.

"I have a message for the Admiral of the fleet," he shouted, as soon as he came within hail.

"Who are you, and from whom is your message?" came the reply.

"Konstantin Volnow, of the Imperial Arsenal at Petersburg, brings the message from the Tsar in writing.'

"His Majesty's messenger is welcome. Come alongside."

The *Ariel* ran ahead until her prow touched the rail of the hurricane deck, and the Professor advanced with the Tsar's letter in his hand, and gave it to the Admiral, saying—

"You are acquainted with me, Admiral Prabylov. Though I bear it unwillingly, I can vouch for the letter being authentic. I saw his Majesty write it, and he gave it into my hands."

"Then how do you come to be an unwilling bearer of it?" asked the Admiral, scowling and gnawing his moustache as he read the unwelcome letter. "What are these terms, and with whom were they made?"

"Pardon me, Admiral," interrupted Mazanoff, "that is not the question. I presume you recognise his Majesty's signature, and see that he desires the air-ship to be given up."

"His Majesty's signature can be forged, just as Nihilists' passports can be, Mr. Terrorist, for that's what I presume you are, and"—

"Admiral, I solemnly assure you that that letter is genuine, and that it is really his Majesty's wish that the air-ship should be given up," the Professor broke in before Mazanoff had time to reply. "It is to be given in exchange for nine war-balloons which these air-ships captured before daybreak this morning."

"How do you come to be the bearer of it, sir? Please answer me that first."

"I am a prisoner of war. I surrendered to save the Arsenal and perhaps Petersburg from destruction under circumstances which I cannot now explain"—

"Thank you, sir, that is quite enough! A pretty story, truly! And you ask me to believe this, and to give up that priceless air-ship on such grounds as these—a story that would hardly deceive a child? You captured nine of the Tsar's war-balloons this morning, had an interview with his Majesty, got this letter from him at Cüstrin—more than five hundred miles away, and bring it here, and it is barely two in the afternoon!

"No, gentlemen, I am too old a sailor to be taken in by a yarn like that. I believe this letter to be a forgery, and I will not give the air-ship up on its authority."

"That is your last word, is it?" asked Mazanoff, white with passion, but still forcing himself to speak coolly.

"That is my last word, sir, save to tell you that if you do not haul that flag you are masquerading under down at once I will fire upon you," shouted the Admiral, tearing the Tsar's letter into fragments as he spoke.

"If I haul that flag down it will be the signal for the air-ships up yonder to open fire upon you, so your blood be on your own heads!" said Mazanoff, stamping thrice on the deck as he spoke. The propellers of the *Ariel* whirled round in a reverse direction, and she sprang swiftly back from the battle-ship, at the same time rising rapidly in the air.

Before she had cleared a hundred yards, and before the flag of truce was hauled down, there was a sharp, grinding report from one of the tops of the man-of-war, and a hail of bullets from a machine gun swept across the deck. Mazanoff heard a splintering of wood and glass, and a deep groan beside him. He looked round and saw the Professor clasp his hand to a great red wound in his breast, and fall in a heap on the deck.

This was the event of an instant. The next he had trained one of the bow-guns downwards on the centre of the deck of the Russian flagship and sent the projectile to its mark. Then quick as thought he sprang over and discharged the other gun almost at random. He saw the dazzling green flash of the explosions, then came a shaking of the atmosphere, and a roar as of a hundred thunder-claps in his ears, and he dropped senseless to the deck beside the corpse of the Professor.

"There was a sharp, grinding report from one of the tops of the man-of-war."

See page 232.

CHAPTER XXXI.

A RUSSIAN RAID.

MAZANOFF came to himself about ten minutes later, lying on one of the seats in the after saloon, and all that he saw when he first opened his eyes was the white anxious face of Radna bending over him.

"What is the matter? What has happened? Where am I?" he asked, as soon as his tongue obeyed his will. His voice, although broken and unsteady, was almost as strong as usual, and Radna's face immediately brightened as she heard it. A smile soon chased away her anxious look, and she said cheerily—

"Ah, come! you're not killed after all. You are still on board the *Ariel*, and what has happened is this as far as I can see. In your hurry to return the shot from the Russian flagship you fired your guns at too close range, and the shock of the explosion stunned you. In fact, we thought for the moment you had blown the *Ariel* up too, for she shook so that we all fell down; then her engines stopped, and she almost fell into the water before they could be started again."

"Is she all right now? Where's the Russian fleet, and what happened to the flagship? I must get on deck," exclaimed Mazanoff, sitting up on the seat. As he did so he put his hand to his head and said: "I feel a bit shaky still. What's that—brandy you've got there? Get me some champagne, and put the brandy into it. I shall be all right when I've had a good drink. Now I think of it, I wonder that explosion didn't blow us to bits. You haven't told me what became of the flagship," he continued, as Radna came back with a small bottle of champagne and uncorked it.

"Well, the flagship is at the bottom of the German Ocean. When Petroff told me that you had fallen dead, as he said, on deck, I ran up in defiance of your orders and saw the battleship just going down. The shells had blown the middle of her right out, and a cloud of steam and smoke and fire was rising out of a great ragged space where the funnels had been. Before I got you down here she broke right in two and went down."

"That serves that blackguard Prabylov right for saying we forged the Tsar's letter, and firing on a flag of truce. Poor Volnow's dead, I suppose?"

"Oh yes," replied Radna sadly. "He was shot almost to pieces by the volley from the machine gun. The deck saloon is riddled with bullets, and the decks badly torn up, but fortunately the hull and propellers are almost uninjured. But come, drink this, then you can go up and see for yourself."

So saying she handed him a tumbler of champagne well dashed with brandy. He drank it down at a gulp, like the Russian that he was, and said as he put the glass down—

"That's better. I feel a new man. Now give me a kiss, *batiushka,* and I'll be off."

When he reached the deck he found the *Ariel* ascending towards the *Ithuriel,* and about a mile astern of the Russian fleet, the vessels of which were blazing away into the air with their machine guns, in the hope of "bringing him down on the wing," as he afterwards put it. He could hear the bullets singing along underneath him; but the *Ariel* was rising so fast, and going at such a speed through the air, that the moment the Russians got the range they lost it again, and so merely wasted their ammunition.

Neither the *Ithuriel* nor the *Orion* seemed to have taken any part in the battle so far, or to have done anything to avenge the attack made upon the *Ariel.* Mazanoff wondered not a little at this, as both Arnold and Tremayne must have seen the fate of the Russian flagship. As soon as he got within speaking distance of the *Ithuriel,* he sang out to Arnold, who was on the deck—

"I got in rather a tight place down there. That scoundrel

fired upon us with the flag of truce flying, and when I gave him a couple of shells in return I thought the end of the world was come."

"You fired at too close range, my friend. Those shells are sudden death to anything within a hundred yards of them. Are you all well on board? You've been knocked about a bit, I see."

"No; poor Volnow's dead. He was killed standing close beside me, and I wasn't touched, though the explosion of the shell knocked the senses out of me completely. However, the machinery's all right, and I don't think the hull is hurt to speak of. But what are you doing? I should have thought you'd have blown half the fleet out of the water by this time."

"No. We saw that you had amply avenged yourself, and the Master's orders were not to do anything till you returned. You'd better come on board and consult with him."

Mazanoff did so, and when he had told his story to Natas, the latter mystified him not a little by replying—

"I am glad that none of you are injured, though, of course, I'm sorry that I sent Volnow to his death; but that is the fortune of war. If one of us fell into his master's hands his fate would be worse than that. You avenged the outrage promptly and effectively.

"I have decided not to injure the Russian fleet more than I can help. It has work to do which must not be interfered with. My only object is to recover the *Lucifer*, if possible, and so we shall follow the fleet for the present across the North Sea on our way to the rendezvous with the other vessels from Aeria which are to meet us on Rockall Island, and wait our opportunity. Should the opportunity not come before then, we must proceed to extremities, and destroy her and the cruiser that has her on board.

"And do you think we shall get such an opportunity?"

"I don't know," replied Natas. "But it is possible. I don't think it likely that the fleet will have coal enough for a long cruise in the Atlantic, and therefore it is possible that they will make a descent on Aberdeen, which they are quite strong enough to capture if they like, and coal up there. In that case it is extremely probable that they will make use of the air-ship to terrorise the town into surrender, and as soon as she takes the air we must make a dash for her, and either take her or blow her to pieces."

Arnold expressed his entire agreement with this idea, and, as the event proved, it was entirely correct. Instead of steering nor'-nor'-west, as they would have done had they intended to go round the Shetland Islands, or north-west, had they chosen the course between the Orkneys and the Shetlands, the Russian vessels kept a due westerly course during the rest of the day, and this course could only take them to the Scotch coast near Aberdeen.

The distance from where they were was a little under five hundred miles, and at their present rate of steaming they would reach Aberdeen about four o'clock on the following afternoon. The air-ships followed them at a height of four thousand feet during the rest of the day and until shortly before dawn on the following morning.

They then put on speed, took a wide sweep to the northward, and returned southward over Banffshire, and passing Aberdeen to the west, found a secluded resting-place on the northern spur of the Kincardineshire Hills, about five miles to the southward of the Granite City.

Here the repairs which were needed by the *Ariel* were at once taken in hand by her own crew and that of the *Ithuriel*, while the *Orion* was sent out to sea again to keep a sharp look-out for the Russian fleet, which she would sight long before she herself became visible, and then to watch the movements of the Russians from as great a distance as possible until it was time to make the counter-attack.

As Aberdeen was then one of the coaling depots for the North Sea Squadron, it was defended by two battleships, the *Ascalon* and the *Menelaus*, three powerful coast-defence vessels, the *Thunderer*, the *Cyclops*, and the *Pluto*, six cruisers, and twelve torpedo-boats. The shore defences consisted of a fort on the north bank at the mouth of the Dee, mounting ten heavy guns, and the Girdleness fort, mounting twenty-four 9-inch twenty-five ton guns, in connection with which was a station for working navigable torpedoes of the Brennan type, which had been considerably improved during the last ten years.

Shortly after two o'clock on the afternoon of the 30th the *Orion* returned to her consorts with the news that the Russian fleet was forty miles off the land, heading straight for Aberdeen, and that there were no other warships in sight as far as could be seen to the southward. From this fact it was concluded that the Russians had escaped the notice of the North Sea Squadron, and so would only have the force defending Aberdeen to reckon with.

Even had they not possessed the air-ship, this force was so far inferior to their own that there would be little chance of successfully defending the town against them. They had eleven battleships, twenty-five cruisers, eight of which were very large and heavily armed, and forty torpedo-boats, to pit against the little British force and the two forts.

But given the assistance of the *Lucifer*, and the town practically lay at their mercy. They evidently feared no serious opposition in their raid, for, without even waiting for nightfall, they came on at full speed, darkening the sky with their smoke, the battleships in the centre, a dozen cruisers on either side of them, and one large cruiser about a mile ahead of their centre.

When the captain of the *Ascalon*, who was in command of the port, saw the overwhelming force of the hostile fleet, he at once came to the conclusion that it would be madness for him to attempt to put to sea with his eleven ships and six torpedo-boats. The utmost that he could do was to remain inshore and assist the forts to keep the Russians at bay, if possible, until the assistance, which had already been telegraphed for to Dundee and the Firth of Forth, where the bulk of the North Sea Squadron was then stationed, could come to his aid.

Five miles off the land the Russian fleet stopped, and the *Lucifer* rose from the deck of the big cruiser and stationed herself about a mile to seaward of the mouth of the river at an elevation of three thousand feet. Then a torpedo-boat flying a flag of truce shot out from the Russian line and ran to within a mile of the shore.

The Commodore of the port sent out one of his torpedo-boats to meet her, and this craft brought back a summons to surrender the port for twelve hours, and permit six of the Russian cruisers to fill up with coal. The alternative would be bombardment of the town by the fleet and the air-ship, which alone, as the Russians said, held the fort and the ships at its mercy.

To this demand the British Commodore sent back a flat refusal, and defiance to the Russian Commander to do his worst.

Where the *Ithuriel* and her consorts were lying the hills between them and the sea completely screened them from the observation of those on board the *Lucifer*. Arnold and Tremayne had climbed to the top of a hill above their ships, and watched the movements of the Russians through their glasses. As soon as they saw the *Lucifer* rise into the air they returned to the *Ithuriel* to form their plans for their share in the conflict that they saw impending.

"I'm afraid we can't do much until it gets a good deal darker than it is now," said Arnold, in reply to a question from Natas as to his view of the situation. "If we take the air now the *Lucifer* will see us; and we must remember that she is armed with the same weapons as we have, and a shot from one of her guns would settle any of us that it struck. Even if we hit her first we should destroy her, and we could have done that easily yesterday.

"It has felt very like thunder all day, and I see there are some very black-looking clouds rolling up there over the hills to the south-west. My advice is to wait for those. I'm afraid we can't do anything to save the town under the circumstances, but in this state of the atmosphere a heavy bombardment is practically certain to bring on a severe thunderstorm, and to fetch those clouds up at the double quick.

"I don't for a moment think that the British will surrender, big and all as the Russian force is, and as they have never seen the effects of our shells they won't fear the *Lucifer* much until she commences operations, and then it will be too late. Listen! They've begun. There goes the first gun!"

A deep, dull boom came rolling up the hills from the sea as he spoke, and was almost immediately followed by a rapid series of similar reports, which quickly deepened into a continuous roar. Every one who could be spared from the air-ship at once ran up to the top of the hill to watch the progress of the fight. The Russian fleet had advanced to within three miles of the land, and had opened a furious cannonade on the British ships and the forts, which were manfully replying to it with every available gun.

By the time the watchers on the hill had focussed their glasses on the scene, the *Lucifer* discharged her first shell on the fort on Girdleness. They saw the blaze of the explosion gleam through the smoke that already hung thick over the low building. Another and another followed in quick succession, and the firing from the fort ceased. The smoke drifted slowly away, and disclosed a heap of shapeless ruins.

"That is horrible work, isn't it?" said Arnold to Tremayne through his clenched teeth. "Anywhere but on British ground would not be so bad, but the sight of that makes my blood boil. I would give my ears to take our ships into the air, and smash up that Russian fleet as we did the French Squadron in the Atlantic."

"There spoke the true Briton, Captain Arnold," said Natasha, who was standing beside him under a clump of trees. "Yes, I can quite understand how you feel watching a scene like that, for country is country after all. Even my half-English blood is pretty near boiling point; and though I wouldn't give my ears, I would give a good deal to go with you and do as you say.

"But you may rest assured that the Master's way is the best, and will prove the shortest road to the universal peace which can only come through universal war. Courage, my friend, and patience! There will be a heavy reckoning to pay for this sort of thing one day, and that before very long."

"Ha!" exclaimed Tremayne. "There goes the other fort. I suppose it will be the turn of the ships next. What a frightful scene! Twenty minutes ago it was as peaceful as these hills, and look at it now."

The second fort had been destroyed as rapidly as the first, and the cessation of the fire of both had made a very perceptible difference in the cannonade, though the great guns of the Russian fleet still roared continuously and poured a hurricane of shot and shell into the mouth of the river across which the British ships were drawn, keeping up the unequal conflict like so many bull-dogs at bay.

Over them and the river hung a dense pall of bluish-white

smoke, through which the *Lucifer* sent projectile after projectile in the attempt to sink the British ironclads. As those on board her could only judge by the flash of the guns, the aim was very imperfect, and several projectiles were wasted, falling into the sea and exploding there, throwing up mountains of water, but not doing any further damage. At length a brilliant green flash shot up through the smoke clouds over the river mouth.

"He's hit one of the ships at last!" exclaimed Tremayne, as he saw the flash. "It'll soon be all up with poor old Aberdeen."

"I don't think so," exclaimed Arnold. "At any rate the *Lucifer* won't do much more harm. There comes the storm at last! Back to the ships all of you at once, it's time to go aloft!"

As he spoke a brilliant flash of lightning split the inky clouds which had now risen high over the western hills, and a deep roll of thunder came echoing up the valleys as if in answer to the roar of the cannonade on the sea. The moment every one was on board, Arnold gave the signal to ascend. As soon as the fan-wheels had raised them a hundred feet from the ground he gave the signal for full speed ahead, and the three air-ships swept upwards to the west as though to meet the coming storm.

CHAPTER XXXII.

THE END OF THE CHASE.

HE flight of the *Ithuriel* and her consorts was so graduated, that as they rose to the level of the storm-cloud they missed it and passed diagonally beyond it at a sufficient distance to avoid disturbing the electrical balance between it and the earth. The object of doing so was not so much to escape a discharge of electricity, since all the vital parts of the machinery and the power-cylinders were carefully insulated, but rather in order not to provoke a lightning flash which might have revealed their rapid passage to the occupants of the *Lucifer*.

As it was, they swept upwards and westward at such a speed that they had gained the cover of the thunder-cloud, and placed a considerable area of it between themselves and the town, long before the storm broke over Aberdeen, and so they were provided with ample shelter under, or rather over, which they were to make their attack on the *Lucifer*.

They waited until the clouds coming up from the westward joined those which had begun to gather thick and black and threatening over the Russian fleet soon after the tremendous cannonade had begun. The shock of the meeting of the two cloud-squadrons formed a fitting counterpart to the drama of death and destruction that was being played on land and sea.

The brilliant sunshine of the midsummer afternoon was suddenly obscured by a darkness born of smoke and cloud like that of a midwinter night. The smoke of the cannonade rose heavily and mingled with the clouds, and the atmospheric concussions produced by the discharge of hundreds of heavy guns, brought down the rain in torrents. Almost continuous streams of lightning flashed from cloud to cloud, and from heaven to earth, eclipsing the spouting fire of the guns, while to the roar of the bombardment was added an almost unbroken roll of thunder.

Above all this hideous turmoil of human and elemental strife, the three air-ships floated for awhile in a serene and sunlit atmosphere. But this was only for a time. Arnold had taken the position and altitude of the *Lucifer* very carefully by means of his sextant and compass before he rose into the air, and as soon as his preparations were complete he made another observation of the angle of the sun's elevation, allowing, of course, for his own, and placed his three ships as nearly perpendicular as he could over the *Lucifer*, floating on the under side of the storm-cloud.

His preparations had been simple in the extreme. Four light strong grappling-irons hung downwards from the *Ithuriel*, two at the bow and two at the stern, by thin steel-wire rope; two similar ones hung from the starboard side of the *Orion*, which was on his left hand, and two from the port side of the *Ariel*, which was on his right hand. As they gained the desired position, a man was stationed at each of the ropes, with instructions how to act when the word was given. Then the fan-wheels were slowed down, and the three vessels sank swiftly through the cloud.

Through the mist and darkness underneath they saw the white shape of the *Lucifer* almost immediately below them, so accurately had the position been determined. They sank a hundred feet farther, and then Arnold shouted—

"Now is your time. Cast!"

Instantly the eight grappling-irons dropped and swung towards the *Lucifer*, hooking themselves in the stays of her masts and the railing that ran completely round her deck.

"Now, up again, and ahead!" shouted Arnold once more, and the fan-wheels of the three ships revolved at their utmost speed; the air-planes had already been inclined to the full, the nine propellers whirled round, and the recaptured *Lucifer* was dragged forward and upwards through the mist and darkness of the thunder-cloud into the bright sunshine above.

So suddenly had the strange manœuvre been executed that

"Now is your time, cast!"

See page 242.

those on board her had not time to grasp what had really happened to them before they found themselves captured and utterly helpless. As she hung below her three captors it was impossible to bring one of the *Lucifer's* guns to bear upon them, while four guns, two from the *Ariel* and two from the *Orion*, grinned down upon her ready to blow her into fragments at the least sign of resistance.

Added to this, a dozen magazine rifles covered her deck, threatening sudden death to the six bewildered men who were still staring helplessly about them in wonderment at the strange thing that had happened to them.

"Who are the Russian officers in command of that airship?" hailed Mazanoff from the *Ariel*.

Two men in Russian uniform raised their hands in reply, and Mazanoff hailed again—

"Which will you have—surrender or death? If you surrender your lives are safe, and we will put you on to the land as soon as possible; if not you will be shot."

"We surrender!" exclaimed one of the officers, drawing his sword and dropping it on the deck. The other followed suit, and Mazanoff continued—

"Very good. Remain where you are. The first man that moves will be shot down."

Almost before the last words had left his lips half a dozen men had slid down the wire ropes and landed on the deck of the *Lucifer*. The moment their feet had touched the deck each whipped a magazine pistol out of his belt and covered his man.

Within a couple of minutes the captives were all disarmed; indeed, most of them had thrown their weapons down on the first summons. The arms were tossed overboard, and all but the two Russian officers were rapidly bound hand and foot. Then three of the six men descended to the engine-room, and one went to the wheel-house. In another minute the fan-wheels of the *Lucifer* began to spin round faster, and quickly raised her to the level of the other three ships, and so the recapture of the deserter was completed.

The two officers were at once summoned on board the *Ithuriel* and shut up under guard in separate cabins. The rest of the crew of the *Lucifer* was found to consist of the four traitors who had carried her away, and two Russian engineers who had been put on board to assist in the working of the vessel.

As soon as these had been replaced by a crew drafted from the *Ithuriel* and her consorts under the command of Lieutenant Marston, Arnold gave the order to go ahead at fifty miles an hour to the northward, and the four air-ships immediately sped away in that direction, leaving Aberdeen to its fate, and within a little over an hour the sounds of both storm and battle had died away in silence behind them.

When they were fairly under way Natas ordered the four deserters to be brought before him in the after saloon of the flagship. He sat at one end of the table, and they were placed in a line in front of him at the other, each with a guard behind him, and the muzzle of a pistol at his head.

"Peter Tamboff, Amos Vornjeh, Ivan Tscheszco, and Paul Oreloff! you have broken your oaths, betrayed your companions, deserted the Cause to which you devoted your lives, and placed in the hands of the Russian tyrant the means of destruction which has enabled him to break the blockade of the Baltic, and so perhaps to change the whole course of the war which he is now waging, as you well know, with the object of conquering Europe and enslaving its peoples.

"Already the lives of thousands of better men than you have been lost through this vile treason of yours, the vilest of all treason, for it was committed for love of money. By the laws of the Brotherhood your lives are forfeit, and if you had a hundred lives each they would be forfeited again by the calamities that your treason has brought, and will bring, upon the world. You will die in half an hour. If you have any preparations to make for the next world, make them. I have done with you. Go!"

Half an hour later the four deserters were taken up on to the deck of the *Ithuriel*. The signal was given to stop the flotilla, which was then flying three thousand feet above the waters of the Moray Firth. As soon as they came to a standstill their crews were summoned on deck. The three smaller vessels floated around the *Ithuriel* at a distance of about fifty yards from her. The traitors, bound hand and foot, were stood up facing the rail of the flagship, and four of her crew were stationed opposite to them on the other side of the deck with loaded rifles.

They were allowed one last look upon sun and sky, and then their eyes were bandaged. As soon as this was done Arnold raised his hand; the four rifles came up to the ready; a stream of flame shot from the muzzles, and the bodies of the four traitors lurched forward over the rail and disappeared into the abyss beneath.

"Now, gentlemen," said Arnold in French, turning to the two Russian officers who had been spectators of the scene, "that is how we punish traitors. Your own lives are spared because we do not murder prisoners of war. You will, I hope, in due time return to your master, and you will tell him why we have been obliged to retake the air-ship which he surrendered to us by force, and therefore why we destroyed his flagship in the North Sea. If Admiral Prabylov had obeyed his orders, the *Lucifer* would have been surrendered to us quietly, and there would have been for the present no further trouble.

"Tell him also from me, as Admiral of the Terrorist fleet, that, so far as matters have now gone, we shall take no further part in the war; but that the moment he brings his war-balloons across the waters which separate Britain from Europe, the last hour of his empire will have struck.

"If he neglects this warning with which I now intrust you, I will bring a force against him before which he shall be as helpless as the armies of the Alliance have so far been before him and his war-balloons; and, more than this, tell him that if I conquer I will not spare. I will hold him and his advisers strictly to account for all that may happen after that moment.

"There will be no treaties with conquered enemies in the hour of our victory. We will have blood for blood, and life for life. Remember that, and bear the message to him faithfully. For the present you will be prisoners on parole; but I warn you that you will be watched night and day, and at the first suspicion of treachery you will be shot, and cast into the air as those traitors were just now.

"You will remain on board this ship. The two engineers will be placed one on board of each of two of our consorts. In twenty-four hours or so you will be landed on Spanish soil and left to your own devices. Meanwhile we shall make you as comfortable as the circumstances permit."

The two Russian officers bowed their acknowledgments, and Arnold gave the signal for the flotilla to proceed.

It was then about seven o'clock in the evening. Flying at the rate of a hundred miles an hour, the squadron crossed the mouth of the Moray Firth trending to the westward until they passed over Thurso, and then took a westerly course to Rockall Island, four hundred miles to the west. Here they met the two other air-ships which had been despatched from Aeria with extra power-cylinders and munitions of war in case they had been needed for a prolonged campaign.

The cylinders, which had been exhausted on board the *Ithuriel* and her three consorts, were replaced, and then the whole squadron rose into the air from one of the peaks of Rockall Island and winged its way southward to the north-western coast of Spain. They made the Spanish land near Corunna shortly before eight on the following evening, and here the four Russian prisoners were released on the sea-shore and provided with money to take them as far as Valladolid, whence they would be able to communicate with the French military authorities at Toulouse.

The Terrorist Squadron then rose once more into the air, ascended to a height of two thousand feet, skirted the Portuguese coast, and then took a south-easterly course over Morocco through one of the passes of the Atlas Mountains, and so across the desert of Sahara and the wilds of Central Africa to Aeria.

CHAPTER XXXIII.

THE BREAKING OF THE CHARM.

HE first news of the Russian attack on Aberdeen was received in London soon after five o'clock on the afternoon of the 30th, and produced an effect which it is quite beyond the power of language to describe. The first telegram containing the bare announcement of the fact fell like a bolt from the blue on the great Metropolis. It ran as follows:—

              Aberdeen, 4.30 P.M.

A large fleet, supposed to be the Russian fleet which broke the blockade of the Baltic on the morning of the 28th, has appeared off the town. About forty large vessels can be made out. Our defences are quite inadequate to cope with such an immense force, but we shall do our best till help comes.

After that the wires were kept hot with messages until well into the night. The newspapers rushed out edition after edition to keep pace with them, and in all the office windows of the various journals copies of the telegrams were posted up as soon as they arrived.

As the messages multiplied in number they brought worse and worse tidings, until excitement grew to frenzy and frenzy degenerated into panic. The thousand tongues of rumour wagged faster and faster as each hour went by. The raid upon a single town was magnified into a general invasion of the whole country.

Very few people slept in London that night, and the streets were alive with anxious crowds till daybreak, waiting for the confidently-expected news of the landing of the Russian troops, in spite of the fact that the avowed and real object of the raid had been made public early in the evening. The following are the most important of the telegrams which were received, and will suffice to inform the reader of the course of events after the departure of the four air-ships from the scene of action—

5 P.M.

A message has been received from the Commander of the Russian fleet demanding the surrender of the town for twelve hours to allow six of his ships to fill up with coal. The captain of the *Ascalon*, in command of the port, has refused this demand, and declares that he will fight while he has a ship that will float or a gun that can be fired. The Russians are accompanied by the air-ship which assisted them to break the blockade of the Sound. She is now floating over the town. The utmost terror prevails among the inhabitants, and crowds are flying into the country to escape the bombardment. Aid has been telegraphed for to Edinburgh and Dundee; but if the North Sea Squadron is still in the Firth of Forth, it cannot get here under nearly twelve hours' steaming.

5.30 P.M.

The bombardment has commenced, and fearful damage has been done already. With three or four shells the air-ship has blown up and utterly destroyed the fort on Girdleness, which mounted twenty-four heavy guns. But for the ships, this leaves the town almost unprotected. News has just come from the North Shore that the batteries there have met with the same fate. The Russians are pouring a perfect storm of shot and shell into the mouth of the river where our ships are lying, but the town has so far been spared.

5.45 P.M.

We have just received news from Edinburgh that the North Sea Squadron left at daybreak this morning under orders to proceed to the mouth of the Elbe to assist in protecting Hamburg from an anticipated attack by the same fleet which has attacked us. There is now no hope that the town can be successfully defended, and the Provost has called a towns-meeting to consider the advisability of surrender, though it is feared that the Russians may now make larger demands. The whole country side is in a state of the utmost panic.

7 P.M.

The towns-meeting empowered the Provost to call upon Captain Marchmont, of the *Ascalon*, to make terms with the Russians in order to save the town from destruction. He refused point blank, although one of the coast-defence ships, the *Thunderer*, has been disabled by shells from the air-ship, and all his other vessels have been terribly knocked about by the incessant cannonade from the fleet, which has now advanced to within two miles of the shore, having nothing more to fear from the land batteries. A terrific thunderstorm is raging, and no words can describe the horror of the scene. The air-ship ceased firing nearly an hour ago.

10 P.M.

Five of our eleven ships—two battleships and three cruisers—have been sunk; the rest are little better than mere wrecks, and seven torpedo-boats have been destroyed in attempting to torpedo some of the enemy's ships. Heavy firing has been heard to the southward, and we have learnt from Dundee that four battleships and six cruisers have been sent to our relief. A portion of the Russian fleet has been detached to meet them. We cannot hope anything from them. Captain Marchmont has now only four ships capable of fighting, but refuses to strike his flag. The storm has ceased, and a strong land breeze has blown the clouds and smoke to seaward. The air-ship has disappeared. Six large Russian ironclads are heading at full speed towards the mouth of the river—

The telegram broke off short here, and no more news was received from Aberdeen for several hours. Of this there was only one possible explanation. The town was in the hands of the Russians, and they had cut the wires. The long charm was broken, and the Isle Inviolate was inviolate no more. The next telegram from the North came from Findon, and was published in London just before ten o'clock on the following morning. It ran thus—

Findon, N.B., 9.15.

About ten o'clock last night the attack on Aberdeen ended in a rush of six ironclads into the river mouth. They charged down upon the four half-crippled British ships that were left, and in less than five minutes rammed and sank them. The Russians then demanded the unconditional surrender of the town, under pain of bombardment and destruction. There was no other course but to yield, and until eight o'clock this morning the town has been in the hands of the enemy.

The Russians at once landed a large force of sailors and marines, cut the telegraph wires and the railway lines, and fired without warning upon every one who attempted to leave the town. The stores of coal and ammunition were seized, and six large cruisers were taking in coal all night. The banks were also entered, and the specie taken possession of, as indemnity for the town. At eight o'clock the cruisers and battleships steamed out of the river without doing further damage. The squadron from the Tay was compelled to retire by the overwhelming force that the Russians brought to bear upon it after Aberdeen surrendered.

Half an hour ago the Russian fleet was lost sight of proceeding at full speed to the north-eastward. Our loss has been terribly heavy. The fort and batteries have been destroyed, all the ships have been sunk or disabled, and of the whole defending force scarcely three hundred men remain. Captain Marchmont went down on the *Ascalon* with his flag flying, and fighting to the last moment.

While the excitement caused by the news of the raid upon Aberdeen was at its height, that is to say, on the morning of the 2nd of July, intelligence was received in London of a tremendous disaster to the Anglo-Teutonic Alliance. It was nothing less, in short, than the fall of Berlin, the collapse of the German Empire, and the surrender of the Kaiser and the Crown Prince to the Tsar. After nearly sixty hours of almost continuous fighting, during which the fortifications had been wrecked by the war-balloons, the German ammunition-trains burnt and blown up by the fire-shells rained from the air, and the heroic defenders of the city disorganised by the aërial bombardment of melinite shells and cyanogen poison-bombs, and crushed by an overwhelming force of not less than four million assailants. So fell like a house of cards the stately fabric built up by the genius of Bismarck and Moltke; and so, after bearing his part gallantly in the death-struggle of his empire, had the grandson of the conqueror of Sedan yielded up his sword to the victorious Autocrat of the Russias.

The terrible news fell upon London like the premonitory echo of an approaching storm. The path of the triumphant Muscovites was now completely open to the forts of the Belgian Quadrilateral, under the walls of which they would form a junction, which nothing could now prevent, with the beleaguering forces of France. Would the Belgian strongholds be able to resist any more effectually than the fortifications of Berlin had done the assaults of the terrible war-balloons of the Tsar?

CHAPTER XXXIV.

THE PATH OF CONQUEST.

HIS narrative does not in any sense pretend to be a detailed history of the war, but only of such phases of it as more immediately concern the working out of those deep-laid and marvellously-contrived plans designed by their author to culminate in nothing less than the collapse of the existing fabric of Society, and the upheaval of the whole basis of civilisation.

It will therefore be impossible to follow the troops of the Alliance and the League through the different compaigns which were being simultaneously carried out in different parts of Europe. The most that can be done will be to present an outline of the leading events which, operating throughout a period of nearly three months, prepared the way for the final catastrophe in which the tremendous issues of the world-war were summed up.

The fall of Berlin was the first decisive blow that had been struck during the war. Under it the federation of kingdoms and states which had formed the German Empire fell asunder almost instantly, and the whole fabric collapsed like a broken bubble. The shock was felt throughout the length and breadth of Europe, and it was immediately seen that nothing but a miracle could save the whole of Central Europe from falling into the hands of the League.

Its immediate results were the surrender of Magdeburg, Brunswick, Hanover, and Bremen. Hamburg, strongly garrisoned by British and German troops, supported by a powerful squadron in the Elbe, and defended by immense fortifications on the landward side, alone returned a flat defiance to the summons of the Tsar. The road to the westward, therefore, lay entirely open to his victorious troops. As for Hamburg, it was left for the present under the observation of a corps of reconnaissance to be dealt with when its time came.

When Berlin fell the position of affairs in Europe may be briefly described as follows:—The French army had taken the field nearly five millions strong, and this immense force had been divided into an Army of the North and an Army of the East. The former, consisting of about two millions of men, had been devoted to the attack on the British and German forces holding an almost impregnable position behind the chain of huge fortresses known at present as the Belgian Quadrilateral.

This Army of the North, doubtless acting in accordance with the preconceived schemes of operations arranged by the leaders of the League, had so far contented itself with a series of harassing attacks upon different points of the Allied position, and had made no forward movement in force. The Army of the East, numbering nearly three million men, and divided into fifteen army corps, had crossed the German frontier immediately on the outbreak of the war, and at the same moment that the Russian Armies of the North and South had crossed the eastern Austro-German frontier, and the Italian army had forced the passes of the Tyrol.

The whole of the French fleet of war-balloons had been attached to the Army of the East with the intention, which had been realised beyond the most sanguine expectations, of overrunning and subjugating Central Europe in the shortest possible space of time. It had swept like a destroying tempest through the Rhine Provinces, leaving nothing in its track but the ruins of towns and fortresses, and wide wastes of devastated fields and vineyards.

Before the walls of Munich it had effected a junction with the Italian army, consisting of ten army corps, numbering two million men. The ancient capital of Bavaria fell in three days under the assault of the aërial fleet and the overwhelming numbers of the attacking force. Then the Franco-Italian armies advanced down the valley of the Danube and invested Vienna, which, in spite of the heroic efforts of what had been left of the Austrian army after the disastrous conflicts on the Eastern frontier, was stormed and sacked after three days and nights of almost continuous fighting, and the most appalling scenes of bloodshed and destruction, four days after the surrender of the German Emperor to the Tsar had announced the collapse of what had once been the Triple Alliance.

From Vienna the Franco-Italian armies continued their way down the valley of the Danube, and at Budapest was joined by the northern division of the Russian Army of the South, and from there the mighty flood of destruction rolled south-eastward until it overflowed the Balkan peninsula, sweeping everything before it as it went, until it joined the force investing Constantinople.

The Turkish army, which had retreated before it, had concentrated upon Gallipoli, where, in conjunction with the allied British and Turkish Squadrons holding the Dardanelles, it prepared to advance to the relief of Constantinople.

The final attack upon the Turkish capital had been purposely delayed until the arrival of the French war-balloons, and as soon as these appeared upon the scene the work of destruction instantly recommenced. After four days of bombardment by sea and land, and from the air, and a rapid series of what can only be described as wholesale butcheries, the ancient capital of the Sultan shared the fate of Berlin and Vienna, and after four centuries and a half the Turkish dominion in Europe died in its first stronghold.

Meanwhile one of the wings of the Franco-Italian army had made a descent upon Gallipoli, and after forty-eight hours' incessant fighting had compelled the remnant of the Turkish army, which it thus cut off from Constantinople, to take refuge on the Turkish and British men-of-war under the protection of the guns of the fleet. In view of the overwhelming numbers of the enemy, and the terrible effectiveness of the war-balloons, it was decided that any attempt to retake Constantinople, or even to continue to hold the Dardanelles, could only result in further disaster.

The forts of the Dardanelles were therefore evacuated and blown up, and the British and Turkish fleet, with the remains of the Turkish army on board, steamed southward to Alexandria to join forces with the British Squadron that was

The victory had, it is true, been bought at a tremendous price, but it was complete and decisive, and at the moment that the last of the ships of the League struck her flag, Admiral Beresford stood in the same glorious position as Sir George Rodney had done a hundred and twenty-two years before, when he saved the British Empire in the ever-memorable victory of the 12th of April 1782.

The triumph in the Mediterranean was, however, only a set-off to a disaster which had occurred more than five weeks previously in the Atlantic. The Russian fleet, which had broken the blockade of the Sound, with the assistance of the *Lucifer*, had, after coaling at Aberdeen, made its way into the Atlantic, and there, in conjunction with the Franco-Italian fleets operating along the Atlantic steamer route, had, after a series of desperate engagements, succeeded in breaking up the line of British communication with America and Canada.

This result had been achieved mainly in consequence of the contrast between the necessary methods of attack and defence. On the one hand, Britain had been compelled to maintain an extended line of ocean defence more than three thousand miles in length, and her ships had further been hampered by the absolute necessity of attending, first, to the protection of the Atlantic liners, and, secondly, to warding off isolated attacks which were directed upon different parts of the line by squadrons which could not be attacked in turn without breaking the line of convoy which it was all-essential to preserve intact.

For two or three weeks there had been a series of running fights; but at length the ocean chain had broken under the perpetual strain, and a repulse inflicted on the Irish Squadron by a superior force of French, Italian, and Spanish warships had settled the question of the command of the Atlantic in favour of the League. The immediate result of this was that food supplies from the West practically stopped.

Now and then a fleet Atlantic greyhound ran the blockade and brought her priceless cargo into a British port; but as the weeks went by these occurrences became fewer and further between, till the time news was received in London of the investment of the fortresses of the Quadrilateral by the innumerable hosts of the League, brought together by the junction of the French and Russian Armies of the North and the conquerors of Vienna and Constantinople, who had returned on their tracks after garrisoning their conquests in the East.

Food in Britain, already at war prices, now began to rise still further, and soon touched famine prices. Wheat, which in the last decade of the nineteenth century had averaged about £9 a ton, rose to over £31 a ton, its price two years before the Battle of Waterloo. Other imported food-stuffs, of course, rose in proportion with the staple commodity, and the people of Britain saw, at first dimly, then more and more clearly, the real issue that had been involved in the depopulation of the rural districts to swell the populations of the towns, and the consequent lapse of enormous areas of land either into pasturage or unused wilderness.

In other words, Britain began to see approaching her doors an enemy before whose assault all human strength is impotent and all valour unavailing. Like Imperial Rome, she had depended for her food supply upon external sources, and now these sources were one by one being cut off.

The loss of the command of the Atlantic, the breaking of the Baltic blockade, and the consequent closing of all the continental ports save Hamburg, Amsterdam, Rotterdam, and Antwerp, had left her entirely dependent upon her own miserably insufficient internal resources and the Mediterranean route to India and the East.

More than this, too, only Hamburg, Antwerp, and the fortresses of the Quadrilateral now stood between her and actual invasion,—that supreme calamity which, until the raid upon Aberdeen, had been for centuries believed to be impossible.

Once let the League triumph in the Netherlands, as it had done in Central and South-Eastern Europe, and its legions would descend like an avalanche upon the shores of England, and the Lion of the Seas would find himself driven to bay in the stronghold which he had held inviolate for nearly a thousand years.

CHAPTER XXXV.

FROM CHAOS TO ARCADIE.

URING the three months of incessant strife and carnage which deluged the plains and valleys of Europe with blood after the fall of Berlin, the Terrorists took no part whatever in the war. At long intervals an air-ship was seen from the earth flying at full speed through the upper regions of the atmosphere, now over Europe, now over America, and now over Australia or the Cape of Good Hope; but if they held any communication with the earth they did so secretly, and only paid the briefest of visits, the objects of which could only be guessed at.

When one was sighted the fact was mentioned in the newspapers, and vague speculations were indulged in; but there was soon little room left for these in the public attention, especially in Britain, for as the news of disaster after disaster came pouring in, and the hosts of the League drew nearer and nearer to the western shores of Europe, all eyes were turned more and more anxiously across "the silver streak" which now alone separated the peaceful hills and valleys of England and Scotland from the destroying war-storm which had so swiftly desolated the fields of Europe, and all hearts were heavy with apprehension of coming sorrows.

The rapidity of their movements had naturally led to the supposition that several of the air-ships had taken the air for some unknown purpose, but in reality there were only two of them afloat during nearly the whole of the three months.

Of these, one was the *Orion*, on board of which Tremayne was visiting the various centres of the Brotherhood throughout the English-speaking world, making everything ready for the carrying out at the proper time of the great project to which he had devoted himself since the memorable night at Alanmere, when he had seen the vision of the world's Armageddon. The other was under the command of Michael Roburoff, who was busy in America and Canada perfecting the preparations for checkmating the designs of the American Ring, which were described in a former chapter.

The remainder of the members of the Inner Circle and those of the Outer Circle, living in Aeria, were quietly pursuing the most peaceful avocations, building houses and water-mills, clearing fields and laying out gardens, fishing in the lake and streams, and hunting in the forests as though they had never heard of the horrors of war, and had no part or share in the Titanic strife whose final issue they would soon have to go forth and decide.

One of the hardest workers in the colony was the Admiral of the aërial fleet. Morning after morning he shut himself up in his laboratory for three or four hours experimenting with explosives of various kinds, and especially on a new form of fire-shell which he had invented, and which he was now busy perfecting in preparation for the next, and, as he hoped, final conflict that he would have to wage with the forces of despotism and barbarism.

The afternoons he spent supervising the erection of the mills, and the construction of new machinery, and in exploring the mountain sides in search of mineral wealth, of which he was delighted to find abundant promise that was afterwards realised beyond his expectations.

On these exploring expeditions he was frequently accompanied by Natasha and Radna and her husband. Sometimes Arnold would be enticed away from his chemicals, and his designs on the lives of his enemies, and after breakfasting soon after sunrise would go off for a long day's ramble to some unknown part of their wonderful domain, in which, like children in a fairyland, they were always discovering some new wonders and beauties And, indeed, no children could have been happier or freer from care than they were during this delightful interval in the tragedy in which they were so soon to play such conspicuous parts.

The two **wedded** lovers, with the dark past put far behind hem for ever, **found** perfect happiness in **each** other's society, and so left, it is almost needless to add, Arnold and Natasha pretty much **to their own** devices. Indeed, Natasha had more than once **declared that she would** have to get the Princess to **join the party, as Radna had** proved herself **a hopeless failure as a chaperone.**

Every one in the valley by this time looked upon Arnold **and Natasha as lovers, though their** rank in the Brotherhood was so high that **no one** ventured to speak of them as betrothed **save** by implication. **How** Natas regarded **them was known** only to himself. He, **of** course, saw their intimacy, and since **he** said nothing he doubtless looked upon it with approval; but whether he regarded it **as an** intimacy of friends or of lovers, remained a mystery **even to** Natasha herself, for he never **by** any chance made an allusion to it.

As for **Arnold,** he had scrupulously observed the compact tacitly made between them on the first and only occasion that he had ever spoken words of love to her. They were the best of friends, the closest companions, and their intercourse with each other was absolutely frank and unrestrained, just as it would have been between **two** close friends of the same sex; but they understood **each other** perfectly, and by no word or deed did **either cross the line** that divides friendship from love.

She trusted him absolutely **in** all things, and he took this **trust as a** sacred pledge **between** them that until his part of **their** compact had been performed, love was a forbidden subject, **not even** to be approached.

So perfectly did Natasha play her part that though he spent **hours and** hours alone with her on their exploring expeditions, and in rowing and sailing on the lake, and though he spent many another hour **in** solitude, weighing her every word and action, **he** was utterly unable to truthfully congratulate himself on having made the slightest progress towards gaining that love without which, even if he held her to the compact in the day of victory, victory itself would be robbed of its crowning glory and dearest prize.

To a weaker man it would have been an impossible situation, **this constant** and familiar companionship with a girl whose wonderful beauty dazzled his eyes and fired his blood as he looked upon it, and whose winning charm of manner and grace of speech and action seemed to glorify her beauty until she seemed a being almost beyond the reach of merely human love —rather one of those daughters of men whom the sons of God looked upon in the early days of the world, and found so fair that they forsook heaven itself to woo them.

Trained and disciplined as he had been in the sternest of all schools, and strengthened as he was by the knowledge of the compact that existed between them, there were moments when his self-control was very sorely tried, moments when her hand would be clasped in his, or rested on his shoulder as he helped her across a stream or down some steep hillside, or when in the midst of some animated discussion she would stop short and face him, and suddenly confound his logic with a flash from her eyes and a smile on her lips that literally forced him to put forth a muscular effort to prevent himself from catching her in his arms and risking everything for just one kiss, one taste of the forbidden fruit within his reach, and yet parted from him by a sea of blood and flame that still lay between the world and that empire of peace which he had promised to win for her sweet sake.

Once, and once only, she had tried him almost too far. They had been discussing the possibility of ruling the world without the ultimate appeal to force, when the nations, weary at length of war, should have consented to disarm, and she, carried away by her own eloquent pleading for the ultimate triumph of peace and goodwill on earth, had laid her hand upon his arm, and was looking up at him with her lovely face aglow with the sweetest expression even he had ever seen upon it.

Their eyes met, and there was a sudden silence between them. The eloquent words died upon her lips, and a deep flush rose to her cheeks and then faded instantly away, leaving her pale and with a look almost of terror in her eyes. He took a quick step backwards, and, turning away as though he feared to look any longer upon her beauty, said in a low tone that trembled with the strength of his repressed passion—

"Natasha, for God's sake remember that I am only made of flesh and blood!"

In a moment she was by his side again, this time with her eyes downcast and her proud little head bent as though in acknowledgment of his reproof. Then she looked up again, and held out her hand and said—

"Forgive me; I have done wrong! Let us be friends again!"

There was a gentle emphasis on the word "friends" that was irresistible. He took her hand in silence, and after a pressure that was almost imperceptibly returned, let it go again, and they walked on together; but there was very little more said between them that evening.

This had happened one afternoon towards the middle of September, and two days later their delightful companionship came suddenly to an end, and the bond that existed between them was severed in a moment without warning, as a nerve thrilling with pleasure might be cut by an unexpected blow with a knife.

On the 16th of September the *Orion* returned from Australia. She touched the earth shortly after mid-day, and before sunset the *Azrael*, the vessel in which Michael Roburoff had gone to America, also returned, but without her commander. Her lieutenant, however, brought a despatch from him, which he delivered at once to Natas, who, immediately on reading it, sent for Tremayne.

It evidently contained matters of great importance, for they remained alone together discussing it for over an hour. At the end of that time Tremayne left the Master's house and went to look for Arnold. He found him just helping Natasha out of a skiff at a little landing-stage that had been built out into the lake for boating purposes. As soon as greetings had been exchanged, he said—

"Natasha, I have just left your father. He asked me, if I saw you, to tell you that he wishes to speak to you at once."

"Certainly," said Natasha. "I hope you have not brought bad news home from your travels. You are looking very serious about something," and without waiting for an answer, she was gone to obey her father's summons. As soon as she was out of earshot Tremayne put his arm through Arnold's, and, drawing him away towards a secluded portion of the shore of the lake, said—

"Arnold, old man, I have some very serious news for you. You must prepare yourself for the severest strain that, I believe, could be put on your loyalty and your honour."

"What is it? For Heaven's sake don't tell me that it has to do with Natasha!" exclaimed Arnold, stopping short and facing round, white to the lips with the sudden fear that possessed him. "You know"—

"Yes, I know everything," replied Tremayne, speaking almost as gently as a woman would have done, "and I am sorry to say that it has to do with her. I know what your hopes have been with regard to her, and no man on earth could have wished to see those hopes fulfilled more earnestly than I have done, but"—

"What do you mean, Tremayne? Speak out, and let me know the worst. If you tell me that I am to give her up, I tell you that I am"—

"'That I am an English gentleman, and that I will break my heart rather than my oath'—that is what you will tell me when I tell you that you must not only give up your hopes of winning Natasha, but that it is the Master's orders that you shall have the *Ithuriel* ready to sail at midnight to take her to America to Michael Roburoff, who has written to Natas to ask her for his wife."

Arnold heard him out in dazed, stupefied silence. It seemed too monstrous, too horrible, to be true. The sudden blow had stunned him. He tried to speak, but the words would not come. Tremayne, still standing with his arm through his, felt his whole body trembling, as though stricken with some sudden palsy. He led him on again, saying in a sterner tone than before—

"Come, come! Play the man, and remember that the work nearest to your hand is war, and not love. Remember the tremendous issues that are gathering to their fulfilment, and the part that you have to play in working them out. This is not a question of the happiness or the hopes of one man or woman, but of millions, of the whole human race. You, and you alone, hold in your hands the power to make the defeat of the League certain."

"And I will use it, have no fear of that!" replied Arnold, stopping again and passing his hand over his eyes like a man waking from an evil dream. "What I have sworn to do I will do; I am not going back from my oath. I will obey to the end, for she will do the same, and what would she think of me if I failed! Leave me alone for a bit now, old man. I must fight this thing out with myself, but the *Ithuriel* shall be ready to start at twelve."

Tremayne saw that he was himself again, and that it was better that he should do as he said; so with a word of farewell he turned away and left him alone with his thoughts. Halfway back to the settlement he met Natasha coming down towards the lake. She was deadly pale, but she walked with a firm step, and carried her head as proudly erect as ever. As they met she stopped him and said—

"Where is he?'

Tremayne's first thought was to try and persuade her to go back and leave Arnold to himself, but a look at Natasha's white set face and burning eyes warned him that she was not in a mood to take advice, and so he told her, and without another word she went on swiftly down the path that led to the lake.

The brief twilight of the tropics had passed before he reached a grove of palms on the western shore of the lake, towards which he had bent his steps when he left Tremayne. He walked with loose, aimless strides, now quickly and now slowly, and now stopping to watch the brightening moon shining upon the water.

He caught himself thinking what a lovely night it would be to take Natasha for a row, and then his mind sprang back with a jerk to the remembrance of the horrible journey that he was to begin at midnight—to take Natasha to another man, and leave her with him as his wife.

No, it could not be true. It was impossible that he should have fought and triumphed as he had done, and all for this. To give up the one woman he had ever loved in all his life, the woman he had snatched from slavery and degradation when not another man on earth could have done it.

What had this Roburoff done that she should be given to him for the mere asking? Why had he not come in person like a man to woo and win her if he could, and then he would have stood aside and bowed to her choice. But this curt order to take her away to him as though she were some piece of merchandise—no, if such things were possible, better that he had never—

"Richard!"

He felt a light touch on his arm, and turned round sharply. Natasha was standing beside him. He had been so engrossed by his dark thoughts that he had not heard her light step on the soft sward, and now he seemed to see her white face and great shining eyes looking up at him in the moonlight as though there was some mist floating between him and her. Suddenly the mist seemed to vanish. He saw tears under the long dark lashes, and the sweet red lips parted in a faint smile.

Lose her he might to-morrow, but for this one moment she was his and no other man's, let those who would say nay. That instant she was clasped helpless and unresisting in his arms, and her lips were giving his back kiss for kiss. Wreck and chaos might come now for all he cared. She loved him, and had given herself to him, if only for that one moonlit hour.

After that he could plunge into the battle again, and slay and spare not—yes, and he would slay without mercy. He would hurl his lightnings from the skies, and where they struck there should be death. If not love and life, then hate and death—it was not his choice. Let those who had chosen see to that; but for the present love and life were his, why should he not live? Then the mad, sweet delirium passed, and saner thoughts came. He released her suddenly, almost brusquely, and said with a harsh ring in his voice—

"Why did you come? Have you forgotten what so nearly happened the day before yesterday?"

"No, I have not forgotten it. I have remembered it, and that is why I came to tell you—what you know now."

Her face was rosy enough now, and she looked him straight in the eyes as she spoke, proud to confess the mastery that he had won.

"Now listen," she went on, speaking in a low, quick, passionate tone. "The will of the Master must be done. There is no appeal from that, either for you or me. He can dispose of me as he chooses, and I shall obey, as I warned you I should when you first told me that you would win me if you could.

"Well, you have won me, so far as I can be won. I love you, and I have come to tell you so before the shadow falls between us. And I have come to tell you that what you have won shall belong to no one else. I will obey my father to the letter, but the spirit is my affair. Now kiss me again, dear, and say good-bye. We have had our glimpse of heaven, and this is not the only life."

For one more brief moment she surrendered herself to him again. Their lips met and parted, and in an instant she had slipped out of his arms and was gone, leaving him dazed with her beauty and her winsomeness.

CHAPTER XXXVI.

LOVE AND DUTY.

A N hour later he walked back to the settlement, looking five years older than he had done a couple of hours before, but with his nerves steady and with the light of a solemn resolve burning in his eyes. He went straight to the *Ithuriel*, and made a minute personal inspection of the whole vessel, inside and out. He saw that every cylinder was charged, and that there was an ample supply of spare ones and ammunition on board, including a number of his new fire-shells. Then he went to Lieutenant Marston's quarters, and told him to have the crew in their places by half-past eleven; and this done, he paid a formal visit to the Master to report all ready.

Natas received him as usual, just as though nothing out of the common had happened; and if he noticed the change that had come over him, he made no sign that he did so. When Arnold had made his report, he merely said—

"Very good. You will start at twelve. The Chief has told you the nature and purpose of the voyage you are about to make, I presume?"

He bowed a silent affirmative, and Natas went on—

"The Chief and Anna Ornovski will go with you as witnesses for Michael Roburoff and Natasha, and the Chief will be provided with my sealed orders for your guidance in the immediate future. The rendezvous is a house on one of the spurs of the Alleghany Mountains. What time will it take to reach there?"

"The distance is about seven thousand miles. That will be

from thirty to thirty-five hours' flight according to the wind. With a fair wind we shall reach the Alleghanies a little before sunrise on the 18th."

"Then to make sure of that, if possible, you had better start an hour earlier. Natasha is making her preparations, and will be on board at eleven."

"Very well; I will be ready to start then," replied Arnold, speaking as calmly and formally as Natas had done. Then he saluted and walked out.

When he got into the open air he drew a deep breath. His teeth came together with a sharp snap, and his hands clenched. So it was true, then, this horrible thing, this sacrilege, this ruin, that had fallen upon his life and hers. Natas had spoken of giving her to this man as quietly as though it had been the most natural proceeding possible, an understood arrangement about which there could be no question. Well, he had sworn, and he would obey, but there would be a heavy price to pay for his obedience.

He did not see Natasha again that night. When the *Ithuriel* rose into the air she was in her cabin with the Princess, and did not appear during the voyage save at meals, when all the others were present, and then she joined in the conversation with a composure which showed that, externally at least, she had quite regained her habitual self-control.

Arnold spent the greater part of the voyage in the deck-saloon with Tremayne, talking over the events of the war, and arranging plans of future action. By mutual consent the object of their present voyage was not mentioned. As Arnold was more than two months and a half behind the news, he found not a little relief in hearing from Tremayne of all that had taken place since the recapture of the *Lucifer*.

The two men, who were now to be the active leaders of the Revolution which, as they hoped, was soon to overturn the whole fabric of Society, and introduce a new social order of things, conversed in this fashion, quietly discussing the terrific tragedy in which they were to play the leading parts, and arranging all the details of their joint action, until well into the night of the 17th.

About eleven Tremayne went to his cabin, and Arnold, going

to the conning-tower, told the man on the look-out to go below until he was called. Then he took his place, and remained alone with his thoughts as the *Ithuriel* sped on her way a thousand feet above the deserted waters of the Atlantic, until the dark mass of the American Continent loomed up in front of him to the westward.

As soon as he sighted land he went aft to the wheel-house, and slightly inclined the air-planes, causing the *Ithuriel* to soar upwards until the barometer marked a height of 6000 feet. At this elevation he passed over the mouth of the Chesapeake, and across Virginia; and a little more than an hour before sunrise the *Ithuriel* sank to the earth on one of the spurs of the Alleghanies, in sight of a lonely weather-board house, in one of the windows of which three lights were burning in the form of a triangle.

This building was used ostensibly as a shooting and hunting-box by Michael Roburoff and a couple of his friends, and in reality as a meeting-place for the Inner Circle or Executive Council of the American Section of the Brotherhood. This Section was, numerically speaking, the most important of the four branches into which the Outer Circle of the Brotherhood was divided—that is to say, the British, Continental, American, and Colonial Sections.

All told, the Terrorists had rather more than five million adherents in America and Canada, of whom more than four millions were men in the prime of life, and nearly all of Anglo-Saxon blood and English speech. All these men were not only armed, but trained in the use of firearms to a high degree of skill; their organisation, which had gradually grown up with the Brotherhood for twenty years, was known to the world only under the guise of the different forms of industrial unionism, but behind these there was a perfect system of discipline and command which the outer world had never even suspected.

The Section was divided first into squads of ten under the command of an eleventh, who alone knew the leaders of the other squads in his neighbourhood. Ten of these squads made a company, commanded by one man, who was only known to the squad-captains, and who alone knew the captain of the regiment, which was composed of ten companies.

The next step in the **organisation was** the brigade, consisting of ten regiments, the **captains** of which alone knew the commander of **the** brigade, **while the commanders** of the brigades were **alone** acquainted with **the members of** the Inner Circle or Executive Council which **managed the affairs of** the whole Section, **and** whose Chief **was the only man in the** Section **who could hold any** communication **with the Inner** Circle **of the Brotherhood itself, which, under the** immediate command **of Natas, governed the** whole organisation throughout the world.

This description will serve for all the Sections, as all **were** modelled upon **exactly** the same plan. The advantages of such an organisation **will** at once be obvious. In the first place, no member of the rank and file could possibly betray **more than** ten of his fellows, including his captain; while his treachery could, if necessary, be made known **in a few hours to ten** thousand others, not one of **whom he knew, and thus it would** be impossible for him **to escape the invariable** death penalty. The same is, **of course, equally true of the** captains and the commanders.

On the other hand, **the system was** equally convenient for the transmission **of** orders **from headquarters.** An order given **to ten commanders** of brigades **could, in** a **single** night, be **transmitted** individually to the **whole of** the Section, and yet **those** in command of the various divisions would not know **whence the orders came, save as** regards their immediate **superiors.**

It will be necessary for the **reader** to bear these few particulars **in mind** in order to understand future developments, which, without them, might **seem to** border on the impossible. **It is** only necessary to add **that** the full fighting **strength** of **the four** Sections of the Brotherhood amounted **to about twelve millions of** men, a considerable proportion **of whom were serv**ing as soldiers in **the** armies of the League **and the Alliance,** and that in its cosmopolitan aspect **it was known to the rank** and file as the Red International, whose members knew each other only by the possession **of** a little knot **of** red ribbon tied **into** the button-hole in **a** peculiar fashion on occasions of meetings for instruction **or** drill.

The three lights burning in the **form** of a triangle in the **window of** the house were a prearranged signal to avoid mistake on the part of those on board the air-ship. When they reached the earth, Arnold, acting under the instructions of Tremayne, who was his superior on land though his voluntary subordinate when afloat, left the *Ithuriel* and her crew in charge of Lieutenant Marston and Andrew Smith, the coxswain.

The remainder disembarked, and then the air-ship rose from the ground and ascended out of sight through a layer of clouds that hung some eight hundred feet above the high ground of the hills. Lieutenant Marston's orders were to remain out of sight for an hour and then return.

Arnold had not seen Natasha for several hours previous to the landing, and he noticed with wonder, by no means unmixed with something very like anger, that she looked a great deal more cheerful than she had done during the voyage. She had preserved her composure all through, but the effort of restraint had been visible. Now this had vanished, although the supreme hour of the sacrifice that her father had commanded her to make was actually at hand. When her feet touched the earth she looked round with a smile on her lips and a flush on her cheeks, and said, in a voice in which there was no perceptible trace of anxiety or suffering—

"So this is the place of my bridal, is it? Well, I must say that a more cheerful one might have been selected; yet perhaps, after all, such a gloomy spot is more suitable to the ceremony. Come along; I suppose the bridegroom will be anxiously waiting the coming of the bride. I wonder what sort of a reception I shall have. Come, my Lord of Alanmere, your arm; and you, Captain Arnold, bring the Princess. We have a good deal to do before it gets light."

These were strange words to be uttered by a girl who but a few hours before had voluntarily confessed her love for one man, and was on the eve of compulsorily giving herself up to another one. Had it been any one else but Natasha, Arnold could have felt only disgust; but his love made it impossible for him to believe her guilty of such unworthy lightness as her words bespoke, even on the plain evidence before him, so he simply choked back his anger as best he might, and followed towards the house, speechless with astonishment at the marvellous change that had come over the daughter of Natas.

Tremayne knocked in a peculiar fashion on the window, and then repeated the knock on the door, which was opened almost immediately.

"Who stands there?" asked a voice in French.

"Those who bring the expected bride," replied Tremayne in German.

"And by whose authority?" This time the question was in Spanish.

"In the Master's name," said Tremayne in English.

"Enter! you are welcome."

A second door was now opened inside the house, and through it a light shone into the passage. The four visitors entered, and, passing through the second door, found themselves in a plainly-furnished room, down the centre of which ran a long table, flanked by five chairs on each side, in each of which, save one, sat a masked and shrouded figure exactly similar to those which Arnold had seen when he was first introduced to the Council-chamber in the house on Clapham Common. In a chair at one end of the table sat another figure similarly draped.

The door was closed as they entered, and the member of the Circle who had let them in returned to his seat. No word was spoken until this was done. Then Natasha, leaving her three companions by the door, advanced alone to the lower end of the table.

As she did so, Arnold for the first time noticed that she carried her magazine pistol in a sheath at her belt. He and Tremayne were, as a matter of course, armed with a brace of these weapons, but this was the first time that he had ever seen Natasha carry her pistol openly. Wondering greatly what this strange sight might mean, he waited with breathless anxiety for the drama to begin.

As Natasha took her stand at the opposite end of the table, the figure in the chair at the top rose and unmasked, displaying the pallid countenance of the Chief of the American Section. He looked to Arnold anything but a bridegroom awaiting his bride, and the ceremony which was to unite him to her for ever. His cheeks and lips were bloodless, and his eyes wandered restlessly from Natasha to Tremayne and back again. He glanced to and fro in silence for several moments, and when he at last found his voice he said, in half-choked, broken accents—

"What is this? Why am I honoured by the presence of the Chief and the Admiral of the Air? I asked only that if the Master consented to grant my humble petition in reward for my services, the daughter of Natas should come attended simply by a sister of the Brotherhood and the messenger that I sent."

They let him finish, although it was with manifest difficulty that he stammered to the end of his speech. Arnold, still wondering at the strange turn events had taken, saw Tremayne's lips tighten and his brows contract in the effort to repress a smile. The other masked figures at the table moved restlessly in their seats, and glanced from one to another. Seeing this, Tremayne stepped quickly forward to Natasha's side, and said in a stern, commanding tone—

"I am the Chief of the Central Council, and I order every one here to keep his seat and remain silent until the daughter of Natas has spoken."

The ten masked and hooded heads instantly bowed consent. Then Tremayne stepped back again, and Natasha spoke. There was a keen, angry light in her eyes, and a bright flush upon her cheek, but her voice was smooth and silvery, and in strange contrast to the words that she used, almost to the end.

"Did you think, Michael Roburoff, that the Master of the Terror would send his daughter to her bridal so poorly escorted as you say? Surely that would have been almost as much of a slight as you put upon me when, instead of coming to woo me as a true lover should have done, you contented yourself with sending a messenger as though you were some Eastern potentate despatching an envoy to demand the hand of the daughter of a vassal.

"It would seem that this sudden love which you do me the honour to profess for me has destroyed your manners as well as your reason. But since you have assumed so high a dignity, it is not seemly that you should stand to hear what I have to say; sit down, for it looks as though standing were a trouble to you."

Michael Roburoff, who by this time could scarcely support

himself on his trembling limbs, sank suddenly back into his chair and covered his face with his hands.

"That is not very lover-like to cover your eyes when the bride that you have asked for is standing in front of you; but as long as you don't cover your ears as well, I will forgive you the slight. Now, listen.

"I have come, as you see, and I have brought with me the answer of the Master to your request. Until an hour ago I did not know what it was myself, for, like the rest of the faithful members of the Brotherhood, I obey the word of the Master blindly.

"You, as it would appear, maddened by what you are pleased to call your love for me, have dared to attempt to make terms where you swore to obey blindly to the death. You have dared to place me, the daughter of Natas, in the balance against the allegiance of the American Section on the eve of the supreme crisis of its work, thus imperilling the results of twenty years of labour.

"If you had not been mad you would have foreseen the results of such treachery. As it is you must learn them now. What I have said has been proved by your own hand, and the proof is here in the hand of the Chief. This is the answer of Natas to the servant who would have betrayed him in the hour of trial."

She took a folded paper from her belt as she spoke, and, unfolding it, read in clear, deliberate tones—

> Michael Roburoff, late chief of the American Section of the Brotherhood. When you joined the Order, you took an oath to obey the directions of its chiefs to the death, and you acknowledged that death would be the just penalty of perjury. My orders to you were to complete the arrangements for bringing the American Section into action when you received the signal to do so. Instead of doing that, you have sought to bargain with me for the price of its allegiance. That is treachery, and the penalty of treachery is death.
>
> NATAS.

"Those are the words of the Master," continued Natasha, throwing the paper down upon the table with one hand, and drawing her pistol with the other. "It rests with the Chief to say when and where the sentence of the Master shall be carried out."

"Let it be carried out here, and now," said Tremayne, "and

"He dropped back into his chair with a bullet in his brain."

let him who has anything to say against it speak now, or for ever hold his peace."

The ten heads bowed once more in silence, and Natasha went on still addressing the trembling wretch who sat huddled in the chair in front of her.

"You have asked for a bride, Michael Roburoff, and she has come to you, and I can promise you that you shall sleep soundly in her embrace. Your bride is Death, and I have chosen to bring her to you with my own hand, that all here may see how the daughter of Natas can avenge an insult to her womanhood.

"You have been guilty of treachery to the Brotherhood, and for that you might have been punished by any hand; but you would also have condemned me to the infamy of a loveless marriage, and that is an insult that no one shall punish but myself. Look up, and, if you can, die like a man."

Roburoff took his hands from his face, and with an inarticulate cry started to his feet. The same instant Natasha's hand went up, her pistol flashed, and he dropped back again into his chair with a bullet in his brain. Then she replaced the pistol in her belt, and going up to Arnold held out both her hands and said, as he clasped them in his own—

"If the Master's reply had been different, that bullet would by this time have been in my own heart."

CHAPTER XXXVII.

THE CAPTURE OF A CONTINENT.

ITHIN an hour after the execution of Michael Roburoff the *Ithuriel* was winging her way back to Aeria, and at least two of her company were anticipating their return to the valley with feelings very different to those with which they had contemplated their departure.

When the last farewells and congratulations had been spoken, and the air-ship rose from the earth, Tremayne returned to the house to commence forthwith the great task which now developed upon him; for in addition to being Chief of the Central Executive, he now assumed the direct command of the American Section, which, after long consideration, had been selected as the nucleus of the Federation of the English-speaking peoples of the world.

For a fortnight he worked almost night and day, attending to every detail with the utmost care, and bringing into play all those rare powers of mind which in the first instance had led Natas to select him as the visible head of the Executive. In this way the chief consequence of the love-madness of Roburoff had been to place at the head of affairs in America the one man of all others most fitted by descent and ability to carry out such a work, and to this fact its complete success must in a great measure be attributed.

So perfectly were his plans laid and executed, that right up to the moment when the signal was given and the plans became actions, American society went about its daily business without the remotest suspicion that it was living on the slope of a slumbering volcano whose fires were so soon to burst forth and finally consume the social fabric which, despite its splendid exterior, was inwardly as rotten as were the social fabrics of Rome and Byzantium on the eve of their fall.

On the 1st of October the cables brought the news of the fall of the Quadrilateral, the storming of Hamburg, and the retreat of the British forces on Antwerp. Four days later came the tidings of a great battle under the walls of Antwerp, in which the British and German forces, outnumbered ten to one by the innumerable hosts of the League, had suffered a decisive defeat, which rendered it imperative for them to fall back upon the Allied fleets in the Scheldt, and to leave the Netherlands to the mercy of the Tsar and his allies, who were thus left undisputed masters of the continent of Europe.

This last and crowning victory had been achieved by exactly the same means which had accomplished all the other triumphs of the campaign, and therefore there will be no need to enter into any detailed description of it. Indeed, the fall of the Quadrilateral and the defeat of the last army of the Alliance round Antwerp would have been accomplished much more easily and speedily than it had been but for the fact that the weather, which had been fine up to the end of July, had suddenly broken, and a succession of violent storms and gales from the north and north-west had made it impossible for the war-balloons to be brought into action with any degree of effectiveness.

During the last week of September the storms had ceased, and then the work of destruction began. Not even the hitherto impregnable fortresses of Tournay, Mons, Namur, and Liége had been able to withstand the assault from the air any better than the forts of Berlin or the walls of Constantinople. A day's bombardment had sufficed to reduce them to ruins, and, the chain once broken, the armies of the League swept in wave after wave across the plains which they had guarded.

The loss of life had been unparalleled even in this the greatest of all wars, for the British and Germans had fought with a dogged resolution which, but for the vastly superior numbers and the irresistible means of destruction employed against them, must infallibly have triumphed. As it was, it was only when valour had achieved its last sacrifice, and further resistance became rather madness than devotion, that the retreat was finally **sounded in time to embark the** remnants **of the armies of the Alliance on board** the warships. Happily at **the very hour when this** was being done the weather broke **again, and the ships of the** Allied fleets were therefore able to **make their way to sea through** storm and darkness, **unmolested by the war-balloons.**

While the American press was teeming with columns **of description telegraphed at** enormous cost from the seat of **war, and with absolutely misleading** articles **as to the** policy **of the League and the attitude of** studious neutrality **that was to be observed by the United States** Government, **the dockyards, controlled directly and indirectly** by the American Ring, **were working night and day putting** the **finishing touches to the flotilla of dynamite cruisers and other war-vessels intended to carry** out **the plan revealed by Michael Roburoff on board the** *Ithuriel,* **after he had been taken off the** *Aurania* **in the Mid-Atlantic.**

Briefly described, **this was as follows:—Representative government in America** had **by this time become a complete sham.** The whole **political machinery and internal resources of the United States were now** virtually at the **command of** a great Ring **of capitalists who,** through **the medium of** the huge **monopolies which** they controlled, **and the** enormous sums of **money at their** command, held the **country in** the hollow of **their hand. These** men **were as** totally devoid of all human **feeling or public sentiment as it was** possible for human beings **to be. They had** grown **rich in** virtue of their contempt of **every principle of** justice and mercy, and they had **no** other **object in life** than to still further increase their gigantic hoards **of wealth, and to** multiply the enormous powers which they already wielded. The then condition of affairs in Europe had presented them with **such an** opportunity **as no** other combination **of** circumstances could have given them, and ignoring, as such wretches would naturally do, **all ties** of blood and kindred **speech, they had** determined to **take** advantage of the situation **to the utmost.**

In **the guise of the United States** Government the Ring had **concluded a secret** treaty **with the** commanders of the League, **in virtue of** which, at a stipulated point in the struggle, America **was to declare war on** Britain, invade Canada by land, and send to sea an immense flotilla of swift dynamite cruisers of tremendously destructive power, which had been constructed openly in the Government dockyards, ostensibly for coast defence, and secretly in private yards belonging to the various Corporations composing the Ring.

This flotilla was to co-operate with the fleet of the League as soon as England had been invaded, and complete the blockade of the British ports. Were this once accomplished nothing could save Britian from starvation into surrender, and the British Empire from disintegration and partition between the Ring and the Commanders of the League, who would then practically divide the mastery of the world among them.

On the night of the 4th of October the five words: "The hour and the man," went flying over the wires from Washington throughout the length and breadth of the North American Continent. The next morning half the industries of the United States were paralysed; all the lines of communication by telegraph and rail between the east and west were severed, the shore ends of the Atlantic cables were cut, no newspapers appeared, and every dockyard on the eastern coast was in the hands of the Terrorists.

To complete the stupor produced by this swift succession of astounding events, when the sun rose an air-ship was seen floating high in the air over the ten arsenals of the United States—that is to say, over Portsmouth, Charlestown, Brooklyn, League Island, New London, Washington, Norfolk, Pensacola, Mare Island, and Port Royal, while two others held Chicago and St. Louis, the great railway centres for the west and south, at their mercy, and the *Ithuriel*, with a broad red flag flying from her stern, swept like a meteor along the eastern coast from Maine to Florida.

To attempt to describe the condition of frenzied panic into which the inhabitants of the threatened cities, and even the whole of the Eastern States were thrown by the events of that ever-memorable morning, would be to essay an utterly hopeless task. From the millionaire in his palace to the outcasts who swarmed in the slums, not a man or a woman kept a cool head save those who were in the councils of the Terrorists. The blow had fallen with such stupefying suddenness that as far as America was concerned the Revolution was practically accomplished before any one very well knew what had happened.

Out of the midst of an apparently peaceful and industrious population five millions of armed men had sprung in a single night. Factories and workshops had opened their doors, but none entered them; ships lay idle by the wharves, offices were deserted, and the great reels of paper hung motionless beside the paralysed machines which should have converted them into newspapers.

It was not a strike, for no mere trade organisation could have accomplished such a miracle. It was the force born of the accumulation of twenty years of untiring labour striking one mighty blow which shattered the commercial fabric of a continent in a single instant. Those who had been clerks or labourers yesterday, patient, peaceful, and law-abiding, were to-day soldiers, armed and disciplined, and obeying with automatic regularity the unheard command of some unknown chief.

This of itself would have been enough to throw the United States into a panic; but, worse than all, the presence of the air-ships, holding at their mercy the arsenals and the richest cities in the Eastern States, proved that tremendous and all as it was, this was only a phase of some vast and mysterious cataclysm which might as easily involve the whole civilised world as it could overwhelm the United States of America.

By noon, almost without striking a blow, every dynamite cruiser and warship on the eastern coast had been seized and manned by the Terrorists. To the dismay of the authorities, it was found that more than half the army and navy, officers and men alike, had obeyed the mysterious summons that had gone throughout the land the night before; and matters reached a climax when, as the clocks of Washington were striking twelve, the President himself was arrested in the White House.

All the streets of Washington were in the hands of the Terrorists, and at one o'clock Tremayne, after posting guards at all the approaches, entered the Senate, and in the name of Natas proclaimed the Constitution of the United States null and void, and the Government dissolved.

Then with a copy of the Constitution in his hand he proceeded to the steps of the Capitol, and, in the presence of a vast throng of the armed members of the American Section, he proclaimed the Federation of the English-speaking races of the world, in virtue of their bonds of kindred blood and speech and common interests; and amidst a scene of the wildest enthusiasm called upon all who owned those bonds to forget the artificial divisions that had separated them into hostile nations and communities, and to follow the leadership of the Brotherhood to the conquest of the earth.

Then in a few strong and simple phrases he exposed the subservience of the Government to the capitalist Ring, and described the inhuman compact that it had entered into with the arch-enemies of national freedom and personal liberty to crush the motherland of the Anglo-Saxon nations, and for the sake of sordid gain to rivet the fetters of oppression upon the limbs of the race which for a thousand years had stood in the forefront of the battle for freedom.

As he concluded his appeal, one mighty shout of wrath and execration rose up to heaven from a million throats. He waited until this died away into silence, then, raising the copy of the Constitution above his head, he cried in clear ringing tones—

"For a hundred and fifty years this has been boasted as the bulwark of liberty, and used as the instrument of social and commercial oppression. The Republic of America has been governed, not by patriots and statesmen, but by millionaires and their hired political puppets. It is therefore a fraud and a sham, and deserves no longer to exist!"

So saying, he tore the paper into fragments and cast them into the air amidst a storm of cheers and volley after volley of musketry. While the enthusiasm was at its height the *Ithuriel* suddenly swept downwards from the sky in full view of the mighty assemblage that swarmed round the Capitol. She was greeted with a roar of wondering welcome, for her appearance was the fulfilment of a promise upon which the success of the Revolution in America had largely depended.

This was the promise, issued by Tremayne several days previously through the commanders of the various divisions of the Section, that as soon as the Anglo-Saxon Federation was proclaimed and accepted in America, the whole Brotherhood throughout the world would fall into line with it, and place its aërial navy at the disposal of its leaders. Practically this was giving the empire of the world in exchange for a money-despotism, of which every one save the millionaires and their servants had become heartily sick.

There were few who in their hearts did not believe the Republic to be a colossal fraud, and therefore there were few who regretted it.

The *Ithuriel* passed slowly over the heads of the wondering crowd, and came to a standstill alongside the steps on which Tremayne was standing. The crowd saw a man on her deck shake hands with Tremayne and give him a folded paper. Then the air-ship swept gracefully upward again in a spiral curve until she hung motionless over the dome of the Capitol.

Amidst a silence born of breathless interest to know the import of this message from the sky, Tremayne opened the paper, glanced at its contents, and handed it to the senior officer in command of the brigades, who stood beside him. This man, a veteran who had grown grey in the service of the Brotherhood, advanced with the open paper in his hand, and read out in a loud voice—

Natas sends greeting to the Brotherhood in America. The work has been well done, and the reward of patient labour is at hand. This is to name Alan Tremayne, Chief of the Central Executive, first President of the Anglo-Saxon Federation throughout the world, and to invest him with the supreme authority for the ordering of its affairs. The aërial navy of the Brotherhood is placed at his disposal to co-operate with the armies and fleets of the Federation.

NATAS.

When the mighty shout of acclamation which greeted the reading of this commission had died away, Tremayne stepped forward again and spoke the few words that now remained to be said—

"I accept the office and all that it implies. The fate of the world lies in our hands, and as we decide it so will the future lot of humanity be good or evil. The armies of the Franco-Slavonian League are now masters of the continent of Europe, and are preparing for the invasion of Britain. The first use that I shall make of the authority now vested in me will be to summon the Tsar in the name of the Federation to sheathe the sword at once, and relinquish his designs on Britain. The moment that one of his soldiers sets foot on the sacred soil of our motherland I shall declare war upon him, and it shall be a war, not of conquest, but of extermination, and we will make an end of tyranny on earth for ever.

"Now let those who are not on guard-duty go to their homes, and remember that they are now citizens of a greater realm than the United States, and endowed with more than national duties and responsibilities. Let every man's person and property be respected, and let the penalty of all violence be death. Those who have plotted against the public welfare will be dealt with in due course, and yonder air-ship will be despatched with our message to the Tsar at sundown. Long live the Federation!"

Millions of throats took up the cry as the last words left his lips until it rolled away from the Capitol in mighty waves of sound, flowing along the crowded streets and overrunning the utmost confines of the capital.

Thus, without the loss of a hundred lives, and in a space of less than twelve hours, was the Revolution in America accomplished. The triumph of the Terrorists was as complete as it had been unexpected. Menaced by air and sea and land, the great centres of population made no resistance, and, when they learnt the true object of the Revolution, wanted to make none. No one really believed in the late Government, and every one in his soul hated and despised the millionaires.

There was no bond between them and their fellow-men but money, and the moment that was snapped they were looked upon in their true nature as criminals and outcasts from the pale of humanity. By sundown, when the *Ithuriel* left for the seat of war, the members of the Ring and those of the late Government who refused to acknowledge the Federation were lodged in prison, and news had been received from Montreal that the simultaneous rising of the Canadian Section had been completely successful, and that all the railways and arsenals and ships of war were in the hands of the Terrorists, so completing the capture of the North American continent.

The President of the Federation and his faithful subordinates went to work, without losing an hour, to reorganise as far as was necessary the internal affairs of the continent of which they had so suddenly become the undisputed masters.

There was some trouble with the British authorities in Canada, who, from mistaken motives of duty to the mother country, at first refused to recognise the Federation.

The consequence of this was that Tremayne went north the next day and had an interview with the Governor General at Montreal. At the same time he ordered six air-ships and twenty-five dynamite cruisers to blockade the St. Lawrence and the eastern ports. The Canadian Pacific Railway and the telegraph lines to the west were already in the hands of the Terrorists, and a million men were under arms waiting his commands.

A very brief explanation, therefore, sufficed to show the Governor that forcible resistance would not only be the purest madness, but that it would also seriously interfere with the working of the great scheme of Federation, the object of which was, not merely to place Britain in the first place among the nations, but to make the Anglo-Saxon race the one dominant power in the whole world.

To all the Governor's objections on the score of loyalty to the British Crown, Tremayne, who heard him to the end without interruption, simply replied in a tone that precluded all further argument—

"The day of states and empires, and therefore of loyalty to sovereigns, has gone by. The history of nations is the history of intrigue, quarrelling, and bloodshed, and we are determined to put a stop to warfare for good and all. We hold in our hands the only power that can thwart the designs of the League and avert an era of tyranny and retrogression. That power we intend to use whether the British Government likes it or not.

"We shall save Britain, if necessary, in spite of her rulers. If they stand in the way, so much the worse for them. They will be called upon to resign in favour of the Federation and its Executive within the next seven days. If they consent, the forces of the League will never cross the Straits of Dover. If they refuse we shall allow Britain to taste the results of their choice, and then settle the matter in our own way."

The next day the Governor dissolved the Canadian Legislatures "under protest," and retired into private life for the present. He felt that it was no time to argue with a man who had millions of men behind him, to say nothing of an aërial fleet which alone could reduce Montreal to ruins in twelve hours.

After arranging matters in Canada the President returned to Washington in the *Ariel*, which he had taken into his personal service for the present, and set about disposing of the Ring and those members of the late Government who were most deeply implicated in the secret alliance with the leaders of the League. When the facts of this scheme were made public they raised such a storm of popular indignation, that if those responsible for it had been turned loose in the streets of Washington they would have been torn to pieces like vermin.

As it was, however, they were placed upon their trial before a Commission of seven members of the Inner Circle of the American Section, presided over by the President. Their guilt was speedily proved beyond the shadow of a doubt. Documents, memoranda, and telegrams were produced by men who had seemed their most trusted servants, but had been in reality members of the Brotherhood told off to unearth their schemes.

Cyphers were translated which showed that they had practically sold the resources of the country in advance to the Tsar and his allies, and that they were only waiting the signal to declare war without warning and without cause upon Britain, blockade her ports, and starve her into surrender and acceptance of any terms that the victors might choose to impose. Last of all, the terms of the bargain between the League and the Ring were produced, signed by the late President and the Secretary of State, and countersigned by the Russian Minister at Washington.

The Court sat for three days, and reassembled on the fourth to deliver its verdict and sentence. Fifteen members of the late Government, including the President, the Vice-President, and the Secretary of State, and twenty-four great capitalists composing the Ring, were found guilty of giving and receiving bribes, directly and indirectly, and of betraying and conspiring to betray the confidence of the American people in its elected representatives, and also of conspiring to make war without due cause on a friendly Power for purely commercial reasons.

At eleven o'clock on the morning of the 9th of October the

President of the Federation rose in the Senate House, amidst breathless silence, to pronounce the sentence of the Court.

"All the accused," he said, speaking in slow, deliberate tones, "have been proved guilty of such treason against their own race and the welfare of humanity as no men ever were guilty of before in all the disreputable history of state-craft. In view of the suffering and misery to millions of individuals, and the irreparable injury to the cause of civilisation that would have resulted from the success of their schemes, it would be impossible for human wit to devise any punishment which in itself would be adequate. The sentence of the Court is the extreme penalty known to human justice—Death!"

A shudder passed through the vast assembly as he pronounced the ominous word, and the accused, who but a few days before had looked upon the world as their footstool, gazed with blanched faces and terror-stricken eyes upon each other. He paused for a moment, and looked sternly upon them. Then he went on—

"But the Federation does not seek a punishment of revenge, but of justice; nor shall its first act of government be the shedding of blood, however guilty. Therefore, as President I override the sentence of death, and instead condemn you, who have been proved guilty of this unspeakable crime, to confiscation of the wealth that you have acquired so unscrupulously and used so mercilessly, and to perpetual banishment with your wives and families, who have shared the profits of your infamous traffic.

"You will be at once conveyed to Kodiak Island, off the south coast of Alaska, and landed there. Once every six months you will be visited by a steamer, which will supply you with the necessaries of life, and the original penalty of death will be the immediate punishment of any one of you who attempts to return to a world of which you from this moment cease to be citizens."

The sentence was carried out without an hour's delay. The exiles, with their wives and families, were placed under a strong guard in a special train, which conveyed them from Washington *viâ* St. Louis to San Francisco, where they were transferred to a steamer which took them to the lonely and desolate island in the frozen North which was to be their home for the rest of their lives. They were followed by the execrations of a whole people and the regrets of none save the money-worshippers who had respected them, not as men, but as incarnations of the purchasing power of wealth.

The huge fortunes which they had amassed, amounting in the aggregate to more than three hundred millions in English money, were placed in the public treasury for the immediate purposes of the war which the Federation was about to wage for the empire of the world. All their real estate property was transferred to the various municipalities in which it was situated, and their rents devoted to the relief of taxation, while the railways and other enterprises which they had controlled were declared public property, and placed in the hands of boards of management composed of their own officials.

Within a week everything was working as smoothly as though no Revolution had ever taken place. All officials whose honesty there was no reason to suspect were retained in their offices, while those who were dismissed were replaced without any friction. All the affairs of government were conducted upon purely business principles, just as though the country had been a huge commercial concern, save for the fact that the chief object was efficiency and not profit-making.

Money was abundantly plentiful, and the necessaries of life were cheaper than they had ever been before. Perhaps the principal reason for this happy state of affairs was the fact that law and politics had suddenly ceased to be trades at which money could be made. People were amazed at the rapidity with which public business was transacted.

The President and his Council had at one stroke abrogated every civil and criminal law known to the old Constitution, and proclaimed in their place a simple, comprehensive code which was practically identical with the Decalogue. To this a final clause was added, stating that those who could not live without breaking any of these laws would not be considered as fit to live in civilised society, and would therefore be effectively removed from the companionship of their fellows.

While the internal affairs of the Federation in America were being thus set in order, events had been moving rapidly in other parts of the world. The Tsar, the King of Italy, and General le Gallifet, who was now Dictator of France in all but name, were masters of the continent of Europe. The Anglo-Teutonic Alliance was a thing of the past. Germany, Austria, and Turkey were completely crushed, and the minor Powers had succumbed.

Britain, crippled by the terrible cost in ships and men of the victory of the Nile, had evacuated the Mediterranean after dismantling the fortifications of Gibraltar and Malta, and had concentrated the remains of her fleets in the home waters, to prepare for the invasion which was now inevitable as soon as fair winds and fine weather made it possible for the war-balloons of the League to cross the water and co-operate with the invading forces.

The Tsar, as had been expected, had not even deigned to reply to Tremayne's summons to disarm, and so the last arrangements for bringing the forces of the Federation into action at the proper time were pushed on with the utmost speed. The blockade of the American and Canadian coasts was rigidly maintained, and no vessels allowed to enter or leave any of the ports. All the warships of the League had been withdrawn from the Atlantic, and the great ocean highway remained unploughed by a single keel.

On the 10th of October the *Ithuriel* had returned from her second trip to the West, with the refusal of the British Government to recognise the Federation as a duly constituted Power, or to have any dealings with its leaders. "Great Britain," the reply concluded, "will stand or fall alone; and even in the event of ultimate defeat, the King of England will prefer to make terms with the sovereigns opposed to him rather than with those whose acts have proved them to be beyond the pale of the law of nations."

"Ah!" said Tremayne to Arnold, as he read the royal words, "the policy which lost the American Colonies for the sake of an idea still rules at Westminster, it seems. But I'm not going to let the old Lion be strangled in his den for all that.

"Natas was right when he said that Britain would have to pass through the fire before she would accept the Federation, and so I suppose she must, more's the pity. Still, perhaps it will be all for the best in the long run. You can't expect to root up a thousand-year-old oak as easily as a mushroom that only came up the day before yesterday."

CHAPTER XXXVIII.

THE BEGINNING OF THE END.

IT is now time to return to Britain, to the land which the course of events had so far appeared to single out as the battle-ground upon which was to be fought the Armageddon of the Western World—that conflict of the giants, the issue of which was to decide whether the Anglo-Saxon race was still to remain in the forefront of civilisation and progress, or whether it was to fall, crushed and broken, beneath the assaults of enemies descending upon the motherland of the Anglo-Saxon nations; whether the valour and personal devotion, which for a thousand years had scarcely known a defeat by flood or field, was still to pursue its course of victory, or whether it was to succumb to weight of numbers and mechanical discipline, reinforced by means of assault and destruction which so far had turned the world-war of 1904 into a succession of colossal and unparalleled butcheries, such as had never been known before in the history of human strife.

When the Allied fleets, bearing the remains of the British and German armies which had been driven out of the Netherlands, reached England, and the news of the crowning disaster of the war in Europe was published in detail in the newspapers, the popular mind seemed suddenly afflicted with a paralysis of stupefaction.

Men looked back over the long series of triumphs in which British valour and British resolution had again and again proved themselves invulnerable to the assaults of overwhelming numbers. They thought of the glories of the Peninsula, of the unbreakable strength **of the thin red line** at Waterloo, of the magnificent madness **of** Balaclava, **and** the invincible steadiness and discipline that had made Inkermann a word to be remembered with **pride as long as** the **English** name endured.

Then their thoughts reverted to the immediate past, **and they heard the shock of** colossal armaments, compared **with which the armies of the past** appeared but pigmies in strength. **They saw empires defended** by millions **of** soldiers crushed in **a few weeks, and** a wave of conquest sweep in one **unbroken roll from end** to end of a continent in less time than **it would have taken** Napoleon **or** Wellington to have fought **a single** campaign. Huge fortresses, rendered, as men had believed, impregnable by the employment of every resource known to the most advanced military science, had been reduced to heaps of defenceless ruins in a few hours by a bombardment, under which their magnificent guns had lain as impotent as though they had been the culverins of three hundred years ago.

It seemed like **some** hideous nightmare **of** the nations, in which Europe had gone **mad**, revelling **in superhuman** bloodshed and destruction,—a conflict in **which more than** earthly forces had **been let** loose, accomplishing a **carnage so** immense that **the mind** could only form **a dim and imperfect conception of it. And now** this red tide of desolation **had swept** up to the western verge of the Continent, and was there **gathering** strength and volume **day** by day against the hour **when** it should burst and oversweep the narrow strip of water **which** separated the inviolate fields of England from the blackened and blood-stained waste that it had left behind it from the Russian frontier to the German Ocean.

It seemed impossible, and yet it was true. **The** first line of defence, the hitherto invincible fleet, magnificently **as it** had been managed, and heroically as it had been fought, **had** failed in the supreme hour of trial. It had failed, not because the sailors of Britain had done their duty **less** valiantly than they had done in the **days of** Rodney and Nelson, but simply because the conditions of naval warfare had been entirely changed, **because** the personal equation had been almost eliminated from the problem of battle, and because the new **warfare** of the seas had been waged rather with machinery **than with men.**

In all the war not a single battle had been fought at close quarters; there had been plenty of instances of brilliant manœuvring, of torpedo-boats running the gauntlet and hurling their deadly missiles against the sides of battleships and cruisers, and of ships rammed and sunk in a few instants by consummately-handled opponents; but the days of boarding and cutting out, of night surprises and fire-ships, had gone by for ever.

The irresistible artillery with which modern science had armed the warships of all nations had made these feats impossible, and so had placed the valour which achieved them out of court. Within the last few weeks scarcely a day had passed but had witnessed the return of some mighty ironclad or splendid cruiser, which had set out a miracle of offensive and defensive strength, little better than a floating ruin, wrecked and shattered almost beyond recognition by the awful battle-storm through which she had passed.

The magnificent armament which had held the Atlantic route had come back represented only by a few crippled ships almost unfit for any further service. True, they and those which never returned had rendered a splendid account of themselves before the enemy, but the fact remained—they were not defeated, but they were no longer able to perform the Titanic task which had been allotted to them.

So, too, with the Mediterranean fleet, which, so far as sea-fighting was concerned, had achieved the most splendid triumph of the war. It had completely destroyed the enemy opposed to it, but the victory had been purchased at such a terrible price that, but for the squadron which had come to its aid, it would hardly have been able to reach home in safety.

In a word, the lesson of the struggle on the sea had been, that modern artillery was just as effective whether fired by Englishmen, Frenchmen, or Russians; that where a torpedo struck a warship was crippled, no matter what the nationality or the relative valour of her crew; and that where once the ram found its mark the ship that it struck went down, no matter what flag she was flying.

And then, behind and beyond all that was definitely known in England of the results of the war, there were vague rumours of calamities and catastrophes in more distant parts of the

world, which seemed to promise nothing less than universal
anarchy, and the submergence of civilisation under some all-
devouring wave of barbarism.

All regular communications with the East had been stopped
for several weeks; that India was lost, was guessed by intuition
rather than known as a certainty. Australia was as isolated
from Britain as though it had been on another planet, and
now every one of the Atlantic cables had suddenly ceased to
respond to the stimulus of the electric current. No ships
came from the East, or West, or South. The British ports
were choked with fleets of useless merchantmen, to which the
markets of the world were no longer open.

Some few venturesome craft that had set out to explore
the now silent ocean had never returned, and every warship
that could be made fit for service was imperatively needed to
meet the now inevitable attack on the shores of the English
Channel and the southern portions of the North Sea. Only
one messenger had arrived from the outside world since the
remains of Admiral Beresford's fleet had returned from the
Mediterranean, and she had come, not by land or sea, but
through the air.

On the 6th of October an air-ship had been seen flying at an
incredible speed across the south of England. She had reached
London, and touched the ground during the night on Hampstead
Heath; the next day she had descended again in the same
place, taken a single man on board, and then vanished into
space again. What her errand had been is well known to the
reader; but outside the members of the Cabinet Council no one
in England, save the King and his Ministers, knew the object of
her mission.

For fifteen days after that event the enemy across the water
made no sign, although from the coast of Kent round about
Deal and Dover could be seen fleets of transports and war-
vessels hurrying along the French coast, and on clear days a
thousand telescopes turned towards the French shore made
visible the ominous clusters of moving black spots above the
land, which betokened the presence of the terrible machines which
had wrought such havoc on the towns and fortresses of Europe.

It was only the calm before the final outburst of the storm.
The Tsar and his allies were marshalling their hosts for the

invasion, and collecting transports and fleets of war-vessels to convoy them. For several days strong north-westerly gales had made the sea impassable for the war-balloons, as though to the very last the winds and waves were conspiring to defend their ancient mistress. But this could not last for ever.

Sooner or later the winds must sink or change, and then these war-hawks of the air would wing their flight across the silver streak, and Portsmouth, and Dover, and London would be as defenceless beneath their attack as Berlin, Vienna, and Hamburg had been. And after them would come the millions of the League, descending like a locust swarm upon the fields of eastern England; and after that would come the deluge.

But the old Lion of the Seas was not skulking in his lair, or trembling at the advent of his enemies, however numerous and mighty they might be. On sea not a day passed but some daring raid was made on the transports passing to and fro in the narrow seas, and all the while a running fight was kept up with cruisers and battleships that approached too near to the still inviolate shore. So surely as they did so the signals flashed along the coast; and if they escaped at all from the fierce sortie that they provoked, it was with shot-riddled sides and battered top-works, sure signs that the Lion still had claws, and could strike home with them.

On shore, from Land's End to John o' Groats, and from Holyhead to the Forelands, everything that could be done was being done to prepare for the struggle with the invader. It must, however, be confessed that, in comparison with the enormous forces of the League, the ranks of the defenders were miserably scanty. Forty years of universal military service on the Continent had borne their fruits.

Soldiers are not made in a few weeks or months; and where the League had millions in the field, Britain, even counting the remnant of her German allies, that had been brought over from Antwerp, could hardly muster hundreds of thousands. All told, there were little more than a million men available for the defence of the country; and should the landing of the invaders be successfully effected, not less than six millions of men, trained to the highest efficiency, and flushed with a rapid succession of unparalleled victories, would be hurled against them.

This was the legitimate outcome of the policy to which Britain had adhered since first she had maintained a standing army, instead of pursuing the ancient policy of making every man a soldier, which had won the triumphs of Crecy and Agincourt. She had trusted everything to her sea-line of defence. Now that was practically broken, and it seemed inevitable that her second line, by reason of its miserable inadequacy, should fail her in a trial which no one had ever dreamt it would have to endure.

A very grave aspect was given to the situation by the fact that the great mass of the industrial population seemed strangely indifferent to the impending catastrophe which was hanging over the land. It appeared to be impossible to make them believe that an invasion of Britain was really at hand, and that the hour had come when every man would be called upon to fight for the preservation of his own hearth and home.

Vague threats of "eating the Russians alive" if they ever did dare to come, were heard on every hand; but beyond this, and apart from the regular army and the volunteers, men went about their daily avocations very much as usual, grumbling at the ever-increasing price of food, and here and there breaking out into bread riots wherever it was suspected that some wealthy man was trying to corner food for his own commercial benefit, but making no serious or combined efforts to prepare for a general rising in case the threatened invasion became a fact.

Such was the general state of affairs in Britain when, on the night of the 27th of October, the north-west gales sank suddenly to a calm, and the dawn of the 28th brought the news from Dover to London that the war-balloons of the League had taken the air, and were crossing the Straits.

CHAPTER XXXIX.

THE BATTLE OF DOVER.

NTIL the war of 1904, it had been an undisputed axiom in naval warfare that a territorial attack upon an enemy's coast by a fleet was foredoomed to failure unless that enemy's fleet had been either crippled beyond effective action, or securely blockaded in distant ports. As an axiom secondary to this, it was also held that it would be impossible for an invading force, although convoyed by a powerful fleet, to make good its footing upon any portion of a hostile coast defended by forts mounting heavy long-range guns.

These principles have held good throughout the history of naval warfare from the time when Sir Walter Raleigh first laid them down in the early portion of his *History of the World*, written after the destruction of the Spanish Armada.

But now two elements had been introduced which altered the conditions of naval warfare even more radically than one of them had changed those of military warfare. Had it not been for this the attack upon the shores of England made by the commanders of the League would probably either have been a failure, or it would have stopped at a demonstration of force, as did that of the great Napoleon in 1803.

The portion of the Kentish coast selected for the attack was that stretching from Folkestone to Deal, and it would perhaps have been difficult to find in the whole world any portion of sea-coast more strongly defended than this was on the morning of October 28, 1904; and yet, as the event proved, the fortresses which lined it were as useless and impotent for defence as the old Martello towers of a hundred and fifty years before would have been.

As the war-balloons rose into the air from the heights above

Boulogne, good telescopes at Dover enabled their possessors to count no less than seventy-five of them. Fifty of these were quite newly constructed, and were of a much improved type, as they had been built in view of the practical experience gained by the first fleet.

This aërial fleet divided into three squadrons; one, numbering twenty-five, steered south-westward in the direction of Folkestone, twelve shaped their course towards Deal, and the remaining thirty-eight steered directly across the Sraits to Dover. As they approached the English coast they continually rose, until by the time they had reached the land, aided by the light south-easterly breeze which was then blowing, they floated at a height of more than five thousand feet.

All this while not a warship or a transport had put to sea. The whole fleet of the League lay along the coast of France between Calais and Dieppe, under the protection of shore batteries so powerful that it would have been madness for the British fleet to have assumed the offensive with regard to them. With the exception of two squadrons reserved for a possible attack upon Portsmouth and Harwich, all that remained from the disasters and costly victories of the war of the once mighty British naval armament was massed together for the defence of that portion of the coast which would evidently have to bear the brunt of the attack of the League.

Ranged along the coast from Folkestone to Deal was an armament consisting of forty-five battleships of the first, second, and third classes, supported by fifteen coast-defence ironclads, seventy armoured and thirty-two unarmoured cruisers, forty gunboats, and a hundred and fifty torpedo-boats.

Such was the still magnificent fleet that patrolled the waters of the narrow sea,—a fleet as impotent for the time being as a flotilla of Thames steamboats would have been in face of the tactics employed against it by the League. Had the enemy's fleet but come out into the open, as it would have been compelled to do under the old conditions of warfare, to fight its way across the narrow strip of water, there is little doubt but that the issue of the day would have been very different, and that what had been left of it would have been driven back, shattered and defeated, to the shelter of the French shore batteries.

But, in accordance with the invariable tactics of the League, the first and most deadly assault was delivered from the air. The war-balloons stationed themselves above the fortifications on land, totally ignoring the presence of the fleet, and a few minutes after ten o'clock began to rain their deadly hail of explosives down upon them. Fifteen were placed over Dover Castle, and five over the fort on the Admiralty Pier, while the rest were distributed over the town and the forts on the hills above it. In an hour everything was in a state of the most horrible confusion. The town was on fire in a hundred places from the effects of the fire-shells. The Castle hill seemed as if it had been suddenly turned into a volcano; jets of bright flame kept leaping up from its summit and sides, followed by thunderous explosions and masses of earth and masonry hurled into the air, mingled with guns and fragments of human bodies.

The end of the Admiralty Pier, with its huge blocks of stone wrenched asunder and pulverised by incessant explosions of dynamite and emmensite, collapsed and subsided into the sea, carrying fort, guns, and magazine with it; and all along the height of the Shakespeare cliff the earthworks had been blown up and scattered into dust, and a huge portion of the cliff itself had been blasted out and hurled down on to the beach.

Meanwhile the victims of this terrible assault had, in the nature of the case, been able to do nothing but keep up a vertical fire, in the hope of piercing the gas envelopes of the balloons, and so bringing them to the earth. For more than an hour this fusilade produced no effect; but at length the concentrated fire of several Maxim and Nordenfelt guns, projecting a hail of missiles into the sky, brought about a result which was even more disastrous to the town than it was to its assailants.

Four of the aerostats came within the zone swept by the bullets. Riddled through and through, their gas-holders collapsed, and their cars plunged downwards from a height of more than 5000 feet. A few seconds later four frightful explosions burst forth in different parts of the town, for the four cargoes exploded simultaneously as they struck the earth.

The emmensite and dynamite tore whole streets of houses to fragments, and hurled them far and wide into the air, to fall back again on other parts of the town, and at the same time the fire-shells ignited, and set the ruins blazing like so many furnaces. No more shots were fired into the air after that.

There was nothing for it but for British valour to bow to the inevitable, and evacuate the town and what remained of its fortifications; and so with sad and heavy hearts the remnant of the brave defenders turned their faces inland, leaving Dover to its fate. Meanwhile exactly the same havoc had been wrought upon Folkestone and Deal. Hour after hour the merciless work continued, until by three o'clock in the afternoon there was not a gun left upon the whole range of coast that was capable of firing a shot.

All this time the ammunition tenders of the aërial fleet had been winging their way to and fro across the Strait constantly renewing the shells of the war-balloons.

As soon as it began to grow dusk the naval battle commenced. Numerically speaking the attacking force was somewhat inferior to that of the defenders, but now the second element, which so completely altered the tactics of sea fighting, was for the first time in the war brought into play.

As the battleships of the League steamed out to engage the opponents, who were thirsting to avenge the destruction that had been wrought upon the land, a small flotilla of twenty-five insignificant-looking little craft, with neither masts nor funnels, and looking more like half-submerged elongated turtles than anything else, followed in tow close under their quarters. Hardly had the furious cannonade broken out into thunder and flame along the two opposing lines, than these strange craft sank gently and silently beneath the waves. They were submarine vessels belonging to the French navy, an improved type of the *Zédé* class, which had been in existence for more than ten years.[1]

These vessels were capable of sinking to a depth of twenty feet, and remaining for four hours without returning to the surface. They were propelled by twin screws worked by electricity at a speed of twenty knots, and were provided with an electric searchlight, which enabled them to find the hulls of hostile ships in the dark.

[1] The *Naval Annual* for 1893 mentions two types of submarine boats, the *Zédé* and the *Goubet*, both belonging to the French navy, which had then been tried with success. The same work mentions no such vessels belonging to Britain, nor yet any prospect of her possessing one. The effects described here as produced by these terrible machines are little, if at all, exaggerated. Granted ten years of progress, and they will be reproduced to a certainty.—AUTHOR.

Each carried three torpedoes, which could be launched from a tube forward so as to strike the hull of the doomed ship from beneath. As soon as the torpedo was discharged the submarine boat spun round on her heel and headed away at full speed in an opposite direction out of the area of the explosion.

The effects of such terrible and, indeed, irresistible engines of naval warfare were soon made manifest upon the ships of the British fleet. In the heat of the battle, with every gun in action, and raining a hail of shot and shell upon her adversary, a great battleship would receive an unseen blow, struck in the dark upon her most vulnerable part, a huge column of water would rise up from under her side, and a few minutes later the splendid fabric would heel over and go down like a floating volcano, to be quenched by the waves that closed over her.

But as if it were not enough that the defending fleet should be attacked from the surface of the water and the depths of the sea, the war-balloons, winging their way out from the scene of ruin that they had wrought on shore, soon began to take their part in the work of death and destruction.

Each of them was provided with a mirror set a little in front of the bow of the car, at an angle which could be varied according to the elevation. A little forward of the centre of the car was a tube fixed on a level with the centre of the mirror. The ship selected for destruction was brought under the car, and the speed of the balloon was regulated so that the ship was relatively stationary to it.

As soon as the glare from one of the funnels could be seen through the tube reflected in the centre of the mirror, a trap was sprung in the floor of the car, and a shell charged with dynamite, which, it will be remembered, explodes vertically downwards, was released, and, where the calculations were accurately made, passed down the funnel and exploded in the interior of the vessel, bursting her boilers and reducing her to a helpless wreck at a single stroke.

Every time this horribly ingenious contrivance was successfully brought into play a battleship or a cruiser was either sunk or reduced to impotence. In order to make their aim the surer, the aerostats descended to within three hundred yards of their prey, and where the missile failed to pass through the funnel it invariably struck the deck close to it, tearing up the armour sheathing, and wrecking the funnel itself so completely that the steaming-power of the vessel was very seriously reduced.

All night long the battle raged incessantly along a semicircle some twelve miles long, the centre of which was Dover. Crowds of anxious watchers on the shore watched the continuous flashes of the guns through the darkness, varied ever and anon by some tremendous explosion which told the fate of a warship that had fired her last shot.

All night long the incessant thunder of the battle rolled to and fro along the echoing coast, and when morning broke the light dawned upon a scene of desolation and destruction on sea and shore such as had never been witnessed before in the history of warfare. On land were the smoking ruins of houses, still smouldering in the remains of the fires which had consumed them; forts which twenty-four hours before had grinned defiance at the enemy were shapeless heaps of earth and stone, and armour-plating torn into great jagged fragments; and on sea were a few half-crippled wrecks, the remains of the British fleet, with their flags still flying, and such guns as were not disabled firing their last rounds at the victorious foe.

To the eastward of these about half the fleet of the League, in but little better condition, was advancing in now overwhelming force upon them, and behind these again a swarm of troopships and transports were heading out from the French shore. About an hour after dawn the *Centurion*, the last of the British battleships, was struck by one of the submarine torpedoes, broke in two, and went down with her flag flying and her guns blazing away to the last moment. So ended the battle of Dover, the most disastrous sea-fight in the history of the world, and the death-struggle of the Mistress of the Seas.

The last news of the tremendous tragedy reached the now panic-stricken capital half an hour before the receipt of similar tidings from Harwich, announcing the destruction of the defending fleet and forts, and the capture of the town by exactly the same means as those employed against Dover. Nothing now lay between London and the invading forces but the utterly inadequate army and the lines of fortifications, which could not be expected to offer any more effective resistance to the assault of the war-balloons than had those of the three towns on the Kentish coast.

CHAPTER XL.

BELEAGUERED LONDON.

 A MONTH had passed since the battle of Dover. It had been a month of incessant fighting, of battles by day and night, of heroic defences and dearly-bought victories, but still of constant triumphs and irresistible progress for the ever-increasing legions of the League. From sunrise to sunrise the roar of artillery, the rattle of musketry, and the clash of steel had never ceased to sound to the north and south of London as, over battlefield after battlefield, the two hosts which had poured in constant streams through Harwich and Dover had fought their way, literally mile by mile, towards the capital of the modern world.

Day and night the fighting never stopped. As soon as two hostile divisions had fought each other to a standstill, and from sheer weariness of the flesh the battle died down in one part of the huge arena, the flame sprang up in another, and raged on with ever renewed fury. Outnumbered four and five to one in every engagement, and with the terrible war-balloons raining death on them from the clouds, the British armies had eclipsed all the triumphs of the long array of their former victories by the magnificent devotion that they showed in the hour of what seemed to be the death-struggle of the Empire.

The glories of Inkermann and Balaclava, of Albuera and Waterloo, paled before the achievements of the whole-souled heroism displayed by the British soldiery standing, as it were, with its back to the wall, and fighting, not so much with any hope of victory, for that was soon seen to be a physical impossibility, but with the invincible determination not to permit the invader to advance on London save over the dead bodies of its defenders.

Such a gallant defence had never been made before in the face of such irresistible odds. When the soldiers of the League first set foot on British soil the defending armies of the North and South had, with the greatest exertions, been brought up to a fighting strength of about twelve hundred thousand men. So stubborn had been the heroism with which they had disputed the progress of their enemies that by the time that the guns of the League were planted on the heights that commanded the Metropolis, more than a million and a half of men had gone down under the hail of British bullets and the rush of British bayonets.

Of all the battlefields of this the bloodiest war in the history of human strife, none had been so deeply dyed with blood as had been the fair and fertile English gardens and meadows over which the hosts of the League had fought their way to the confines of London. Only the weight of overwhelming numbers, reinforced by engines of destruction which could strike without the possibility of effective retaliation, had made their progress possible.

Had they met their heroic foes as they had met them in the days of the old warfare, their superiority of numbers would have availed them but little. They would have been hurled back and driven into the sea, and not a man of them all would have left British soil alive had it been but a question of military attack and defence.

But this was not a war of men. It was a war of machines, and those who wielded the most effective machinery for the destruction of life won battle after battle as a matter of course, just as a man armed with a repeating rifle would overcome a better man armed with a bow and arrow.

Natas had formed an entirely accurate estimate of the policy of the leaders of the League when he told Tremayne, in the library at Alanmere, that they would concentrate all their efforts on the reduction of London. The rest of the kingdom had been for the present entirely ignored.

London was the heart of the British Empire and of the

English-speaking world, for the matter of that, and therefore it had been determined to strike one deadly blow at the vital centre of the whole huge organism. That paralysed, the rest must fall to pieces of necessity. The fleet was destroyed, and every soldier that Britain could put into the field had been mustered for the defence of London. Therefore the fall of London meant the conquest of Britain.

After the battles of Dover and Harwich the invading forces advanced upon London in the following order: The Army of the South had landed at Deal, Dover, and Folkestone in three divisions, and after a series of terrific conflicts had fought its way *viâ* Chatham, Maidstone, and Tunbridge to the banks of the Thames, and occupied all the commanding positions from Shooter's Hill to Richmond. These three forces were composed entirely of French and Italian army corps, and numbered from first to last nearly four million men.

On the north the invading force was almost wholly Russian, and was under the command of the Tzar in person, in whom the supreme command of the armies of the League had by common consent been now vested. A constant service of transports, plying day and night between Antwerp and Harwich, had placed at his disposal a force about equal to that of the Army of the South, although he had lost over seven hundred thousand men before he was able to occupy the line of heights from Hornsey to Hampstead, with flanking positions at Brondesbury and Harlesden to the west, and at Tottenham, Stratford, and Barking to the east.

By the 29th of November all the railways were in the hands of the invaders. A chain of war-balloons between Barking and Shooter's Hill closed the Thames. The forts at Tilbury had been destroyed by an aërial bombardment. A flotilla of submarine torpedo-vessels had blown up the defences of the estuary of the Thames and Medway, and led to the fall of Sheerness and Chatham, and had then been docked at Sheerness, there being no further present use for them.

The other half of the squadron, supported by a few battle-ships and cruisers which had survived the battle of Dover, had proceeded to Portsmouth, destroyed the booms and submarine defences, while a detachment of aerostats shelled the land defences, and then in a moment of wanton revenge had blown up the venerable hulk of the *Victory*, which had gone down at her moorings with her flag still flying as it had done a hundred years before at the fight of Trafalgar. After this inglorious achievement they had been laid up in dock to wait for their next opportunity of destruction, should it ever occur.

London was thus cut off from all communication, not only with the outside world, but even from the rest of England. The remnants of the armies of defence had been gradually driven in upon the vast wilderness of bricks and mortar which now held more than eight millions of men, women, and children, hemmed in by long lines of batteries and entrenched camps, from which thousands of guns hurled their projectiles far and wide into the crowded masses of the houses, shattering them with bursting shells, and laying the whole streets in ruins, while overhead the war-balloons slowly circled hither and thither, dropping their fire-shells and completing the ruin and havoc wrought by the artillery of the siege-trains.

Under such circumstances surrender was really only a matter of time, and that time had very nearly come. The London and North-Western Railway, which had been the last to fall into the hands of the invaders, had been closed for over a week, and food was running very short. Eight millions of people massed together in a space of thirty or forty square miles' area can only be fed and kept healthy under the most favourable conditions. Hemmed in as London now was, from being the best ordered great city in the world, it had degenerated with frightful rapidity into a vast abode of plague and famine, a mass of human suffering and misery beyond all conception or possibility of description.

Defence there was now practically none; but still the invaders did not leave their vantage ground on the hills, and not a soldier of the League had so far set foot in London proper. Either the besiegers preferred to starve the great city into surrender at discretion, and then extort ruinous terms, or else they hesitated to plunge into that tremendous gulf of human misery, maddened by hunger and made desperate by despair. If they did so hesitate they were wise, for London was too vast to be carried by assault or by any series of assaults.

No army could have lived in its wilderness of streets swarming with enemies, who would have fought them from house to house and street to street. Once they had entered that mighty maze of streets and squares both their artillery and their war-balloons would have been useless, for they would only have buried friend and foe in common destruction. There were plenty of ways into London, but the way out was a very different matter.

Had a general assault been attempted, not a man would ever have got out of London alive. The commanders of the League saw this clearly, and so they kept their position on the heights, wasted the city with an almost constant bombardment, and, while they drew their supplies from the fertile lands in their rear, lay on their arms and waited for the inevitable.

Within the besieged area martial law prevailed universally. Riots were of daily, almost hourly, occurrence, but they were repressed with an iron hand, and the rioters were shot down in the streets without mercy; for, though siege and famine were bad enough, anarchy breaking out amidst that vast sweltering mass of human beings would have been a thousand times worse, and so the King, who, assisted by the Prime Minister and the Cabinet Council, had assumed the control of the whole city, had directed that order was to be maintained at any price.

The remains of the army were quartered in the parks under canvas, and billeted in houses throughout the various districts, in order to support the police in repressing disorder and protecting property. Still, in spite of all that could be done, matters were rapidly coming to a terrible pass. In a week, at the latest, the horses of the cavalry would be eaten. For a fortnight London had almost lived upon horse-flesh. In the poorer quarters there was not a dog to be seen, and a sewer rat was considered a delicacy.

Eight million mouths had made short work of even the vast supplies that had been hurriedly poured into the city as soon as the invasion had become a certainty, and absolute starvation was now a matter of a few days at the outside. There were millions of money lying idle, but very soon a five-pound note would not buy even a little loaf of bread.

But famine was by no means the only horror that afflicted

London during those awful days and nights. All round the heights the booming of cannon sounded incessantly. Huge shells went screaming through the air overhead to fall and burst amidst some swarming hive of humanity, scattering death and mutilation where they fell, and high up in the air the fleet of aerostats perpetually circled, dropping their fire-shells and blasting cartridges on the dense masses of houses, until a hundred conflagrations were raging at once in different parts of the city.

No help had come from outside. Indeed none was to be expected. There was only one Power in the world that was now capable of coping with the forces of the victorious League, but its overtures had been rejected, and neither the King nor any of his advisers had now the slightest idea as to how those who controlled it would now use it. No one knew the real strength of the Terrorists, or the Federation which they professed to control.

All that was known was that, if they choose, they could with their aërial fleet sweep the war-balloons from the air in a few moments and destroy the batteries of the besiegers; but they had made no sign after the rejection of their President's offer to prevent the landing of the forces of the League on condition that the British Government accepted the Federation, and resigned its powers in favour of its Executive.

The refusal of those terms had now cost more than a million British lives, and an incalculable amount of human suffering and destruction of property. Until the news of the disaster of Dover had actually reached London, no one had really believed that it was possible for an invading force to land on British soil and exist for twenty-four hours. Now the impossible had been made possible, and the last crushing blow must fall within the next few days. After that who knew what might befall?

So far as could be seen, Britain lay helpless at the mercy of her foes. Her allies had ceased to exist as independent Powers, and the Russian and the Gaul were thundering at her gates as, fifteen hundred years before, the Goth had thundered at the gates of the Eternal City in the last days of the Roman Empire.

If the terms of the Federation could have been offered again, it is probable that the King of England would have been the first man to own his mistake and that of his advisers and accept them, for now the choice lay between utter and humiliating defeat and the breaking up of the Empire, and the recognition of the Federation. After all, the kinship of a race was a greater fact in the supreme hour of national disaster than the maintenance of a dynasty or the perpetuation of a particular form of government.

It was not now a question of nation against nation, but of race against race. The fierce flood of war had swept away all smaller distinctions. It was necessary to rise to the altitude of the problem of the Government, not of nations, but of the world. Was the genius of the East or of the West to shape the future destinies of the human race? That was the mighty problem of which the events of the next few weeks were to work out the solution, for when the sun set on the Field of Armageddon the fate of Humanity would be fixed for centuries to come.

CHAPTER XLI.

AN ENVOY OF DELIVERANCE.

FROM the time that the Tsar had received the conditional declaration of war from the President of the Anglo-Saxon Federation in America to nightfall on the 20th of November, when the surrender of the capital of the British Empire was considered to be a matter of a few days only, the Commander-in-Chief of the forces of the League was absolutely in the dark, not only as to the actual intentions of the Terrorists, if they had any, but also as to the doings of his allies in America.

According to the stipulations arranged between himself and the confidential agent of the American Government, the blockading flotilla of dynamite cruisers ought to have sailed from America as soon as the cypher message containing the news of the battle of Dover reached New York. The message had been duly sent *via* Queenstown and New York, and had been acknowledged in the usual way, but no definite reply had come to it, and a month had elapsed without the appearance of the promised squadron. The explanation of this will be readily guessed. The American end of the Queenstown cable had been reconnected with Washington, but it was under the absolute control of Tremayne, who permitted no one to use it save himself.

Other messages had been sent to which no reply had been received, and a swift French cruiser, which had been launched at Brest since the battle of Dover, had been despatched across the Atlantic to discover the reason of this strange silence. She had gone, but she had never returned. The Atlantic highway appeared to be barred by some invisible force. No vessels came from the westward, and those which started from the east were never heard of again.

His Majesty had treated the summons of the President of the Federation with silent contempt, just as such a victorious autocrat might have been expected to do. True, he knew the terrific power wielded by the Terrorists through their aërial fleet, and he had an uncomfortable conviction, which refused to be entirely stifled, that in the days to come he would have to reckon with them and it.

But that a member of the Terrorist Brotherhood could by any possible means have placed himself at the head of any body of men sufficiently numerous or well-disciplined to make them a force to be seriously reckoned with in military warfare, his Majesty had never for a moment believed.

And, more than this, however disquieting might be the uncertainty due to the ominous silence on the other side of the Atlantic, and the non-arrival of the expected fleet, there stood the great and significant fact that the army of the League had been permitted, without molestation either from the Terrorists or the Federation in whose name they had presumed to declare war upon him, not only to destroy what remained of the British fleet, but to completely invest the very capital of Anglo-Saxondom itself.

All this had been done; the sacred soil of Britain itself had been violated by the invading hosts; the army of defence had been slowly, and at a tremendous sacrifice of life on both sides, forced back from line after line, and position after position, into the city itself; his batteries were raining their hail of shot and shell from the heights round London, and his aerostats were hurling ruin from the sky upon the crowded millions locked up in the beleaguered space; and yet the man who had presumed to tell him that the hour in which he set foot on British soil would be the last of his Empire, had done absolutely nothing to interrupt the march of conquest.

From this it will be seen that Alexander Romanoff was at least as completely in the dark as to the possible course of the events of the near future as was the King of England himself, shut up in his capital, and cut off from all communication from the rest of the world.

On the morning of the 29th of November there was held at the Prime Minister's rooms in Downing Street a Cabinet Council, presided over by the King in person. After the Council had remained for about an hour in earnest consultation, a stranger was admitted to the room in which they were sitting.

The reader would have recognised him in a moment as Maurice Colston, otherwise Alexis Mazanoff, for he was dressed almost exactly as he had been on that memorable night, just thirteen months before, when he made the acquaintance of Richard Arnold on the Thames Embankment.

Well-dressed, well-fed, and perfectly at ease, he entered the Council Chamber without any aggressive assumption, but still with the quiet confidence of a man who knows that he is practically master of the situation. How he had even got into London, beleaguered as it was on every side in such fashion that no one could get out of it without being seen and shot by the besiegers, was a mystery; but how he could have in his possession, as he had, a despatch dated thirty-six hours previously in New York was a still deeper mystery; and upon neither of these points did he make the slightest attempt to enlighten the members of the British Cabinet.

All that he said was that he was the bearer of a message from the President of the Anglo-Saxon Federation in America, and that he was instructed to return that night to New York with such answer as the British Government might think fit to make to it. It was this message that had been the subject of the deliberations of the Council before his admission, and its net effect was as follows.

It was now practically certain, indeed proved to demonstration, that the forces at the command of the British Government were not capable of coping with those brought against them by the commanders of the League, and that therefore Britain, if left to her own resources, must inevitably succumb, and submit to such terms as her conquerors might think fit to impose upon her. The choice before the British Government thus lay between surrender to her foreign enemies, whose objects were well known to be dismemberment of the Empire and the reduction of Great Britain to the rank of a third-class Power,—to say nothing of the payment of a war indemnity which could not fail to be paralysing,—and the consent of those who controlled the destinies of the mother country to accept a Federation of the whole Anglo-Saxon race, to waive the merely national idea in favour of the racial one, and to permit the Executive Council of the Federation to assume those governmental functions which were exercised at present by the King and the British Houses of Parliament.

In a word, the choice lay between conquest by a league of foreign powers and the merging of Britain into the Federation of the English-speaking peoples of the world.

If the former choice were taken, the only prospect possible under the condition of things was a possibly enormous sacrifice of human life on the side of both Britain and its enemies, a gigantic loss in money, the crippling of British trade and commerce, and then a possible, nay probable, social revolution to which the message distinctly pointed.

If the latter choice were taken, the forces of the Federation would be at once brought into the field against those of the League, the siege of London would be raised, the power of the invaders would be effectually broken for ever, and the stigma of conquest finally wiped away.

It is only just to record the fact that in this supreme crisis of British history the man who most strongly insisted upon the acceptance of the terms which he had previously, as he now confessed in the most manly and outspoken fashion, rejected in ignorance of the true situation of affairs, was the man who believed that he would lose a crown by accepting them.

When the Ambassador of the Federation had been presented to the Council, the King rose in his place and handed to him with his own hands a sealed letter, saying as he did so—

"Mr. Mazanoff, I am still to a great extent in ignorance as to the inexplicable combination of events which has made it necessary for me to return this affirmative answer to the message of which you are the bearer. I am, however, fully aware that the Earl of Alanmere, whose name I have seen at the foot of this document with the most profound astonishment, is in a position to do what he says.

"The course of events has been exactly that which he predicted. I know, too, that whatever causes may have led him to unite himself to those known as the Terrorists, he is an English nobleman, and a man to whom falsehood or bad faith is absolutely impossible. In your marvellous aërial fleet I know also that he wields the only power capable of being successfully opposed to those terrible machines which had wrought such havoc upon the fleets and armies, not only of Britain, but of Europe.

"To a certain extent this is a surrender, but I feel that it will be better to surrender the destinies of Britain into the hands of her own blood and kindred than to the tender mercies of her alien enemies. My own personal feelings must weigh as nothing in the balance where the fate, not only of this country, but perhaps of the whole world, is now poised.

"After all, the first duty of a Constitutional King is not to himself and his dynasty, but to his country and his people, and therefore I feel that it will be better for me and mine to be citizens of a free Federation of the English-speaking peoples, and of the nations to which Britain has given birth, than the titular sovereign and Royal family of a conquered country, holding the mockery of royalty on the sufferance of their conquerors.

"Tell Lord Alanmere from me that I now accept the terms he has offered as President of the Anglo-Saxon Federation, first, because at all hazards I would see Britain delivered from her enemies; and, secondly, because I have chosen rather to be an English gentleman without a crown, than to wear a crown which after all would only be gift from my conquerors."

Edward VII. spoke with visible emotion, but with a dignity which even Mazanoff, little and all as he respected the name of king, felt himself compelled to recognise and respect. He took the letter with a bow that was more one of reverence than of courtesy, and as he put it into his breast-pocket of his coat he said—

"The President will receive your Majesty's reply with as genuine pleasure and satisfaction as I shall give it to him. Though I am a Russian without a drop of English blood in my veins, I have always looked upon the British race as the real bulwark of freedom, and I rejoice that the King of England has not permitted either tradition or personal feeling to stand in the way of the last triumph of the Anglo-Saxon race.

"As long as the English language is spoken your Majesty's name will be held in greater honour for this sacrifice which you make to-day, than will that of any other English king for the greatest triumph of arms ever achieved in the history of your country.

"I must now take my leave, for I must be in New York to-morrow night. I have your word that I shall not be watched or followed after I leave here. Hold the city for six days more at all costs, and on the seventh at the latest the siege shall be raised and the enemies of Britain destroyed in their own entrenchments."

So saying, the envoy of the Federation bowed once more to the King and the astonished members of his Council, and was escorted to the door.

Once in the street he strode away rapidly through Parliament Street and the Strand, then up Drury Lane, until he reached the door of a mean-looking house in a squalid court, and entering this with a latch-key, disappeared.

Three hours later a Russian soldier of the line, wearing an almost imperceptible knot of red ribbon in one of the buttonholes of his tunic, passed through the Russian lines on Hampstead Heath unchallenged by the sentries, and made his way northward to Northaw Wood, which he reached soon after nightfall.

Within half an hour the *Ithuriel* rose from the midst of a thick clump of trees like a grey shadow rising into the night, and darted southward and upward at such a speed that the keenest eyes must soon have lost sight of her from the earth.

She passed over the beleaguered city at a height of nearly ten thousand feet, and then swept sharply round to the eastward. She stopped immediately over the lights of Sheerness, and descended to within a thousand feet of the dock, in which could be seen the detachment of the French submarine vessels lying waiting to be sent on their next errand of destruction.

As soon as those on board her had made out the dock clearly she ascended a thousand feet and went about half a mile to the southward. From that position she poured a rapid hail of shells into the dock, which was instantly transformed into a cavity vomiting green flame and fragments of iron and human bodies. In five minutes nothing was left of the dock or its contents but a churned-up swamp of muddy water and shattered stonework.

Then, her errand so far accomplished, the air-ship sped away to the south-westward, and within an hour she had destroyed in like fashion the submarine squadron in the Government dock at Portsmouth, and was winging her way westward to New York with the reply of the King of England to the President of the Federation.

CHAPTER XLII.

THE EVE OF ARMAGEDDON.

WHEN the news of the destruction of the two divisions of the submarine squadron reached the headquarters of the League on the night of the 29th, it would have been difficult to say whether anger or consternation most prevailed among the leaders. A council of war was hurriedly summoned to discuss an event which it was impossible to look upon as anything less than a calamity.

The destruction which had been wrought was of itself disastrous enough, for it deprived the League of the chief means by which it had destroyed the British fleet and kept command of the sea. But even more terrible than the actual destruction was the unexpected suddenness with which the blow had been delivered.

For five months, that is to say, from the recapture of the *Lucifer* at Aberdeen, the Tsar and his coadjutors had seen nothing of the operations of the Terrorists; and now, without a moment's warning, this apparently omnipresent and yet almost invisible force had struck once more with irresistible effect, and instantly vanished back into the mystery out of which it had come.

Who could tell when the next blow would fall, or in what shape the next assault would be delivered? In the presence of such enemies, invisible and unreachable, the commanders of the League, to their rage and disgust, felt themselves, on the eve of their supreme victory, as impotent as a man armed with a sword would have felt in front of a Gatling gun.

Consternation naturally led to divided councils. The

French and Italian commanders were for an immediate general assault on London at all hazards, and the enforcement of terms of surrender at the point of the sword. The Tsar, on the other hand, insisted on the pursuance of the original policy of reduction by starvation, as he rightly considered that, great as the attacking force was, it would be practically swamped amidst the infuriated millions of the besieged, and that, even if the assault were successful, the loss of life would be so enormous that the conquest of the rest of Britain—which in such a case would almost certainly rise to a man—would be next door to impossible.

He, however, so far yielded as to agree to send a message to the King of England to arrange terms of surrender, if possible at once, in order to save further bloodshed, and then, if these terms were rejected, to prepare for a general assault on the seventh day from then.

These terms were accepted as a compromise, and the next morning the bombardment ceased both from the land batteries and the air. At daybreak on the 30th an envoy left the Tsar's headquarters in one of the war-balloons, flying a flag of truce, and descended in Hyde Park. He was received by the King in Council at Buckingham Palace, and, after a lengthy deliberation, an answer was returned to the effect that on condition the bombardment ceased for the time being, London would be surrendered at noon on the 6th of December if no help had by that time arrived from the other cities of Britain. These terms, after considerable opposition from General le Gallifet and General Cosensz, the Italian Commander-in-Chief, were adopted and ratified at noon that day, almost at the very moment that Alexis Mazanoff was presenting the reply of the King of England to the President of the Federation in New York.

As the relief expedition had been fully decided upon, whether the British Government recognised the Federation or not, everything was in readiness for an immediate start as soon as the *Ithuriel* brought definite news as to the acceptation or rejection of the President's second offer. For the last seven weeks the ten dockyards of the east coast of America, and at Halifax in Nova Scotia, had been thronged with shipping, and swarming with workmen and sailors.

All the vessels which had been swept off the Atlantic by the war-storm, and which were of sufficient size and speed to take part in the expedition, had been collected at these eleven ports. Whole fleets of liners of half a dozen different nationalities, which had been laid up since the establishment of the blockade, were now lying alongside the quays, taking in vast quantities of wheat and miscellaneous food-stuffs, which were being poured into their holds from the glutted markets of America and Canada. Every one of these vessels was fitted up as a troopship, and by the time all arrangements were complete, more than a thousand vessels, carrying on an average twelve hundred men each, were ready to take the sea.

In addition to these there was a fleet of warships as yet unscathed by shot or shell, consisting of thirty battleships, a hundred and ten cruisers, and the flotilla of dynamite cruisers which had been constructed by the late Government at the expense of the capitalist Ring. There were no less than two hundred of these strange but terribly destructive craft, the lineal descendants of the *Vesuvius*, which, as the naval reader will remember, was commissioned in 1890.

They were double-hulled vessels built on the whale-back plan, and the compartments between the inner and outer hull could be wholly or partially filled with water. When they were entirely filled the hull sank below the surface, leaving nothing as a mark to an enemy save a platform standing ten feet above the water. This platform, constructed throughout of 6-inch nickel-steel, was of oval shape, a hundred feet long and thirty broad in its greatest diameter, and carried the heavily armoured wheel-house and conning-tower, two funnels, six ventilators, and two huge pneumatic guns, each seventy-five feet long, working on pivots nearly amidships.

These weapons, with an air-charge of three hundred atmospheres, would throw four hundred pounds of dynamite to a distance of three miles with such accuracy that the projectile would invariably fall within a space of twenty feet square. The guns could be discharged once a minute, and could thus hurl 48,000 lbs. of dynamite an hour upon a hostile fleet or fortifications.

Each cruiser also carried two under-water torpedo tubes ahead and two astern. The funnels emitted no smoke, but merely supplied draught to the petroleum furnaces, which burned with practically no waste, and developed a head of steam which drove the long submerged hulls through the water at a rate of thirty-two knots, or more than thirty-six miles an hour.

Such was the enormous naval armament, manned by nearly a hundred thousand men, which hoisted the Federation flag at one o'clock on the afternoon of the 30th of November, when orders were telegraphed north and south from Washington to get ready for sea. Two hours later the vast flotilla of war-ships and transports had cleared American waters, and was converging towards a point indicated by the intersection of the 41st parallel of latitude with the 40th meridian of longitude.

At this ocean rendezvous the divisions of the fleet and its convoys met and shaped their course for the mouth of the English Channel. They proceeded in column of line abreast three deep, headed by the dynamite cruisers, after which came the other warships which had formed the American Navy, and after these again came the troopships and transports properly protected by cruisers on their flanks and in their rear.

The commander of every warship and transport had the most minute instructions as to how he was to act on reaching British waters, and what these were will become apparent in due course. The weather was fairly good for the time of year, and, as there was but little danger of collision on the now deserted waters of the Atlantic, the whole flotilla kept at full speed all the way. As, however, its speed was necessarily limited by that of its slowest steamer until the scene of action was reached, it was after midnight on the 5th of December when its various detachments had reached their appointed stations on the English coast.

At the entrance of the English Channel and St. George's Channel a few scouting cruisers, flying French, Russian, and Italian colours, had been run down and sunk by the dynamite cruisers. Strict orders had been given by Tremayne to destroy everything flying a hostile flag, and not to permit any news to be taken to England of the approach of the flotilla. The Federation was waging a war, not merely of conquest and revenge, but of extermination, and no more mercy was to be shown to its enemies than they had shown in their march of victory from one end of Europe to the other.

While the Federation fleet had been crossing the Atlantic, other events no less important had been taking place in England and Scotland. The hitherto apparently inert mass of the population had suddenly awakened out of its lethargy. In town and country alike men forsook their daily avocations as if by one consent. As in America, artisans, pitmen, clerks, and tradesmen were suddenly transformed into soldiers, who drilled, first in squads of ten, and then in hundreds and thousands, and finally in tens of thousands, all uniformed alike in rough grey breeches and tunics, with a knot of red ribbon in the buttonhole, and all armed with rifle, bayonet, and revolver, which they seemed to handle with a strange and ominous familiarity.

All the railway traffic over the island was stopped, and the rolling-stock collected at the great stations along the lines to London, and at the same time all the telegraph wires communicating with the south and east were cut. As day after day passed, signs of an intense but strongly suppressed excitement became more and more visible all over the provinces, and especially in the great towns and cities.

In London very much the same thing had happened. Hundreds of thousands of civilians vanished during that seven days of anxious waiting for the hour of deliverance, and in their place sprang up orderly regiments of grey-clad soldiers, who saw the red knot in each other's button-holes, and welcomed each other as comrades unknown before.

To the surprise of the commanders of the regular army, orders had been issued by the King that all possible assistance was to be rendered to these strange legions, which had thus so suddenly sprang into existence; and the result was that when the sun set on the 5th of December, the twenty-first day of the total blockade of London, the beleaguered space contained over two millions of armed men, hungering both for food and vengeance, who, like the five millions of their fellow-countrymen outside London, were waiting for a sign from the sky to fling themselves upon the entrapped and unsuspecting invader.

That night countless eyes were upturned throughout the length and breadth of Britain to the dun pall of wintry cloud that overspread the land. Yet so far, so perfect was the discipline of this gigantic host, not a sign of overt hostile movement had been made, and the commanders of the armies of the League looked forward with exulting confidence to the moment, now only a few hours distant, when the capital of the British Empire, cut off from all help, should be surrendered into their hands in accordance with the terms agreed upon.

When night fell the *Ithuriel* was floating four thousand feet above Aberdeen. Arnold and Natasha, wrapped in warm furs, were standing on deck impatiently watching the sun sinking down over the sea of clouds which lay between them and the earth.

"There it goes at last!" exclaimed Natasha, as the last of the level beams shot across the cloud-sea and the rim of the pale disc sank below the surface of the vapoury ocean. "The time that we have waited and worked for so long has come at last. This is the eve of Armageddon! Who would think it, floating up here above the clouds and beneath those cold, calmly shining stars! And yet the fate of the whole world is trembling in the balance, and the doings of the next twenty-four hours will settle the destiny of mankind for generations to come. The hour of the Revolution has struck at last"—

"And therefore it is time that the Angel of the Revolution should give the last signal with her own hand!" said Arnold, seized with a sudden fancy, "Come, you shall start the dynamo yourself."

"Yes I will, and, I hope, kindle a flame that shall purge the earth of tyranny and oppression for ever. Richard, what must my father be thinking of just now down yonder in the cabin?"

"I dare not even guess. To-morrow or the next day will be the day of reckoning, and then God help those of whom he demands payment, for they will need it. The vials of wrath are full, and before long the oppressors of the earth will have drained them to the dregs. Come, it is time we went down."

They descended together to the engine-room, and meanwhile the air-ship sank through the clouds until the lights of Aberdeen lay about a thousand feet below. A lens of red glass had been fitted to the searchlight of the *Ithuriel*, and all that

The Eve of Armageddon.

was necessary was to connect the forward engine with the dynamo.

Arnold put Natasha's hand on a little lever. As she took hold of it she thought with a shudder of the mighty forces of destruction which her next movement would let loose. Then she thought of all that those nearest and dearest to her had suffered at the hands of Russian despotism, and of all the nameless horrors of the rule whose death-signal she was about to give.

As she did so her grip tightened on the lever, and when Arnold, having given his orders to the head engineer as to speed and course, put his hand on her shoulder and said, "Now!" she pulled it back with a sharp, determined motion, and the next instant a broad fan of blood-red light shot over the *Ithuriel's* bows.

At the same moment the air-ship's propellers began to spin round, and then with the flood of red light streaming in front of her, she headed southward at full speed towards Edinburgh. The signal flashed over the Scottish capital, and then the *Ithuriel* swerved round to the westward.

Half an hour later Glasgow saw it, and then away she sped southward across the Border to Carlisle; and so through the long December night she flew hither and thither, eastward and westward, flashing the red battle-signal over field and village and town; and wherever it shone armed men sprang up like the fruit of the fabled dragon's teeth, companies were mustered in streets and squares and fields and marched to railway stations; and soon long trains, one after another in endless succession, got into motion, all moving towards the south and east, all converging upon London.

Last of all, after it had made a swift circuit of northern and central and western England, the red light swept along the south coast, and then swerved northward again till it flashed thrice over London, and then it vanished into the darkness of the hour before the dawn of Armageddon.

Since the ever-memorable night of Thursday the 29th of July 1588, three hundred and sixteen years before, when "The beacon blazed upon the roof of Edgcumbe's lofty Hall," and the answering fires sprang up "From Eddystone to Berwick bounds, from Lynn to Milford Bay," to tell that the Spanish

Armada was in sight, there had been no such night in England, nor had men ever dreamed that there should be.

But great as had been the deeds done by the heroes of the sixteenth century with the pigmy means at their command, they were but the merest child's play to the awful storm of devastation which, in a few hours, was to burst over southern England. Then it was England against Spain; now it was Anglo-Saxondom against the world; and the conquering race of earth, armed with the most terrific powers of destruction that human wit had ever devised, was rising in its wrath, millions strong, to wipe out the stain of invasion from the sacred soil of the motherland of the Anglo-Saxon nations.

CHAPTER XLIII.

THE OLD LION AT BAY.

T HE morning of the 6th of December dawned grey and cold over London and the hosts that were waiting for its surrender. Scarcely any smoke rose from the myriad chimneys of the vast city, for the coal was almost all burnt, and what was left was selling at £12 a ton. Wood was so scarce that people were tearing up the woodwork of their houses to keep a little fire going.

So the steel-grey sky remained clear, for towards daybreak the clouds had been condensed by a cold north-easter into a sharp fall of fine, icy snow, and as the sun gained power it shone chilly over the whitened landscape, the innumerable roofs of London, and the miles of tents lining the hills to the north and south of the Thames valley.

The havoc wrought by the bombardment on the public buildings of the great city had been terrible. Of the Houses of Parliament only a shapeless heap of broken stones remained, the Law Courts were in ruins, what had been the Albert Hall was now a roofless ring of blackened walls, Nelson's Column lay shattered across Trafalgar Square, and the Royal Exchange, the Bank of England, and the Mansion House mingled their fragments in the heart of the almost deserted city.

Only three of the great buildings of London had suffered no damage. These were the British Museum, Westminster Abbey, and St Paul's, which had been spared in accordance with special orders issued by the commanders of the League. The two former were spared for the same reason that the Germans had spared Strasburg Cathedral in 1870—because their destruction would have been a loss, not to Britain alone, but to the world.

The great church of the metropolis had been left untouched chiefly because it had been arranged that, on the fall of London, the Tsar was to be proclaimed Emperor of Asia under its dome, and at the same time General le Gallifet was to assume the Dictatorship of France and abolish the Republic, which for more than ten years had been the plaything of unprincipled financiers, and the laughing-stock of Europe. As the sun rose the great golden cross, rising high out of the wilderness of houses, shone more and more brightly under the brightening sky, and millions of eyes looked upon it from within the city and from without with feelings far asunder as triumph and defeat.

At daybreak the last meal had been eaten by the defenders of the city. To supply it almost every animal left in London had been sacrificed, and the last drop of liquor was drunk, even to the last bottle of wine in the Royal cellars, which the King shared with his two commanders-in-chief, Lord Roberts and Lord Wolseley, in the presence of the troops on the balcony of Buckingham Palace. At nine o'clock the King and Queen attended service in St. Paul's, and when they left the Cathedral half an hour later the besiegers on the heights were astounded to hear the bells of all the steeples left standing in London ring out in a triumphant series of peals which rippled away eastward and westward from St. Paul's and Westminster Abbey, caught up and carried on by steeple after steeple, until from Highgate to Dulwich, and from Hammersmith to Canning Town, the beleaguered and starving city might have been celebrating some great triumph or deliverance.

The astonished besiegers could only put the extraordinary manifestation down to joy on the part of the citizens at the near approaching end of the siege; but before the bells of London had been ringing for half an hour this fallacious idea was dispelled from their minds in a very stern and summary fashion.

Since nightfall there had been no communication with the secret agents of the League in the various towns of England and Scotland. At ten o'clock a small company of Cossacks spurred and flogged their jaded horses up the northern slope of Muswell Hill, on which the Tsar had fixed his headquarters. Nearly every man was wounded, and the horses were in the last stages of exhaustion. Their captain was at once admitted to the presence of the Tsar, and, flinging himself on the ground before the enraged Autocrat, gasped out the dreadful tidings that his little company were the sole survivors of the army of occupation that had been left at Harwich, and which, twelve hours before, had been thirty thousand strong.

A huge fleet of strange-looking vessels, flying a plain blood-red flag, had just before four A.M. forced the approaches to the harbour, sunk every transport and warship with guns that were fired without flame, or smoke, or report, and whose projectiles shattered everything that they struck. Immediately afterwards an immense flotilla of transports had steamed in, and, under the protection of those terrible guns, had landed a hundred thousand men, all dressed in the same plain grey uniform, with no facings or ornaments save a knot of red ribbon at the button-hole, and armed with magazine rifle and a bayonet and a brace of revolvers. All were English by their speech, and every man appeared to know exactly what to do with very few orders from his officers.

This invading force had hunted the Russians out of Harwich like rabbits out of a warren, while the ships in the harbour had hurled their shells up into the air so that they fell back to earth on the retreating army and exploded with frightful effect. The general in command had at once telegraphed to London for a detachment of war-balloons and reinforcements, but no response had been received.

After four hours' fighting the Russian army was in full retreat, while the attacking force was constantly increasing as transport after transport steamed into the harbour and landed her men. At Colchester the Russians had been met by another vast army which had apparently sprung from the earth, dressed and armed exactly as the invading force was. What its numbers were there was no possibility of telling.

By this time, too, treachery began to show itself in the Russian ranks, and whole companies suddenly appeared with the red knot of ribbon in their tunics, and instantly turned their weapons against their comrades, shooting them down without warning or mercy. No quarter had been given to those who did not show the ribbon. Most of them died fighting, but those who had thrown away their arms were shot down all the same.

Whoever commanded this strange army had manifestly given orders to take no prisoners, and it was equally certain that its movements were directed by the Terrorists, for everywhere the battle-cries had been, "In the Master's name!" and "Slay, and spare not!"

The whole of the army, save the deserters, had been destroyed, and the deserters had immediately assumed the grey uniforms of those of the Terrorist army who had fallen. The Cossack captain and his forty or fifty followers were the sole remains of a body of three thousand men who had fought their way through the second army. The whole country to the north and east seemed alive with the grey soldiery, and it was only after a hundred hair-breadth escapes that they had managed to reach the protection of the lines round London.

Such was the tale of the bringer of bad tidings to the Tsar at the moment when he was looking forward to the crowning triumph of his reign. Like the good soldier that he was, he wasted no time in thinking at a moment when everything depended on instant action.

He at once despatched a war-balloon to the French and Italian headquarters with a note containing the terrible news from Harwich, and requesting Generals le Gallifet and Cosensz to lose no time in communicating with the eastern and southern ports, and in throwing out corps of observation supported by war-balloons. Evidently the American Government had played the League false at the last moment, and had allied herself with Britain.

As soon as he had sent off this message, the Tsar ordered a fleet of forty aerostats to proceed to the north-eastward, in advance of a force of infantry and cavalry numbering three hundred thousand men, and supported by fifty batteries of field and machine guns, which he detached to stop the progress of the Federation army towards London. Before this force was in motion a reply came back from General le Gallifet to the effect that all communication with the south and east was stopped, and that an aerostat, which had been on scout duty during the night, had returned with the news that the whole country appeared to be up in arms from Portsmouth to Dover. Corps of observation and a fleet of thirty aerostats had been sent out, and three army corps were already on the march to the south and east.

Meanwhile, the hour for the surrender of London was drawing very near, and all the while the bells were sending their mingled melody of peals and carillons up into the clear frosty air with a defiant joyousness that seemed to speak of anything but surrender. As twelve o'clock approached the guns of all the batteries on the heights were loaded and trained on different parts of the city, and the whole of the forces left after the detachment of the armies that had been sent to engage the battalions of the Federation prepared to descend upon the devoted city from all sides after the two hours' incessant bombardment that had been ordered to precede the general attack.

It had been arranged that if the city surrendered a white flag was to be hoisted on the cross of St. Paul's.

Within a few minutes of twelve the Tsar ascended to the roof of the Alexandra Palace on Muswell Hill, and turned his field-glasses on the towering dome. His face and lips were bloodless with repressed but intense anxiety, but the hands that held his glasses to his eyes were as steady as though he had been watching a review of his own troops. It was the supreme moment of his victorious career. He was practically master of Europe. Only Britain held out. The relieving forces would be rent to fragments by his war-balloons, and then decimated by his troops as the legions of Germany and Austria had been. The capital of the English-speaking world lay starving at his feet, and a few minutes would see—

Ha! there goes the flag at last. A little ball of white bunting creeps up from the gallery above the dark dome. It clears the railing under the pedestal, and climbs to the apex of the shining cross. As it does so the wild chorus of the bells suddenly ceases, and out of the silence that follows come the deep booming strokes of the great bell of St. Paul's sounding the hour of twelve.

As the last stroke dies away the ball bursts, and the White Ensign of Britain crossed by the Red Cross of St. George, and with the Jack in the corner, floats out defiantly on the breeze.

greeted by the reawakening clamour of the bells, and a deep hoarse cry from millions of throats, that rolls like a vast sea of sound up the slopes to the encampments of the League.

With an irrepressible cry of rage, Alexander dashed his field-glass to the ground, and shouted, in a voice broken with passion—

"So! They have tricked us. Let the bombardment begin at once, and bring that flag down with the first shots!"

But before the words were out of his mouth, the bombardment had already commenced in a very different fashion to that in which he had intended that it should begin. So intense had been the interest with which all eyes had been turned on the Cross of St. Paul's that no one had noticed twelve little points of shining light hanging high in air over the batteries of the besiegers, six to the north and six to the south.

But the moment that the Ensign of St. George floated from the summit of St. Paul's a rapid series of explosions roared out like a succession of thunder-claps along the lines of the batteries. The hills of Surrey, and Kent, and Middlesex were suddenly transformed into volcanoes spouting flame and thick black smoke, and flinging clouds of dust and fragments of darker objects high into the air.

The order of the Tsar was obeyed in part only, for by the time that the word to recommence the bombardment had been flashed round the circuit of the entrenchments, more than half the batteries had been put out of action. The twelve air-ships stationed at equal intervals round the vast ellipse, and discharging their No. 3 shell from their four guns ahead and astern, from an elevation of four thousand feet, had simultaneously wrecked half the batteries of the besiegers before their occupants had any clear idea of what was really happening.

Wherever one of those shells fell and exploded, earth and stone and iron melted into dust under the terrific force of the exploding gases, and the air-ships, moving with a velocity compared with which the utmost speed of the aerostats was as a snail's pace, flitted hither and thither wherever a battery got into action, and destroyed it before the second round had been fired.

There were still twenty-five aerostats at the command of the

Tsar which had not been sent against the relieving forces, and as soon as it was realised that the aërial bombardment of the batteries came from the air-ships of the Terrorist fleet, they were sent into the air to engage them at all hazards. They outnumbered them two to one, but there was no comparison between the manœuvring powers of the two aërial squadrons.

As soon as the aerostats rose into the air, the Terrorist fleet receded northward and southward from the batteries. Their guns had a six-mile range, and it did not matter to them which side of the assailed area they lay. They could still hurl their explosives with the same deadly precision on the appointed mark. But with the aerostats it was a very different matter. They could only drop their shells vertically, and where they were not exactly above the object of attack their shells exploded with comparative harmlessness.

As a natural consequence they had to follow the air-ships, not only away from London, but over their own encampments, in order to bring them to anything like close quarters. The aerostats possessed one advantage, and one only, over the air-ships. They were able to rise to a much greater height. But this advantage the air-ships very soon turned into a disadvantage by reason of their immensely superior speed and ease of handling. They darted about at such a speed over the heads of the massed forces of the League on either side of London, that it was impossible to drop shells upon them without running the inevitable risk of missing the small and swiftly-moving air-ship, and so causing the shell to burst amidst friends instead of foes.

Thus the Terrorist fleet, sweeping hither and thither, in wide and ever changing curves, lured the most dangerous assailants of the beleaguered city farther and farther away from the real scene of action, at the very time when they were most urgently needed to support the attacking forces which at that moment were being poured into London.

To destroy the air-ships seemed an impossibility, since they could move at five times the speed of the swiftest aerostat, and yet to return to the bombardment of the city was to leave them free to commit what havoc they pleased upon the encampments of the armies of the League. So they were drawn farther and farther away from the beleaguered city, while their agile enemies, still keeping within their six-mile range, evaded their shells, and yet kept up a constant discharge of their own projectiles upon the salient points of the attack on London.

By four o'clock in the afternoon all the batteries of the besiegers had been put out of action by the aërial bombardment. It was now a matter of man to man and steel to steel, and so the gage of final battle was accepted, and as dusk began to fall over the beleaguered city, the Russian, French and Italian hosts left their lines, and descended from their vantage ground to the assault on London, where the old Lion at bay was waiting for them with claws bared and teeth grinning defiance.

CHAPTER XLIV.

THE TURN OF THE BATTLE-TIDE.

THE force which the Tsar had detached to operate against the Federation Army of the North left the headquarters at eleven o'clock, and proceeded in four main divisions by Edmonton, Chingford, Chigwell, and Romford. The aerostats, regulating their speed so as to keep touch with the land force, maintained a position two miles ahead of it at three thousand feet elevation.

Strict orders had been given to press on at the utmost speed, and to use every means to discover the Federationists, and bring them to an engagement with as little delay as possible; but they marched on hour after hour into the dusk of the early winter evening, with the sounds of battle growing fainter in their rear, without meeting with a sign of the enemy.

As it would have been the height of imprudence to have advanced in the dark into a hostile country occupied by an enemy of great but unknown strength, General Pralitzin, the Commander of the Russian force, decided to bring his men to a halt at nightfall, and therefore took up a series of positions between Cheshunt, Epping, Chipping Ongar, and Ingatestone. From these points squadrons of Cossacks scoured the country in all directions, north, east, and west, in search of the so far invisible army; and at the same time he sent mounted messengers back to headquarters to report that no enemy had been found, and to ask for further orders.

The aerostats slowed down their engines until their propellers just counteracted the force of the wind and they hung motionless at a height of a thousand feet, ranged in a semicircle about fifteen miles long over the heads of the columns.

All this time the motions of the Russian army had been watched by the captain of the *Ithuriel* from an elevation of eight thousand feet, five miles to the rear. As soon as he saw them making preparations for a halt, and had noticed the disposition of the aerostats, he left the conning-tower which he had occupied nearly all day, and went into the after saloon, where he found Natas and Natasha examining a large plan of London and its environs.

"They have come to a halt at last," he said. "And if they only remain where they are for three hours longer, we have the whole army like rats in a trap, war-balloons and all. They have not seen us so far, for if they had they would certainly have sent an aerostat aloft to reconnoitre, and, of course, I must have destroyed it. The whole forty are arranged in a semicircle over the heads of the four main columns in divisions of ten."

"And what do you propose to do with them now you have got them?" said Natasha, looking up with a welcoming smile.

"Give me a cup of coffee first, for I am cold to the marrow, and then I'll tell you," replied Arnold, seating himself at the table, on which stood a coffee-urn with a spirit lamp beneath it, something after the style of a Russian samovar.

Natasha filled a cup and passed it to him, and he went on—

"You remember what I said to Tremayne in the Princess's sitting-room at Petersburg about the eagle and the crows just before the trial of the Tsar's first war-balloon. Well, if you like to spend a couple of hours with me in the conning-tower as soon as it is dark enough for us to descend, I will show you what I meant then. I suppose the original general orders stand good?" he said, turning to Natas.

"Yes," replied the Master gravely. "They must all be destroyed. This is the day of vengeance and not of mercy. If my orders have been obeyed, all the men belonging to the International in this force will have managed to get to the rear by nightfall. They can be left to take care of themselves. Mazanoff assured me that all the members in the armies of the League fully understood what they are to do. Some of the war-balloons have been taken possession of by our men, but we don't know how many. As soon as you destroy the first of the fleet, these will rise and commence operations on the army, and they will also fly the red flag, so there will be no fear of your mistaking them."

"Very well," said Arnold, who had been quietly sipping his coffee while he listened to the utterance of this death sentence on more than a quarter of a million of men. "If our fellows to the northward only obey orders promptly, there will not be many of the Russians left by sunrise. Now, Natasha, you had better put on your furs and come to the conning-tower; it's about time to begin."

It did not take her many moments to wrap up, and within five minutes she and Arnold were standing in the conning-tower watching the camp fires of the Russian host coming nearer and nearer as the *Ithuriel* sank down through the rapidly increasing darkness towards the long dotted line which marked the position of the aerostats, whose great gas-holders stood out black and distinct against the whitened earth beneath them.

By means of electric signals to the engineers the captain of the *Ithuriel* was able to regulate both the speed and the elevation of the air-ship as readily as though he had himself been in charge of the engine-room. Giving Natasha a pair of night-glasses, and telling her to keep a bright look-out ahead, he brought the *Ithuriel* round by the westward to a position about five miles west of the extremity of the line of war-balloons, and as soon as he got on a level with it he advanced comparatively slowly, until Natasha was able to make it out distinctly with the night-glass.

Then he signalled to the wheel-house aft to disconnect the after-wheel, and at the same moment he took hold of the spokes of the forward-wheel in the conning-tower. The next signal was "Full speed ahead," and as the *Ithuriel* gathered way and rushed forward on her errand of destruction he said hurriedly to Natasha—

"Now, don't speak till it's over. I want all my wits for this work, and you'll want all your eyes."

Without speaking, Natasha glanced up at his face, and saw on it somewhat of the same expression that she had seen at the moment when he put the *Ariel* at the rock-wall which barred the entrance to Aeria. His face was pale, and his lips were set, and his eyes looked straight out from under his frowning brows with an angry gleam in them that boded ill for the fate of those against whom he was about to use the irresistible engine of destruction under his command

Twenty feet in front of them stretched out the long keen ram of the air-ship, edged and pointed like a knife. This was the sole weapon that he intended to use. It was impossible to train the guns at the tremendous speed at which the *Ithuriel* was travelling, but under the circumstance the ram was the deadliest weapon that could have been employed.

In four minutes from the time the *Ithuriel* started on her eastward course the nearest war-balloon was only fifty yards away. The air-ship, travelling at a speed of nearly two hundred miles an hour, leapt out of the dusk like a flash of white light. In ten seconds more her ram had passed completely through the gas-holder without so much as a shock being felt. The next one was only five hundred yards away. Obedient to her rudder the *Ithuriel* swerved, ripped her gas-holder from end to end, and then darted upon the next one even before a terrific explosion in their rear told that the car of the first one had struck the earth.

So she sped along the whole line, darting hither and thither in obedience to the guiding hand that controlled her, with such inconceivable rapidity that before any of the unwieldy machines, saving only those whose occupants had been prepared for the assault, had time to get out of the way of the destroying ram, she had rent her way through the gas-holders of twenty-eight out of the forty balloons, and flung them to the earth to explode and spread consternation and destruction all along the van of the army encamped below.

From beginning to end the attack had not lasted ten minutes. When the last of the aerostats had gone down under his terrible ram, Arnold signalled "Stop, and ascend," to the engine-room. A second signal turned on the search-light in the bow, and from this a rapid series of flashes were sent up to the sky to the northward and eastward.

The effect was as fearful as it was instantaneous. The twelve war-balloons which had escaped by flying the red flag took up their positions above the Russian lines, and began to

"Her ram had passed completely through the gasholder."

drop their fire-shell and cyanogen bombs upon the masses of men below. The air-ship, swerving round again to the westward, with her fan-wheels aloft, moved slowly across the wide area over which men and horses were wildly rushing hither and thither in vain attempts to escape the rain of death that was falling upon them from the sky.

Her searchlight, turned downwards to the earth, sought out the spots where they were crowded most thickly together, and then the air-ship's guns came into play also. Arnold had given orders to use the new fire-shell exclusively, and its effects proved to be frightful beyond description. Wherever one fell a blaze of intense light shone for an instant upon the earth. Then this burst into a thousand fragments, which leapt into the air and spread themselves far and wide in all directions, burning with inextinguishable fury for several minutes, and driving men and horses mad with agony and terror.

No human fortitude or discipline could withstand the fearful rain of fire, in comparison with which even the deadly hail from the aerostats seemed insignificant. For half an hour the eight guns of the *Ithuriel* hurled these awful projectiles in all directions, scattering death and hopeless confusion wherever they alighted, until the whole field of carnage seemed ablaze with them.

At the end of this time three rockets soared up from her deck into the dark sky, and burst into myriads of brilliant white stars, which for a few moments shed an unearthly light upon the scene of indescribable confusion and destruction below. But they made more than this visible, for by their momentary light could be seen seemingly interminable lines of grey-clad figures swiftly closing in from all sides, chasing the Cossack scouts before them in upon the completely disorganised Russian host.

A few minutes later a continuous roll of musketry burst out on front, and flank, and rear, and a ceaseless hail of rifle bullets began to plough its way through the helpless masses of the soldiers of the Tsar. They formed as well as they could to confront these new enemies, but the moment that the searchlight of the air-ship, constantly sweeping the field, fell upon a company in anything like order, a shell descended in the midst of it and broke it up again.

All night long the work of death and vengeance went on; the grey lines ever closing in nearer and nearer upon the dwindling remnants of the Russian army. Hour after hour the hail of bullets never slackened. There was no random firing on the part of the Federation soldiers. Every man had been trained to use his rifle rapidly but deliberately, and never to fire until he had found his mark; and the consequence was that the long nickel-tipped bullets, fired point-blank into the dense masses of men, rent their way through half a dozen bodies before they were spent.

At last the grey light began to break over an indescribably hideous scene of slaughter. Scarcely ten thousand men remained of the three hundred thousand who had started the day before in obedience to the order of the Tsar; and these were split up into formless squads and ragged companies fighting desperately amidst heaps of corpses for dear life, without any pretence at order or formation.

The cannonade from the air had ceased, and the last scene in the drama of death had come. With bayonets fixed and rifles lowered to the charge, the long grey lines closed up, and, as the bugles rang out the long-awaited order, they swept forward at the double, horses and men went down like a field of standing corn under the irresistible rush of a million bayonets, and in twenty minutes all was over. Not a man of the whole Russian army was left alive, save those whose knot of red ribbon at the button-hole proclaimed them members of the International.

As soon as it was light enough for Arnold to see clearly that the fate of the Russians was finally decided, he descended to the earth, and, after complimenting the commander and officers of the Federation troops on the splendid effectiveness of their force, and their admirable discipline and coolness, he gave orders for a two hours' rest and then a march on the Russian headquarters at Muswell Hill with every available man. The Tsar and his Staff were to be taken alive at all hazards; every other Russian who did not wear the International ribbon was to be shot down without mercy.

These orders given, the *Ithuriel* mounted into the air again, and disappeared in the direction of London. She passed over the now shattered and silent entrenchments of the Russians at a speed which made it possible to remain on deck without discomfort or danger, and at an elevation of two thousand feet. Natas was below in the saloon, alone with his own thoughts, the thoughts of twenty years of waiting and working and gradual approach to the hour of vengeance which was now so near. Andrew Smith was steering in the wheel-house, Lieutenant Marston was taking his watch below, after being on deck nearly the whole of the previous night, and Arnold and Natasha, wrapped in their warm furs, were pacing up and down the deck engaged in conversation which had not altogether to do with war.

The sun had risen before the *Ithuriel* passed over London, and through the clear, cold air they could see with their field-glasses signs of carnage and destruction which made Natasha's soul sicken within her to gaze upon them, and even shook Arnold's now hardened nerves. All the main thoroughfares leading into London from the north and south were choked with heaps of dead bodies in Russian, French, and Italian uniforms, in the midst of which those who still survived were being forced forward by the pressure of those behind. Every house that remained standing was spouting flames upon them from its windows; and where the streets opened into squares and wider streets there were barricades manned with British and Federation troops, and from their summits and loopholes the quick-firing guns were raining an incessant hail of shot and shell upon the struggling masses pent up in the streets.

A horrible chorus of the rattle of small arms, the harsh, grinding roar of the machine guns, the hurrahs of the defenders, and the cries of rage and agony from the baffled and decimated assailants, rose unceasingly to their ears as they passed over the last battlefield of the Western nations, where the Anglo-Saxon, the Russ, and the Gaul were locked in the death struggle.

"There is some awful work going on down there," said Arnold, as they headed away towards the south, where, from behind the Surrey hills, soon came the sound of some tremendous conflict. "For the present we must leave them to fight it out. They don't seem to have had such easy work of it to the south as we have had to the north; but I didn't expect they would, for they have probably detached a very much larger force of French and Italians to attack the Army of the South than the Russian lot we had to deal with."

"Is all this frightful slaughter really necessary?" asked Natasha, slipping her arm through his, and looking up at him with eyes which for the first time were moistened by the tears of pity for her enemies.

"Necessary or not," replied Arnold, "it is the Master's orders, and I have only to obey them. This is the day of vengeance for which he has waited so long, and you can hardly expect him to show much mercy. It lies between him and Tremayne. For my part I will stay my hand only when I am ordered to do so.

"Still, if any one can influence Natas to mercy, you can. Nothing can now stop the slaughter on the north, I'm afraid, for the Russians are caught in a hopeless trap. The Londoners are enraged beyond control, and if the men spared them I believe the women would tear them to pieces. But there are two or three millions of lives or so to be saved at the south, and perhaps there is still time to do it. It would be a task worthy of the Angel of the Revolution; why should you not try it?"

"I will do so," said Natasha, and without another word she turned away and walked quickly towards the entrance to the saloon.

CHAPTER XLV.

ARMAGEDDON.

ON the southern side of London the struggle between the Franco-Italian armies and the troops of the Federation had been raging all night with unabated fury along a curved line extending from Bexley to Richmond.

The railways communicating with the ports of the south and east had, for their own purposes, been left intact by the commanders of the League; and so sudden and utterly unexpected had been the invasion of the force from America, and the simultaneous uprising of the British Section of the Brotherhood, that they had fallen into the hands of the Federationists almost without a struggle. This had enabled the invaders and their allies to concentrate themselves rapidly along the line of action which had been carefully predetermined upon.

Landing almost simultaneously at Southampton, Portsmouth, Shoreham, Newhaven, Hastings, Folkestone, Dover, Deal, Ramsgate, and Margate, they had been joined everywhere by their comrades of the British Section, whose first action, on receiving the signal from the sky, had been to seize the railways and shoot down, without warning or mercy, every soldier of the League who opposed them.

What had happened at Harwich had at the same time and in the same fashion happened at Dover and Chatham. The troops in occupation had been caught and crushed at a blow between overwhelming forces in front and rear. Added to this, the International was immensely stronger in France and Italy than in Russia, and therefore the defections from the ranks of the League had been far greater than they had been in the north.

Tens of thousands had donned the red ribbon as the Signal flashed over their encampments, and when the moment came to repel the assault of the mysterious grey legions that had sprung from no one knew where, the bewildered French and Italian officers found their regiments automatically splitting up into squads of tens and companies of hundreds, obeying other orders, and joining in the slaughter of their former comrades with the most perfect *sang froid*. By daybreak on the 6th the various divisions of the Federationists were well on their way to the French and Italian positions to the south of London. The utmost precautions had been taken to prevent any news reaching headquarters, and these, as has been seen, were almost entirely successful.

The three army corps sent southward by General le Gallifet met with a ruinous disaster long before they came face to face with the enemy. Ten of the fleet of thirty war-balloons which had been sent to co-operate with them, had been manned and commanded by men of the International. They were of the newest type and the swiftest in the fleet, and their crews were armed with the strangest weapons that had yet been used in the war. These were bows and arrows, a curious anachronism amidst the elaborate machinery of destruction evolved by the science of the twentieth century, but none the less effective on that account. The arrows, instead of being headed in the usual way, carried on the end of the shaft two little glass tubes full of liquid, bound together, and tipped with fulminate.

When the fleet had been in the air about an hour these ten aerostats had so distributed themselves that each of them, with a little manœuvring, could get within bowshot of two others. They also rose a little higher than the rest. The flutter of a white handkerchief was the signal agreed upon, and when this was given by the man in command of the ten, each of them suddenly put on speed, and ran up close to her nearest neighbour. A flight of arrows was discharged at the gas-holder, and then she headed away for the next nearest, and discharged a flight at her.

Considering the apparent insignificance of the means

employed, the effects were absolutely miraculous. The explosion of the fulminate on striking either the hard cordage of the net or one of the steel ribs used to give the gas-holder rigidity, broke the two tubes full of liquid. Then came another far more violent explosion, which tore great rents in the envelope. The imprisoned gas rushed out in torrents, and the crippled balloons began to sink, at first slowly, and then more and more rapidly, till the cars, weighted with crews, machinery, and explosives, struck the earth with a crash, and exploded, like so many huge shells, amidst the dense columns of the advancing army corps. In fifteen minutes each of the ten captured aerostats had sent two others to the earth, and then, completely masters of the position, those in charge of them began their assault on the helpless masses below them. This was kept up until the Federation troops appeared. Then they retired to the rear of the French and Italian columns, and devoted themselves to burning their stores and blowing up their ammunition trains with fire-shell.

Assailed thus in front and rear, and demoralised by the defection of the thousands who, as soon as the battle became general, showed the red ribbon and echoed the fierce battle-cry of the Federation, the splendid force sent out by General le Gallifet was practically annihilated by midnight, and by daybreak the Federationists, after fifteen hours of almost continuous fighting, had stormed all the outer positions held by the French and Italians to the south of London, the batteries of which had already been destroyed by the air-ships.

Thus, when the *Ithuriel* passed over London on the morning of the 7th the position of affairs was as follows: The two armies which had been detached by the Tsar and General le Gallifet to stop the advance of the Federationists had been destroyed almost to a man. Of the two fleets of war-balloons there remained twenty-two aerostats in the hands of the Terrorists, while the twenty-five sent by the Tsar against the air-ships had retired at nightfall to the depot at Muswell Hill to replenish their stock of fuel and explosives. Their ammunition-tenders, slow and unwieldy machines, adapted only for carrying large cargoes of shells, had been rammed and destroyed with ease by the air-ships during the running, or rather flying, fight of the previous afternoon.

At sunset on the 6th the whole available forces of the League which could be spared from the defence of the positions, numbering more than three million men, had descended to the assault on London at nearly fifty different points.

No human words could convey any adequate conception of that night of carnage and terror. The assailants were allowed to advance far into the mighty maze of streets and by-ways with so little resistance, that they began to think that the great city would fall an easy prey to them after all. But as they approached the main arteries of central London they came suddenly upon barricades so skilfully disposed that it was impossible to advance without storming them, and from which, as they approached them, burst out tempests of rifle and machine gunfire, under which the heads of their columns melted away faster than they advanced.

Light, quick-firing guns, posted on the roofs of lofty buildings, rained death and mutilation upon them. The air-ships, flying hither and thither a few hundred feet above the house-tops, like spirits of destruction, sent their shells into their crowded masses and wrought the most awful havoc of all with their frightful explosives, blowing hundreds of men to indistinguishable fragments at every shot, while from the windows of every house that was not in ruins came a ceaseless hail of missiles from every kind of firearm, from a magazine rifle to a shot-gun.

When morning came the Great Eastern Railway and the Thames had been cleared and opened, and the hearts of the starving citizens were gladdened by the welcome spectacle of train after train pouring in laden with provisions from Harwich, and of a fleet of steamers, flying the Federation flag, which filled the Thames below London Bridge, and was rapidly discharging its cargoes of food at the wharves and into lighters.

As fast as the food could be unloaded it was distributed first to the troops manning the barricades, and then to the markets and shops, whence it was supplied free in the poorer districts, and at the usual prices in the richer ones. All that day London feasted and made merry, for now the Thames was open there seemed to be no end to the food that was being poured into the city which twelve hours before had eaten its last scanty provisions. As soon as one vessel was discharged another took its place, and opened its hold filled with the necessaries and some of the luxuries of life.

The frightful butcheries at the barricades had stopped for the time being from sheer exhaustion on both sides. One cannot fight without food, and the defenders were half-starved when they began. Rage and the longing for revenge had lent them strength for the moment, but twelve hours of incessant street fighting, the most wearing of all forms of battle, had exhausted them, and they were heartily glad of the tacit truce which gave them time to eat and drink.

As for the assailants, as soon as they saw conclusive proof that the blockade had been broken and the city victualled, they found themselves deserted by the ally on whose aid they had most counted. While the grip of famine remained on London they knew that its fall was only a matter of time; but now—if food could get in so could reinforcements, and they had not the remotest idea as to the number of the mysterious forces which had so suddenly sprung into existence outside their own lines.

Added to this their losses during the night had been something appalling. The streets were choked with their dead, and the houses into which they had retired were filled with their wounded. So they, too, were glad of a rest, and many spoke openly of returning to their lines and abandoning the assault. If they did so it might be possible to fight their way to the coast, and escape out of this huge death-trap into which they had fallen on the very eve of their confidently-anticipated victory.

So, during the whole of the 7th there was little or no hard fighting in London, but to the north and south the grey legions of the Federation fought their way mile by mile over the field of Armageddon, gradually driving in the two halves of the Russian and the Franco-Italian armies which had been faced about to oppose their progress while the other halves were making their assault on London.

As soon as news reached the Tsar that the blockade of the river had been broken, he had ordered twelve of his remaining war-balloons to destroy the ships that were swarming below London Bridge. Their fuel and cargoes of explosives had been renewed, and they rose into the air to execute the Autocrat's command just as Natasha had taken leave of Arnold on her errand of mercy. He fathomed their design at once, swung the *Ithuriel* rapidly round to the northward, and said to his lieutenant, who had just come on deck—

"Mr. Marston, those fellows mean mischief. Put a three-minute time fuze on a couple of No. 3 fire-shell, and load the bow guns."

The order was at once executed. He trained one of the guns himself, giving it an elevation sufficient to throw the shell over the rising balloons. As the sixtieth second of the first minute passed, he released the projectile. It soared away through the air, and burst with a terrific explosion about fifty feet over the ascending aerostats.

The rain of fire spread out far and wide, and showered down upon the gas-holders. Then came a concussion that shook the air like a thunder-clap as the escaping gas mixed with the air, took fire, and exploded. Seven of the twelve aerostats instantly collapsed and plunged back again to the earth, spending the collective force of their explosives on the slopes of Muswell Hill. Meanwhile the second gun had been loaded and fired with the same effect on the remaining five.

Arnold then ran the *Ithuriel* up to within a mile of Muswell Hill, and found the remaining thirteen war-balloons in the act of making off to the northward.

"Two more time-shells, quick!" he cried. "They are off to take part in the battle to the north, and must be stopped at once. Look lively, or they'll see us and rise out of range!"

Almost before the words were out of his mouth one of the guns was ready. A moment later the messenger of destruction was speeding on its way, and they saw it explode fairly in the midst of the squadron. The second followed before the glare of the first explosion had passed, and this was the last shot fired in the aërial warfare between the air-ships and the war-balloons.

The effects of these two shots were most extraordinary. The accurately-timed shells burst, not over, but amidst the aerostats, enveloping their cars in a momentary mist of fire. The intense heat evolved must have suffocated their crews instantaneously. Even if it had not done so their fate would have been scarcely

"The rain of fire spread out far and wide."

See page 344

less sudden or terrible, for the fire falling in the cars exploded their own shells even before it burst their gas-envelopes. With a roar and a shock as though heaven and earth were coming together, a vast dazzling mass of flame blazed out, darkening the daylight by contrast, and when it vanished again there was not a fragment of the thirteen aerostats to be seen.

"So ends the Tsar's brief empire of the air!" said Arnold, as the smoke of the explosion drifted away. "And twenty-four hours more should see the end of his earthly Empire as well."

"I hope so," said Natasha's voice at his elbow. "This awful destruction is sickening me. I knew war was horrible, but this is more like the work of fiends than of men. There is something monstrous, something superhumanly impious, in blasting your fellow-creatures with irresistible lightnings like this, as though you were a god instead of a man. Will you not be glad when it is over, Richard?"

"Glad beyond all expression," replied her lover, the angry light of battle instantly dying out of his eyes as he looked upon her sweetly pitiful face. "But tell me, what success has my angel of mercy had in pleading for the lives of her enemies?" he continued, slipping his arm through hers, and leading her aft.

"I don't know yet, but my father told me to ask you to go to him as soon as you could leave the deck. Go now, and, Richard, remember what I said to you when you offered me the empire of the world as we were going to Aeria. No one has such influence with the Master as you have, for you have given him the victory and delivered his enemies into his hands. For my sake, and for Humanity's, let your voice be for mercy and peace—surely we have shed blood enough now!"

"It shall, angel mine! For your sweet sake I would spare even Alexander Romanoff himself and all his Staff."

"You will never be asked to do that," said Natasha quietly, as Arnold disappeared down the companion-way.

It was nearly an hour before he came on deck again, and by this time the *Ithuriel*, constantly moving to and fro over London, so that any change in the course of events could be at once reported to Natas, had shifted her position to the southward, and was hanging in the air over Sydenham Hill, the headquarters of General le Gallifet, whence could be plainly heard the roar of the tide of battle as it rolled ever northward over the hills of Surrey.

An air-ship came speeding up from the southward as he reached the deck. He signalled to it to come alongside. It proved to be the *Mercury* taking a message from Tremayne, who was personally commanding the Army of the South in the *Ariel*, to the air-ships operating with the Army of the North.

"What is the message?" asked Arnold.

"To engage and destroy the remaining Russian war-balloons, and then come south at once," replied the captain of the *Mercury*. "I am sorry to say both the *Lucifer* and the *Azrael* have been disabled by chance shots striking their propellers. The *Lucifer* was so badly injured that she fell to the earth, and blew up with a perfectly awful explosion; but the *Azrael* can still use her fan-wheels and stern propeller, though her air-planes are badly broken and twisted."

Arnold frowned at the bad news, but took no further notice of it beyond saying—

"That is unfortunate; but, I suppose, some casualties were inevitable under the circumstances." Then he added: "I have already destroyed all that were left of the Tsar's war-balloons, but you can take the other part of the message. Where is the *Ariel* to be found?"

The captain of the *Mercury* gave him the necessary directions, and the two air-ships parted. Within an hour a council of war, consisting of Natas, Arnold, and Tremayne, was being held in the saloon of the *Ithuriel*, on the issue of which the lives of more than two millions of men depended.

CHAPTER XLVI.

VICTORY.

IT was a little after three o'clock in the afternoon when Natas, Tremayne, and Arnold ended their deliberations in the saloon of the *Ithuriel*. At the same hour a council of war was being held by Generals le Gallifet and Cosensz at the Crystal Palace Hotel, Sydenham, where the two commanders had taken up their quarters.

Since daybreak matters had assumed a very serious, if not desperate aspect for the troops of the League to the south of London. Communication had entirely ceased with the Tsar since the night before, and this could only mean that his Majesty had lost the command of the air, through the destruction or disablement of his fleet of aerostats. News from the force which had descended upon London told only of a fearful expenditure of life that had not purchased the slightest advantage.

The blockade had been broken on the east, and, therefore, all hope of reducing the city by famine was at an end. Their own war-balloons had been either captured or destroyed, thousands of their men had deserted to the enemy, and multitudes more had been slain. Every position was dominated by the captured aerostats and the air-ships of the Terrorists. Even the building in which the council was being held might be shattered to fragments at any moment by a discharge of their irresistible artillery.

Finally, it was practically certain that within the next few hours their headquarters must be surrounded, and then their only choice would lie between unconditional surrender and swift and inevitable destruction by an aërial bombardment. Manifestly the time had come to make terms if possible, and purchase their own safety and that of their remaining troops. Both the generals and every member of their respective staffs saw clearly that victory was now a physical impossibility, and so the immediate issue of the council was that orders were given to hoist the white flag over the tricolour and the Italian standard on the summits of the two towers of the Crystal Palace, and on the flagstaffs over the headquarters.

These were at once seen by a squadron of air-ships coming from the north in obedience to Tremayne's summons, and within half an hour the same squadron was seen returning from the south headed by the flagship, also flying, to the satisfaction of the two generals, the signal of truce. The air-ships stopped over Sydenham and ranged themselves in a circle with their guns pointing down upon the headquarters, and the *Ariel*, with Tremayne on board, descended to within twenty feet of the ground in front of the hotel.

As she did so an officer wearing the uniform of a French General of Division came forward, saluted, and said that he had a message for the Commander-in-Chief of the Federation forces. Tremayne returned the salute, and said briefly—

"I am here. What is the message?"

"I am commissioned by General Gallifet, Commander-in-Chief of the Southern Division, to request on his behalf the honour of an audience. He awaits you with General Cosensz in the hotel," replied the Frenchman, gazing in undisguised admiration at the wonderful craft which he now for the first time saw at close quarters.

"With pleasure. I will be with you in a moment," said Tremayne, and as he spoke the *Ariel* settled gently down to the earth, and the gangway steps dropped from her bow.

As he entered the room in which the two generals were awaiting him, surrounded by their brilliantly-uniformed staffs, he presented a strange contrast to the men whose lives he held in the hollow of his hand. He was dressed in a dark tweed suit, with Norfolk jacket and knickerbockers, met by long shooting boots, just as though he was fresh from the moors, instead of from the battlefield on which the fate of the world was being decided. General le Gallifet advanced to meet him with a puzzled look of half-recognition on his face, which was at once banished by Tremayne holding out his hand without the slightest ceremony, and saying—

"Ah, I see you recognise me, General!"

"I do, my Lord Alanmere, and, you will permit me to add, with the most profound astonishment," replied the General, taking the proffered hand with a hearty grasp. "May I venture to hope that with an old acquaintance our negotiations may prove all the easier?"

Tremayne bowed and said—

"Rest assured, General, that they shall be as easy as my instructions will permit me to make them."

"Your instructions! But I thought"—

"That I was in supreme command. So I am in a sense, but I am the lieutenant of Natas for all that, and in a case like this his word is law. But come, what terms do you propose?"

"That truce shall be proclaimed for twenty-four hours; that the commanders of the forces of the League shall meet this mysterious Natas, yourself, and the King of England, and arrange terms by which the armies of France, Russia, and Italy shall be permitted to evacuate the country with the honours of war."

"Then, General, I may as well tell you at once that those terms are impossible," replied the Chief of the Federation quietly, but with a note of inflexible determination in his voice. "In the first place, 'the honours of war' is a phrase which already belongs to the past. We see no honour in war, and if we can have our way this shall be the last war that shall ever be waged on earth.

"Indeed, I may tell you that we began this war as one of absolute extermination. Had it not been for the intercession of Natasha, the daughter of Natas, you would not even have been given the opportunity of making terms of peace, or even of unconditional surrender. Our orders were simply to slay, and spare not, as long as a man remained in arms on British soil. You are, of course, aware that we have taken no prisoners."—

"But, my lord, this is not war, it is murder on the most colossal scale!" exclaimed the General, utterly unable to control the agitation that these terrible words evoked, not only in his own breast, but in that of every man who heard them.

"To us war and murder are synonymous terms, differing only as wholesale and retail," replied Tremayne drily; "for the mere names we care nothing. This world-war is none of our seeking; but if war can be cured by nothing but war, then we will wage it to the point of extermination. Now here are my terms. All the troops of the League on this side of the river Thames, on laying down their arms, shall be permitted to return to their homes, not as soldiers, but as peaceful citizens of the world, to go about their natural business as men who have sworn never to draw the sword again save in defence of their own homes."

"And his Majesty the Tsar?"

"You cannot make terms for the Tsar, General, and let me beg of you not to attempt to do so. No power under heaven can save him and his advisers from the fate that awaits them."

"And if we refuse your terms, the alternative is what?"

"Annihilation to the last man!"

A dead silence followed these fearful words so calmly and yet so inflexibly spoken. General le Gallifet and the Italian Commander-in-Chief looked at one another and at the officers standing about them. A murmur of horror and indignation passed from lip to lip. Then Tremayne spoke again quickly but impressively—

"Gentlemen, don't think that I am saying what I cannot do. We are inflexibly determined to stamp the curse of war out here and now, if it cost millions of lives to do so. Your forces are surrounded, your aerostats are captured or destroyed. It is no use mincing matters at a moment like this. It is life or death with you. If you do not believe me, General le Gallifet, come with me and take a flight round London in my air-ship yonder, and your own eyes shall see how hopeless all further struggle is. I pledge my word of honour as an English gentleman that you shall return in safety. Will you come?"

"I will," said the French commander. "Gentlemen, you will await my return"; and with a bow to his companions, he followed the Chief out of the room, and embarked on the air-ship without further ado.

The *Ariel* at once rose into the air. Tremayne reported to

"Do you understand now why you could not make terms for Russia?"

See page 351.

Natas what had been done, and then took the General into the deck saloon, and gave orders to proceed at full speed to Richmond, which was reached in what seemed to the Frenchman an inconceivably short space of time. Then the *Ariel* swung round to the eastward, and at half speed traversed the whole line of battle over hill and vale, at an elevation of eight hundred feet, from Richmond to Shooter's Hill.

What General le Gallifet saw more than convinced him that Tremayne had spoken without exaggeration when he said that annihilation was the only alternative to evacuation on his terms. The grey legions of the League seemed innumerable. Their long lines lapped round the broken squadrons of the League, mowing them down with incessant hailstorms of magazine fire, and overhead the air-ships and aerostats were hurling shells on them which made great dark gaps in their formations wherever they attempted anything like order. Every position of importance was either occupied or surrounded by the Federationists. There was no way open save towards London, and that way, as the General knew only too well, lay destruction.

To the east of Shooter's Hill the air-ship swerved round to the northward. The Thames was alive with steamers flying the red flag, and carrying food and men into London. To the north of the river the battle had completely ceased as far as Muswell Hill.

There the Black Eagle of Russia still floated from the roof of the Palace, and a furious battle was raging round the slopes of the hill. But the Russians were already surrounded, and manifestly outnumbered five to one, while six aerostats were circling to and fro, doing their work of death upon them with fearful effectiveness.

"You see, General, that the aerostats do not destroy the Palace and bury the Tsar in its ruins, nor do I stop and do the same, as I could do in a few minutes. Do you understand now why you could not make terms for Russia?"

"What your designs are Heaven and yourselves only know," replied the General, with quivering lips. "But I see that all is hopelessly lost. For God's sake let this carnage stop! It is not war, it is butchery, and we have deserved this retribution for employing those infernal contrivances in the first place.

I always said it was not fair fighting. It is murder to drop death on defenceless men from the clouds. We will accept your terms. Let us get back to the south and save the lives of what remain of our brave fellows. If this is scientific warfare, I, for one, will fight no more!"

"Well spoken, General!" said Tremayne, laying his hand upon his shoulder. "Those words of yours have saved two millions of human lives, and by this time to-morrow war will have ceased, I hope for ever, among the nations of the West."

The *Ariel* now swerved southward again, crossed London at full speed, and within half an hour General le Gallifet was once more standing in front of the Crystal Palace Hotel. As it was now getting dusk the searchlights of the air-ships were turned on, and they swept along the southern line of battle flashing the signal, "Victory! Cease firing!" to the triumphant hosts of the Federation, while at the same time the French and Italian commanders set the field telegraph to work and despatched messengers into London with the news of the terms of peace. By nightfall all fighting south of the Thames had ceased, and victors and vanquished were fraternising as though they had never struck a blow at each other, for war is a matter of diplomacy and Court intrigue, and not of personal animosity. The peoples of the world would be good enough friends if their rulers and politicians would let them.

Meanwhile the battle raged with unabated fury round the headquarters of the Tsar. Here despotism was making its last stand, and making it bravely, in spite of the tremendous odds against it. But as twilight deepened into night the numbers of the assailants of the last of the Russian positions seemed to multiply miraculously.

A never-ceasing flood of grey-clad soldiery surged up from the south, overflowed the barricades to the north, and swept the last of the Russians out of the streets like so much chaff. All the hundred streams converged upon Muswell Hill, and joined the ranks of the attacking force, and so the night fell upon the last struggle of the world-war. Even the Tsar himself now saw that the gigantic game was virtually over, and that the stake of world-empire had been played for—and lost.

A powerful field searchlight had been fixed on the roof of

"A vision which no one who saw it forgot to the day of his death."

VICTORY.

the Palace, and, as it flashed hither and thither round the area of the battle, he saw fresh hosts of the British and Federation soldiers pouring in upon the scene of action, while his own men were being mown down by thousands under the concentrated fire of millions of rifles, and his regiments torn to fragments by the incessant storm of explosives from the sky.

Hour after hour the savage fight went on, and the grey and red lines fought their way up and up the slopes, drawing the ring of flame and steel closer and closer round the summit of the hill on which the Autocrat of the North stood waiting for the hour of his fate to strike.

The last line of the defenders of the position was reached at length. For an hour it held firm in spite of the fearful odds. Then it wavered and bent, and swayed to and fro in a last agony of desperation. The encircling lines seemed to surge backwards for a space. Then came a wild chorus of hurrahs, a swift forward rush of levelled bayonets, the clash of steel upon steel—and then butchery, vengeful and pitiless.

The red tide of slaughter surged up to the very walls of the Palace. Only a few yards separated the foremost ranks of the victorious assailants from the little group of officers, in the midst of which towered the majestic figure of the White Tsar—an emperor without an empire, a leader without an army. He strode forward towards the line of bayonets fringing the crest of the hill, drew his sword, snapped the blade as a man would break a dry stick, and threw the two pieces to the ground, saying in English as he did so—

"It is enough, I surrender!"

Then he turned on his heel, and with bowed head walked back again to his Staff.

Almost at the same moment a blaze of white light appeared in the sky, a hundred feet above the heads of the vast throng that encircled the Palace. Millions of eyes were turned up at once, and beheld a vision which no one who saw it forgot to the day of his death.

The ten air-ships of the Terrorist fleet were ranged in two curves on either side of the *Ithuriel*, which floated about twenty feet below them, her silvery hull bathed in a flood of light from their electric lamps. In her bow, robed in glistening white fur, stood Natasha, transfigured in the full blaze of the concentrated searchlights. A silence of wonder and expectation fell upon the millions at her feet, and in the midst of it she began to sing the Hymn of Freedom. It was like the voice of an angel singing in the night of peace after strife.

Men of every nation in Europe listened to her entranced, as she changed from language to language; and when at last the triumphant strains of the Song of the Revolution came floating down from her lips through the still night air, an irresistible impulse ran through the listening millions, and with one accord they took up the refrain in all the languages of Europe, and a mighty flood of exultant song rolled up in wave after wave from earth to heaven,—a song at once of victory and thanksgiving, for the last battle of the world-war had been lost and won, and the valour and genius of Anglo-Saxondom had triumphed over the last of the despotisms of Europe.

CHAPTER XLVII.

THE JUDGMENT OF NATAS.

THE myriad-voiced chorus of the Song of the Revolution ended in a mighty shout of jubilant hurrahs, in the midst of which the *Ariel* dropped lightly to the earth, and Tremayne, dressed now in the grey uniform of the Federation, with a small red rosette on the left breast of his tunic, descended from her deck to the ground with a drawn sword in his hand.

He was at once recognised by several of the leaders, and as the words, "The Chief, the Chief," ran from lip to lip, those in the front ranks brought their rifles to the present, while the captains saluted with their swords. The British regulars and volunteers followed suit as if by instinct, and the chorus of cheers broke out again. Tremayne acknowledged the salute, and raised his hand to command silence. A hush at once fell upon the assembled multitude, and in the deep silence of anticipation which followed, he said in clear, ringing tones—

"Soldiers of the Federation and the Empire! that which I hope will be the last battle of the Western nations has been fought and won. The Anglo-Saxon race has rallied to the defence of its motherland, and in the blood of its invaders has wiped out the stain of conquest. It has met the conquerors of Europe in arms, and on the field of battle it has vindicated its right to the empire of the world.

"Henceforth the destinies of the human race are in its keeping, and it will worthily discharge the responsibility. It may yet be necessary for you to fight other battles with other races; but the victory that has attended you here will wait upon your arms elsewhere, and then the curse and the shame of war will be removed from the earth, let us hope for ever. European despotism has fought its last battle and lost, and those who have appealed to the sword shall be judged by the sword."

As he said this, he pointed with his weapon towards the Tsar and his Staff, and continued, with an added sternness in his voice—

"In the Master's name, take those men prisoners! Their fate will be decided to-morrow. Forward a company of the First Division; your lives will answer for theirs!"

As the Chief ended his brief address to the victorious troops ten men, armed with revolver and sword, stepped forward, each followed by ten others armed with rifle and fixed bayonet, and immediately formed in a hollow square round the Tsar and his Staff. This summary proceeding proved too much for the outraged dignity of the fallen Autocrat, and he stepped forward and cried out passionately—

"What is this? Is not my surrender enough? Have we not fought with civilised enemies, that we are to be treated like felons in the hour of defeat?"

Tremayne raised his sword and cried sharply, "To the ready!" and instantly the prisoners were encircled by a hedge of levelled bayonets and rifle-barrels charged with death. Then he went on, in stern commanding tones—

"Silence there! We do not recognise what you call the usages of civilised warfare. You are criminals against humanity, assassins by wholesale, and as such you shall be treated."

There was nothing for it but to submit to the indignity, and within a few minutes the Tsar and those who with him had essayed the enslavement of the world were lodged in separate rooms in the building under a strong guard to await the fateful issue of the morrow.

The rest of the night was occupied in digging huge trenches for the burial of the almost innumerable dead, a task which, gigantic as it was, was made light by the work of hundreds of thousands of willing hands. Those of the invaders who had fallen in London itself were taken down the Thames on the ebb tide in fleets of lighters, towed by steamers, and were buried at sea. Happily it was midwinter, and the temperature remained some degrees below freezing point, and so the great city was saved from what in summer would infallibly have brought pestilence in the track of war.

At twelve o'clock on the following day the vast interior of St. Paul's Cathedral was thronged with the anxious spectators of the last scene in the tremendous tragedy which had commenced with the destruction of Kronstadt by the *Ariel*, and which had culminated in the triumph of Anglo-Saxondom over the leagued despotism and militarism of Europe.

At a long table draped with red cloth, and placed under the dome in front of the chancel steps, sat Natas, with Tremayne and Natasha on his right hand, and Arnold and Alexis Mazanoff on his left. Radna, Anna Ornovski, and the other members of the Inner Circle of the Terrorists, including the President, Nicholas Roburoff, who had been pardoned and restored to his office at the intercession of Natasha, occupied the other seats, and behind them stood a throng of the leaders of the Federation forces.

Neither the King of England nor any of his Ministers or military officers were present, as they had no voice in the proceedings which were about to take place. It had been decided, at a consultation with them earlier in the day, that it would be better that they should be absent.

That which was to be done was unparalleled in the history of the world, and outside the recognised laws of nations; and so their prejudices were respected, and they were spared what they might have looked upon as an outrage on international policy, and the ancient but mistaken traditions of so-called civilised warfare.

In front of the table two double lines of Federation soldiers, with rifles and fixed bayonets, kept a broad clear passage down to the western doors of the Cathedral. The murmur of thousands of voices suddenly hushed as the Cathedral clock struck the first stroke of twelve. It was the knell of an empire and a despotism. At the last stroke Natas raised his hand and said—

"Bring up the prisoners!"

There was a quick rustling sound, mingled with the clink of steel, as the two grey lines stiffened up to attention. Twelve commanders of divisions marched with drawn swords down to the end of the nave, a few rapid orders were given, and then they returned heading two double files of Federation guards, between which, handcuffed like common felons, walked the once mighty Tsar and the ministers of his now departed tyranny.

The footsteps of the soldiers and their captives rang clearly upon the stones in the ominous breathless silence which greeted their appearance. The fallen Autocrat and his servants walked with downcast heads, like men in a dream, for to them it was a dream, this sudden and incomprehensible catastrophe which had overwhelmed them in the very hour of victory and on the threshold of the conquest of the world. Three days ago they had believed themselves conquerors, with the world at their feet; now they were being marched, guarded and in shackles, to a tribunal which acknowledged no law but its own, and from whose decision there was no appeal. Truly it was a dream, such a dream of disaster and calamity as no earthly despot had ever dreamt before.

Four paces from the table they were halted, the Tsar in the centre, facing his unknown judge, and his servants on either side of him. He recognised Natasha, Anna Ornovski, Arnold, and Tremayne, but the recognition only added to his bewilderment.

There was a slight flush on the face of Natas, and an angry gleam in his dark magnetic eyes, as he watched his captives approach; but when he spoke his tones were calm and passionless, the tones of the conqueror and the judge, rather than of the deeply injured man and a personal enemy. As the prisoners were halted in front of the table, and the rifle-butts of the guards rang sharply on the stone pavement, so deep a hush fell upon the vast throng in the Cathedral, that men seemed to hold their breath rather than break it until the Master of the Terror began to speak.

"Alexander Romanoff, late Tsar of the Russias, and now prisoner of the Executive of the Brotherhood of Freedom, otherwise known to you as the Terrorists—you have been brought here with your advisers and the ministers of your tyranny that your crimes may be recounted in the presence of this congregation, and to receive sentence of such punishment as it is possible for human justice to mete out to you"—

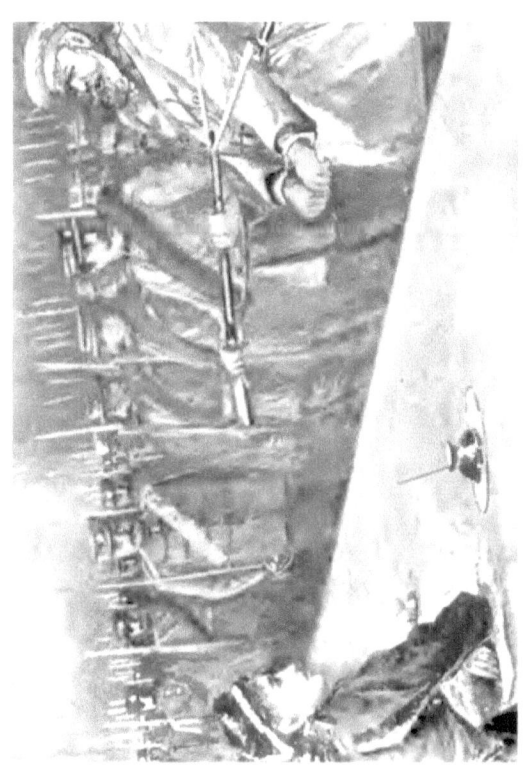

"I deny both your justice and your right to judge. It is you who are the criminals, conspirators, and enemies of Society. I am a crowned King, and above all earthly laws"—

Before he could say any more two bayonets crossed in front of him with a sharp clash, and he was instantly thrust back into his place.

"Silence!" said Natas, in a tone of such stern command that even he instinctively obeyed. "As for our justice, let that be decided between you and me when we stand before a more awful tribunal than this. My right to judge even a crowned king who has no longer a crown, rests, as your own authority and that of all earthly rulers has ever done, upon the power to enforce my sentence, and I can and will enforce it upon you, you heir of a usurping murderess, whose throne was founded in blood and supported by the bayonets of her hired assassins. You have appealed to the arbitration of battle, and it has decided against you; you must therefore abide by its decision.

"You have waged a war of merciless conquest at the bidding of insatiable ambition. You have posed as the peace-keeper of Europe until the train of war was laid, as you and your allies thought, in secret, and then you let loose the forces of havoc upon your fellow-men without ruth or scruple. Your path of victory has been traced in blood and flames from one end of Europe to the other; you have sacrificed the lives of millions, and the happiness of millions more, to a dream of world-wide empire, which, if realised, would have been a universal despotism.

"The blood of the uncounted slain cries out from earth to heaven against you for vengeance. The days are past when those who made war upon their kind could claim the indulgence of their conquerors. You have been conquered by those who hold that the crime of aggressive war cannot be atoned for by the transfer of territory or the payment of money.

"If this were your only crime we would have blood for blood, and life for life, as far as yours could pay the penalty. But there is more than this to be laid to our charge, and the swift and easy punishment of death would be too light an atonement for Justice to accept.

"Since you ascended your throne you have been as the visible shape of God in the eyes of a hundred million subjects. Your hands have held the power of life and death, of freedom and slavery, of happiness and misery. How have you used it, you who have arrogated to yourself the attributes of a vicegerent of God on earth? As the power is, so too is the responsibility, and it will not avail you now to shelter yourself from it behind the false traditions of diplomacy and statecraft.

"Your subjects have starved, while you and yours have feasted. You have lavished millions in vain display upon your palaces, while they have died in their hovels for lack of bread; and when men have asked you for freedom and justice, you have given them the knout, the chain, and the prison.

"You have parted the wife from her husband"—

Here for the moment the voice of Natas trembled with irrepressible passion, which, before he could proceed, broke from his heaving breast in a deep sob that thrilled the vast assembly like an electric shock, and made men clench their hands and grit their teeth, and wrung an answering sob from the breast of many a woman who knew but too well the meaning of those simple yet terrible words. Then Natas recovered his outward composure and went on; but now there was an angrier gleam in his eyes, and a fiercer ring in his voice.

"You have parted the wife from her husband, the maid from her lover, the child from its parents. You have made desolate countless homes that once were happy, and broken hearts that had no thought of evil towards you—and you have done all this, and more, to maintain as vile a despotism as ever insulted the justice of man, or mocked at the mercy of God.

"In the inscrutable workings of Eternal Justice it has come to pass that your sentence shall be uttered by the lips of one of your victims. For no offence known to the laws of earth or Heaven my flesh has been galled by your chains and torn by your whips. I have toiled to win your ill-gotten wealth in your mines, and by the hands of your brutal servants the iron has entered into my soul. Yet I am but one of thousands whose undeserved agony cries out against you in this hour of judgment.

"Can you give us back what you have taken from us—the years of life and health and happiness, our wives and our children, our lovers and our kindred? You have ravished, but you cannot restore. You have smitten, but you cannot heal. You have killed, but you cannot make alive again. If you had ten thousand lives they could not atone, though each were dragged out to the bitter end in the misery that you have meted out to others.

"But so far as you and yours can pay the debt it shall be paid to the uttermost farthing. Every pang that you have inflicted you shall endure. You shall drag your chains over Siberian snows, and when you faint by the wayside the lash shall revive you, as in the hands of your brutal Cossacks it has goaded on your fainting victims. You shall sweat in the mine and shiver in the cell, and your wives and your children shall look upon your misery and be helpless to help you, even as have been the fond ones who have followed your victims to exile and death.

"They have seen your crimes without protest, and shared in your wantonness. They have toyed with the gold and jewels which they knew were bought with the price of misery and death, and so it is just that they should see your sufferings and share in your doom.

"To the mines for life! And when the last summons comes to you and me, may Eternal Justice judge between us, and in its equal scales weigh your crimes against your punishment! Begone! for you have looked your last on freedom. You are no longer men; you are outcasts from the pale of the brotherhood of the humanity you have outraged!

"Alexis Mazanoff, you will hold yourself responsible for the lives of the prisoners, and the execution of their sentence. You will see them in safe keeping for the present, and on the thirtieth day from now you will set out for Siberia."

The sentence of Natas, the most terrible one which human lips could have uttered under the circumstances, was received with a breathless silence of awe and horror. Then Mazanoff rose from his seat, drew his sword, and saluted. As he passed round the end of the table the guards closed up round the prisoners, who were staring about them in stupefied bewilderment at the incredible horror of the fate which in a moment had hurled them from the highest pinnacle of earthly power and splendour down to the degradation and misery of the most wretched of their own Siberian convicts. No time was given for protest or appeal, for Mazanoff instantly gave the word "Forward!" and, surrounded by a hedge of bayonets, the doomed men were marched rapidly down between the two grey lines.

As they reached the bottom of the nave the great central doors swung open, and through them came a mighty roar of execration from the multitude outside as they appeared on the top of the Cathedral steps.

From St. Paul's Churchyard, down through Ludgate Hill and up the Old Bailey to the black frowning walls of Newgate, they were led through triple lines of Federation soldiers amidst a storm of angry cries from the crowd on either side,—cries which changed to a wild outburst of savage, pitiless exultation as the news of their dreadful sentence spread rapidly from lip to lip. They had shed blood like water, and had known no pity in the hour of their brief triumph, and so none was shown for them in the hour of their fall and retribution.

The hour following their disappearance from the Cathedral was spent in a brief and simple service of thanksgiving for the victory which had wiped the stain of foreign invasion from the soil of Britain in the blood of the invader, and given the control of the destinies of the Western world finally into the hands of the dominant race of earth.

The service began with a short but eloquent address from Natas, in which he pointed out the consequences of the victory and the tremendous responsibilities to the generations of men in the present and the future which it entailed upon the victors. He concluded with the following words—

"My own part in this world-revolution is played out. For more than twenty years I have lived solely for the attainment of one object, the removal of the blot of Russian tyranny upon European civilisation, and the necessary punishment of those who were guilty of the unspeakable crime of maintaining it at such a fearful expense of human life and suffering.

"That object has now been accomplished; the soldiers of freedom have met the hirelings of despotism on the field of the world's Armageddon, and the God of Battles has decided between them. Our motives may have been mistaken by those who only saw the bare outward appearance without knowing their inward intention, and our ends have naturally been misjudged by those who fancied that their accomplishment meant their own ruin.

"Yet, as the events have proved, and will prove in the ages to come, we have been but as intelligent instruments in the hands of that eternal wisdom and justice which, though it may seem to sleep for a season, and permit the evildoer to pursue his wickedness for a space, never closes the eye of watchfulness or sheathes the sword of judgment. The empire of the earth has been given into the hands of the Anglo-Saxon race, and therefore it is fitting that the supreme control of affairs should rest in the hands of one of Anglo-Saxon blood and lineage.

"For that reason I now surrender the power which I have so far exercised as the Master of the Brotherhood of Freedom into the hands of Alan Tremayne, known in Britain as Earl of Alanmere and Baron Tremayne, and from this moment the Brotherhood of Freedom ceases to exist as such, for its ends are attained, and the objects for which it was founded have been accomplished.

"With the confidence born of intimate knowledge, I give this power into his keeping, and those who have shared his counsels and executed his commands in the past will in the future assist him as the Supreme Council, which will form the ultimate tribunal to which the disputes of nations will henceforth be submitted, instead of to the barbarous and bloody arbitration of battle.

"No such power has ever been delivered into the hands of a single body of men before; but those who will hold it have been well tried, and they may be trusted to wield it without pride and without selfishness, the twin curses that have hitherto afflicted the divided nations of the earth, because, with the fate of humanity in their hands and the wealth of earth at their disposal, it will be impossible to tempt them with bribes, either of riches or of power, from the plain course of duty which will lie before them."

As Natas finished speaking, he signed with his hand to

Tremayne, who rose in his place and briefly addressed the assembly—

"I and those who will share it with me accept alike the power and the responsibility—not of choice, but rather because we are convinced that the interests of humanity demand that we should do so. Those interests have too long been the sport of kings and their courtiers, and of those who have seen in selfish profit and aggrandisement the only ends of life worth living for.

"Under the pretences of furthering civilisation and progress, and maintaining what they have been pleased to call law and order, they have perpetrated countless crimes of oppression, cruelty, and extortion, and we are determined that this shall have an end.

"Henceforth, so far as we can insure it, the world shall be ruled, not by the selfishness of individuals, or the ambitions of nations, but in accordance with the everlasting and immutable principles of truth and justice, which have hitherto been burlesqued alike by despots on their thrones and by political partisans in the senates of so-called democratic countries.

"To-morrow, at mid-day in this place, the chief rulers of Europe will meet us, and our intentions will be further explained. And now before we separate to go about the rest of the business of the day let us, as is fitting, give due thanks to Him who has given us the victory."

He ceased speaking, but remained standing; the same instant the organ of the Cathedral pealed out the opening notes of the familiar Normanton Chant, and all those at the table, saving Natas, rose to their feet. Then Natasha's voice soared up clear and strong above the organ notes, singing the first line of the old well-known chant—

The strain upraise of joy and praise.

And as she ceased the swell of the organ rolled out, and a mighty chorus of hallelujahs burst by one consent from the lips of the vast congregation, filling the huge Cathedral, and flowing out from its now wide-open doors until it was caught up and echoed by the thousands who thronged the churchyard and the streets leading into it.

As this died away Radna sang the second line, and so the Psalm of Praise was sung through, as it were in strophe and anti-strophe, interspersed with the jubilant hallelujahs of the multitude who were celebrating the greatest victory that had ever been won on earth.

That night the inhabitants of the delivered city gave themselves up to such revelry and rejoicing as had never been seen or heard in London since its foundation. The streets and squares blazed with lights and resounded with the songs and cheerings of a people delivered from an impending catastrophe which had bidden fair to overwhelm it in ruin, and bring upon it calamities which would have been felt for generations.

CHAPTER XLVIII.

THE ORDERING OF EUROPE.

HILE these events had been in progress three squadrons of air-ships had been speeding to St. Petersburg, Vienna, and Rome. Three vessels had been despatched to each city, and the instructions of those in command of the squadrons were to bring the German Emperor, the Emperor of Austria, and the King of Italy to London.

The news of the defeat of the League had preceded them by telegraph, and all three monarchs willingly obeyed the summons which they carried to attend a Conference for the ordering of affairs of Europe.

The German Emperor was at once released from his captivity, although only under a threat of the destruction of the city by the air-ships, for the Grand Duke Vladimir, who ruled at St. Petersburg as deputy of the Tsar, had first refused to believe the astounding story of the defeat of his brother and the destruction of his army. The terrible achievements of the air-ships were, however, too well and too certainly known to permit of resistance by force, and so the Kaiser was released, and made his first aërial voyage from St. Petersburg to London, arriving there at ten o'clock on the evening of the 8th, in the midst of the jubilations of the rejoicing city.

The King of England had sent a despatch to the Emperor of Austria inviting him to the Conference, and General Cosensz had sent a similar one to the King of Italy, and so there had been no difficulty about their coming. At mid-day on the 9th the Conference was opened in St. Paul's, which was the only public building left intact in London capable of containing the vast audience that was present, an audience composed of men of every race and language in Europe.

Natas was absent, and Tremayne occupied his seat in the centre of the table; the other members of the Inner Circle, now composing the Supreme Council of the Federation, were present, with the exception of Natasha, Radna, and Anna Ornovski, and the other seats at the table were occupied by the monarchs to whom the purposes of the Conference had been explained earlier in the day. France was represented in the person of General le Gallifet.

The body of the Cathedral was filled to overflowing, with the exception of an open space kept round the table by the Federation guards.

The proceedings commenced with a brief but impressive religious service conducted by the Primate of England, who ended it with a short but earnest appeal, delivered from the altar steps, to those composing the Conference, calling upon them to conduct their deliberations with justice and moderation, and reminding them of the millions who were waiting in other parts of Europe for the blessings of peace and prosperity which it was now in their power to confer upon them. As the Archbishop concluded the prayer for the blessing of Heaven upon their deliberation, with which he ended his address, Tremayne, after a few moments of silence, rose in his place and, speaking in clear deliberate tones, began as follows:—

"Your Majesties have been called together to hear the statement of the practical issues of the conflict which has been decided between the armies of the Federation of the Anglo-Saxon peoples and those of the late Franco-Slavonian League.

"Into the motives which led myself and those who have acted with me to take the part which we have done in this tremendous struggle, there is now no need for me to enter. It is rather with results than with motives that we have to deal, and those results may be very briefly stated.

"We have demonstrated on the field of battle that we hold in our hands means of destruction against which it is absolutely impossible for any army fortress or fleet to compete with the slightest hope of victory; and more than this, we are in command of the only organised army and fleet now on land or sea. We have been compelled by the necessities of the case to use our powers unsparingly up to a certain point. That we have not used them beyond that point, as we might have done, to enslave the world, is the best proof that I can give of the honesty of our purposes with regard to the future.

"But it must never be forgotten that these powers remain with us, and can be evoked afresh should necessity ever arise.

"It is not our purpose to enter upon a war of conquest, or upon a series of internal revolutions in the different countries of Europe, the issue of which might be the subversion of all order, and the necessity for universal conquest on our part in order to restore it.

"With two exceptions the internal affairs of all the nations of Europe, saving only Russia, which for the present we shall govern directly, will be left undisturbed. The present tenure of land will be abolished, and the only rights to the possession of it that will be recognised will be occupation and cultivation. Experience has shown that the holding of land for mere purposes of luxury or speculative profit leads to untold injustices to the general population of a country. The land on which cities and towns are built will henceforth belong to the municipalities, and the rents of the buildings will be paid in lieu of taxation.

"The other exception is even more important than this. We have waged war in order that it may be waged no more, and we are determined that it shall now cease for ever. The peoples of the various nations have no interest in warfare. It has been nothing but an affliction and a curse to them, and we are convinced that if one generation grows up without drawing the sword, it will never be drawn again as long as men remain upon the earth. All existing fortifications will therefore be at once destroyed, standing armies will be disbanded, and all the warships in the world, which cannot be used for peaceful purposes, will be sent to the bottom of the deepest part of the ocean.

"For the maintenance of peace and order each nation will maintain a body of police, in which all citizens between the ages of twenty and forty will serve in rotation, and this police will be under the control, first of the Sovereign and Parliament of the country, and ultimately of an International Board, which will sit once a year in each of the capitals of Europe in turn, and from whose decision there will be no appeal.

"The possession of weapons of warfare, save by the members of this force, will be forbidden under penalty of death, as we shall presuppose that no man can possess such weapons save with intent to kill, and all killing, save execution for murder, will henceforth be treated as murder. Declaration of war by one country upon another will be held to be a national crime, and, should such an event ever occur, the forces of the Anglo-Saxon Federation will be at once armed by authority of the Supreme Council, and the guilty nation will be crushed and its territories will be divided among its neighbours.

"Such are the broad outlines of the course which we intend to pursue, and all I have now to do is to commend them to your earnest consideration in the name of those over whom you are the constituted rulers."

As the President of the Federation sat down the German Emperor rose and said in a tone which showed that he had heard the speech with but little satisfaction—

"From what we have heard it would seem that the Federation of the Anglo-Saxon peoples considers itself as having conquered the world, and as being, therefore, in a position to dictate terms to all the peoples of the earth. Am I correct in this supposition?"

Tremayne bowed in silence, and he continued—

"But this amounts to the destruction of the liberties of all peoples who are not of the Anglo-Saxon race. It seems impossible to me to believe that free-born men who have won their liberty upon the battlefield will ever consent to submit to a despotism such as this. What if they refuse to do so?"

Tremayne was on his feet in an instant. He turned half round and faced the Kaiser, with a frown on his brow and an ominous gleam in his eyes—

"Your Majesty of Germany may call it a despotism if you choose, but remember that it is a despotism of peace and not of war, and that it affects only those who would be peace-breakers and drawers of the sword upon their fellow-creatures. I regret that you have made it necessary for me to remind you that we have conquered your conquerors, and that the despotism from which we have delivered the nations of Europe would infallibly have been ten thousand times worse than that which you are pleased to miscall by the name.

"You deplore the loss of the right and the power to draw the sword one upon another. Well, now, take that right back again for the last time! Say here, and now, that you will not acknowledge the supremacy of the Council of the Federation, and take the consequences!

"Our soldiers are still in the field, our aërial fleet is still in the air, and our sea-navy is under steam. But, remember, if you appeal to the sword it shall be with you as it was with Alexander Romanoff and the Russian force which invaded England. We have annihilated the army to a man, and exiled the Autocrat for life. Choose now, peace or war, and let those who would choose war with you take their stand beside you, and we will fight another Armageddon!"

The pregnant and pitiless words brought the Kaiser to his senses in an instant. He remembered that his army was destroyed, his strongest fortresses dismantled, his treasury empty, and the manhood of his country decimated. He turned white to the lips and sank back into his chair, covered his face with his hands, and sobbed aloud. And so ended the last and only protest made by the spirit of militarism against the new despotism of peace.

One by one the monarchs now rose in their places, bowed to the inevitable, and gave their formal adherence to the new order of things. General le Gallifet came last. When he had affixed his signature to the written undertaking of allegiance which they had all signed, he said, speaking in French—

"I was born and bred a soldier, and my life has been passed either in warfare or the study of it. I have now drawn the sword for the last time, save to defend France from invasion. I have seen enough of modern war, or, as I should rather call it, murder by machinery, for such it only is now. They spoke truly who prophesied that the solution of the problem of aërial navigation would make war impossible. It has made it impossible, because it has made it too unspeakably horrible for humanity to tolerate it.

"In token of the honesty of my belief I ask now that

France and Germany shall bury their long blood-feud on their last battlefield, and in the persons of his German Majesty and myself shake hands in the presence of this company as a pledge of national forgiveness and perpetual peace."

As he ceased speaking, he turned and held out his hand to the Kaiser. All eyes were turned on William II., to see how he would receive this appeal. For a moment he hesitated, then his manhood and chivalry conquered his pride and national prejudice, and amidst the cheers of the great assembly, he grasped the outstretched hand of his hereditary enemy, saying in a voice broken by emotion—

"So be it. Since the sword is broken for ever, let us forget that we have been enemies, and remember only that we are neighbours."

This ended the public portion of the Conference. From St. Paul's those who had composed it went to Buckingham Palace, in the grounds of which the aërial fleet was reposing on the lawns under a strong guard of Federation soldiers. Here they embarked, and were borne swiftly through the air to Windsor Castle, where they dined together as friends and guests of the King of England, and after dinner discussed far on into the night the details of the new European Constitution which was to be drawn up and formally ratified within the next few days.

Shortly after noon on the following day the *Ithuriel*, with Natas, Natasha, Arnold, and Tremayne on board, rose into the air from the grounds of Buckingham Palace and headed away to the northward. The control of affairs was left for the time being to a committee of the members of what had once been the Inner Circle of the Terrorists, and which was now the Supreme Council of the Federation.

This was under the joint presidency of Alexis Mazanoff and Nicholas Roburoff, who was exerting his great and well-proved administrative abilities to the utmost in order to atone for the fault which had led to the desertion of the *Lucifer*, and to amply justify the intercession of Natasha which had made it possible for him to be present at the last triumph of the Federation and the accomplishment of the long and patient work of the Brotherhood. There was an immense amount of work to be got through in the interval between the pronouncement of the judgment of Natas on the Tsar and his Ministers and the execution of the sentence. After twenty-four hours in Newgate they were transferred to Wormwood Scrubs Prison, and there, under a guard of Federation soldiers, who never left them for a moment day or night, they awaited the hour of their departure to Siberia.

Communication with all parts of the Continent and America was rapidly restored. The garrisons of the League were withdrawn from the conquered cities, gave up their arms at the depots of their respective regiments, and returned to their homes. The French and Italian troops round London were disarmed and taken to France in the Federation fleet of transports. Meanwhile three air-ships were placed temporarily at the disposal of the Emperor of Austria, the Kaiser, and the King of Italy, to convey them to their capitals, and furnish them with the means of speedy transit about their dominions, and to and from London during the drawing up of the new European Constitution.

A fleet of four air-ships and fifteen aerostats was also despatched to the Russian capital, and compelled the immediate surrender of the members of the Imperial family and the Ministers of the Government, and the instant disarmament of all troops on Russian soil, under pain of immediate destruction of St. Petersburg and Moscow, and invasion and conquest of the country by the Federation armies. The Council of State and the Ruling Senate were then dissolved, and the Executive passed automatically into the hands of the controllers of the Federation. Resistance was, of course, out of the question, and as soon as it was once known for certain that the Tsar had been taken prisoner and his army annihilated, no one thought seriously of it, as it would have been utterly impossible to have defended even Russia against the overwhelming forces of the Federation and the British Empire, assisted by the two aërial fleets.

The *Ithuriel*, after a flight of a little more than an hour, stopped and descended to the earth on the broad, sloping, and now snow-covered lawn in front of Alanmere Castle. Lord Marazion and his daughter, who, as it is almost needless to say, had been kept well informed of the course of events since the Federation forces landed in England, had also been warned by telegraph of the coming of their aërial visitors, and before the *Ithuriel* had touched the earth, the new mistress of Alanmere had descended the steps of the terrace that ran the whole length of the Castle front to welcome its lord and hers back to his own again.

Then there were greetings of lovers and friends, well known to each other by public report and familiar description, yet never seen in the flesh till now, and of others long parted by distance and by misconception of aims and motives. But however pleasing it might be to dwell at length upon the details of such a meeting, and its delightful contrast to the horrors of unsparing war and merciless destruction, there is now no space to do so, for the original limits of this history of the near future have already been reached and overpassed, and it is time to make ready for the curtain to descend upon the last scenes of the world-drama of the Year of Wonders—1904.

Tremayne was the first to alight, and he was followed by Natasha and Arnold at a respectful distance, which they kept until the first greeting between the two long and strangely-parted lovers was over. When at length Lady Muriel got out of the arms of her future lord, she at once ran to Natasha with both her hands outstretched, a very picture of grace and health and blushing loveliness.

She was Natasha's other self, saving only for the incomparable brilliance of colouring and contrast which the daughter of Natas derived from her union of Eastern and Western blood. Yet no fairer type of purely English beauty than Muriel Penarth could have been found between the Border and the Land's End, and what she lacked of Natasha's half Oriental brilliance and fire she atoned for by an added measure of that indescribable blend of dignity and gentleness which makes the English gentlewoman perhaps the most truly lovable of all women on earth.

"I could not have believed that the world held two such lovely women," said Arnold to Tremayne, as the two girls met and embraced. "How marvellously alike they are, too! They might be sisters. Surely they must be some relation."

"Yes, I am sure they are," replied Tremayne; "such a resemblance cannot be accidental. I remember in that queer double life of mine, when I was your unconscious rival, I used to interchange them until they almost seemed to be the same identity to me. There is some little mystery behind the likeness which we shall have cleared up before very long now. Natas told me to take Lord Marazion to him in the saloon, and said he would not enter the Castle till he had spoken with him alone. There he is at the door! You go and make Muriel's acquaintance, and I will take him on board at once."

So saying, Tremayne ran up the terrace steps, shook hands heartily with the old nobleman, and then came down with him towards the air-ship. As they met Lady Muriel coming up with Arnold on one side of her and Natasha on the other, Lord Marazion stopped suddenly with an exclamation of wonder. He took his arm out of Tremayne's, strode rapidly to Natasha, and, before his daughter could say a word of introduction, put his hands on her shoulders, and looked into her lovely upturned face through a sudden mist of tears that rose unbidden to his eyes.

"It is a miracle!" he said, in a low voice that trembled with emotion. "If you are the daughter of Natas, there is no need to tell me who he is, for you are Sylvia Penarth's daughter too. Is not that so, Sylvia di Murska—for I know you bear your mother's name?"

"Yes, I bear her name—and my father's. He is waiting for you in the air-ship, and he has much to say to you. You will bring him back to the Castle with you, will you not?"

Natasha spoke with a seriousness that had more weight than her words, but Lord Marazion understood her meaning. He stooped down and kissed her on the brow, saying—

"Yes, yes; the past is the past. I will go to him, and you shall see us come back together."

"And so we are cousins!" exclaimed Lady Muriel, slipping her arm round Natasha's waist as she spoke. "I was sure we must be some relation to each other; for, though I am not so beautiful"—

"Don't talk nonsense, or I shall call you 'Your Ladyship' for the rest of the day. Yes, of course we are alike, since our mothers were twin-sisters, and the very image of each other, according to their portraits."

While the girls were talking of their new-found relationship, Arnold had dropped behind to wait for Tremayne, who, after he had taken Lord Marazion into the saloon of the *Ithuriel*, had left him with Natas. and returned to the Castle alone.

CHAPTER XLIX.

THE STORY OF THE MASTER.

THAT evening, when the lamps were lit and the curtains drawn in the library at Alanmere, in the same room in which Tremayne had seen the Vision of Armageddon, Natas told the story of Israel di Murska, the Jewish Hungarian merchant, and of Sylvia Penarth, the beautiful English wife whom he had loved better than his own faith and people, and how she had been taken from him to suffer a fate which had now been avenged as no human wrongs had ever been before.

"Twenty-five years ago," he began, gazing dreamily into the great fire of pine-logs, round the hearth of which he and his listeners were sitting, "I, who am now an almost helpless, half-mutilated cripple, was a strong, active man, in the early vigour of manhood, rich, respected, happy, and prosperous even beyond the average of earthly good fortune.

"I was a merchant in London, and I had inherited a large fortune from my father, which I had more than doubled by successful trading. I was married to an English wife, a woman whose grace and beauty are faithfully reflected in her daughter"—

As Natas said this, the fierce light that had begun to shine in his eyes softened, and the hard ring left his voice, and for a little space he spoke in gentler tones, until sterner memories came and hardened them again.

"I will not deny that I bought her with my gold and fair promises of a life of ease and luxury. But that is done every day in the world in which I then lived, and I only did as my Christian neighbours about me did. Yet I loved my beautiful

Christian wife very dearly,—more dearly even than my people and my ancient faith,—or I should not have married her.

"When Natasha was two years old the black pall of desolation fell suddenly on our lives, and blasted our great happiness with a misery so utter and complete that we, who were wont to count ourselves among the fortunate ones of the earth, were cast down so low that the beggar at our doors might have looked down upon us.

"It was through no fault of mine or hers, nor through any circumstance over which either of us had any control, that we fell from our serene estate. On the contrary, it was through a work of pure mercy, intended for the relief of those of our people who were groaning under the pitiless despotism of Russian officialism and superstition, that I fell, as so many thousands of my race have fallen, into that abyss of nameless misery and degradation that Russian hands have dug for the innocent in the ghastly solitudes of Siberia, and, without knowing it, dragged my sweet and loving wife into it after me.

"It came about in this wise.

"I had a large business connection in Russia, and at a time when all Europe was ringing with the story of the persecution of the Russian Jews, I, at the earnest request of a committee of the leading Jews in London, undertook a mission to St. Petersburg, to bring their sufferings, if possible, under the direct notice of the Tsar, and to obtain his consent to a scheme for the payment of a general indemnity, subscribed to by all the wealthy Jews of the world, which should secure them against persecution and official tyranny until they could be gradually and completely removed from Russia.

"I, of course, found myself thwarted at every turn by the heartless and corrupt officialism that stands between the Russian people and the man whom they still regard as the vicegerent of God upon earth.

"Upon one pretext and another I was kept from the presence of the Tsar for weeks, until he left his dominions on a visit to Denmark.

"Meanwhile I travelled about, and used my eyes as well as the officials would permit me, to see whether the state of things was really as bad as the accounts that had reached England had made it out to be.

"I saw enough to convince me that no human words could describe the awful sufferings of the sons and daughters of Israel in that hateful land of bondage.

"Neither their lives nor their honour, their homes nor their property, were safe from the malice and the lust and the rapacity of the brutal ministers of Russian officialdom.

"I conversed with families from which fathers and mothers, sons and daughters had been spirited away, either never to return, or to come back years afterwards broken in health, ruined and dishonoured, to the poor wrecks of the homes that had once been peaceful, pure, and happy.

"I saw every injury, insult, and degradation heaped upon them that patient and long-suffering humanity could bear, until my soul sickened within me, and my spirit rose in revolt against the hateful and inhuman tyranny that treated my people like vermin and wild beasts, for no offence save a difference in race and creed.

"At last the shame and horror of it all got the better of my prudence, and the righteous rage that burned within me spoke out through my pen and my lips.

"I wrote faithful accounts of all I had seen to the committee in England. They never reached their destination, for I was already a marked man, and my letters were stopped and opened by the police.

"At last I one day attended a court of law, and heard one of those travesties of justice which the Russian officials call a trial for conspiracy.

"There was not one tittle of anything that would have been called evidence, or that would not have been discredited and laughed out of court in any other country in Europe; yet two of the five prisoners, a man and a woman, were sentenced to death, and the other three, two young students and a girl who was to have been the bride of one of them in a few weeks' time, were doomed to five years in the mines of Kara, and after that, if they survived it, to ten years' exile in Sakhalin.

"So awful and so hideous did the appalling injustice seem to me, accustomed as I was to the open fairness of the English criminal courts, that, overcome with rage and horror, I rose to my feet as the judge pronounced the frightful sentence, and poured forth a flood of passionate denunciations and wild appeals to the justice of **humanity to revoke the** doom of the innocent

"Of **course I was** hustled **out of the court and** flung into the street **by** the police attendants, and I groped my way back to my hotel with **eyes blinded** with tears of rage and sorrow.

"**That afternoon I was** requested by **the** proprietor of the hotel **to leave** before nightfall. I expostulated in vain. **He** simply **told me** that he dared **not** have in his house a man **who** had brought himself into collision with the police, and **that I must** find other lodgings **at once.** This, however, I found to be **no easy matter.** Wherever **I went** I was met with cold looks, **and** was refused admittance.

"Lower and lower **sank my** heart within me at each **refusal, and the** terrible conviction forced itself upon **me** that I was a marked man amidst **all-powerful** and unscrupulous enemies whom no Russian dare **offend.** I was a Jew **and** an outcast, and there **was** nothing **left for me but** to seek **for** refuge such as I could **get among my own** persecuted **people.**

"Far on **into the night I** found one, a **modest** lodging, in which I hoped **I could remain** for a day or two while waiting for my passport, **and** making the necessary preparations to **return to** England **and** shake the mire of Russia off my feet for ever. It would have been a thousand times better for me and my **dear ones, and** for those whose sympathy and kindness involved them in my ruin, if, instead of going to that ill-fated **house, I had flung** myself into **the** dark waters of the Neva, **and so ended my sorrows ere they** had well begun.

"I applied for my passport the next day, and **was** informed **that it would** not be ready for **at** least three days. The delay **was,** of course, purposely created, and before **the time** had **expired a police** visit **was paid to** the house **in** which I was **lodging, and papers** written in cypher were found within the lining of one of my hats.

"**I was arrested, and a guard** was placed over the house. Without **any further ceremony I** was thrown **into** a cell in **the fortress of Peter and Paul to** await the translation of **the** cypher. **Three days later I was** taken before the chief **of** police, and **accused of having in** my possession papers proving that I was an emissary **from** the Nihilist headquarters in London.

"I was told that my conduct had been so suspicious and of late so disorderly, that I had been closely watched during my stay in St. Petersburg, with the result that conclusive evidence of treason had been found against me.

"As I was known to be wealthy, and to have powerful friends in England, the formality of a trial was dispensed with, and after eating my heart out for a month in my cell in the fortress, I was transferred to Moscow to join the next convict train for Siberia. Arrived there, I for the first time learned my sentence —ten years in the mines, and then ten in Sakhalin.

"Thus was I doomed by the trick of some police spy to pass what bade fair to be the remainder of a life that had been so bright and full of fair promise in hopeless exile, torment, and degradation—and all because I protested against injustice and made myself obnoxious to the Russian police.

"As the chain-gang that I was attached to left Moscow, I found to my intense grief that the good Jew and his wife who had given me shelter were also members of it. They had been convicted of 'harbouring a political conspirator,' and sentenced to five years' hard labour, and then exile for life, as 'politicals,' which, as you no doubt know, meant that, if they survived the first part of their sentence, they would be allowed to settle in an allotted part of Southern Siberia, free in everything but permission to leave the country.

"Were I to talk till this time to-morrow I could not properly describe to you all the horrors of that awful journey along the Great Siberian road, from the Pillar of Farewells that marks the boundary between Europe and Asia across the frightful snowy wastes to Kara.

"The hideous story has been told again and again without avail to the Christian nations of Europe, and they have permitted that awful crime against humanity to be committed year after year without even a protest, in obedience to the miserable principles that bade them to place policy before religion and the etiquette of nations before the everlasting laws of God.

"After two years of heartbreaking toil at the mines my health utterly broke down. One day I fell fainting under the lash of the brutal overseer, and as I lay on the ground he ran at me and kicked me twice with his heavy iron-shod boots, once on the hip, breaking the bone, and once on the lower part of the spine, crushing the spinal cord, and paralysing my lower limbs for ever.

"As this did not rouse me from my fainting-fit, the heartless fiend snatched a torch from the wall of the mine-gallery and thrust the burning end in my long thick beard, setting it on fire and scorching my flesh horribly, as you can see. I was carried out of the mine and taken to the convict hospital, where I lay for weeks between life and death, and only lived instead of died because of the quenchless spirit that was within me crying out for vengeance on my tormentors.

"When I came back to consciousness, the first thing I learnt was that I was free to return to England on condition that I did not stop on my way through Russia.

"My friends, urged on by the tireless energy of my wife's anxious love, had at last found out what had befallen me, and proceedings had been instituted to establish the innocence that had been betrayed by a common and too well-known device used by the Russian police to secure the conviction and removal of those who have become obnoxious to the bureaucracy

"Whether my friends would ever have accomplished this of themselves is doubtful, but suddenly the evidence of a pope of the Orthodox Church, to whom the spy who had put the forged letters in my hat had confessed the crime on his deathbed, placed the matter in such a strong clear light that not even the officialism of Russia could cloud it over. The case got to the ears of the Tsar, and an order was telegraphed to the Governor of Kara to release me and send me back to St. Petersburg on the conditions I have named.

"Think of the mockery of such a pardon as that! By the unlawful brutality of an official, who was not even reprimanded for what he had done, I was maimed, crippled, and disfigured for life, and now I was free to return to the land I had left on an errand of mercy, which tyranny and corruption had wilfully misconstrued into a mission of crime, and punished with the ruin of a once happy and useful life. That was bad enough, but worse was to come before the cup of my miseries should be full."

Natas was silent for a moment, and as he gazed into the fire the spasm of a great agony passed over his face, and two great tears welled up in his eyes and overflowed and ran down his cheeks on to his breast.

"On receiving the order the governor telegraphed back that I was sick almost to death, and not able to bear the fatigue of the long, toilsome journey, and asked for further orders. As soon as this news reached my devoted wife she at once set out, in spite of all the entreaties of her friends and advisers, to cross the wastes of Siberia, and take her place at my bedside.

"It was winter time, and from Ekaterinenburg, where the rail ended in those days, the journey would have to be performed by sledge. She, therefore, took with her only one servant and a courier, that she might travel as rapidly as possible.

"She reached Tiumen, and there all trace was lost of her and her attendants. She vanished into that great white wilderness of ice and snow as utterly as though the grave had closed upon her. I knew nothing of her journey until I reached St. Petersburg many months afterwards.

"All that money could do was done to trace her, but all to no avail. The only official news that ever came back out of that dark world of death and misery was that she had started from one of the post-stations a few hours before a great snowstorm had come on, that she had never reached the next station—and after that all was mystery.

"Five years passed. I had returned to find my little daughter well and blooming into youthful beauty, and my affairs prospering in skilful and honest hands. I was richer in wealth than I had ever been, and in happiness poorer than a beggar, while the shadow of that awful uncertainty hung over me.

"I could not believe the official story, for the search along the Siberian road had been too complete not to have revealed evidences of the catastrophe of which it told when the snows melted, and none such were ever found.

"At length one night, just as I was going to bed, I was told that a man who would not give his name insisted on seeing me on business that he would tell no one but myself. All that he would say was that he came from Russia. That was enough. I ordered him to be admitted.

"He was a stranger, ragged and careworn, and his face was stamped with the look of sullen, unspeakable misery that men's faces only wear in one part of the world.

"'You are from Siberia,' I said, stretching out my hand to him. 'Welcome, fellow-sufferer! Have you news for me?'

"'Yes, I am from Siberia,' he replied, taking my hand; 'an escaped Nihilist convict from the mines. I have been four years getting from Kara to London, else you should have had my news sooner. I fear it is sad enough, but what else could you expect from the Russian prison-land? Here it is.'

"As he spoke, he gave me an envelope, soiled and stained with long travel, and my heart stood still as I recognised in the blurred address the handwriting of my long-lost wife.

"With trembling fingers I opened it, and through my tears I read a letter that my dear one had written to me on her deathbed four years before.

"It has lain next my heart ever since, and every word is burnt into my brain, to stand there against the day of vengeance. But I have never told their full tale of shame and woe to mortal ears, nor ever can.

"Let it suffice to say that my wife was beautiful with a beauty that is rare among the daughters of men; that a woman's honour is held as cheaply in the wildernesses of Siberia as is the life of a man who is a convict.

"The official story of her death was false—false as are all the ten thousand other lies that have come out of that abode of oppression and misery, and she whom I mourned would have been well-favoured of heaven if she had died in the snowdrifts, as they said she did, rather than in the shame and misery to which her brutal destroyer brought her.

"He was an official of high rank, and he had had the power to cover his crime from the knowledge of his superiors in St. Petersburg.

"If it was ever known, it was hushed up for fear of the trouble that it would have brought to his masters; but two years later he visited Paris, and was found one morning in bed with a dagger in his black heart, and across his face the mark that told that he had died by order of the Nihilist Executive.

"When I read those awful tidings from the grave, sorrow became quenchless rage, and despair was swallowed up in revenge. I joined the Brotherhood, and thenceforth placed a great portion of my wealth at their disposal. I rose in their councils till I commanded their whole organisation. No brain was so subtle as mine in planning schemes of revenge upon the oppressor, or of relief for the victims of his tyranny.

"In a word, I became the brain of the Brotherhood which men used to call Nihilists, and then I organised another Society behind and above this which the world has known as the Terror, and which the great ones of the earth have for years dreaded as the most potent force that ever was arrayed against the enemies of humanity. Of this force I have been the controlling brain and the directing will. It was my creature, and it has obeyed me blindly; but ever since that fatal day in the mine at Kara I have been physically helpless, and therefore obliged to trust to others the execution of the plans that I conceived.

"It was for this reason that I had need of you, Alan Tremayne, and this is why I chose you after I had watched you for years unseen as you grew from youth to manhood, the embodiment of all that has made the Anglo-Saxon the dominant factor in the development of present-day humanity.

"I have employed a power which, as I firmly believe, was given to me when eternal justice made me the instrument of its vengeance upon a generation that had forgotten alike its God and its brother, to bend your will unconsciously to mine, and to compel you to do my bidding. How far I was justified in that let the result show.

"It was once my intention to have bound you still closer to the Brotherhood by giving Natasha to you in marriage while you were yet under the spell of my will; but the Master of Destiny willed it otherwise, and I was saved from doing a great wrong, for the intention to do which I have done my best to atone."

He paused for a moment and looked across the fireplace at Arnold and Natasha, who were sitting together on a big, low lounge that had been drawn up to the fire. Natasha raised her eyes for a moment and then dropped them. She knew what was coming, and a bright red flush rose up from her white throat to the roots of her dusky, lustrous hair.

"Richard Arnold, in the first communication I ever had

with you, I told you that if you used the powers you held in your hand well and wisely, you should, in the fulness of time, attain to your heart's desire. You have proved your faith and obedience in the hour of trial, and your strength and discretion in the day of battle. Now it is yours to ask and to have."

For all answer Arnold put out his hand and took hold of Natasha's, and said quietly but clearly—

"Give me this!"

"So be it!" said Natas. "What you have worthily won you will worthily wear. May your days be long and peaceful in the world to which you have given peace!"

And so it came to pass that three days later, in the little private chapel of Alanmere Castle, the two men who held the destinies of the world in their hands, took to wife the two fairest women who ever gave their loveliness to be the crown of strength and the reward of loyal love.

For a week the Lord of Alanmere kept open house and royal state, as his ancestors had done five hundred years before him. The conventional absurdity of the honeymoon was ignored, as such brides and bridegrooms might have been expected to ignore it. Arnold and Natasha took possession of a splendid suite of rooms in the eastern wing of the Castle, and the two new-wedded couples passed the first days of their new happiness under one roof without the slightest constraint; for the Castle was vast enough for solitude when they desired it, and yet the solitude was not isolation or self-centred seclusion.

Tremayne's private wire kept them hourly informed of what was going on in London, and when necessary the *Ithuriel* was ready to traverse the space between Alanmere and the capital in an hour, as it did more than once to the great delight and wonderment of Tremayne's bride, to whom the marvellous vessel seemed a miracle of something more than merely human skill and genius.

So the days passed swiftly and happily until the Christmas bells of 1904 rang out over the length and breadth of Christendom, for the first time proclaiming in very truth and fact, so far as the Western world was concerned, "Peace on earth, Goodwill to Man."

. . . .

On the 8th of January a swift warship, attended by two

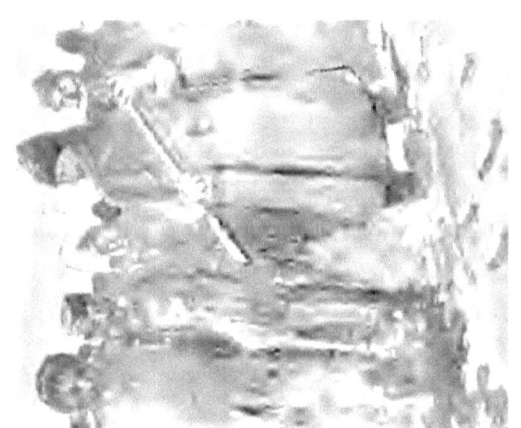

tion and Control, composed of all the Sovereigns of Europe and their Prime Ministers for the time being, with the new President of the United States, the Governor-General of Canada, and the President of the now federated Australasian Colonies. This Board was to meet in sections every year in the various capitals of Europe, and collectively every five years in London, Paris, Berlin, Vienna, Rome, and New York in rotation. There was no appeal from its decision save to the Supreme Council of the Federation, and this appeal could only be made with the consent of the President of that Council, given after the facts of the matter in dispute had been laid before him in writing.

The third clause dealt with the rearrangement of the European frontiers. The Rhine from Karlsruhe to Basle was made the political as well as the natural boundary between France and Germany. The ancient kingdom of Poland was restored, with the frontiers it had possessed before the First Partition in 1773, and a descendant of Kosciusko, elected by the votes of the adult citizens of the reconstituted kingdom, was placed upon the throne. Turkey in Europe ceased to exist as a political power. Constantinople was garrisoned by British and Federation troops, and the country was administered for the time being by a Provisional Government under the presidency of Lord Cromer, who was responsible only to the Supreme Council. The other States were left undisturbed.

The fourth and fifth clauses dealt with land, property, and law. All tenures of land existing before the war were cancelled at a stroke, and the soil of each country was declared to be the sole and inalienable property of the State. No occupiers were disturbed who were turning the land to profitable account, or who were making use of a reasonable area as a residential estate; but the great landowners in the country and the ground landlords in the towns ceased to exist as such, and all private incomes derived from the rent of land were declared illegal and so forfeited.

All incomes unearned by productive work of hand or brain were subjected to a progressive tax, which reached fifty per cent. when the income amounted to £10,000 a year. It is almost needless to say that these clauses raised a tremendous outcry among the limited classes they affected; but the only reply made to it by the President of the Supreme Council was "that honestly earned incomes paid no tax, and that the idle and useless classes ought to be thankful to be permitted to exist at any price. The alternative of the tax would be compulsory labour paid for at its actual value by the State." Without one exception the grumblers preferred to pay the tax.

All rents, revised according to the actual value of the produce or property, were to be paid direct to the State. As long as he paid this rent-tax no man could be disturbed in the possession of his holding. If he did not pay it the non-payment was to be held as presumptive evidence that he was not making a proper use of it, and he was to receive a year's notice to quit; but if at the end of that time he had amended his ways the notice was to be revoked.

In all countries the Civil and Criminal Codes of Law were to be amalgamated and simplified by a committee of judges appointed directly by the Parliament with the assent of the Sovereign. The fifth clause of the Constitution plainly stated that no man was to be expected to obey a law that he could not understand, and that the Supreme Council would uphold no law which was so complicated that it needed a legal expert to explain it.

It is almost needless to say that this clause swept away at a blow that pernicious class of hired advocates who had for ages grown rich on the weakness and the dishonesty of their fellow-men. In after years it was found that the abolition of the professional lawyer had furthered the cause of peace and progress quite as efficiently as the prohibition of standing armies had done.

On the conclusion of the war the aërial fleet was increased to twenty-five vessels exclusive of the flagship. The number of war-balloons was raised to fifty, and three millions of Federation soldiers were held ready for active service until the conclusion of the war in the East between the Moslems and Buddhists. By November the Moslems were victors all along the line, and during the last week of that month the last battle between Christian and Moslem was fought on the Southern shore of the Bosphorus.

All communications with the Asiatic and African shores of the Mediterranean were cut as soon as it became certain that Sultan Mohammed Reshad, at the head of a million and a half of victorious Moslems, and supported by Prince Abbas of Egypt at the head of seven hundred thousand more, was marching to the reconquest of Turkey. The most elaborate precautions were taken to prevent any detailed information as to the true state of things in Europe reaching the Sultan, as Tremayne and Arnold had come to the conclusion that it would be better, if he persisted in courting inevitable defeat, that it should fall upon him with crushing force and stupefying suddenness, so that he might be the more inclined to listen to reason afterwards.

The Mediterranean was patrolled from end to end by airships and dynamite cruisers, and aërial scouts marked every movement of the victorious Sultan until it became absolutely certain that his objective point was Scutari. Meanwhile, two millions of men had been concentrated between Galata and Constantinople, while another million occupied the northern shore of the Dardanelles. An immense force of warships and dynamite cruisers swarmed between Gallipoli and the Golden Horn. Twenty air-ships and forty-five war-balloons lay outside Constantinople, ready to take the air at a moment's notice.

The conqueror of Northern Africa and Southern Asia had only a very general idea as to what had really happened in Europe. His march of conquest had not been interrupted by any European expedition. The Moslems of India had exterminated the British garrisons, and there had been no attempt at retaliation or vengeance, as there had been in the days of the Mutiny. England, he knew, had been invaded, but according to the reports which had reached him, none of the invaders had ever got out of the island alive, and then the English had come out and conquered Europe. Of the wonderful doings of the aërial fleets only the vaguest rumours had come to his ears, and these had been so exaggerated and distorted, that he had but a very confused idea of the real state of affairs.

The Moslem forces were permitted to advance without the slightest molestation to Scutari and Lamsaki, and on the evening of the 28th of November the Sultan took up his quarters in Scutari. That night he received a letter from the President of the Federation, setting forth succinctly, and yet very clearly, what had actually taken place in Europe, and calling upon him to give his allegiance to the Supreme Council, as the other sovereigns had done, and to accept the overlordship of Northern Africa and Southern Asia in exchange for Turkey in Europe. The letter concluded by saying that the immediate result of refusal to accept these terms would be the destruction of the Moslem armies on the following day. Before midnight, Tremayne received the Sultan's reply. It ran thus—

In the name of the Most Merciful God.
From MOHAMMED RESHAD, Commander of the Faithful, to ALAN TREMAYNE, Leader of the English.
I have come to retake the throne of my fathers, and I am not to be turned back by vain and boastful threats. What I have won with the sword I will keep with the sword, and I will own allegiance to none save God and His holy Prophet who have given me the victory. Give me back Stamboul and my ancient dominions, and we will divide the world between us. If not we must fight. Let the reply to this come before daybreak.
MOHAMMED.

No reply came back; but during the night the dynamite cruisers were drawn up within half a mile of the Asiatic shore with their guns pointing southward over Scutari, while other warships patrolled the coast to detect and frustrate any attempt to transport guns or troops across the narrow strip of water. With the first glimmer of light, the two aërial fleets took the air, the war-balloons in a long line over the van of the Moslem army, and the air-ships spread out in a semicircle to the southward. The hour of prayer was allowed to pass in peace, and then the work of death began. The war-balloons moved slowly forward in a straight line at an elevation of four thousand feet, sweeping the Moslem host from van to rear with a ceaseless hail of melinite and cyanogen bombs. Great projectiles soared silently up from the water to the north, and where they fell buildings were torn to fragments, great holes were blasted into the earth, and every human being within the radius of the explosion was blown to pieces, or hurled stunned to the ground. But more mysterious and terrible than all were the effects of the assault delivered by the air-ships, which divided into squadrons and swept hither and thither in wide curves, with the sunlight shining on their silvery hulls and their long slender guns, smokeless and flameless, hurling the most awful missiles of all far and wide, over a scene of butchery and horror that beggared all description.

In vain the gallant Moslems looked for enemies in the flesh to confront them. None appeared save a few sentinels across the Bosphorus. And still the work of slaughter went on, pitiless and passionless as the earthquake or the thunderstorm. Millions of shots were fired into the air without result, and by the time the rain of death had been falling without intermission for two hours, an irresistible panic fell upon the Moslem soldiery. They had never met enemies like these before, and, brave as lions and yet simple as children, they looked upon them as something more than human, and with one accord they flung away their weapons and raised their hands in supplication to the sky. Instantly the aërial bombardment ceased, and within an hour East and West had shaken hands, Sultan Mohammed had accepted the terms of the Federation, and the long warfare of Cross and Crescent had ceased, as men hoped, for ever.

Then the proclamation was issued disbanding the armies of Britain and the Federation and the forces of the Sultan. The warships steamed away westward on their last voyage to the South Atlantic, beneath whose waves they were soon to sink with all their guns and armaments for ever. The war-balloons were to be kept for purposes of transportation of heavy articles to Aeria, while the fleet of air-ships was to remain the sole effective fighting force in the world.

While these events were taking place in Europe, those who had been banished as outcasts from the society of civilised men by the terrible justice of Natas had been plodding their weary way, in the tracks of the thousands they had themselves sent to a living grave, along the Great Siberian Road to the hideous wilderness, in the midst of which lie the mines of Kara. From the Pillar of Farewells to Tiumen, from thence to Tomsk,—where they met the first of the released political exiles returning in a joyous band to their beloved Russia,—and thence to Irkutsk, and then over the ice of Lake Baikal, and through the awful frozen desert of the Trans-Baikal Provinces, they had been driven like cattle until the remnant that had survived the horrors of the awful journey reached the desolate valley of the Kara and were finally halted at the Lower Diggings.

Of nearly three hundred strong and well-fed men who had said good-bye to liberty at the Pillar of Farewells, only a hundred and twenty pallid and emaciated wretches stood shivering in their rags and chains when the muster was called on the morning after their arrival at Kara. Mazanoff and his escort had carried out their part of the sentence of Natas to the letter. The arctic blasts from the Tundras, the forced march, the chain and the scourge had done their work, and more than half the exile-convicts had found in nameless graves along the road respite from the long horrors of the fate which awaited the survivors.

The first name called in the last muster was Alexander Romanoff. "Here," came in a deep hollow tone from the gaunt and ragged wreck of the giant who twelve months before had been the stateliest figure in the brilliant galaxy of European Royalty.

"Your sentence is hard labour in the mines for"— The last word was never spoken, for ere it was uttered the tall and still erect form of the dethroned Autocrat suddenly shrank together, lurched forward, and fell with a choking gasp and a clash of chains upon the hard-trampled snow. A stream of blood rushed from his white, half-open lips, and when they went to raise him he was dead.

If ever son of woman died of a broken heart it was Alexander Romanoff, last of the tyrants of Russia. Never had the avenging hand of Nemesis, though long-delayed, fallen with more precise and terrible justice. On the very spot on which thousands of his subjects and fellow-creatures, innocent of all crime save a desire for progress, had worn out their lives in torturing toil to provide the gold that had gilded his luxury, he fell as the Idol fell of old in the temple of Dagon.

He had seen the blasting of his highest hopes in the hour of their apparent fruition. He had beheld the destruction of his army and the ruin of his dynasty. He had seen kindred and friends and faithful servants sink under the nameless horrors of a fate he could do nothing to alleviate, and with the knowledge that nothing but death could release them from it, and now at the last moment death had snatched from him even the poor consolation of sharing the sufferings of those nearest and dearest to him on earth.

This happened on the 1st of December 1905, at nine o'clock in the morning. At the same hour Arnold leapt the *Ithuriel* over the Ridge, passed down the valley of Aeria like a flash of silver light, and dropped to earth on the shores of the lake. In the same grove of palms which had witnessed their despairing betrothal he found Natasha swinging in a hammock, with a black-eyed six-weeks'-old baby nestling in her bosom, and her own loveliness softened and etherealised by the sacred grace of motherhood.

"Welcome, my lord!" she said, with a bright flush of pleasure and the sweetest smile even he had ever seen transfiguring her beauty, as she stretched out her hand in welcome at his approach. "Does the King come in peace?"

"Yes, Angel mine! the empire that you asked for is yours. There is not a regiment of men under arms in all the civilised world. The last battle has been fought and won, and so there is peace on earth at last!"

THE END

Now Ready, Third Edition.

308 pages, demy 8vo, cloth gilt, 6s.,

THE CAPTAIN OF THE MARY ROSE.

A TALE OF TO-MORROW

By W. LAIRD CLOWES,
U.S. NAVAL INSTITUTE.

With 60 Illustrations by **the Chevalier** de Martino **and** Fred. T. Jane.

A most graphic and enthralling description of the next Naval War between France and Great Britain.

THE FOLLOWING ARE A FEW PRESS OPINIONS.

"Deserves something more than a mere passing notice."—*The Times.*

"Full of exciting situations. . . . Has manifold attractions for all sorts of readers."—*Army and Navy Gazette.*

"The most notable book of the season."—*The Standard.*

"A clever book. Mr. Clowes is pre-eminent for literary touch and practical knowledge of naval affairs."—*Daily Chronicle.*

"Mr. W. Laird Clowes' exciting story."—*Daily Telegraph.*

"We read 'The Captain of the Mary Rose' at a sitting."—*The Pall Mall Gazette.*

"Written with no little spirit and imagination. . . . A stirring romance of the future."—*Manchester Guardian.*

"Is of a realistic and exciting character. . . . Designed to show what the naval warfare of the future may be."—*Glasgow Herald.*

"One of the most interesting volumes of the year."—*Liverpool Journal of Commerce.*

"It is well told and magnificently illustrated."—*United Service Magazine.*

"Full of absorbing interest."—*Engineer's Gazette.*

"Is intensely realistic, so much so that after commencing the story every one will be anxious to read to the end."—*Dundee Advertiser.*

"The book is splendidly illustrated."—*Northern Whig.*

TOWER PUBLISHING CO. LIMITED,
91 MINORIES, LONDON, E C.;
And all Booksellers throughout the Kingdom.

www.ingramcontent.com/pod-product-compliance
Lightning Source LLC
Chambersburg PA
CBHW051739300426
44115CB00007B/628